Order and Surprise

Order and Surprise

Martin Gardner

Prometheus Books

700 East Amherst St.
Buffalo, New York 14215

Library of Congress Card Catalog No. 83-61117
ISBN: 0-87975-219-X

For my good old friend
John Bennett Shaw

Contents

Preface

Order and Surprise is a sort of sequel to *Science: Good, Bad and Bogus,* published in 1981 by Prometheus Books. The earlier volume reprinted almost everything I had written about pseudoscience since 1952, when my *Fads and Fallacies in the Name of Science* first appeared. The present book comprises other essays and reviews, most of them about topics other than parascience.

Here and there I have modified original texts, sometimes restoring passages removed by editors, sometimes adding new footnotes to update the material. In many cases I have appended a postscript that allows me to comment on an article or review. Like the previous anthology, the book is divided into two parts. The first contains articles in chronological order of publication; the second, book reviews in similar order. As before, I have made no effort to eliminate overlapping, where something said earlier is repeated.

It takes, I must admit, a considerable ego to put together a collection of previously published essays for a new book. I can only say that few things give a writer more satisfaction than a chance to reprint fugitive earlier scribblings, if for no other reason than to correct those inevitable copy changes made by editors and absent-minded printers.

9

Part One

1

The Strange Case
of Robert Maynard Hutchins

"The most striking fact about the higher learning in America," began Robert Hutchins, speaking at Yale University in 1936, "is the confusion that besets it." He then proceeded to add to that confusion by delivering a series of four bewildering lectures that were later reprinted in book form under the title, *The Higher Learning in America*. This small volume soon became one of the most controversial documents in contemporary educational literature.

No one was quite sure what the president of the University of Chicago had intended his words to mean, but nearly everyone was dismayed by the book. Most of the reviews in both popular and scholarly publications were unfavorable. Harvard's distinguished philosopher Alfred North Whitehead wrote an article for the *Atlantic Monthly* that, without mentioning Hutchins by name, took sharp issue with his basic point of view.[1] John Dewey, at Columbia University, in two articles for *Social Frontier,* intimated that Hutchins was obscurantist, anti-scientific, reactionary, authoritarian, and badly educated.[2] At Hutchins's own university, opposition to his educational theories grew in intensity. Almost every member of the faculty disagreed with him. James Weber Linn of the English department wrote an article for the alumni magazine that chided "Bob" for his immature ideas.[3] Charles E. Clark, dean of the Yale Law School (to whom Hutchins had dedicated his book), arrived at the university in December 1937 to give the annual Moody lecture. He announced his subject to be "The Higher Learning in a Democracy." Hutchins introduced him, then sat courageously on the platform to endure a friendly castigation by one of his former law teachers.

The strongest attack came from Harry D. Gideonse of the economics

This essay originally appeared in the *University Review,* Winter 1938, published by the University of Kansas City.

department, who wrote a book with the same title as Clark's lecture.[4] Two years later Gideonse became a full professor at Columbia University. "I would certainly not have left the University of Chicago," he told an alumni group in Washington, "because Columbia offered me a higher rank and higher salary. I left because I disagreed with the intellectual and administrative ideas and practices of President Hutchins."

Throughout these attacks (I have mentioned only a few of them), Hutchins maintained that he was seriously misunderstood. To the *Atlantic Monthly* he contributed "A Reply to Professor Whitehead." For the *Social Frontier* he wrote an answer to John Dewey, sarcastic in tone and accusing Dewey of "still fighting nineteenth-century German philosophy."

To see this conflict of ideas in better perspective, it will be worthwhile to glance briefly at some earlier history. After graduating from the Yale Law School at age twenty-seven, Hutchins became a professor of law at Yale and was soon appointed dean of the Law School. In 1929, when he was thirty, the University of Chicago made him president. There were many reasons. He was brilliant, handsome, and articulate. As the youngest college president in America he was great publicity. Above all, he had a reputation as a money-getter.

He was everything the university wanted—and more. Things began to happen fast. The now well-known Chicago Plan of undergraduate instruction (four survey courses, noncompulsory class attendance, advance at your own speed, and so on) had been lying about on office desks for years.[5] Hutchins picked it up, believed it to be essentially sound, and after making a few minor changes railroaded it into actuality. When the Big Crash occurred, he was effective in preventing salary cuts. He condensed eighty budgets into twelve. During the thirties he defended the academic freedom of radicals on the faculty who came under fire from conservatives in the city and state governments, aided by conservative Chicago newspapers. And he began to make speeches.

They were strange speeches. For one thing, they contained none of the platitudes and cliches that normally grace the lectures of college presidents. He told a graduating class that they were nearer to truth now than they would ever be again. He told students that the purpose of the university was to unsettle their minds. He told science departments that they were too concerned with fact-finding and not enough concerned with ideas. He maintained that the world was bewildered because it had forgotten how to read and think. He proposed a return to philosophy. He sprinkled his lectures with quotations from Plato and Aristotle and Thomas Aquinas. He had even been reading Gilbert Chesterton.

As Hutchins himself once said, he talked more than any other college president in captivity. But it was invigorating and refreshing talk. It was a new kind of talk. Thornton Wilder, an old schoolmate of Hutchins at Yale (Hutchins brought him to the University of Chicago to teach in the English department), suggested that the president's epitaph should read, "Here lies a college president who never used the word *ideals.*"

At first the campus enjoyed the president's speeches. Then gradually an awful rumor began to take shape and run about "The Grey City on the Midway."[6] The president—yes, it was true—the president had developed an intense interest in Catholic theology! Students and professors rubbed their ears and listened more carefully to what Hutchins was saying. Who could believe it? The little Baptist school that had grown into a great center of unbelief had a president who was studying books by Catholic theologians!

The first intimation the campus had of the president's interest in neo-Thomism—the modern version of the philosophy and theology of Saint Thomas Aquinas—was in 1930 when Hutchins brought Mortimer J. Adler to the university. Adler had been teaching Great Books courses in New York with his friend Scott Buchanan, and he had written a book, *Dialectic,* which (as Hutchins once described it in a speech) "proved there was nothing true, but that there were a great many ways of talking about things, and that you could have a lot of fun seeing how many consistent universes of discourse you could construct to talk about them in . . . . It was this great man whom at this critical juncture in my educational career I had the good fortune to meet."

By the time Adler came to Chicago he had made a 180-degree turn. He had discovered the *Summa Theologica* of Thomas Aquinas.[7] Although Jewish, and unwilling to become a practicing Catholic, Adler had brought himself intellectually to a position in which he was willing to defend the doctrines of Catholicism as God-given truth.[8] Word spread around the country that the University of Chicago was a former Baptist school where Jewish professors were now teaching Catholic theology to atheists.

How the president had become acquainted with Adler, no one knew. They did know that he had placed Adler in the university's department of philosophy without anticipating the furor it would arouse. George Mead, a leading pragmatist, was then head of the department. He objected to Adler's appointment, and when Hutchins turned a deaf ear Mead stomped out of the department in great disgust, never to return. With him went two other philosophers. This historic occasion became known as the great walkout of the philosophers. It left the department in a crippled condition from which it did not recover for years.

When Hutchins realized that he had made an executive blunder, he withdrew Adler from the philosophy department to make him an associate professor of the philosophy of law. It was a title and department created on the spot. Soon he and Adler were teaching an honors course in the intellectual history of western Europe. It was the first of their Great Books seminars, modeled on the courses Adler had been teaching in New York, which in turn had been modeled on courses that had been introduced at Columbia by John Erskine.

Jacques Maritain, one of the world's most respected Catholic Thomists, came from the University of Paris to lecture on the Midway. When his speech was printed as a booklet by the University of Chicago Press, it was observed that Maritain had dedicated it to Hutchins, and Mrs. Hutchins, a talented artist, had drawn a sketch of the author for the frontispiece. Hutchins gave an address somewhere. It sounded so much like a speech by a neo-Thomist that a prominent Catholic journal of philosophy ran an editorial welcoming Hutchins into the ranks.

Hutchins's first book, *No Friendly Voice,* was enthusiastically reviewed in Catholic journals. The reception on the Midway was not so friendly. The university's *International Journal of Ethics* carried a vitriolic criticism by its editor, T. V. Smith.[9] When Hutchins's second book, *The Higher Learning in America,* came off the press, the reactions were similar. Catholic universities placed it on required reading lists, but secular philosophers and educators around the nation were profoundly shocked by it.

It is not difficult to understand why. They had heard of Adler and the great walkout of the philosophers. They knew Adler had become a Thomist and that his influence on Hutchins was increasing. It was only natural that when Hutchins set forth a scheme for reforming the higher learning, expressing it in a Thomist vocabulary, they would assume that behind the scheme was a Catholic philosophy that Hutchins for some reason did not want to make explicit.

The modern world, said Hutchins, is "anti-intellectual." Not only is truth "everywhere the same," but there is a "hierarchy of truths." The book proposed that universities revive the medieval trivium of grammar, rhetoric, and logic. It repeated most of the central ideas expressed in Cardinal John Newman's classic work, *The Idea of a University.* Medieval schools and Catholic theology were viewed with what one critic called "a disturbingly fond backward look." For example, consider the following passage:

> Saddest of all is the fate that has overtaken theology itself. Displaced from its position as the queen of the sciences, it now finds itself a feeble imitator of all the rest. In general its students are its students in name only . . . . Its nominal followers, frightened out of their wits by the scientific spirit, have thrown theology overboard and have transferred their affections to those overdressed hoydens, the modern versions of the natural and social sciences.

Statements such as these, in the book and in Hutchins's speeches, gave the impression that behind his cautiously expressed public utterances were unexpressed private convictions hardly in step with the trends of modern thought. To discuss, as Hutchins did, the decline of theological schools implies that before the decline, when the schools were orthodox, they were somehow better than they are now. Hutchins began to emerge as a man who had deep religious convictions but was shy of writing about them. Like Cardinal Newman before him, it seemed as if Hutchins had written a book on education that he hoped would be favorably received by both the faithful and the unbeliever.

The Higher Learning in America falls roughly into two parts. The first section stresses the evils of today's higher learning, especially its confusion as to ends. There is no single, unifying aim. Like a "service station" it reflects every passing need and desire of the populace. The book's second section outlines a new curriculum designed to eliminate this confusion. There must be, said Hutchins, a unifying field of study. In the middle ages, universities were unified by Catholic theology. But theology implies dogma, and dogma implies a church; and our secular age has neither. "To look to theology to unify the modern university is futile and vain." We must turn, therefore, to the next best thing, the discipline that unified the thinking of the ancient Greeks. We must turn to metaphysics.

Perhaps that word *metaphysics,* more than anything else, aroused the ire of Hutchins's critics. It is, of course, a word that has been used with many meanings. But in the absence of a clear understanding of what Hutchins meant by the word, his critics assumed he was using it in a Thomist sense. He had quoted from Aquinas in making statements about metaphysics. As Dewey pointed out, it seemed absurd for Hutchins to refer to Saint Thomas unless he regarded metaphysics in the same way Aquinas did. It seemed that Hutchins was asking modern universities to adopt a final, eternally true metaphysical system that would unify the higher learning in the way Catholic theology had unified medieval schools.

Herbert Spencer, in his influential treatise on education, had maintained that human opinion usually goes through three historical phases: the unanimity of the ignorant, the disagreement of the inquiring, and the unanimity of the wise.

It is manifest [said Spencer] that the second is parent of the third. They are not sequences in time only; they are sequences in causation. However impatiently, therefore, we may witness the present conflict of educational systems, and however much we may regret its accompanying evils, we must recognize it as a transition stage needful to be passed through and beneficent in its ultimate effects.

Most modern educators, following Spencer, look on contemporary bewilderment in education, deplorable though it may be, as a necessary prelude, something in which we can take a kind of pride. But Hutchins, by his use of the word *metaphysics,* by his disturbingly fond backward look, seemed to view present-day bewilderment as the loss of something splendid.

Hutchins later insisted that he was not using *metaphysics* in the medieval sense. He merely meant to say that a university should be unified by a vigorous search for broad, general truths. The university would be integrated not by an imposed metaphysical system, but by the fact that its faculty and students would be engaged in the cooperative task of seeking a philosophy that might someday provide an intellectual synthesis for the world. Hutchins put it this way in a speech delivered on April 9, 1937:

> We may then hope to have a unified university, not because an official dogma has been imposed upon it, but because teachers and students can know what they are talking about and can have some hope of understanding one another. As I have said before, the ideal of a university is an understood diversity.

The trouble with our chaotic world, Hutchins said, is not that we have wrong ideologies, but that we have no ideology. That is, the average educated man has none. Hutchins had no quarrel, he made clear, with the view that education should be concerned with the reconstruction of society. He agreed with Dewey and with the Marxists that the end of education was "intelligent action." His message was simply that we should put first things first. Intelligent action is impossible without intelligent, well-educated citizens.

Dewey and Hutchins, it seems to me, differ largely not in what they believe to be the end of education, but in the methods they think will best achieve that end. It is mainly a difference of emphasis. Hutchins wants the higher learning to concentrate on the history of ideas. The modern university, he believes, is too preoccupied by empirical science, vocational training, and contemporary writing. It should put more stress on a liberal education, which is best provided by reading the classics. In this stress on the classics Hutchins is close to the American literary humanist movement, whose leading spokesmen were Paul Elmer More and Irving Babbitt. His views are in substantial agreement with those of Norman Foerster, the movement's surviving voice.[10] Dewey agrees on the virtues of a liberal education, but for him such an education requires an understanding of modern science where reading the classics (books by Galileo, Newton, Harvey, and so on) has little value. The two points of view may not be so far apart as one might suppose.

In any case, Hutchins is certainly far from the Thomism of his friend Adler, although his critics can hardly be blamed for thinking otherwise. His insistence that the university become a "unified diversity," with no imposed metaphysics, seems belied by his repeated expressions of admiration for philosophers who defended vast metaphysical systems and by his constant denigration of anti-metaphysical schools such as pragmatism, empiricism, and positivism.

The history of philosophy from the Renaissance to the present has been one of increasing weariness with the web-spinning of metaphysicians. Because of Hutchins's fascination with the language of Thomism, perhaps because of private religious convictions about which we know nothing, he made the fatal mistake of expressing his views in a terminology that was only too easy to misinterpret. The word *philosophy* would surely have had a less ominous sound than *metaphysics*. Its use might have avoided much of the strident opposition by educators who perhaps would have agreed with Hutchins if they had better understood him. As it was, Hutchins's use of the word *metaphysics* only added to the confusion in educational theory that he was trying to disperse.

It was once a good word, but Hutchins was in the wrong age.

POSTSCRIPT

Aside from some trivial articles in University of Chicago undergraduate publications, in magic magazines, and in a few other obscure periodicals, this was my first published piece of nonfiction. I have revised it and added the footnotes.

Hutchins left the University of Chicago in 1951, much to the satisfaction of the faculty, to become an officer of the Ford Foundation. In 1954 he was made president of the foundation's Fund for the Republic, and in 1959 he became the founder and first president of the Center for the Study of Democratic Institutions, in Santa Barbara, California. This think tank, to which Hutchins invited over the years an odd assortment of old friends and other thinkers, came to an inglorious end shortly before Hutchins died in 1977.[11]

By 1975 the center was in shambles. It had run out of funds, associates had been let go or had quit, and those who remained were squabbling furiously. The new president, Malcolm Moos, resigned in opposition to Hutchins's plan to sell the large Santa Barbara estate and move the center to the University of Chicago, where Hutchins would resume leadership. For several years the center had been kept solvent by, of all things, royalties from Dr. Alexander Comfort's best-selling sex manual *The Joy of Sex*.

A former British pediatrician, Comfort had been an associate fellow of the center since 1969. In 1974, after the whopping commercial success of his sex manual, he moved to Santa Barbara as a permanent senior fellow. For tax purposes and other complicated reasons, he assigned 20 percent of his book's royalties to the center, which was supposed to pass the rest along to Comfort in U.S. dollars.

When Hutchins planned to sell the estate and move the center to Chicago, Comfort decided that the center had broken his contract. He sued for $406,000 he claimed was owed him. The center responded with a counter suit of $3.8 million, contending that Dr. Comfort had "intentionally and maliciously" written a second book, *More Joy*, in order to cut down sales of the first one. In 1976 a federal district judge ruled mostly in favor of Comfort's action. The judge called the pact between Comfort and the center a "shabby" one in which the doctor had untruthfully claimed to have written *Joy of Sex* under the center's auspices. The center, said the judge, had "winked at the fraud."

"Hutchins may have set out to study democratic institutions," declared Dr. Comfort, "but he ran this place like a Byzantine harem . . . . The center has no future—it is a fiction and a sham." To outsiders, the imbroglio was high comedy. Here was a distinguished think tank, presided over by a man who believed that an education could be obtained only by reading the great books, keeping itself Comfortably alive with royalties from a book that sold mainly because it was filled with erotic drawings.

As an undergraduate major in philosophy at Chicago during the legendary Hutchins–Adler epoch, and on the staff of the university's public relations office during the years in which Hutchins passionately opposed the nation's entrance into the war against Germany, I have since followed the careers of Hutchins and Adler with more than usual interest. On the whole, I admired Hutchins. He was surely right in deploring the increasing trivialization of America's higher learning, in insisting that a university should provide a liberal education before it allows students to choose courses, and in stressing the importance of philosophy and the Great Books. He may have been naive about communism, but he had the courage to take a strong stand against the crude tactics of Senator Joseph McCarthy and other anti-communists who knew even less about the red menace than he did. Above all, he had an admirable sense of humor. "The faculty doesn't amount to much," he once said about his University of Chicago, "but the president and the students are wonderful." After his divorce and remarriage he told a reporter, "I think I'll try it every year."

What prevented Hutchins from becoming the great educator he had always hoped to be? For one thing, his caustic tongue and arrogant, high-handed ways made endless enemies. For another, he constantly exaggerated. American universities may be in bad shape, but they surely are a bit more than what Hutchins once called "high-class flophouses where parents send their children to keep them off the labor market and out of their own hair." Perhaps more than anything else, he never took the time to learn much about modern science or philosophy. "I have been permitted to glory in the possession of an unmathematical mind," he said in a commencement address at Saint John's College, in Annapolis, the only university that tried to carry out his Great Books program. "My scientific attainments were of the same order." Because Hutchins knew so little about science, his constant sniping at the scientific community for being concerned only with what they could measure, obsessed by facts instead of ideas, could hardly have been persuasive.

In my opinion, Adler might have become a great philosopher if he had not been sidetracked by Aquinas, and Hutchins might have become a great educator if he had not been sidetracked by Adler. Consider, for example, Hutchins's annual Aquinas lecture at Marquette University in 1949. He had been preceded by such distinguished Catholic theologians as Jacques Maritain and Etienne Gilson, and by Adler. Marquette University Press issued the lecture as a small book entitled *St. Thomas and the World State,* and dedicated "To Mortimer Adler for twenty-two years." Hutchins described Aquinas's *Treatise on Law* as "that greatest of all books on the philosophy of law." He urged the Catholic church to assume leadership in working for "a universal church and world state."

Of course this does not mean that Hutchins believed in the doctrines of Rome, or was even close to believing. But just what *did* he believe? I have always agreed with what Chesterton said in his introduction to *Heretics:*

> But there are some people, nevertheless—and I am one of them—who think that the most practical and important thing about a man is still his view of the universe. We think that for a landlady considering a lodger, it is important to know his income, but still more important to know his philosophy. We think that for a general about to fight an enemy, it is important to know the enemy's numbers, but still more important to know the enemy's philosophy. We think the question is not whether the theory of the cosmos affects matters, but whether, in the long run, anything else affects them.

To me the strangest aspect of the strange case of Robert Maynard Hutchins is that he never talked about his own theology except in the haziest way. That he believed in a creator God, transcendent yet personal, there can be no doubt. Indeed, he often sounded like an Old Testament prophet. Civilization, he said in a convocation address at Chicago in 1946, is doomed unless there is a worldwide "moral, intellectual, and spiritual reformation." There is no way, he said, that we can learn to love our neighbors unless we first love God. "The brotherhood of man must rest on the fatherhood of God. If God is denied . . . the basis of community disappears. . . . Unless we believe that every man is the child of God, we cannot love our neighbors. Most cats and most dogs are more attractive than most men. Unless we see men as children of God, they appear to us as rivals, or customers, or foreigners, unrelated to us except as means to our ends."

Hutchins's attack on the very possibility of a naturalistic ethics was unremitting. He admitted that if the world practiced Aristotle's ethics it would be much better off, but he added: "I doubt if any single man, to say nothing of the whole world, can practice Aristotle's ethics without the support and inspiration of religious faith. . . . It is very late; perhaps nothing can save us."

Surely a man who talks so apocalyptically, like Noah warning of the Deluge, owes it to his listeners to let them in on what religious faith he has in mind. Protestants, Catholics, Jews, and Muslims, all believe in the fatherhood of God, yet Protestants and Catholics are now killing each other in Ireland, and Jews and Muslims are killing each other in the Near East. Did Hutchins have a particular faith in mind? Or was he a philosophical theist who did not place any great religious tradition above any other?

In a speech on "Morals, Religion, and Higher Education" (you'll find it in *Freedom, Education, and the Fund,* 1956) Hutchins writes: "By religion I mean belief in and obedience to God. This may not require adherence to a church or creed; but it demands religious faith. Faith is not reason, but it is something more than a vague, sentimental desire to do good and be good." He then cites Saint Augustine as an example of a man whose conversion "followed after tremendous wrestling with the intellectual difficulties of Christianity." Metaphysics and natural theology, he goes on, can throw little light on "the existence and nature of God, the character and destiny of the human soul, and the salvation of man." Naturalistic ethical doctrines "overlook the fallen nature of man and assume that without grace he can reach a terrestrial end to which, almost by definition, no being with such a nature can ever obtain."

The curriculum of an ideal university, Hutchins continues, must include more than a study of morals. "It should include both natural and sacred theology." Scientism, skepticism, and secularism—especially what Hutchins elsewhere called the "anti-philosophies" of pragmatism and positivism—deny that there are objective moral and religious truths. "If higher education is to take morality and religion seriously, it must repudiate these dogmas; for the truths of morality and religion never have been and never can be discovered by experiment or by any allegedly 'scientific' means. Morality and religion cannot be taken seriously unless the possibility of attaining truth by philosophical inquiry and by revelation is admitted."

Revelation? I find it hard to read this 1948 lecture without assuming that Hutchins then believed in the same revelation in which Augustine and Aquinas believed. But wait! There is a curious footnote to the paragraph from which I just quoted. It is a long statement by the vice-chancellor of the University of Punjab declaring education to be "incomplete" unless it is "illuminated" by God's revelation to Islam! Was Hutchins trying to tell us that the Muslim tradition is as true as the Christian? This seems unlikely. Did he believe the Christian revelation to be true and that this ultimately would become clear after, say, a century or two of world dialogue? Did he merely want us to know that even Muslim educators held views similar to his own? Or was he unsure of just what he believed?

This hesitancy to put on the record one's core beliefs was also characteristic of the men with whom Hutchins and Adler were most closely associated. Did Scott Buchanan believe in God? Does Richard McKeon? (I will say more about McKeon in Chapter 2.) As for Stringfellow Barr, who died in 1982, we know he was a practicing Episcopalian, but today this tells us nothing about a person's doctrinal beliefs. For ten years Barr was president of Saint John's College, with Buchanan as his dean. In a Penguin paperback titled *Christianity Takes a Stand* (1946), edited by Bishop William Scarlett, Barr has an essay on "The Duty of a Christian in the Modern World." His theme is this. The world is moving toward disaster, and this may be God's will. On the other hand, perhaps we can avert it. The only way to do so is by a return to Christ. That the world can solve its problems without seeking first the Kingdom of God strikes him, he says, as harder to believe than the mystery of the Incarnation. He finds very little in modern efforts to build a better world that "is relevant if the Incarnation did indeed take place." The future is, of course, in God's hands. "This fact we must learn to welcome or else we must deny Christ and go it alone. I doubt whether in modern history the choice before us has been clearer."

Note that Barr did not say outright that he personally believed in the Incarnation, but how can you make much sense of his remarks unless he did? With statements like these coming from Hutchins's associates, and from Hutchins himself, it is understandable why American philosophers and educators suspected that behind the Hutchins-Adler rhetoric for the Great Books was an unstated motive. Could it be that the motive, especially in Adler's mind, was not so much to introduce students to the great ideas as it was to introduce them to the great Roman Catholic ideas?

We know that Hutchins's father was an evangelical Presbyterian minister in whose home there were morning prayers and daily Bible readings. We also know that Hutchins early stopped going to church even though, as he said, he often found himself "singing, humming, or moaning third-rate hymns . . . while shaving, while waiting on the platform to make a speech, or in other moments of abstraction or crisis." Milton Mayer, a good friend of Hutchins who often wrote Hutchins's articles for mass-circulation magazines, likes to recall an occasion when Hutchins startled him by saying, "The trouble with you, Mayer, is that you don't believe in God."

But what sort of God? A God who walked the earth as Jesus? I recall a banquet in the University of Chicago's Commons at which Hutchins gave a short speech that was followed by questions from the guests. I asked if he would mind telling us something about his religious beliefs. Yes, Hutchins answered, he would mind. Everybody laughed, and Hutchins went on to the next question.

I did not think this funny. Hutchins, I am persuaded, damaged his career by concealing his religious views. Perhaps someday a biographer will interview those who knew him best and tell us exactly what sort of light he chose to keep hidden under the bushel of his books and speeches.

NOTES

1. Whitehead, "Harvard and the Future," *Atlantic Monthly,* September 1936. Hutchins's "Reply to Professor Whitehead" appeared in November.

2. Dewey, "Rationality in Education," *Social Frontier,* December 1936; "President Hutchins' Proposals to Remake Higher Education," ibid., January 1937. Hutchins responded with "Grammar, Rhetoric, and Mr. Dewey" in the February issue, and Dewey had the final word in March with "The Higher Learning in America."

In my opinion Dewey came out far ahead. See also Dewey's essay, "Challenge to Liberal Thought," reprinted in *Problems of Men* (1946).

3. Linn, "Notes on a Textbook," *University of Chicago Magazine,* December 1936.

4. Gideonse, *The Higher Learning in a Democracy* (Farrar and Rinehart, 1937).

5. The Chicago Plan was outlined in an anonymous novel, *Grey Towers* (Covici-McGee, 1923). This book created a sensation at the time because of its revelations about the sex lives of prominent faculty members who appeared in the novel under thin disguises. The author was Miss Zo Flannagan, a young English instructor at the University of Chicago, where she had graduated in 1911.

6. The university's *Alma Mater* song contains a line about "the city grey that ne'er shall die." Having called the university "Grey City" throughout my novel, *The Flight of Peter Fromm,* I was pleased when in 1977 Hanna Holborn Gray became the university's tenth president.

7. In the fifth chapter of his autobiography, *Philosopher at Large* (1977), Adler tells how he made this about-face. It was his friend Richard McKeon, then teaching a course on medieval philosophy at Columbia, who sent Adler to a Catholic bookstore in downtown Manhattan, where he bought the first of twenty-one volumes of an English translation of *Summa Theologica.* Adler describes the effect this book had on him as "cataclysmic."

As for the view he had taken in *Dialectic,* Adler writes: "I cannot now give a wholly satisfactory explanation of why this incorrect view of philosophy should have taken so strong a hold on my mind and dominated it for a number of years." He attributes it in part to the influence of his good friends Arthur Rubin and Scott Buchanan. Buchanan had written a book called *Possibility,* published the same year as Adler's, which took a similar line. (Years later he and Adler had a falling-out over Adler's embracing of Thomism.) Adler says he went through a short period of "intellectual schizophrenia" before completely repudiating his earlier view.

Dialectic is a curious work. Its thesis is that philosophy, rightly viewed, is a dialectical process without end that explores the internal consistency and implications of all points of view without dogmatically affirming that one vision is truer than another. Truth is logical coherence, not correspondence with an external reality. The true philosopher sees his efforts as a game, a comic play of thought, a verbal fencing. Reading his books you can hear the "quiet laughter" of Plato, the supreme dialectician. "The aim of philosophy," wrote Adler, "might almost be described as the attempt to achieve an empty mind, a mind free from any intellectual prepossessions, and unhampered by one belief or another."

Back in 1908, in the section on metaphysics in his book *First and Last Things,* H. G. Wells argued for an approach to philosophy almost indistinguishable from Adler's early vision. Here is how Wells expressed it with a metaphor:

> It will perhaps give a clearer idea of what I am seeking to convey if I suggest a concrete image for the whole world of a man's thought and knowledge. Imagine a large clear jelly, in which at all angles and in all states of simplicity or contortion his ideas are imbedded. They are all valid and possible ideas as they lie, none incompatible with any. If you imagine the direction of up or down in this clear jelly being as it were the direction in which one moves by analysis or by synthesis, if you go down for example from matter to atoms and centres of force and up to men and states and countries—if you will imagine the ideas lying in that manner—you will get the beginnings of my intention.

But our Instrument, our process of thinking, like a drawing before the discovery of perspective, appears to have difficulties with the third dimension, appears capable only of dealing with or reasoning about ideas by projecting them upon the same plane. It will be obvious that a great multitude of things may very well exist together in a solid jelly, which would be overlapping and incompatible and mutually destructive, when projected together upon one plane. Through the bias in our Instrument to do this, through reasoning between terms not in the same plane, an enormous amount of confusion, perplexity and mental deadlocking occurs.

8. Some notion of how close Adler came to becoming a Catholic may be gleaned from passages in "Religion in a Modern World," a speech he gave on April 3, 1935. Adler shared the platform with two secular humanists, Max Carl Otto and Albert Eustace Haydon. I have forgotten where this symposium was held, but I have a mimeographed typescript of the speech that was provided later by a Chicago lecture service. Said Adler:

There is only one true religion because there cannot be opposed truths of faith. There is only one orthodox or right theology because there cannot be two or more opposed correct understandings of those truths. Because of this, religion must be organized by a church and its dogma and ritual must be prescribed by church doctors. It is by the authority of the doctors of the church that infidels are converted. . . . It seems to me that liberal Protestantism and Judaism are heretical. . . . The true religion I wish to expound for you is the Catholic Christianity.

Then comes the most incredible paragraph of all:

I now want to suggest the possibility of choosing between the religions. As I survey the religions of the Western World, it seems to me that Catholicism is the true religion. The sin of heresy is not the intellectual sin but it is the sin of pride, of egotism. When a church council succeeded in answering a theological question, then a heretic was he who willfully set his opinion against the church. It is this pride that constitutes his error. I am not sure that I would hesitate to say that the church was right in burning heretics.

In hesitating to condemn the Inquisition, Adler was being a faithful Thomist. Saint Augustine had opposed the death penalty for heresy; he thought the church should limit its punishments to flogging, fines, and exile. "To put a heretic to death would be to introduce upon earth an inexpiable crime," declared Saint John Chrysostom. But Saint Thomas thought otherwise. "If false coiners or other felons are justly committed to death without delay by worldly princes," he wrote in his *Summa Theologica* (II, xi), "much more may heretics, from the moment that they are convicted, be not only excommunicated, but slain justly out of hand." By the end of the sixteenth century hundreds of thousands of poor souls had been savagely tortured and burned alive, or otherwise murdered, for holding opinions contrary to those of the church. Public executions of heretics and witches became festive occasions, like watching the deaths of gladiators.

If it is right to execute those who kill the body, so went the reasoning of devout Christians, how much more right it is to execute those who send souls to eternal punishment. Moreover, killing a heretic does even the heretic a favor. Will it not prevent him from causing greater harm and thereby lighten his torment in hell? Protestants were, of course, just as intolerant. Luther and Calvin followed Aquinas in believing that heretics deserved death; but because the Protestants came later, were fewer in number, and had less political clout, their victims were fewer.

I would guess that Adler is now much ashamed of his 1935 speech, but it helps one to understand why James Farrell, writing in *Partisan Review* in 1940, would call Adler "a provincial Torquemada without an Inquisition." (The article is reprinted in Farrell's *League of Frightened Philistines,* 1945.) "Thanks very much for the chance to see your blast against Mortimer J. Adler," said H. L. Mencken in a letter to Farrell. "You describe him precisely. I hear confidentially that Holy Church is full of hopes that he will submit to baptism anon. If the ceremony is public I'll certainly attend. I invite you herewith to come along in my private plane. I assure you there will be plenty of stimulants aboard" *(Letters of H. L. Mencken,* 1961, p. 451).

In the last chapter of his autobiography Adler struggles manfully to explain why he never became a Catholic. (I have more to say about this in Chapter 12 of my *Whys of a Philosophical Scrivener.*) "This whole matter was complicated," Adler writes, ". . . by the conversion to Roman Catholicism of a number of students who had been introduced to the *Summa Theologica* in the great books class that Bob Hutchins and I taught, or in the Trivium course I taught with Malcolm Sharp."

Many of Adler's students who converted were Jewish. Although Adler's rhetoric played a role in these conversions, there were others on the campus who were even more influential, such as Adler's close associate William Gorman, an Irish Catholic from birth, and Herbert Schwartz, a Jewish convert to the church who had obtained his doctorate at Columbia under Richard McKeon. Schwartz, whose official position at Chicago was on the faculty of music, had an enormous influence on the Jewish students who converted. Later he became the leader of a Catholic community in New Jersey. He died in 1981, leaving a raft of manuscripts that his disciples are publishing in a periodical called *Filoque* (issued by the Mount Hope Foundation, Middletown, N.Y.). Other Jewish converts included Herbert Ratner, Kenneth Simon, Janet Kalven, Peggy Stern, Paula Myers, and Alice Zucker, all of whom have retained their faith. Ratner, who became a medical doctor, is now director of public health, Oak Park, Illinois, and editor of *Child and Family Quarterly.* Simon became Father M. Raphael, at Saint Joseph's Abbey, Spencer, Massachusetts, where he is a Trappist monk. His book, *The Glory of Thy People* (Macmillan, 1948), tells of his conversion.

Miss Kalven, at age 17, was one of twenty students chosen for the first Hutchins-Adler Great Books class. After graduation, she taught for five years in the Chicago Great Books program before joining a Catholic lay women's movement called the Grail. She is now an administrator in the Grail's educational center at Grailville, in Loveland, Ohio.

Among the dozen or so Gentiles who converted after Adler introduced them to Saint Thomas was Winston Ashley, who came to the University of Chicago from a Protestant background in Blackwell, Oklahoma. I admired his poems and published some of them in *Comment,* a campus literary magazine I edited in 1936. Winston joined the Dominican order, became a priest in 1948, and is now Father Benedict M. Ashley, a teacher of moral theology at the order's Aquinas Institute, St. Louis University. He was president of the institute from 1962 to 1969. Of his several books, the most recent (written with a fellow Dominican) is *Health Care Ethics* (second edition, 1982).

In a recent letter to me, Father Ashley expressed his debt to Adler, not only "for having awakened in me so early in life to the breadth of our western intellectual tradition," but also for financial support. Ashley and his Catholic friend Leo Shields (who was killed in the Normandy invasion of World War II) had worked for two years as Adler assistants, along with Quentin ("Bud") Ogren, another Catholic convert, who married Paula Myers and became a professor of law at Loyola University of Los Angeles.

Miss Kalven, in response to my query, eloquently summed up her debt to Hutchins and Adler as follows:

> The thirties were a time of extraordinary intellectual ferment at Chicago, in large measure due to Hutchins and Adler. Their stance ran counter to the prevailing campus culture and was propaedeutic so far as Catholicism was concerned. From them I learned to question the received wisdom of the semanticists, psychologists, sociologists, cultural relativists; to respect the intellectual rigor of the Greeks and the medievals; to suspect the reductionism of the physical and biological scientists; to read a text on its own terms, define a concept, and analyze an argument. I cut my intellectual teeth so to speak on all the big questions: the nature of language, knowledge, truth; the nature of man (I was not a feminist then), of society, of justice; the existence of God. . . . The Hutchins-Adler training was a necessary but not sufficient condition for conversion. It made Catholicism intellectually respectable, but it did not make anyone become a Catholic. A much more powerful and intimate witness is necessary, I think, to enable people to act as contrary to our upbringing and education as our little group did.

9. Thomas Vernor Smith, who died in 1964, was then a philosopher at Chicago and one of Hutchins's most vocal enemies. Later Mr. Smith went to Washington as a senator from Illinois, and in 1948 joined the faculty of Syracuse University. His review of Hutchins's book (*International Journal of Ethics,* April 1936) was harsh enough to make a news report in *Time* (May 4, 1936). Smith enjoyed telling anti-Hutchins anecdotes to his classes, of which I recall only a dull one: The president had sent a note to physicist Arthur Holly Compton ordering him to come to his office. Compton responded with a note saying that if Hutchins wanted to see him he would have to come to *his* office.

The anecdote points up the strong antagonism that almost the entire faculty at Grey City felt toward Hutchins. Although he never fired an opponent ("No faculty member," he once said, "can ever be fired except for rape or murder committed in broad daylight before three witnesses"), he had subtler ways of getting rid of them. When Tulsa University was seeking a new president in the late thirties, my father (a trustee) wrote to Hutchins for advice. He replied with a glowing recommendation of Smith for the post.

10. See Foerster's book, *The American State University* (1937), for views so similar to Hutchins's that I have always been puzzled by the fact that Hutchins never mentioned Foerster or his mentors. Where Hutchins used the word *metaphysics,* Foerster used the word *humanism.* Like Hutchins, whom he quotes with approval, Foerster looked to humanism to unify the higher learning only because theology is no longer possible. Here are some passages from Foerster's book that could almost have been written by Hutchins:

> Any future extension of this two-fold basis [humanism and theology] must depend upon the possibility of a Christian revival—at present a remote possibility, at least in America.

Meanwhile we must still avail ourselves of humanism . . . . [The] modern spirit, if it cannot bring itself to an acceptance of Christianity, will have to express itself once more in the line of humanistic development which it entered upon in the Renaissance . . . . While humanism makes no claim to a knowledge of the divine, the possibility of this supreme knowledge is left open—a stand which, if it does not help the student, at least it does not hinder him.

11. Well, not entirely. The center, now called the Robert M. Hutchins Center for the Study of Democratic Institutions, has been taken over by the University of California, at Santa Barbara. It continues to publish its *Center Magazine.* For a semi-obit, see Edward Engberg's article "Hutchinsland" in the *New Republic*, July 21, 1979. Engberg likens the center to Charles Dickens's Mudfog Association for the Advancement of Everything.

2

Art, Propaganda, and Propaganda Art

Current controversies between Marxian critics and their opponents concerning the nature and value of propaganda in art suffer in general from a melange of linguistic confusions. The same words are used by the opposing sides (sometimes by the same side) with widely different meanings, and different words are used with the same meanings. It is possible, therefore, that a large portion of the conflict may, upon analysis, prove to be verbal in nature and that, once these linguistic confusions are uncovered, something of a genuine synthesis might be initiated.

This is an attempt at such an initiation. The thesis will be that the Marxian and anti-Marxian critics operate within two divergent and ancient critical traditions—the Platonic and the Aristotelian—which do not actually contradict each other but differ only in their respective vocabularies and emphases.[1] In clearing away the verbal contradictions a path may be opened for a consideration of the emphases and the deeper reasons that underlie their divergence.

Before proceeding it will be expedient to examine some of the general terms involved.

The word *art* will be used in reference to the fine arts as distinct from useful or practical arts that concern the making of objects (such as clothing and furniture) which serve purposes primarily utilitarian.

The terms *propaganda* and *rhetoric* will be used interchangeably to refer to the process of persuasion.

This essay originally appeared in the *University Review,* Spring 1944, published by the University of Kansas City.

Important distinctions should be kept in mind between art that contains consciously intended rhetoric, art in which the propaganda is there by unconscious intention, and art that is rhetorical by accident—the rhetoric implied by the subject-matter apart from any intention whatsoever on the part of the artist.

Aesthetics (or any roughly synonymous term such as *critical theory*) is a vague and crucial word. Two fundamental distinctions seem to be involved in any definition of its scope.

The first is made on the basis of whether all things related to the art object, or only the immediate psychological experience (with its strange mixture of pleasures), are proper in the study of art. These two approaches may be distinguished by the terms *universal* and *psychological*.

The universal approach is concerned with anything of significance that relates in any way to the art object. This includes the forces which combined to shape the work of art (the artist's personality and history; the social, economic, and political forces surrounding him; and so on) and the effects that follow from the work (the immediate pleasure experience, and the later effects—moral, political, educational, etc.). The art object is considered in its total context of relations.

The psychological approach is concerned only with the immediate effect of the work of art upon the audience; that is, with the pleasure or delight that persons experience at the time they are contemplating a work of art. It is "art qua art" in the sense of art considered only in its unique function as art.

This immediate experience is far from simple. Three "levels" of pleasures are traditionally distinguished. (1) The purely sensuous, such as the pleasure of seeing a clear blue sky. (2) The formal, which involves a delight in the harmonious order of the parts of the work of art. (3) The meaningful, which includes innumerable and widely different types of pleasures aroused by symbols in the medium that relate to the observer's past experience.

Only the second level seems to be essential to all works of art. The third level has very little relevance to music, for example, in which are concentrated the pleasures of the first and second level. And the first level has very little relevance to fiction, which is rich in the pleasures of the second and third. It is the second level that gives to art its unique value and distinguishes it from other objects also capable of arousing immediate delight.

The adjective *aesthetic* has been used so indiscriminately since it was introduced into philosophic writing that it is almost as useless for analysis as the word *beauty*. For this reason, it will be omitted entirely from the body of the essay. The phrase "art as art," whenever used, will simply mean art functioning on all levels that provide immediate pleasures.[2]

The second distinction stems from the question of whether the causes and effects related to the art object are to be studied in the work itself or outside of it. These two approaches will be distinguished by the terms *intrinsic* and *extrinsic*.

The "extrinsic" approach deals with the forces that shaped the art, and with the effects of the art on the individual and society, studied *apart from the art object*. This study would, of course, bring the work of art into consideration, but only for the purpose of correlating it with the artist's personality and history, and with the manifold effects of the work on individuals and society.

The "intrinsic" approach also considers the causes and effects of the art object, but studies them as they are embedded in the work—as structural features that had antecedent causes and will in turn produce varied effects. It is "art qua art" in the sense that the emphasis is on the structure of the object itself. "Extrinsic" factors are considered, of course, but only for the purpose of better understanding the actual construction of the work of art.

In regard to this last distinction it will be apparent that each "value" which art may possess—moral, political, psychological, etc.—will have a double aspect. It can be studied intrinsically or extrinsically.

In the *Poetics* Aristotle discusses catharsis, the chief psychological value of Greek tragedy, but the discussion is intrinsic—in terms of the principles in a dramatic work that are capable of producing catharsis. For Aristotle, an extrinsic analysis of catharsis would fall more properly within the scope of the science of psychology.

To illustrate with a rhetorical value: a study of the influence of painting in winning converts to the church, or in strengthening the faith of believers, would be an extrinsic study of religious rhetoric. Research on the use of the halo in painting would be an intrinsic rhetorical study.

The problem of where an art value exists—in the work or in the mind—is almost entirely verbal and need not detain us. It is comparable to asking if the color red is really on the apple. The important, though obvious, point is that an analytical distinction can be made between the nature of the apple and what happens in the mind. In the same way, one can distinguish between the structure of a work of art and the effects of that structure on a mind.

On the basis of the two distinctions—the universal-psychological and the intrinsic-extrinsic—it is now possible to formulate with some precision the nature of the two major critical traditions of Western Europe, which had their origins in the teachings of Plato and Aristotle.[3]

Plato approached the criticism of art from the universal point of view without explicit reference to intrinsic and extrinsic distinctions.

This approach was a natural outcome of Plato's dialectic and synthetic method. He was impressed with continuity and interrelatedness. Instead of producing treatises on separate sciences or branches of philosophy, he confined his works to imaginary dialogues in which dialectical discussions took place.

In the absence, therefore, of a treatise by Plato on art criticism, or a work on any topic in which he spoke as himself, it is impossible to know Plato's actual attitudes on the subject. However, in the scattered references to art that occur throughout the dialogues (chiefly the *Republic* and the *Laws*) Plato clearly approached the art object in terms of its total context of relations.

Although Plato recognized that art provided an immediate psychological delight, he seemed to regard this as of little value either to the individual or to society. His chief concern was with the later effects of art, in particular the moral and political.

In the *Republic,* which deals with the ideal state, Socrates finally banished artists from his imaginary city because their art possessed no special value to the state that could not better be provided by other instruments of education. In the *Laws,* concerned with more immediate political reform, artists are permitted to remain in the city, their works carefully censored to prevent moral or political harm.

Aristotle, on the other hand, and for the first time in Greek philosophy, recognized the distinction both between the psychological and other values of art and between intrinsic and extrinsic analysis. His approach to philosophy, unlike that of Plato, involved the division of subject matter into sciences, each of which constituted an independent realm of study. This division was in no sense an artificial compartmentalization of thought, but simply a necessary step to obtain clarity and efficiency in philosophical and scientific analysis.

It is not surprising, then, that one of Aristotle's surviving treatises deals exclusively with the immediate psychological values of Greek tragedy, a fine art that had developed a structure sufficiently stable to permit an inductive analysis.[4] For Aristotle, the science of poetics was confined to the psychological effect of a work of art, considered intrinsically. The reasons for these two restrictions are clear.

He confined poetics to the immediate delight art arouses, because this is the only unique function that art objects possess. Other functions are held in common with other objects, and therefore more readily analyzed by other sciences.

He confined poetics to intrinsic analysis of the psychological value, because an extrinsic study of this aspect of art would fall more conveniently under the science of psychology.

In addition to differing in method and terminology, Aristotle also departed from Plato on the question of the value of art to the state.

Plato's position was, apparently, that art is of small value to the state now, and in the "city in the skies" would be of no value at all. Aristotle answered Plato by discussing the social value of at least one type of art, namely, the value of tragedy in purging emotions that might otherwise find expression in forms harmful to the state.

Other social functions of art (such as communication, education, and propaganda) are discussed (as in Plato) only in connection with the censorship of art to prevent harmful moral and political effects, especially on the youth.

Aristotle also made clear that art possessed the values of arousing delight in the mere fact of imitation (that is, one is pleased by an imitation simply because it imitates), and providing mental relaxation—a value held in common with sleep, wine, and dancing.

We are now in position to discuss the Marxist approach to art and that of its opponents.

Marxism, like Platonism, approaches art in terms of a total context of relations. Although Marxists recognize the positive value of art to the state, even to the perfect state (and in this respect are Aristotelians), in their general approach and emphasis they are Platonists.

Contemporary critics who oppose, or seem to oppose, the Marxists, though differing among themselves in many important respects, in general emphasize the unique functions of art as art and the importance of distinguishing between intrinsic and extrinsic analysis. For these reasons they may be regarded as within the Aristotelian tradition.[5]

If the preceding analyses of the two traditions are accurate, it should be clear that they do not contradict each other in any important respect, but differ chiefly in what they emphasize and what they define as the proper province of aesthetics. An adherent of either point of view can, without hesitation, practice the type of criticism emphasized by the other.

A Platonist, if he wishes, can undertake an Aristotelian investigation of a work of art; but he would tend to regard the results as only a small fraction of what he would like to discover about the work. The "greatness" of a work of art, he would insist, is too comprehensive to be judged solely in terms of immediate delight. "Art is not a pleasure, a solace, or an amusement; art is a great matter," Tolstoy wrote. The Platonist is inclined to regard Aristotelian criticism as "purely formal" or "technical," trivial and narrow in the light of the multiplicity of values that works of art possess.

On the other hand, the Aristotelian critic can, without injuring his conscience, discuss a work of art in terms of its total context of values. But he would regard this as stepping outside his province as an art critic, invading realms in which he might not feel qualified to operate. He inclines, therefore, to ignore the wider aspects of art, relegating this type of criticism to experts in the respective sciences involved.[6]

"But literature is an art. It is not philosophy, it is not social economy, it is not politics: it is an art. And art is for delight." So wrote Somerset Maugham.

With this discussion of the two European critical traditions in the background we can now turn to some of the major points of current controversy. For convenience and clarity, what follows will be presented in the form of three propositions. Each will be stated, then briefly amplified and defended.

1. *Some arts cannot contain propaganda; some arts may or may not con-*

tain it; and others are almost certain to contain it in some degree.

The more purely "formal" or "abstract" arts—music, for example—seem incapable of carrying meanings of sufficient complexity to be meaningful as rhetoric. Music may, of course, arouse certain emotions and establish certain moods. It may also symbolize objects and acts by imitating specific sounds and rhythms. But these emotions, moods, sounds, and acts are not propositions that can be evaluated as to their truth or goodness. It is difficult to be for or against a storm at sea; and even a battle or sex experience is good or bad only in the light of a wider context of ideas. It is this wider context that is too complex for the symbolizing power of pure music.

This does not imply, however, that music cannot be used as a rhetorical instrument. It can, in fact, become an extremely effective instrument when fused with another medium capable of presenting the doctrine, as in the song, opera, ballet, or cinema. In these arts the music creates an emotional atmosphere that may greatly intensify the persuasive quality of rhetoric carried by the symbols of the other medium.

Pure music may also function as a rhetorical aid if it is associated in the minds of the audience in any way with a special doctrine. Thus the music of Palestrina played during High Mass may impress worshipers with the beauty and solemnity of the ritual and consequently with the truth of Catholic doctrine. In a similar way a symphony by Shostakovitch may signify, in vague ways, a story glorifying the Russian state; and, if the audience is aware of this signification, the music may acquire a rhetorical value it could not otherwise possess.

If a composer is known to have strong beliefs, this knowledge alone may tinge his music with rhetoric. Or, again, if the audience is in a special moral or political mood, its members may react in certain moral and political ways to certain types of music. Martial music may contribute to the military fervor of a people about to revolt or fight a war, even though the music itself gives no specific direction to the military action. Or the Bolero played in the open air on a warm night, to an audience of young people, might affect their moral behavior after the concert.

In various ways, then, music can certainly influence, to some degree, the beliefs and behavior of the listener. But the degree is slight, and so dependent on extraneous factors that more confusion than clarity seems to result from regarding music as capable of taking sides on moral, political, or metaphysical topics.

Other arts to which the term *propaganda* does not appear applicable in any meaningful way include the abstract visual arts (abstract two-dimensional, abstract sculpture, and abstract moving arts such as Calder's "mobiles" or the Bach section of *Fantasia*) and architecture. Arts that carry a relatively slight burden of ideas (such as sculpture, painting, dancing, lyric poetry, etc.) may or may not have rhetorical implications.

But arts that cover a wide range of meanings in a single work—such as fiction, drama, and cinema—are almost certain to be shot through with moral, political, and metaphysical implications. These may be reflected in the artist's handling of his subject matter, or simply in his choice of subject matter. If a novel denounces the rich, it is propaganda. If it does not denounce the rich, it is propaganda.

This does not mean of course that novels, plays, and motion pictures must contain consciously intended rhetoric. The political implications in Proust, for example, are there because they are part of the subject matter, because the author wrote from the remembrance of a past lived within a particular social structure. Unconscious and accidental rhetoric of this sort usually calls forth a variety of responses depending on the attitudes of each individual reader. Shakespeare probably never intended to argue for anything. As a result, critics have found evidence that he argued for almost everything.

2. *The presence of consciously intended propaganda in a work of art need not detract from its immediate psychological value.*

This is a truth that Marxists have always recognized, but one that Aristotelians who failed to understand their own position have found difficult to accept.

It is obvious, of course, that an artist, in addition to being an artist, is also a member of society, with many interests that may mingle with his desire (as artist) to create good art. He may (to mention only three) wish to make money, achieve fame, or persuade his audience of the truth of certain doctrines.

There is no reason for assuming that the presence of one or more of these intentions will necessarily weaken his ability to function as an artist.

It is true that in many cases of contemporary political art the rhetorical intention of the artist does detract from—or rather is emphasized at the expense of—other values. This, however, is a criticism of individual artists, not of Marxist critical theory. And critics in the Communist Party have not hesitated, especially in recent years, to make this criticism of the works of overenthusiastic members. There are, in fact, many reasons why a developing revolutionary art should be expected to have deficiencies.

In the first place, a political movement at its inception is small in the number of its followers—and good artists are rare. "A party card," Joseph Freeman once wrote, "does not automatically endow a Communist with artistic genius."

A more important reason is that even a competent artist, when involved in an emotionally tinged political movement, is in constant danger of choking his talent with his enthusiasm for manufacturing rhetoric. This is particularly true in fiction, an art that slides easily into didacticism. Much of the early left-wing writing in America was guilty of this misplaced emphasis. Rather than labor over a manuscript to enhance its value as art, the authors preferred in their political excitement to produce quickly written works of current rhetorical value.

This raises the question of whether, to produce great art, the propaganda intent of the artist should be a "subordinate" one. Critics of Marxism frequently answer yes. A statement by T. S. Eliot, in his essay, "The Function of Criticism" (1934), is typical: "I do not deny that art may be affirmed to serve ends beyond itself; but art is not required to be aware of these ends, and indeed performs its function, whatever that may be, according to various theories of value, much better by indifference to them."

If Eliot is saying simply that, insofar as the artist functions as an artist, he does well to remain "indifferent" to other intentions, then his statement is sound. It is like saying that an industrial designer should be more concerned with designing than with the utility of the industrial products. But the artist himself is more than just an "art department." He is a total personality frequently acting in response to double or multiple motivations. These respective "ends" are of such different species that it seems fruitless to debate the question of which is, or should be, "primary" and which "subordinate" in the artist's mind. As *artists*, of course Dante, Virgil, and Shakespeare were primarily interested in producing art. But as total personalities they were far from ''indifferent'' to the ends of glorifying the church, impressing the reader with the greatness of a city's heritage, and pleasing a diversified audience.

The burden of proof surely lies on the shoulders of those who assert, or seem to assert, that the presence of these nonartistic intentions automatically injures (by some elusive magic law) an artist's ability to function as an artist. And why may not an end that is "beyond" the work actually stimulate the artist to even greater concentration on the task of perfecting his work as art?[7]

It should be emphasized at this point that the revolutionary artist is in no sense "compelled" by his political convictions to twist his art into social rhetoric. He chooses his subject matter because it is to him the material of life that is most significant — the richest in artistic possibilities. Steinbeck was no more compelled by his political views to write about the migratory worker than Dante and Milton were compelled by their theological views to deal with Christian doctrine and mythology.

Joseph Freeman expressed this point when he wrote (in his introduction to *Proletarian Literature in the United States*, 1935):

> ... in an era of bitter class war such as ours, party programs, collective actions, class purposes, when they are enacted in life, themselves become experiences — experiences so great, so far-reaching, so all-inclusive that, *as experiences*, they transcend flirtations and autumn winds and stars and nightingales and getting drunk in Paris cafes.

3. Art may be good art yet contain bad rhetoric, or it may contain good rhetoric and have little value as art.

Before going further it will be necessary to distinguish two meanings of "good" and "bad" rhetoric. Rhetoric may be considered good or bad if (1) it is effective or ineffective as a means of persuasion, (2) it is propaganda for a good or bad cause. It is often stated that the rhetorical effectiveness of a work of art varies directly with its art value. This is undoubtedly true in most cases, though there may be exceptions. It is possible, for instance, to imagine a type of political action desired immediately, and involving artistically insensitive individuals. Such action might best be aroused by a crude, inartistic work of fiction or cinema, perhaps even untrue in its factual implications. At any rate, analysis of the precise relationships between the value of art as art and its effectiveness as rhetoric raises numerous problems that cannot be entered into here. What follows will be confined, therefore, to the second interpretation of good and bad rhetoric.

As now understood, the proposition asserts that the art value of a work and the political value of its propaganda need not vary directly. The importance of this statement is difficult to underestimate.

Just as opposition to the first two propositions (which are stressed by Marxists) can be regarded as bad Aristotelianism, so can Marxist opposition to the third proposition (stressed by Aristotelians) be regarded as bad Marxism.

The proposition rests on the Aristotelian assumption that the political value of a work of art can be analytically separated from other values for purposes of criticism. To say this is not to deny that the values of art are inextricably bound up with one another, influencing each other in numerous obscure ways. An art object is a unit just as the artist's mind is a unit. But this does not mean that distinctions cannot be made for critical purposes, just as we can distinguish between an artist's political views and his ability as an artist.

An analogy with one of the useful arts may be illuminating. Consider the art of chair making. A chair is designed for the primary purpose of producing an object upon which someone may sit. But a chair also may serve other ends. It may be a work of formal beauty; it may function as a barber chair, dental chair, or electric chair. It may be made of expensive woods and so acquire a high economic value. Although these many values inhere in a single unified object, they are nonetheless analytically separable and may vary independently in worth. As Dewey (also speaking of chairs) delicately phrases it in *Art as Experience,* "There is no pre-established harmony that guarantees that what satisfies the need of one set of organs will fulfill that of all the other structures and needs that have a part in the experience."

This Aristotelian method of distinguishing the various values of art, and allowing for their independent variability, should be regarded as little more than the development of a set of distinctions and definitions to facilitate the complete analysis of a work of art. There is no reason why a Marxist, of any party persuasion, should hesitate to accept it as a valuable and workable procedure.

In the earlier days of the Marxist movement, in America and elsewhere, attempts were made by many Marxist critics to deny that art had value apart from social ends. They were reacting (and rightly of course) to the overemphasis of the "art for art's sake" schools, but in their ardor they fell into the equally absurd error of denying that art contained within it elements of value independent of political issues. Fortunately this attitude is vanishing, and Marxian critics are rapidly accepting the commonsense Aristotelian distinctions.

Although it may appear irrelevant to look to Marx, Engels, or Lenin for support of a point of view in the field of criticism (since these men made no pretenses of expertness in that field), there is ample evidence that the three founders of communism did recognize the independent variability of the immediate psychological value of a work, and its later political value. There is no doubt that this was Trotsky's attitude, because he expressed his views clearly in *Literature and Revolution*, published in 1925.

Perhaps it was partly because of this work that admirers of Trotsky in this country were among the first of the left-wing critics to attack openly the ultra-leftist attitude toward art of the Communist Party.

Max Eastman, in 1934, wrote in *Art and the Life of Action*: "You can not pretend that art has no value in itself when you stand humiliated before the perfection of a carved image whose goal outside itself was some funny trick of necromancy dead six thousand years."

In 1938 Edmund Wilson wrote in *Triple Thinkers*: "Marxism by itself can tell us nothing whatever about the goodness or badness of a work of art."

And James Farrell's "A Note on Literary Criticism," 1936, rested its entire argument upon a distinction made in the first chapter between two aspects of literature, which he labeled the "aesthetic" (literature as art) and the "functional" (literature as an instrument of social influence).

It is unfair, however, to suggest that the Stalinists merely followed in the footsteps of their Trotsky-admiring opponents. As early as 1934 John Strachey had written *Literature and Dialectical Materialism,* a clear attack on the early Marxist confusion of values: "It would be indeed a blunder if we tried to pretend that a man was a bad poet because he was a bad Marxist, or a good poet because he was a good Marxist."

It is a startling commentary on our age that these four men, with the possible exception of Eastman, apparently did not realize, or did not feel it important enough to state, that they were defending an attitude as old as Aristotle.[8] But regardless of the label, the left-wing critics have at last discovered it, and the recognition is providing a long overdue check against earlier tendencies to voice wild enthusiasm for even the crudest work with proper social content, to condemn all contemporary works that did not carry the right political message, and to regard the "classics" as of value only for their "craft."[9]

It has been shown that Plato and Aristotle initiated two critical traditions that find expression today in the critical theories of the Marxists and
their "Aristotelian" opponents. An attempt has been made to disclose the
extent to which the conflict between the two groups is verbal in nature, and
to indicate how each group can profit from an understanding of its opponent's approach. The Aristotelian, to be a good Aristotelian, must recognize
the value of a Platonic analysis; and the Marxist, to be a good Marxist, must
recognize the value of an Aristotelian analysis.

This brings us to the real core of the controversy. After the verbal confusions are understood, the question remains concerning the relative values of
the two approaches. Should either be regarded as superior to the other — as
the preferable manner of formulating criticism?

The question can be answered, perhaps, only in reference to the specific
practical ends for which the task of criticism is undertaken.

For example, in the Marxist movement, which assumes that the primary
need of the world today is economic adjustment rather than progress in the
arts, it is natural that art should be enlisted as a "weapon." A man starving
for food may also be starving for art. But he must be fed before he can enjoy a symphony. The unique values of art may be, in some final sense, near
the top of life's hierarchy of values, but the economic problems are more
important now. They come first in time. For this reason the Marxist feels
justified in emphasizing the social effects of art — in encouraging art that he
feels will advance social reconstruction, and discouraging art that will retard
it. A preoccupation with art as art would be as out of place in the periodicals
of a revolutionary movement as an academic discussion of why one woman
seems more beautiful than another. The Marxist feels that there will be time
for this type of analysis — later.

On the other hand, other contexts may find the Aristotelian approach
more appropriate. To give one example — a university, organized on the basis
of a division of disciplines to facilitate teaching and research, may best serve
its ends if departments of art, literature, and music stress an intrinsic approach to the immediate psychological experience.[10]

But these questions take us into the fields of ethics and politics, and
ultimately, perhaps, into metaphysics.

POSTSCRIPT

Rereading this essay for the first time in almost forty years, I find it enormously pretentious and bulging with obviosities. However, because it deals
with a colorful period of American criticism, I have let it stand almost
unaltered, including the footnotes.

At the time I wrote the article I was a sort of fellow-traveler of the Communist Party, incredibly naive about the Soviet Union. Were I writing it to-

day I would be much less kind to Marxist aesthetic theory. I was also under the influence (as my first footnote indicates) of Richard Peter McKeon, a remarkable historian of philosophy then at the University of Chicago, now retired.

McKeon was born in 1900 at Union Hill, New Jersey, of a Catholic father and a Jewish mother. Baptized and raised a Catholic, he studied medieval philosophy under its greatest living historian, Etienne Gilson, at the University of Paris, before returning to Columbia University to obtain a doctorate. Somewhere along the line he abandoned the Catholic faith. His 1928 thesis on Spinoza was published that same year as a book. The following year he compiled the two-volume *Selections from Medieval Philosophers,* and in 1941 edited *The Basic Works of Aristotle.* Both are still in print.

McKeon and Mortimer Adler had been good friends in New York, and (as I noted earlier) it was McKeon who introduced Adler to Aquinas. In 1934, Hutchins brought McKeon to Chicago as a professor of Greek and soon made him dean of the humanities division. McKeon and Ronald Crane, of the English department, became the founders and leaders of the Chicago neo-Aristotelian school of literary criticism. The two friends taught a course on aesthetics, using the Great Books format, which I had the good fortune of attending.

There is much about "my old friend Dick McKeon" in Adler's *Philosopher at Large.* Their relationship cooled (as Adler tells it on pages 173-76) after Adler became a Thomist. "My inclination was now," Adler writes, "to come down flatly in favor of certain propositions as true, rejecting their contraries or contradictories as false. McKeon, on the other hand, now appeared to me to be taking the approach that I had recommended in *Dialectic . . .* Observing Dick straddling issues that Bob Hutchins and I thought required one either to be with us or against us, I wrote Bob a letter in which I criticized Dick:

> He makes the basic issues a matter of difference in method, not a matter of difference in doctrine. He can take any position and justify it by interpreting it as one method of approaching the problem. This, it seems to me, is simply a way of avoiding the dilemma of having to decide which position is true, and which false. Either Aristotle is right, and Plato wrong, or conversely. I'll be damned if they do not contradict one another and I'll be damned if, contradicting one another, one of them isn't right and the other wrong. Dick is today taking the position which I took in *Dialectic* eight years ago, and which I now think is nothing but clever sophistry. It is simply a way of avoiding the obligation to take sides and take the chance of being wrong. If you straddle all issues by Dick's method, you can never be found off-side.

This gulf between Adler's Thomism and McKeon's relativism proved uncrossable. The annual volumes of *The Great Ideas Today,* edited by Hutchins and Adler from 1961 until Hutchins's death, and since by Adler, never contained a contribution by McKeon. This was in marked contrast to contributions by other good friends of Hutchins and Adler, not to mention such Catholic mentors as Gilson and Maritain. Hutchins and Adler even reprinted in its entirety Chesterton's book *St. Thomas Aquinas*!

In the latest edition of *Encyclopaedia Britannica,* edited by Adler, you'll find in the *Micropaedia* a biographical entry on Adler, with his photograph. The entry is seven inches long. There is no entry on McKeon, though he did write the article on censorship in the *Macropaedia.* It is amusing to note that the entry on Whitehead is five inches, on Carnap four, Dewey a bit less than four, Santayana and Quine less than three. Poor Karl Popper has a mere two and one-quarter inches. None of these great philosophers rated a picture. Bertrand Russell exceeds Adler by less than half an inch, but without a photograph. Maritain, the ultraconservative French Catholic philosopher, has an entry of more than eleven inches.

As far as I know, McKeon has never abandoned his relativism. When he taught a course on Hobbes, he was a Hobbesian. When he taught Plato, he was a Platonist. On the level of practical politics, he did take positions; for example, when Hutchins was speaking against American involvement in World War II, McKeon openly opposed him. But on loftier matters it has been impossible to penetrate McKeon's disguises. Even his papers in philosophical journals have not taken sides. Typically, they open by giving Plato's and Aristotle's views on the topic, then move effortlessly through the history of Western philosophy, classifying thinkers as Platonists or Aristotelians or as proponents of variant or new positions. Just when you expect McKeon to arrive at some sort of grand evaluation, he stresses the necessity of knowing what great minds of the past have said about the topic; then the paper abruptly ends.[11]

Because McKeon's erudition is vast, and his insights so penetrating, one longs to know what he actually believes about fundamental metaphysical questions. Is it that he does have opinions but for some reason desires to conceal them, or is he persuaded that in some subtle dialectical way all great philosophical visions are equally valid? This reluctance to express beliefs is almost unique in the annals of philosophy. Does McKeon, for example, believe in God? If so, what sort? I recall an informal lecture by McKeon, at the university's chapel, during which someone asked if he thought Augustine made a wise decision when he became a Catholic. The questioner had couched his query in Freudian terminology. McKeon replied by saying that one could just as well ask, in a Catholic terminology, whether Freud made a wise decision not to become a Catholic.[12]

I once asked one of McKeon's graduate students, who had worked closely with him for years, if he knew whether McKeon believed in God. The student looked surprised — perhaps this is the proper McKeonist response to such a personal question — then shook his head. There is a passage in Adler's autobiography in which he describes a session at which McKeon struggled to justify Adler's Thomism to Scott Buchanan, and Buchanan's skepticism to Adler, "to nobody's satisfaction but his own."

In spite of his reluctance to disclose ontological beliefs, or his inability to hold them, McKeon's influence on students during the Hutchins-Adler era was immense. Two of his graduate students at Columbia, Paul Goodman and William Barrett, followed him to Chicago. Goodman even taught on the Midway for a short time, and some of his early papers acknowledge his debt to McKeon. A few of McKeon's disciples took to imitating his mannerisms, such as puffing on a pipe during lectures, or talking with a slight lisp. When asked about McKeon's personal views, a frequent answer was that everything would become clear in a book or books on which McKeon was reportedly working.

The books never materialized. Andre J. Reck, in his preface to *The New American Philosophers* (1968) apologizes for not having covered so important a thinker as McKeon. He gives as his reason the fact that McKeon's "major work is not yet published."

"The preoccupation with the analysis of older philosophical systems," said Hans Reichenbach (in a 1946 lecture, "Philosophy and Physics"), "has made of many a philosopher a historian rather than a man of philosophical research; the quest for truth has been forgotten and has been replaced by a program of mapping the various conceptions of previous philosophers. ... those who believe that a study of the traditional philosophical systems can compensate for a lack of scientific training will never be able to accomplish the philosophical research of our time."

Carnap made the same point in the autobiographical section of *The Philosophy of Rudolf Carnap*, edited by Paul Schilpp (1963). Carnap singled out the University of Chicago, during the time he was there, as a place where philosophical research was often confined to the great systems of the past. Although such an emphasis has historical value, Carnap wrote, it is marred by a refusal to recognize progress in philosophy. McKeon is not mentioned by name, but Carnap offered as a horrendous example of "historical neutralism" a Ph.D. thesis by one of McKeon's students that concerned the ontological proof of God. "He had no idea of the fact that modern logic, independently of any particular philosophical point of view, had definitely shown the alleged proof to be logically invalid. In his view, as in that of some of my colleagues, the ontological proof was not only of historical importance, which no doubt is the case, but also represented a problem which must still be taken seriously."

Carnap recalled hearing Adler demonstrate in a lecture, by metaphysical reasoning, the impossibility that human beings have a soul that evolved from the brutes. Carnap said he experienced the weird feeling, strengthened by the university's Gothic architecture, that he was back in the Middle Ages; that at any moment he might hear someone debate the question of whether stars influence human lives. In his imagination he would hear himself "expressing a humble doubt whether this problem fitted well into the twentieth century."

The two papers by McKeon cited in my first note were reprinted in *Critics and Criticism* (University of Chicago Press, 1952). An abridged paperback was issued in 1957 with a new preface by Crane. I have more to say about the Chicago neo-Aristotelian school, represented by the papers in Crane's anthology, in Section 4 of my *Annotated Ancient Mariner* (1965).

Since I wrote the article on art and propaganda there have been endless debates between Aristotelian upholders of art for art's sake and Platonists who see art primarily as a social weapon. Perhaps someday a critic will give us an anthology of quotations from the opposing sides of this perennial controversy, and from mediating views.

I was astonished to learn (from Leslie Fiedler's *Love and Death in the American Novel*) that in the early nineteenth century our nation had a widely read novelist of extreme art-as-weapon opinions. He was George Lippard, a socialist, whose best-selling novel, *Quaker City*, appeared in 1844. No one remembers him today, and with good reason. Here is one of his solemn pronouncements: "Literature merely considered as art is a despicable thing. . . . A literature which does not work practically for the advancement of social reform, or which is too dignified or too good to picture the great wrongs of the great mass of humanity, is just good for nothing at all."

Lippard's successor in the early twentieth century was another dedicated socialist, Upton Sinclair. I do not call him a successor merely because he wrote novels of undisguised political rhetoric, but because his aesthetic philosophy was as extreme as Lippard's. Back in the twenties Sinclair's views of art were thoroughly ventilated in the pages of the *Haldeman-Julius Weekly*, a periodical that later changed its name to the *American Freeman*. This lively publication was edited by Emmanuel Haldeman-Julius, an energetic socialist and free-thinker who sold millions of Little Blue Books for five cents each from his headquarters in Girard, Kansas. In 1924 his periodical published (in four installments) Sinclair's *The Goslings*, in which Sinclair argued that all art is propaganda of some sort and that great art must combine good propaganda with technical excellence. The controversy this ignited—letters from readers and replies by Sinclair—filled many pages of the weekly for the first four months of 1925.

All great writers who ever wrote a passage that offended Sinclair's sense of social justice were dismissed as mediocre. Balzac? No good because he wrote mainly about the bourgeoisie. Shakespeare? Sinclair favored the crackpot theory (he was partial to crazy theories of all varieties, including outrageous medical quackery and spiritualism) that Shakespeare's plays were actually written by Francis Bacon. In any case, because the Bard of Avon admired the upper classes, his plays were untrue to life and a burden on humanity. That Marx and Engels admired both Balzac and Shakespeare failed to impress Sinclair. In a later book, *Mammonart*, he lambasted Conrad and other writers with an arrogance and ignorance that would be equaled later only by such Communist Party hacks as Mike Gold.

If you're interested, the Sinclair story is told by Albert Mordell (himself a man of strange tastes) in a rare Big Blue Book published by Haldeman-Julius as number B-850, titled *Haldeman-Julius and Upton Sinclair: The Amazing Record of a Long Collaboration*. Although Haldeman-Julius serialized many of Sinclair's novels, and published his other writings in dozens of little and big blue books, he could never swallow Sinclair's chronic inability to judge the worth of a work of art independent of its political content.

Of course the tendency to dismiss the formal value of a work of art because you dislike the artist's religious or political views is as old as civilization. An amusing essay to read in this connection—it is good in summarizing the vicious attacks on Milton's poetry—is "Political Criticism on Literary Compositions," by Isaac Disraeli (Benjamin's father) in *Miscellanies of Literature* (London, 1840). A more recent essay along similar lines is "Art for Marx's Sake," George Pfeifer's interview with Aleksandr Borisovich Chakovsky, editor of the Soviet newspaper *Literaturnaya Gazeta* (Literary News), in the *New York Times Magazine*, December 20, 1964. It is an excellent summary of Soviet aesthetic theory.

I always liked a remark Chesterton made in a letter to his wife. He would no more fault Omar as a poet, said G. K., because of his metaphysical views than he would criticize a tightrope dancer's skill on the grounds that he was a liar and an atheist. My own favorite analogy is with the sex act. Clearly it has two functions, the successes of which can be rated independently: the giving of pleasure and the production of children. Today the act is not even necessary to produce children.

At the moment, motion picture and television critics seem to me the most prone to confuse rhetoric with formal excellence. Greatness is not automatically conferred on a movie if it is highly successful as political propaganda, or as rhetoric for racial tolerance, women's liberation, sexual freedom, the paranormal, or anything else that concerns a popular trend or belief. Nevertheless, I am enough of a Platonist to forgive film producers for all their mindlessness (in the past few years obligatory sexual bouts have been superseded by obligatory car crashes) because of the truly admirable job they have done and are still doing in combating racial prejudice. It will be a great relief when they get over their childish obsessions with explosions, disasters, blood, witchcraft, demons, ghosts, corpses, and invaders from outer space.

NOTES

1. This thesis is based on the position taken by Dr. Richard P. McKeon, dean of the humanities division at the University of Chicago, in an article, "Literary Criticism and the Concept of Imitation in Antiquity," published in *Modern Philology*, August 1936, and an unpublished lecture, "The Philosophic Bases of Art and Criticism," given in 1941 at the annual meeting of the College Art Association. In addition to

the two basic approaches, McKeon also distinguishes three additional modes of criticism, regarded as "particularizations" of the Platonic, which found their classical expressions in the critical works of Longinus (later given a philosophical basis by Kant), Horace, and Demetrius.

2. It should be noted that the distinction between "immediate" pleasure and "later" effects of art, like all distinctions, develops blurred edges when placed under a microscope. The pleasure of experiencing a work of art may carry over after the work is no longer present, or may be revived on later occasions simply by recalling the work. Or the rhetoric in a novel, which may later influence the political behavior of the reader, may cause immediate pleasure or displeasure depending on whether the reader agrees with it or not. Music and song may cause persons to behave in certain social ways while they are actually experiencing the music (for example, converts at a revival meeting under the influence of group singing). But the rough distinction is good enough for the purposes of the essay. To make sharper distinctions between various functions of art would probably necessitate abandoning traditional terms entirely and approaching the subject with a "semiotic" vocabulary such as that used by Dr. Charles Morris in his pioneering article "Esthetics and the Theory of Signs" in the *Journal of Unified Science*, June 1939.

3. No attempt can be made here to do more than present a bare outline of the two approaches. Other "schools" of aesthetics, past and present, usually fall into one of the two traditions, or emphasize certain aspects of them at the expense of other aspects. Many contemporary opponents of Marxist theory, it should be noted, are Platonists who differ only in the specific moral, political, and metaphysical standards they apply.

4. Because the intrinsic "principles" of art are such by virtue of their power to arouse immediate pleasure, they can be discovered only by inductive study of works of art which do, in fact, arouse such pleasure. Perhaps the most unfortunate error to which Aristotelian critics throughout history have been susceptible is that of failing to recognize that new forms of art call forth new principles, and therefore cannot be judged by standards applicable to the older forms. Works of art are created first; the principles discovered afterward. Aristotle's *Poetics* could not have been written before the development of Greek tragedy. Walt Disney made this point in a recent press interview when he said that he and his staff merely went to work and made a picture, then the "professors" came along to tell them what they had done.

5. The liveliest critical research in America along Aristotelian lines has been taking place in the English Department at the University of Chicago under the guidance of Ronald S. Crane, head of the department. See the *University Review,* Spring 1942, for essays by Elder Olson and Norman F. Maclean, with a prefatory note by Crane. The essays are pioneer attempts to formulate a poetics of lyric poetry.

Another Aristotelian (in the Thomist tradition) at the University of Chicago is Mortimer J. Adler, whose book *Art and Prudence* (1937) is an unusually competent study of the problem of censorship with reference to the motion picture. It contains an excellent historical survey of critical theories, with special emphasis on the Platonic and Aristotelian traditions. The Aristotelian is, of course, defended as superior. A sly criticism of McKeon's position will be found on page 656.

6. It is interesting to note that Dewey, in *Art as Experience*, clearly adopts the Aristotelian approach. On page 316 he points out the "confusion of categories" involved in dealing with art in terms of "non-aesthetic" criticism. Discussing psychoanalytic criticism, he states that the artist's neuroses are "relevant to biography, but

they are wholly impertinent as to the character of the work itself. If the latter has defects, they are blemishes to be detected in the construction of the object itself. If an Oedipus complex is part of the work of art, it can be discovered on its own account." As to sociological criticism, he writes, "Knowledge of social conditions of production is, when it is really knowledge, of genuine value. But it is no substitute for understanding of the object in its own qualities and relations." Of the historic approach, "But historic judgment is not esthetic judgment. There are categories . . . appropriate to history, and only confusion results when they are used to control inquiry into art which also had its own ideas." Mathematical, religious, scientific, and philosophical approaches are similarly rejected from the province of aesthetic criticism because of their "neglect of the intrinsic significance of the medium."

7. Dewey, it appears, like Eliot, is reluctant to admit that an artist may be consciously concerned with the political effect of his work without at the same time weakening his performance as an artist (see the last chapter of *Art as Experience*). One is tempted to state the Marxist case in Dewey's own vocabulary: The aesthetic and moral intentions of the artist fuse and interpenetrate so that the work of art is a genuine artistic expression in which political rhetoric is embedded—the entire substance of the work grounded in the artist's experience as a live creature in dynamic interaction with his environment.

8. Especially startling is the case of Farrell. Although Aristotle took for granted the distinction upon which he rests his entire book, Farrell attributes it to an article by George Herbert Mead, "The Nature of the Aesthetic Experience," in the *International Journal of Ethics*, July 1926.

9. Typical of this type of criticism was Mike Gold's historic outburst against Thornton Wilder in the *New Republic*, October 22, 1930. Wilder was shown to be "silly" and "superficial," destined to quick oblivion. On another page in the same issue, in an advertisement, was quoted Gold's estimate of Mary Heaton Vorse's novel *Strike* as a "burning and imperishable epic." To borrow Edward Bullough's term, Gold lacked "psychic distance." His enthusiasm for the right political content, and rage at its absence, distorted his judgment of the other values of art. But his high-voltage criticism was of timely value in arousing interest in the Marxist approach.

10. For a thorough discussion of this question see Crane's article, "History versus Criticism in the University Study of Literature," in the *English Journal* (college edition), October 1935. Writing before he became head of the department of English at the University of Chicago, Crane deplored the overemphasis in American universities on the "historical" aspects of literature and the consequent neglect of "criticism" in the Aristotelian sense. He outlined the nature of a reform that he implemented a few years later when he became departmental head.

11. McKeon's complex, involuted, opaque writing style has been described several times by his detractors. For two notable descriptions, see Eliseo Vivas, "The Neo-Aristotelians of Chicago," a 1953 paper reprinted in Vivas, *The Artistic Transaction and Essays on the Theory of Literature* (Ohio State University Press, 1963), and Robert Pirsig's novel *Zen and the Art of Motorcycle Maintenance* (William Morrow, 1974), Chapter 28. McKeon is called "The Chairman" throughout this section of the novel. Pirsig offers several hypotheses, none satisfactory, to explain McKeon's curious style.

12. After the death of his first wife, Muriel, McKeon married one of his graduate students, Zahavah, who had obtained her doctorate under him. Janet Kalven tells me that Zahavah is a Catholic convert of orthodox Jewish background. They were married in the church.

3

Sidney Sime of Worplesdon

In his autobiography, *Patches of Sunlight,* Lord Dunsany records that after he completed his first book of fantasy tales, *The Gods of Pegana*, he could think of only two men he would like to have illustrate it.

> . . . one of them I knew was dead and I did not know whether the other still lived or not. The two men that had so impressed me were Dore and Sime, and Mr. S. H. Sime was luckily not only alive in 1904 but is still alive today. This remarkable man consented to do me eight illustrations, and I have never seen a black-and-white artist with a more stupendous imagination. I think he is greater than Beardsley, and I do not know anyone now living who can bring such scenes of wonder down upon paper with lamp-black and Indian ink. Of course the gods and their heavens that he drew for me were totally different from anything that I had imagined, but I knew that it would be impossible to catch Sime's Pegasus and drive it exactly along some track that I had travelled myself, and that if it were possible, it could only be done by clipping its wings. So I left Mr. Sime to do exactly as he liked, and I think the eight pictures he did for my first book are among the most remarkable pictures of his that I have ever seen.

Patches of Sunlight was published in 1938. Four years later, Mr. Sime was dead. Except for a narrow circle of ardent admirers, he died unhonored and unknown. The London papers did not mention his passing. And yet he was perhaps the greatest fantasy artist of modern times. His illustrations for Dunsany's tales and novels were so extraordinary that Frank Harris, in an essay on Dunsany and Sime (in the second series of his *Contemporary Portraits*) calls him "one of the greatest of living artists" and adds that "for sheer imaginative quality his best is without an equal in modern work."

This essay originally appeared in the *Arkham Sampler,* Autumn 1949.

One may question Harris's judgment that Sime "is a far abler man than the Irish lord," but no one familiar with Sime's work can fail to recognize his singular genius. His illustrations for Dunsany's *The Gods of Pegana, Time and the Gods, A Dreamer's Tales, The Sword of Welleran, The Book of Wonder, The Last Book of Wonder;* and many of Dunsany's novels, including *The King of Elfland's Daughter* and *The Blessing of Pan*, are so convincing and satisfying in their bizarre beauty that one looks up from them with sudden shock to find himself back in what Dunsany liked to call "the fields we know."

Sidney H. Sime (pronounced to rhyme with dream) was born in 1867, in Manchester, England, of humble parents. In his youth he worked five years in the gloomy coal mines of Yorkshire, pushing a small "scoop," loaded with coal, along rails to the spot where it was hoisted upward. A number of horrible accidents occurred to fellow workers, and on one occasion he himself narrowly escaped death.

Haldane McFall, British art critic and author of the eight-volume *History of Painting*, writes in that work of Sime: "The Manchester lad who began breathing in the bowels of the earth, must have already with grim Northern humor, been spinning dreams of Heaven and Hell before he came to the surface at the pit's mouth to try sign painting for a change." I do not know if Sime, like the miners in Louis Untermeyer's poem, prayed to the powers above to "fling us a handful of stars," but no one can deny the generosity with which Sime later flung them over his drawings — "blooming great stars" (to borrow a phrase from Dunsany) that glow with unearthly splendor.

After leaving the coal mines, Sime worked for a brief period as a linen draper's assistant and then a barber's apprentice (he did the lathering) before he took up sign painting as a trade. His facility in wielding the brush led him to enroll in the Liverpool School of Art, and finally took him to London.

It was 1893 when Sime as a young man first came to London. For many years he lived in shabby Bohemian garrets, eking out a living by peddling drawings to half-penny comic papers and cheap magazines. This early work was in conscious imitation of Beardsley, whom he greatly admired, and is about as valueless as the early amateurish work of Beardsley himself. The two never met, incidentally, though Sime made an effort to meet him on one ocasion shortly before his fatal illness. Of Beardsley, Sime has said:

> Beardsley's work was generally morbid, and he introduced often into his drawings more than a suggestion of pain and disease. But, apart from his temperament, his technique was extraordinary. I think he has influenced almost every man who is drawing today. The same, of course, may be said of Japanese art.[1]

As Sime's skill improved, he began to break away from the Beardsley influence and his work took on a texture and richness all its own. But the impress of Beardsley, and of Japanese art as well, never left his work. William Blake was another artist much revered by Sime. In a letter to Frank Harris (quoted in *Contemporary Portraits*) he wrote:

> I hope I did not convey any idea that Blake is communicable. The interest of him to me lies in the fact that he isn't. It is one of my delusions that there is not any general truth or value outside the perceptive soul; no intrinsic values.
>
> Blake speaks like the wind in the chimney, which sings with all the voice of all dead poets and always sings the heart's desire without the bondage of words. The commentators will try in vain to pigeonhole Blake as they have failed with others, but they will throw their obfuscating mildew around his dim and unfinished statement without shame.
>
> Blake told his friend Butts that he was bringing a poem to town and what he meant by a poem was a work that intrigued and allured and satisfied the imagination but utterly confounded and bewildered the corporal sense.

By the late 1890s Sime's magazine drawings had become well known. His work included cartoons with gag lines, political satire, caricatures of prominent people (he did a famous series for the walls of the Yorick Club), and drawings of sheer fantasy and whimsy. I do not know if there are Sime collectors, but what a weird and wonderful collection could be garnered from the pages of British publications to which he sold! These magazines include *The Sketch, Pick-Me-Up, The Strand, The Tatler, Punch, The Idler, The Butterfly, Eureka, Illustrated Sporting and Dramatic News, Illustrated London News, The Queen, Pall Mall Magazine,* and *The Unicorn.* For a time Sime was publisher of *The Idler,* having purchased it with money left him by an uncle, but he was unable to make it pay, and finally sold it. He was also one of the editors of *Eureka.* Many of these magazine drawings, especially in *The Idler,* are pictures of high loveliness and grotesque humor. Of special interest to admirers of H. G. Wells are three illustrations for Wells's "A Vision of Judgment," in the September 1899 issue of *The Butterfly.*

Typical of Sime's quaint humor is a picture called *The Dream of the Woman of Char.* In it a charwoman tries desperately to scrub a mammoth stairway. Great clouds of suds billow from her hand as she discovers to her chagrin that the stair is made of soap! A lengthy series of cartoons, depicting amusing scenes from Heaven and Hell, won wide acclaim.

In addition to his black-and-white drawings, Sime also worked in oils and water colors, favoring landscapes of wild Scottish and Welsh scenery. Scores of these strange, brilliantly colored paintings have been exhibited in London galleries, and I sometimes wonder how many are currently available, perhaps at ridiculously low figures, in the stock of London art dealers.

After 1904, when he began illustrating for Dunsany, Sime's fame and income increased enough to enable him to buy a public building in Worplesdon, which he converted into a home for himself and his wife. I have often fancied that he chose this area largely because of its outlandish name. A stable in the garden became an art studio. In a nearby village, his wife gave foxtrot lessons to the farm lads and lassies.

Frank Harris describes Sime, in this period of his life, as:

> . . . a strongly-built man of about five feet seven or eight with a cliff-like, overhanging, tyrannous forehead. His eyes are superlative, grayish blue looking out under heavy brows, eyes with a pathetic patience in them as of one who has lived with sorrow; and realizes—"The weary weight of all this unintelligible world." From time to time humorous gleams light up the eyes and the whole face; mirth on melancholy—a modern combination.

A revealing statement made by Sime in an interview in 1908 was: "I owe everything to omniverous and indiscriminate reading. But perhaps if I mention Poe, Heine, De Quincey, it will give you some indication of my preference in literature. And Meredith—above all, Meredith."

It was this same year, 1908, that Dunsany published *The Sword of Welleran,* in which his story "The Highwayman" appeared. The story had a curious origin, and Dunsany tells of it in his autobiography.

> It came about like this: a man wrote to me to say that he had a picture by Sime that he had bought while up at Cambridge and that he now wanted to sell, but did not know how to do it, or what price to ask. I gladly bought the picture, and it was a picture in lamp-black and Indian ink of a man, much decomposed, hanging in chains, while three villainous people in ancient hats come by the light of such a moon as Mr. Sime draws best, apparently to cut the man down. In reality they were coming, as Mr. Sime told me later, to cut off the man's hand in order to use it for magic; but I took the view that they were his friends, and that they were coming for friendship's sake to give him decent burial. And so I wrote a tale about human beings, and was delighted to find that I could do it.

In addition to being the Irish lord's first story about ordinary people, "The Highwayman" also was his first tale written to fit a Sime drawing. Later, most of the stories in *The Book of Wonder* were produced in this unusual manner. To return to the autobiography:

> It happened like this: I found Mr. Sime one day, in his strange house at Worplesdon, complaining that editors did not offer him very suitable subjects for illustrations; so I said: "Why not do any pictures you like, and I will write stories explaining them, which may add a little to their mystery?" Mr. Sime fortunately agreed; and so, reversing the order of story and illustration which we had followed hitherto, we set about putting together *The Book of Wonder.* Some of Mr. Sime's drawings were finished pictures, others the faintest sketches on bits of paper, and one of them I think may have been inspired in its turn by the three travellers and their mule that came over the mountains in my tale of Bethmoora on their ominous journey to the Emperor Thuba Mleen. I had

Sidney H. Sime's "Tom o' the Roads"

particularly asked Mr. Sime not to tell me what the pictures were about, and he only tried to explain one to me, but I could not quite follow. When I showed him a story and asked him if it accurately described what was going on in the picture he said: "It sounds extremely probable."

To describe those pictures would require another book, as long as *The Book of Wonder,* but I may mention that the illustration for the first tale, or rather the picture for which that tale was an illustration, showed an old woman sitting under a tree; but the tree was rather mineral than vegetable, for it was all full of stars, and was in fact an erect slice of a clear night, and was approached from an abyss by steps of stone, from which it was shut off by a gate. The old woman sitting at the foot of it has just uttered a cough to warn the man who is crossing the abyss by a fallen tree that he is being followed. The forest is full of cobwebs vaster than curtains, and the spider that follows the man, as he puts his great diamond down and turns round with his sword, is the size of one that could easily make such cobwebs. The picture is called The Ominous Cough. You can see by the old woman's face that she knows that her warning will be useless. One of the trees has shining windows in it, and a door, and so common a stove-pipe sticking out further up, that you know that after all it must be somewhere in this world. And now I have only described odd corners of that marvelous picture. The story, as I saw it, did not end happily. . . .

All the tales in *The Book of Wonder,* with the exception of "The Wonderful Window" and "Chubu and Sheemish," were similarly inspired by Sime's pictures. Dunsany adds:

> . . . I think I was sometimes able to give a little of the feeling of Mr. Sime's worlds, as he, when he did the pictures in the more usual order, gave some of the feeling of mine; I think for instance I may have given some indication of the vastness of Sime's spaces when I told how the Old Man Who Looks After Fairyland "used to empty his slops sheer on to the Southern Cross."

Has Sime illustrated books other than those of Lord Dunsany? He has, and doubtless they are many, but the only ones I know are several Arthur Machen novels and William Hope Hodgson's *The Ghost Pirates,* all of which contain, in certain editions, Sime frontispieces. And there is a delightful book of nonsense rhymes for children called *Bogey Beasts,* published in 1893 by Goodwin and Tabb, Ltd., London. Sime wrote fifteen jingles for the book, each about a rare, mythical beast, and the jingles were set to music by Joseph C. Holbrooke. A full-page Sime drawing pictures each animal—the Caush, Seekim, Wily Grasser, Gorobobble, Oop Oop, Zoom, Nunk (the book's preface is by the Nunk), Two-Tailed Sogg, Iffysaurus, Snide, Pst, Moonijim, Snatch, Prapsnot, and the Ta-Ta.

Here is Sime's description of the Pst:

Sidney H. Sime's "The Ominous Cough"

Not for cash
Or glory,
Nor
A conceited whim,
No tradition
Hoary,
A-tittilutes
His limb.
Not to
Please a rabble,
Or
Charm the caltured few,
Or stir up tongues
To gabble
Of things
They never knew.
He
Finds a place
A mile hence
A place
Devoid of lumps
And dances
There
In silence
Because
He has "the Jumps."
I would do as he does
If I
Were just like he;
But
Would he do
What I does,
If he
Resembled
Me?

In the *Fortnightly,* August 1942, shortly after Sime's death, there is a beautifully written tribute by Dunsany. I have space for only a few sentences:

There was in his pictures a sombre grandeur showing all the majesty of night or the mystery of dark forests . . . a doom seems often to haunt the glades of his forests, and sometimes seems to spread over the whole landscape, like a curse laid for a joke by a god whom nobody worships.

And yet his "sombre shadows . . . are always lit by the rays of his merry humor." Dunsany calls attention to Sime's sly little earthly touches. "Cliffs too vast for our world I have seen made terrestrial in one of his pictures by

Sidney H. Sime's "The Edge of the World"

a little iron clamp and a couple of screws fastened over a crack in the cliff . . ."

Perhaps time will someday confirm Dunsany's estimate:

> We have lost . . . a genius whose stupendous imagination has passed across our time little more noticed by most people than the shadow of a bird passing over a lawn would be noticed by most of a tennis party.

. . . .

And now that vast imagination has left us, having enriched our age with dreams that we have not entirely deserved.

POSTSCRIPT

Although today's art world has no interest in Sime, there has been increasing recognition of his work on the part of fantasy buffs in both England and the United States.

At least six books have been published in the past ten years in which you will find a wealth of information about Sime, reproductions of many of his pictures not in books by Dunsany, and detailed bibliographies: *From an Ultimate Dim Thule: A Review of the Early Works of Sidney H. Sime,* by George Locke (London: Ferret Fantasy, Ltd., 1973); *Beasts That Might Have Been,* by S. H. Sime (London: Ferret Fantasy, Ltd., 1974); *Bogey Beasts,* by Sidney H. Sime (Newport News, Va.: Purple Mouth Press, 1975), a reprint of the 1923 edition; *The Land of Dreams: S. H. Sime 1905-1916,* by George Locke (London: Ferret Fantasy, Ltd., 1975); *Sidney H. Sime: Master of Fantasy,* by Paul W. Skeeters, Introduction by Ray Bradbury (Pasadena, Calif.: Ward Ritchie Press, 1978); *Sidney Sime: Master of the Mysterious,* by Simon Heneage and Henry Ford (London: Thames and Hudson, 1980).

I spoke in my essay of Sime's unearthly, glowing stars. In Philip José Farmer's Riverworld Series novel *To Your Scattered Bodies Go,* Sime's stars are mentioned by Peter Jairus Frigate, the name Farmer uses for himself when he enters one of his novels. Here, from Chapter 12, is the passage:

> They drank, and then they sat around the fire for a while and smoked and talked. The shadow darkened, the sky lost its blue, and the gigantic stars and great sheets, which had been dimly seen ghosts just before dusk, blossomed out. The sky was indeed a blaze of glory.
>
> "Like a Sime illustration," Frigate said.
>
> Burton did not know what a Sime was. . . .

NOTE

1. The quotation appears in "Mr. S. H. Sime and His Work," by E. S. Valentine, in *The Strand,* October 1908. In addition to a photograph of Sime, and reproductions of many of his drawings, the article also includes a caricature of Sime by Max Beerbohm. Other articles on Sime can be found in *The Graphic,* November 25, 1922; *Magazine Art,* March 1904; and *The Idler,* January 1898. The last article reproduces a self-caricature.

4

Order and Surprise

"We are in the position of a little child," said Einstein in a press interview, "entering a huge library whose walls are covered to the ceiling with books in many different tongues. . . . The child does not understand the languages in which they are written. He notes a definite plan in the arrangement of the books, a mysterious order which he does not comprehend, but only dimly suspects."

Few empirically minded philosophers today would find fault with Einstein's statement. Bertrand Russell's book *Human Knowledge: Its Scope and Limits* repeats like a refrain: The external world exists; the structure of the world is ordered; we know little about the nature of the order, nothing at all about why it should exist.

If the cosmos were suddenly frozen, so all movement ceased, a survey of its structure would not reveal a random distribution of parts. Simple geometrical patterns, for example, would be found in profusion — from the spirals of galaxies to the hexagonal shapes of snow crystals. Set the clockwork going, and its parts move rhythmically to laws that often can be expressed by equations of surprising simplicity. And there is no logical or a priori reason why these things should be so.

"The most incomprehensible thing about the world is that it is comprehensible," said Einstein, on another occasion; "It is indeed a surprising and fortunate fact that nature can be expressed by relatively low-order mathematical functions," declared Rudolf Carnap in a classroom lecture; and Russell closes his early book on relativity with this sentence: "The final conclusion is that we know very little, and yet it is astonishing that we know so much, and still more astonishing that so little knowledge can give us so much power."[1]

This essay originally appeared in the *Philosophy of Science,* January 1950. © 1950 by the Williams & Wilkins Co. Reprinted with permission.

One more quotation from Russell illustrates how easily these expressions of surprise enter an otherwise technical discussion:

> We are accustomed to the axiom that things that are equal to the same thing are equal to one another. This axiom has a specious and deceptive appearance of obviousness, in spite of the fact that the empirical evidence is against it. You may find that, by the most delicate tests you can apply, A is equal to B, and B to C, but A is noticeably unequal to C. When this happens, we say that A is not *really* equal to B, or B to C. *Oddly enough,* this tends to be confirmed when the technique of measurement is improved.[2] [Last italics added.]

It is this feeling of surprise, with the related emotion of good fortune, that I wish to discuss. First, to show how it arises from the activities of science. Second, to discuss briefly its role in the traditional proof of God from design. Lastly, to examine its psychological basis and state precisely when it is and is not a legitimate emotion.

It is easy to understand the surprise early physicists felt as they found natural phenomena yielding so readily to mathematical formulation. "Nature's great book," said Galileo, "is written in mathematical symbols," and Galileo was well aware that the universe was under no obligation to behave with such polite regularity.

Sextus Empiricus, two centuries before Christ, had no difficulty imagining a less obedient world: "If causes were non-existent, everything would have been produced by everything and at random. Horses, for instance, might be born, perchance, of flies, and elephants of ants; and there would have been severe rains and snow in Egyptian Thebes, while the southern districts would have had no rain. . . ."[3]

In the opening chapter of his book on relativity, Russell allows his imagination similar rein:

> The success of this common-sense point of view [that when you start on a trip to a city, you expect to find it there when you arrive] depends upon a number of things which are really of the nature of luck. Suppose all the houses in London were perpetually moving about, like a swarm of bees; suppose railways moved and changed their shapes like avalanches; and finally suppose that material objects were perpetually being formed and dissolved like clouds. There is nothing impossible in these suppositions: something like them must have been verified when the earth was hotter than it is now. But obviously what we call a journey to Edinburgh would have no meaning in such a world. You would begin, no doubt, by asking the taxi-driver: "Where is King's Cross this morning?" At the station you would have to ask a similar question about Edinburgh, but the booking-office clerk would reply: "What part of Edinburgh do you mean, Sir? Prince's Street has gone to Glasgow, the Castle has moved up into the Highlands, and Waverly Station is under water in the middle of the Firth of Forth."[4]

Observe that Russell speaks of the relative permanence of geography as a "matter of luck." Later in the same book he refers to the notion of "place" as dependent on the "fortunate immovability of most of the large objects on the earth's surface." On an electron or the sun, he points out, we would be in a "higgledy-piggledy" universe in which it would be impossible to formulate natural laws. "It is fortunate for us," he concludes, " that we are not faced with this alternative."

A similar sense of wonder and thankfulness concerning the rigidity of geography is amusingly expressed by a character in one of Gilbert Chesterton's fantasies:

> "I tell you," went on Syme with passion, "that every time a train comes in I feel that it has broken past batteries of besiegers, and that man has won a battle against chaos. You say contemptuously that when one has left Sloane Square one must come to Victoria. I say that one might do a thousand things instead, and that whenever I really come there I have the sense of hair-breadth escape. And when I hear the guard shout out the word 'Victoria,' it is not an unmeaning word. It is to me the cry of a herald announcing conquest. It is to me indeed 'Victoria'; it is the victory of Adam."[5]

It might be thought that relativity physics, with its contracting and expanding bodies, has blasted the notion of rigidity. This is an easy misconception. The fact is that relativity theory provides a triumphant vindication of rigidity. It is only in what Carnap likes to call the "Euclidean language" that bodies in motion or in gravitational fields can be described as altering shape. In the non-Euclidean language of relativity, with its four-dimensional continuum, the bodies remain as fixed and rigid as in Newtonian physics.

Not only does relativity physics maintain the uniformity of solids, but it also retains the striking similarity in the behavior of light rays and the movement of solid bodies. As Reichenbach has pointed out, classical physics assumes that both mechanics and optics rest upon the same geometrical structure of space. Both bodies and light rays move in straight lines. There is no a priori reason why this coincidence should obtain in Newtonian physics; it is equally "surprising" that it should continue to hold true in relativity physics. Experiments that indicate that light is bent by gravity, or maintains a constant speed relative to all observers, seem at first thought to destroy the simplicity of movement that light possessed in Newtonian physics. Again, this is because it is expressed in Euclidean language. In the non-Euclidean syntax of relativity, light does not "bend" any more than solids change their shape. It continues to move along a "geodesic" — the shortest possible route between spacetime points. In the language of relativity, light does not alter its speed as objects move relative to it. It maintains a constant speed, but the spacetime structure of moving objects so alters that measurements of the speed always yield the same result. As Russell puts it, relativity physics upholds the principle of "cosmic laziness" so essential to the Kepler and

Newton tradition. Bodies and light rays alike continue, in the world of Einstein, to move in terms of the simplest possible mathematical formulations.

Closely allied with nature's neatness, perhaps only another way of stating it, is the principle of induction. Mill regarded the uniformity of nature as the "ultimate major premise of all inductions." The universe, as H. G. Wells once phrased it, "seems to play fair upon some vaster system of its own."

Russell, after a lifelong search for a logical basis for induction, has finally decided to agree with Mill. In *Human Knowledge* he states one of his central theses as follows:

> Inference from a group of events to other events can only be justified if the world has certain characteristics which are not logically necessary. So far as deductive logic can show, any collection of events might be the whole universe; if, then, I am ever to be able to infer events, I must accept principles of inference which lie outside deductive logic. All inference from events to events demands some kind of interconnection between different occurrences. Such interconnection is traditionally asserted in the principle of causality or natural law.[6]

One of the major tasks of *Human Knowledge* is to describe more precisely the fundamental features of natural order. Russell finds that it possesses five properties, or what he calls the five basic postulates that underlie scientific method. They are: (1) The postulate of quasi-permanence (Carnap calls it "genidentity"). (2) The postulate of separable causal lines. (3) The postulate of spatio-temporal continuity (no action at a distance). (4) The postulate of the common causal origin of similar structures ranged about a center. (5) The postulate of analogy. There is no logical reason why any of these postulates should be true. They are valid only because that is the way science has found the world behaving.

In an earlier book, writing about the inability of the empiricist to give a logical ground for induction, Russell confessed: "This method has had the most amazing success, amazing because it is as indefensible intellectually as the purely deductive method of the Middle Ages."[7]

Again, the expression of surprise. And Russell is far from the first philosopher to stare with raised eyebrows at the equations of science.

Technicalities aside, thinkers of the past divide roughly into two groups in their attitude toward the fact of a patterned universe.

The oldest and most widespread attitude, implicit in the mythologies of all cultures, is to attribute the order to a mind or minds. The sun rises because Apollo drives his chariot into the sky. If the mythology is monotheistic, it is God who wills the regularity—who "geometrizes." Spinoza's God is not the same as Plato's, but there is still a sense in which the Spinozistic deity "thinks" the laws of nature, a point of view that has fascinated Einstein and Sir James Jeans.

Newton was, of course, a devout theist. He regarded space as a kind of "sensorium" by which God perceived all things. Gravity was God's method of holding the cosmos together. Unlike Leibniz, Newton thought it necessary for God occasionally to adjust the cosmos after it developed imperfections. He accepted the proof of God from design, using as illustrations both the perfection in the bodies of plants and animals and the orderly paths of the planets. The mere fact that the planets revolved in a single plane seemed to him startling enough to require supernatural explanation.

Chesterton, the late and great apologist for the Roman Catholic church, was fond of using nature's uncanny dance as an argument for God:

The modern world as I found it was solid for modern Calvinism, for the necessity of things being as they are. But when I came to ask them I found they had really no proof of this unavoidable repetition in things except the fact that the things were repeated. Now, the mere repetition made the things to me rather more weird than rational. It was as if, having seen a curiously shaped nose in the street and dismissed it as an accident, I had then seen six other noses of the same astonishing shape. I should have fancied for a moment that it must be some local secret society. So one elephant having a trunk was odd; but all elephants having trunks looked like a plot. I speak here only of an emotion, and of an emotion at once stubborn and subtle. But the repetition in Nature seemed sometimes to be an excited repetition, like that of an angry schoolmaster saying the same thing over and over again. The grass seemed signalling to me with all its fingers at once; the crowded stars seemed bent upon being understood. The sun would make me see him if he rose a thousand times. The recurrences of the universe rose to the maddening rhythm of an incantation. . . .[8]

From this initial sense of amazement, Chesterton makes an easy leap into theology: "I had always vaguely felt facts to be miracles in the sense that they are wonderful: now I began to think them miracles in the stricter sense that they were *wilful*. I mean that they were, or might be, repeated exercises of some will."[9]

The weird repetition of nature is attributed by Chesterton to God's inability to tire:

. . . perhaps God is strong enough to exult in monotony. It is possible that God says every morning, "Do it again" to the sun; and every evening, "Do it again" to the moon. It may not be automatic necessity that makes all daisies alike; it may be that God makes every daisy separately, but has never got tired of making them. It may be that He has the eternal appetite of infancy; for we have sinned and grown old, and our father is younger than we. The repetition in Nature may not be a mere recurrence; it may be a theatrical *encore*. Heaven may *encore* the bird who laid an egg. If the human being conceives and brings forth a human child instead of bringing forth a fish, or a bat, or a griffin, the reason may not be that we are fixed in an animal fate without life or purpose. It may be that our little tragedy has touched the gods, that they admire it from their starry galleries, and that at the end of every human drama man is called again and again before the curtain. Repetition may go on for millions of years, by mere choice, and at any instant it may stop. Man may stand on the earth generation after generation, and yet each birth be his positively last appearance.[10]

I have quoted Chesterton at length because it seems to me he expresses with great honesty the psychological motives beneath the traditional proof of God from design. I take for granted that the proof is logically indefensible. But the "pragmatic" or "emotional" meaning of the proof lies precisely in what Chesterton calls a "stubborn and subtle" emotion. This emotion may be compounded of many elements; certainly surprise is one of them. The modern formulation of the proof, by the neo-Thomists for instance, differs from Chesterton's literary description only in that the emotional leap is buried under erudition and technical jargon. But at some point in the demonstration, the subtle emotion creeps between the inferences.

The alternative attitude toward nature's order is characteristic of philosophers in the positivist tradition. There is no need to elaborate it here. From this point of view the leap from pattern to pattern-maker is logically invalid and pragmatically unnecessary. The existence of regularity is simply a given fact. It is accepted. It leads to no further conclusion.

The everyday world of experience is a mixture of order and haphazardry. It is true that solids maintain their shapes, Euclidean geometry applies for all practical purposes to relations between parts, and objects always fall when dropped; but these patterns are enveloped with disorder. Quite apart from the unpredictability of living things, the inorganic world is saturated with chaos. James Branch Cabell has described it vividly:

> It needed only a glance toward the sky the first clear night to show there was no pattern-work in the arrangement of the stars. Nor were the planets moving about the sun at speeds or distances which bore any conceivable relation to one another. It was all at loose ends. . . . To his finicky love of neatness the universe showed on a sudden as a vast disheveled horror. There seemed so little harmony, so faint a sense of order, back of all this infinite torrent of gyrations. . . .
>
> And on earth there was no balancing in the distribution of land and water. Continents approached no regular shape. Mountains stood out like pimples or lay like broken welts across the habitable ground, with no symmetry of arrangement. Rivers ran anywhither. . . . It was all at loose ends, except — bewilderingly — when water froze. For then . . . the ice-crystals were arranged in perfect and very elaborate patterns. And these stellular patterns, to the mused judgment of Kennaston, appeared to have been shaped by the last love-tap of unreason — when, in completing all, unreason made sure that even here the universe should run askew to any conceivable "design" and loose even the coherency of being everywhere irregular.[11]

It is into this world of surface incoherence that science penetrates. The farther it penetrates, the more order it uncovers. It is precisely this contrast between surface muddlement and underlying regularity that is the occasion for surprise.

Let us imagine a world in which our lives and environment are so completely ordered that almost every event can be predicted. Let us suppose also that a science exists to discover areas in nature where predictions are impossible. The aim of this curious science is to introduce disorder — not to control nature, but to break the dullness, to make life interesting. The progress of such a science, assuming it could progress, would be viewed with increasing astonishment. "There is no logical reason why nature should behave at random," one can imagine a well-ordered physicist saying. "How surprising and fortunate to find that it does!" A wild theory might even be proposed that at bottom the universe is completely disorderly — that so-called "laws" are not laws at all, but seem so only because science has not yet disclosed the disorder beneath them.

As a matter of fact the world of physics in recent years has not been dissimilar from this imaginary world. Newtonian physics reduced nature to a complex machine, the parts turning with invariable precision. That was why the Michelson-Morley experiment was such a shock. It suggested that either light behaved in a remarkably disorderly fashion or, if light were orderly, then rigid bodies were no longer rigid. The surprise soon led, as previously indicated, to the formulation of a new physics, in which the uniformity of classical mechanics and optics was restored.

In quantum theory, however, a more basic kind of disorder appeared. The possibility arose that ultimate particles of nature, considered as individuals, may behave in random ways. Fundamental particles and quantum systems seem to acquire definite properties only at the instant they are measured, and certain of those properties are determined not by causal laws but by pure chance — a situation Einstein liked to describe as God playing dice with the universe.

Against the background of the history of science such a fact, if it is a fact, comes with an enormous element of surprise. So much so that many physicists, Einstein among them, insist that the haphazardry of the electron may be due simply to our inability to make the necessary measurements; that, as our techniques improve, laws for the electron's behavior may be forthcoming.

In any case, we must conclude that the discovery of both order and disorder may arouse the emotion of surprise. It all depends on what is expected. Logically, there is no reason that nature should behave in either fashion. Astonishment at finding the world as orderly as it is has psychological meaning only when the patterns are viewed against the haphazardry of most of our experience. When Russell and other empiricists profess this astonishment, it should be taken partly in the above sense, partly as a poetic and rhetorical device to remind the reader that there is no rational justification for the world's regularity.

The associated emotion of "good fortune" results when we imagine the difficulties we would experience if the order were diminished. If enough of it vanished, we could not, of course, exist at all. But, when this is analyzed more fully, we see quickly that it is of a kind with the feeling of good luck Michelet expressed when he wrote: "How beautifully everything is arranged by nature. As soon as the child comes into the world, it finds a mother who is ready to care for it." For nature is the mother of us all, and if there is symmetry in nature an evolving organism will develop habits of behavior and thought that conform to the symmetry of its environment. Clearly, only such habits would have survival value. The apparent coincidence between the order of the cosmos and the advantages such an order has for us is strictly analogous to the happy coincidence that we have lungs and find ourselves on a planet with an atmosphere. When evolution is remembered, the feeling of good fortune in regard to external order becomes as meaningless as the good fortune earlier Christian apologists felt when they observed the ingenious adaptive structures of organisms to the environment.

Note that in the foregoing argument it is assumed that order existed in nature before the beginning of life on this planet and that our minds (and consequently our mathematical habits of thought) evolved to fit this order. This is the sense in which Russell is a "realist." "As mankind have advanced in intelligence," he writes, "their inferential habits have come gradually nearer to agreement with the laws of nature which have made these habits, throughout, more often a source of true expectations than of false ones. The forming of inferential habits which lead to true expectations is part of the adaptation to the environment upon which biological survival depends."[12]

In sharp contrast to this realism is the view that the external world possesses no order whatever except the order that a human mind reads into it in virtue of its interests. This curious view was adroitly defended by William James:

> . . . order and disorder . . . are purely human inventions. . . . If I should throw down a thousand beans at random upon a table, I could doubtless, by eliminating a sufficient number of them, leave the rest in almost any geometrical pattern you might propose to me, and you might then say that that pattern was the thing prefigured beforehand, and that the other beans were mere irrelevance and packing material. Our dealings with nature are just like this. She is a vast *plenum* in which our attention draws capricious lines in innumerable directions. We count and name whatever lies upon the special lines we trace, whilst the other things and the untraced lines are neither named nor counted.[13]

From this point of view the order of nature becomes an illusion, projected upon reality by mind; a viewpoint dangerously close to a subjective idealism James would have vigorously denied. And it is a similar danger that

Russell finds implicit in the views of Carnap. I would not presume to speak for Carnap on this difficult matter, but the following quotation expresses Russell's fear:

> Plato, who was interested in astronomy solely as a body of laws, wished it to be wholly divorced from sense; those who were interested in the actual heavenly bodies that happen to exist would, he said, be punished in the next incarnation by being birds. This point of view is not nowadays adopted by men of science, but it, or something very like it, is to be found in the works of Carnap and some other logical positivists. They are not, I think, conscious of holding any such opinion, and would vehemently repudiate it; but absorption in words, as opposed to what they mean, has exposed them to Platonic temptation, and led them down strange paths toward perdition. . . .[14]

It should be made clear that though we may affirm with Russell the reality of an external order, which has an existence apart from our minds, we have no basis for insisting that the order we find, or any other type of order, permeates the whole of being. In some final sense, the cosmos may be neither ordered nor disordered, but only uniform on certain levels, or in certain spots, or at certain times. Being what we are, we could have evolved only on that level, or in that spot, or at that time. It may be that in quantum mechanics we have already probed a level of disorder. This would be no more astonishing than a trip to the moon, where there is no atmosphere for our lungs. To exist on the moon we would have to carry air with us. Similarly, we can enter the world of the electron only by taking our mathematics with us. But formulating orderly causal laws for an individual electron may be as impossible as breathing empty space.

And it matters not at all if we be atheist or theist. If atheist, it is not surprising that, being what we are, we would have evolved in a corner of being such as we are in. If theist, it is not surprising that God, wanting us to be as we are, would have permitted us to evolve in the corner we inhabit. Perhaps an angel of the Lord surveyed an endless sea of chaos, then troubled it gently with his finger. In this tiny and temporary swirl of equations, our cosmos took shape.

To return to Einstein's library metaphor, we have detected an order in the arrangement of the books. Our discovery leads us to hope that we may in time learn to read a few of their pages. But it may well be that on many shelves are volumes written entirely in nonsense syllables. Atheist, theist, or agnostic, we must agree with Santayana: ". . . a really naked spirit cannot assume that the world is thoroughly intelligible. There may be surds, there may be hard facts, there may be dark abysses before which intelligence must be silent, for fear of going mad."[15]

POSTSCRIPT

After leaving the Navy at the close of World War II, I was able to use the G.I. Bill to pay for a year of graduate work at the University of Chicago.

My most exciting course was a seminar on the philosophy of physics, taught by Rudolf Carnap. "Order and Surprise" was a rewrite of my term paper for this class. It concerns a problem that seems to trouble many philosophers and scientists: How is it that logic and mathematics, constructed by human minds, fits the outside world so well that it provides us with such enormous power over nature?

The best-known expression of amazement by a physicist over this "coincidence" is Eugene Wigner's 1960 paper, "The Unreasonable Effectiveness of Mathematics in the Natural Sciences."[16] A recent article inspired by Wigner's essay is mathematician R. W. Hamming's "The Unreasonable Effectiveness of Mathematics."[17] Hamming ends up almost as surprised as Wigner. Even the counting numbers astonish him:

> The integers seem to us to be so fundamental that we expect to find them wherever we find intelligent life in the universe. I have tried, with little success, to get some of my friends to understand my amazement that the abstraction of integers for counting is both possible and useful. Is it not remarkable that 6 sheep plus 7 sheep make 13 sheep; that 6 stones plus 7 stones make 13 stones? Is it not a mircale that the universe is so constructed that such a simple abstraction as a number is possible? To me this is one of the strongest examples of the unreasonable effectiveness of mathematics. Indeed, I find it both strange and unexplainable.

As an Aristotelian realist who takes for granted that the universe is independent of your mind and mine, and mathematically ordered, I find plenty about the world's structure to be surprised about. And the theorems of mathematics can be equally beautiful and surprising. But what is surprising about the fact that mathematics fits the world? As Raymond L. Wilder crisply put it, "There is nothing mysterious, as some have tried to maintain, about the *applicability* of mathematics. What we get by abstraction from something can be returned!"[18]

Like fellow realist Einstein, it is the disorder of quantum mechanics that I find surprising. But not really. After all, as Charles Peirce and so many others have since shown, the notion of a totally disordered universe is self-contradictory. There is no way to construct a long sequence of patternless numbers. For the same reason, any universe conceivable by the mind will be in some way ordered. Behind the apparent disorder of quantum mechanics is a marvelous order that rests firmly on foundations of probability and statistical laws. "There was a moment," Richard Feynman told a reporter, recalling his discovery of a law about weak interactions, "when I knew how nature worked. It had elegance and beauty. The goddam thing was gleaming."[19]

What truly does amaze me is that any mathematician, scientist, or philosopher could suppose that Feynman and his collaborators had done nothing more than uncover a cultural artifact with no reality outside of human minds. For more on this kind of amazement, see the next chapter.

NOTES

1. Bertrand Russell, *The ABC of Relativity,* 1925.

2. Bertrand Russell, *Human Knowledge: Its Scope and Limits,* 1948, p. 285.

3. Sextus Empiricus, *Outlines of Pyrrhonism,* Book 3, p. 18. A similar paragraph occurs in the same author's *Against the Physicists,* Book 1, p. 203. Both references are to the Loeb Classical Library edition.

4. Bertrand Russell, *The ABC of Relativity,* 1925.

5. Gilbert Chesterton, *The Man Who Was Thursday,* 1908.

6. Bertrand Russell, *Human Knowledge: Its Scope and Limits,* 1948, p. xii.

7. Bertrand Russell, *Philosophy,* 1927.

8. Gilbert Chesterton, *Orthodoxy,* 1927.

9. Ibid.

10. Ibid.

11. James Branch Cabell, *The Cream of the Jest,* 1917.

12. Bertrand Russell, *Human Knowledge: Its Scope and Limits,* 1948, p. 507.

13. William James, *Varieties of Religious Experience,* 1902.

14. Bertrand Russell, *Human Knowledge: Its Scope and Limits,* 1948, p. 245.

15. George Santayana, *Ultimate Religion,* an address reprinted in *Obiter Scripta,* 1936.

16. Wigner's essay is reprinted in *Symmetries and Reflections* (Indiana University Press, 1967).

17. Hamming's paper appeared in the *American Mathematical Monthly,* February 1980, pp. 81-90.

18. Wilder, *Introduction to the Foundations of Mathematics,* 2nd ed. (Wiley, 1965).

19. Lee Edson, "Two Men in Search of a Quark," *New York Times Magazine,* October 8, 1967.

5

Mathematics and the Folkways

If there is any aspect of our culture that one might suppose would lie outside the folkways, grounded in a reality independent of cultural processes, it is mathematics — the Queen of the Sciences. Alas, she has been toppled from her lonely throne! Dr. Leslie Alvin White, professor of anthropology at the University of Michigan, is responsible for this bold deed. In a chapter called "The Locus of Mathematical Reality," in his book *The Science of Culture* (Farrar, Straus, 1949), he banishes her to the region of the folkways to join company with other distinguished exiles from the realms of Truth, Beauty, and Goodness. Because Professor White's chapter carries to an ultimate extreme the approach that in anthropology is called "cultural determinism," marking the conquest of the last outpost of values that were thought to be in contact with a universal, nonsocial reality, it seems worth-while to make a close inspection of the author's arguments.

Professor White opens the chapter with a quotation from *Through the Looking Glass*. It is the section in which Alice is told she is merely a figment of the Red King's dream. The passage is appropriate because the chapter defends a view that leads ultimately, as the author himself apparently realized, to a curious kind of collective solipsism.

Of course Professor White does not put it in those terms. He is concerned only with what he calls "mathematical reality." The laws of mathematics, he writes, are "wholly dependent upon the mind of the species." "Mathematics in its entirety, its 'truths' and its 'realities,' is a part of human culture, nothing more." "The locus of mathematical reality is cultural tradition." "Mathematical concepts are independent of the individual mind but lie wholly within the

This essay originally appeared in the *Journal of Philosophy,* March 30, 1950, and is reprinted with permission.

mind of the species, i.e., culture." "Its [mathematical] reality is cultural: the sort of reality possessed by a code of etiquette, traffic regulations, the rules of baseball, the English language or rules of grammar."

One final quotation: "It is now clear that concepts such as space, straight line, plane, etc., are no more necessary and inevitable as a consequence of the structure of the external world than are the concepts green and yellow — or the relationship term with which you designate your mother's brother, for that matter."

Let us take a more careful look at that last statement. The *term* by which a society designates the kinship of uncle-nephew is, of course, purely cultural. But the relationship itself, the *denotatum* of the sign, is clearly an aspect of the external world that would exist whether anyone gave a term to it or not. Dinosaurs had uncles and nephews long before a species evolved capable of describing the relationship in language symbols.

Similarly with colors. The *term* "green" is obviously a cultural reality. The *sensation* of green is a psychological reality. But the sensation and the symbol are both grounded in an external state of affairs that causes all wave lengths of light to be absorbed by an object except the green which is reflected to the eye of the observer.

When Professor White suggests that colors are not features of the external world he certainly does not mean anything so trivial as that color *sensations* are in the mind. His chapter makes quite clear that he wishes to deny any necessary causal connection between the sensations and outside reality. Colors are not "a consequence of the structure of the external world." You might think so, he adds, until you learn that Creek and Natchez Indians did not distinguish yellow from green, but had a common term for both.

This is an astonishing *non sequitur*. The fact that these Indian tribes used the same word for what we call yellow and green does not mean that a tribesman could not distinguish between green and yellow objects otherwise identical. If someone had shown him a green and a yellow string of beads, pointed to the green saying, "This is yours," then mixed them and asked him to pick out "his," there is no reason for thinking he would have experienced any difficulty. Does Professor White mean to imply that the Creek and Natchez Indians had a culturally conditioned yellow-green color blindness?

One is reminded of the famous controversy over Homer's color sense, provoked by the British statesman William Gladstone. In 1858 Gladstone wrote a book on Homer which suggested that the Greek poet was color blind because of his meager use of color words. In 1870 a German group of evolutionary ethnologists argued that the entire Greek population of Homer's day was color blind, and that ability to discriminate colors did not develop until a culture reached advanced levels of complexity. The first important attack on this view was Grant Allen's *The Colour Sense: Its Origin and Development* (1879). Allen called attention to the fact that a single term for green and blue is common among primitive societies, but he pointed out that the

Highland Scots, who did not verbally distinguish green and blue, were able to discriminate perfectly between the two colors when they were tested for this ability. There was no word for "orange" in the Middle English of Chaucer's time and one might suppose Chaucer unaware of this dubious color had he not referred twice in the *Canterbury Tales* to a shade "bitwixe yelow and reed." Since 1900 the theory that a deficiency of color terms in a language indicates a deficiency in color discrimination has been increasingly discredited, especially by the investigations of the Spanish anthropologist José Perez de Barradas, published in the thirties.

No one questions, of course, that the precise areas of the spectrum signified by color words will vary widely from culture to culture depending on the society's needs. A primitive tribe may demand only a few color words, whereas a modern factory producing women's dresses may require terms for several hundred different shades. Members of a tribe who did not distinguish green from yellow might have an understandable tendency to confuse these colors, just as it is easy for us to confuse shades of brown, but this does not mean that the tribesmen could not see the difference between green and yellow. The basic issue, of course, is whether the process of color vision is culturally determined, as Professor White implies, or whether it is determined by an external structure ordered in such manner that it sends certain wave lengths to the retina that result in certain color sensations in the brain.

Precisely the same issue is involved in regard to "mathematical reality." We do not have to plunge here into the highly technical controversies over the exact meaning of "reality" that divide such philosophers as Carnap, Russell, and Dewey, because the vital point is much simpler. There has been no philosopher of eminence, including the logical empiricists, who has argued that the so-called external world was nothing more than a projection of human minds. Even idealists like Berkeley, who insisted that nothing could exist except as perceived, were quick to restore external reality by making the world a projection of God's mind. Berkeley's stones are just as external and kickable as the stones of a materialist. All we need grant, for purposes of this elementary discussion, is the existence of a world outside of human minds that has a structure that is ordered.[1] We need not concern ourselves with the metaphysical questions of how or why it exists, or exactly how and why it is ordered. It will suffice if we are willing to abandon solipsism, both of the individual and of the group, and confess belief in an outside reality that is more than a vast, nondescript fog in which such features as, say, spiral nebulae, are merely projections of our interests, involving no pattern of parts other than the patterns we infuse into them by our attention.

And what are the consequences of affirming an external order? It follows that mathematical concepts, like colors and family linkages, have at least one foothold in a reality independent of the human species. It is true, of course, that an abstract triangle does not exist in the same sense a cow does, but this does not mean that the concept of triangle is an arbitrary cultural feature unconnected with the structure of the world. Professor White himself admits this connection at the close of his chapter when he discusses briefly the question of how mathematical concepts first arose. They were produced, he says, in the "nervous systems" of our apelike ancestors, and he reminds us that apes "have a fine appreciation of geometric forms." This is a startling admission, because clearly, if an ape appreciates geometric forms, there must be geometric forms outside of human culture for him to appreciate. This is only another way of saying that, if all men vanished, there would still be a sense (exactly *what* sense is another and more difficult problem) in which spiral nebulae could be said to spiral, and hexagonal ice crystals to be hexagonal, even though no human creatures were around to give these forms a name. The only alternative to this view is to insist that all the order we perceive in the universe, whether it be the static geometrical order of structure or the dynamic order of natural laws, is but a projection of our minds upon empty space or, at the most, on a kind of patternless plenum.[2]

And yet the modern ethnologist, with his allergy toward absolutes, is constantly haunted by forms of subjective idealism. I recall an evening at the University of Chicago a few years ago when I tried for hours, totally without success, to persuade a group of anthropology graduate students that two plus two were four in all cultures. It sounded to them suspiciously like a "cultural universal" that might trap them into a value judgment. In the course of the discussion, however, two important misconceptions about mathematics came to light, and since both are to be found in Professor White's chapter, it might be instructive to mention them here.

First, there is the notion that variations in counting systems somehow mean variations in mathematical laws. People inherit methods of counting and calculating from their culture, Professor White explains, just as they inherit ways of cooking and marrying. "Had Newton been reared in Hottentot culture he would have calculated like a Hottentot." The author's choice of Hottentot was unfortunate, because Hottentots have a decimal system and therefore calculate the same way Newton did; but even if Professor White had chosen, say, the African bushmen who use a binary system, the illustration would still have been utterly valueless for his purposes. Counting and calculation in the binary system make use of exactly the same mathematical laws as any other system. In fact most of the giant electronic calculators operate on a binary system because it adapts easily to electronic relays, but this does not imply that the machine is based on a different kind of mathematical reality. Variations in number systems are, in fact, nothing more than variations in methods of symbolization. Whatever is done in the signs of one system can be translated exactly into all the others. Any number can provide a base for counting, though in most cultures the base has been five, ten, or twenty in correspondence with the groupings of fingers and toes. (One of the curiosities of ethnology is the quaternary system of the Yuki Indians in California. They counted on the *spaces* between fingers.) The base number chosen will play a role in determining the sounds used for higher numbers, or the way they are depicted in writing, but this no more changes the underlying mathematical laws than the number designated by "17" changes its properties when it is symbolized by Roman numerals or in the Mayan vigesimal system by two dots above three horizontal lines.

To make this very clear, let us consider for a moment the meaning of "two plus two are four." In everyday experience we find that objects often are grouped as couples. To all classes of couples let us give the generic name of "bing." We further observe another type of configuration of units, which in our culture is designated by the word "four." To this grouping we will give the name "bong." A little experimentation with groups of bings soon establishes an astonishing law. Whenever we add one bing to another bing, producing so to speak "bing bings," the new configuration invariably belongs to the class we have designated "bong." Thus we arrive at a simple arithmetical law, "Bing plus bing are bong." This is what is meant by "two plus two are four."

I am aware of the fact that, if two drops of water are added to two drops, the result may be one large drop. But in so far as the units remain units, the law is universal and invariable. If a tribesman breaks each of two sticks in half he will find he has four sticks. If he extends two fingers of one hand, then two more, he would be surprised indeed to discover, exclusive of his thumb, five fingers.

John Stuart Mill, in an effort to establish logic and mathematics on an empirical basis, imagined a mischievous demon who went about creating fifth objects whenever two things were brought together with two other things. If this were the case, Mill reasoned, our arithmetic books would tell us that two plus two equaled five. Most contemporary empiricists agree that experience provides the psychological origin for our knowledge of mathematical laws, but they prefer to give the laws an absolute validity of their own— analytic, formal, and a priori.[3] We need not concern ourselves, however, with the controversy between those who defend Mill's view, and those who, like Carnap and Russell, regard the laws as true of all possible worlds, because in neither case are the laws subject to cultural variation. The spoken and written signs by which a culture symbolizes mathematical reality are, of course, culturally determined, though one method of symbolization may be more efficient than another. Robert Lowie, in his *Introduction to Cultural Anthropology,* does not hesitate to describe the Roman system as "cumbersome" in comparison with the Mayan, which introduced the valuable zero symbol.

It is important to realize also that the process of addition does not require the witness of a human being. It operates just as effectively when no one is looking. If you drop two pennies in a child's empty bank, then two more pennies, you will discover, on opening the bank, that it contains four pennies. The entire operation could, in fact, be performed mechanically and recorded on film.

The view that mathematics is grounded only in the cultural process slides

easily into the "collective solipsism" that George Orwell satirizes in his novel
Nineteen Eighty-Four. For if mathematics is in the folkways, and the folkways
can be molded by a political party, then it follows that the party can proclaim mathematical laws. "Reality exists in the human mind," declares
O'Brien, member of the Inner Party, "and nowhere else. Not in the individual
mind, which can make mistakes, and in any case soon perishes; only in the
mind of the Party, which is collective and immortal. Whatever the Party holds
to be truth *is* truth." One of the more agonizing episodes in the novel is the
scene in which the protagonist is tortured into the conviction that two plus
two are sometimes five.

A second common source of confusion concerning these topics is the fact
that recent work in mathematics, stimulated by the relativity revolution in
physics, seems to deny an absolute validity to familiar Euclidean laws. For
centuries, Professor White points out, it was thought that Euclid's theorems
were necessary, but "the invention of non-Euclidean geometries . . . has
dispelled this view entirely."

Now there is a sense in which this is entirely correct; but it is a sense wholly
foreign to Professor White's purposes. It is true there is no a priori reason
why a geometrical postulate, such as the famous parallel postulate, must be
true. A coherent non-Euclidean system can be constructed that will violate
this postulate, and the discoveries of modern physics suggest that such a
system is a sounder basis on which to make calculations involving high speeds
and astronomical distances. But on the level of ordinary speeds and distances,
we live very much in an old-fashioned, prosaic, Euclidean world that does
not vary in any *measurable* respect from one geographical area to another.
If a tribesman wishes to shoot a bird with a bow and arrow, it is necessary
for him, whatever his tribal affiliation, to aim the arrow at the bird in strict
accord with Euclidean and Newtonian laws and not, say, to shoot the arrow
in the opposite direction on the grounds that straight lines, prolonged in-
definitely in a closed fourth-dimensional continuum, will circle the cosmos
and return to the starting point.

A moment's reflection and one will realize that any imaginable society,
to exist at all, must constantly make use of elementary mathematical laws
that are everywhere the same but so commonplace we are seldom aware of
them. For example, to exist it is necessary to eat, and to eat it is necessary
that something be placed in the mouth. But the fact that a smaller object
can be pushed through a larger orifice is a fact of geometry. A tribe that
acted on the reverse assumption, i.e., that only larger objects could be placed
through smaller holes, would be acting on a law that, however well grounded
it might be in the mythology of the culture, would be so poorly grounded
in mathematical reality that the tribe would quickly die of starvation.

Of course no native group has ever adopted a belief that stupid, and in
fact ethnological research of recent decades has disclosed members of primitive societies to be not nearly as unlearned in mathematics as earlier anthro-

pologists had supposed. At one time it was assumed that, if a tribe had no words for numbers beyond two or three, members were incapable of counting beyond two or three. Early investigators, however, were puzzled by the uncanny ability of these natives to survey a herd of fifty sheep and immediately know when one was missing. It was supposed that the native had a phenomenal memory in which he retained the entire herd gestalt; or perhaps he knew each sheep personally and recalled the face. But later investigation soon made clear that these natives had elaborate means of counting in which they made use of various parts of their anatomy in a predetermined order. For example, they counted their fingers, wrists, elbows, armpits, nipples, navel, knees, and toes. The counting would be done mentally; then, instead of remembering a word for 27, the native would simply recall that he stopped counting on, say, his left big toe.

Lévy-Bruhl's books on primitive mentality made clear that the savage was much shrewder than the aboriginal idiots described by Spencer in his *Principles of Sociology*. But even Lévy-Bruhl is now regarded as having greatly exaggerated the extent to which savage "pre-logical" thought differs from our own. There is perhaps a more thorough mixing of reality with the religious projective system; but, when it comes to solving practical problems within terms of their own culture, they do as well, if not better, than we do. And they are successful precisely because they make use of laws of logic and mathematics that have their loci, not in the culture, but in external reality. The laws are discovered, not created, just as the laws of the lever or wheel are discovered; and there is no reason an anthropologist should be ashamed to admit this fact.

In fairness to Professor White I should say at this point that I do not doubt for a moment that he believes in an external world, of orderly structure, and that this order plays a necessary role in determining the ways in which cultures formulate mathematical and physical laws. His article contains a great deal of ambiguity, and I suppose it would be possible to twist and force his statements to mean nothing more than that the *cultural* aspect of mathematics is cultural. But this is like saying that all aspects of reality within this room are inside this room, and I have accordingly paid Professor White the compliment of assuming his words to mean something less trivial — to convey what he obviously believes to be a new and revolutionary approach to his topic. I have tried to show that this approach leads to an idealism that Professor White would be the first, I am sure, to disavow.

Since 1900, cultural anthropologists have been in a phase of reaction against the naïve ethnocentrism of their Victorian predecessors. One by one various aspects of culture — art, philosophy, religion, ethics — have fallen into the category of the folkways. Karl Mannheim's "sociology of knowledge" subjected all ideas, including those of science, to sociological investigation. But even Mannheim did not dream of maintaining that the laws of mathematics, or even the knowledge obtained by science, were culturally determined. "Relating individual ideas to the total structure of a given historico-social subject," he wrote in his *Ideology and Utopia,* "should not be confused with a philosophical relativism which denies the validity of any standards and of the existence of order in the world" (p. 254). On page 263 he explicitly cites the law of "two times two equals four" as an example of the sort of truth *not* subject to cultural determination. Even in the social sciences Mannheim believed objective knowledge to be possible. In fact the chief end of the sociology of knowledge, as he saw it, was to "unmask" the unconscious compulsions behind conflicting points of view and so enable the social scientist to arrive at a perspective that would be the most objective possible, and therefore the nearest to reality. Two quotations from *Ideology and Utopia* will suffice:

> No one denies the possibility of empirical research nor does anyone maintain that facts do not exist (nothing seems more incorrect to us than an illusionist theory of knowledge).

> It is, of course, true that in the social sciences, as elsewhere, the ultimate criterion of truth or falsity is to be found in the investigation of the object, and the sociology of knowledge is no substitute for this.

In Mannheim's view the student of the sociology of knowledge is like a man moving among a group of artists who surround a nude model (reality), each painting her from his own perspective. The man studies every canvas, comparing it with what he sees from each artist's perspective, and in this manner tries to arrive at an accurate understanding of the model's shape. The notion that, because each artist paints her differently, therefore her anatomy has no definite shape would have struck Mannheim as a completely indefensible form of subjective idealism. And I need not add that "shape" is geometrical.

Among contemporary anthropologists signs of a long-needed rebellion against extreme cultural determinism are increasingly evident. The work of such men as Kardiner and Linton (Professor White does not mention Kardiner in his 650-page survey of "culturology," and he cites Linton only to disagree with him) is beginning to suggest dimly a basis for setting up standards of mental health that may someday provide a rough yardstick for measuring the degree to which a culture satisfies the basic needs of its members. It is regrettable that Professor White, out of sheer inertia, should let the older trend propel him through the looking glass into a realm of dream and nonsense.

POSTSCRIPT

Leslie Alvin White, one of America's most influential and controversial anthropologists, died in 1975 after a distinguished career at the University of

Michigan. Although he regarded all of mathematics, even the theoretical constructions of physics, as rooted in culture, not in the outside world, he was not a cultural relativist. Far from it! More than any other anthropologist, White was responsible for the revival of the evolutionary views of Lewis Morgan. Like Morgan, White saw all cultures as passing through stages from savagery to barbarism to civilization, thereby achieving genuine progress toward better and better ways of meeting basic human needs.

George Boas and other cultural relativists recognized the importance of environment (that is, the external world) in shaping both individual personalities and cultures. In his vigorous battle against the cultural relativism of Boas, there was (in my opinion) no need whatever for White to abandon epistemological realism. I see his paper on mathematics as an aberration, inconsistent with evolutionary anthropology and written out of philosophical naïveté. It is easy to understand why. In his later years White became so obsessed by his vision of culture as the fundamental reality that he almost forgot there was a big world out there, with its own fixed laws not made by us, that had produced all human cultures. But I will say no more here about White's curious philosophy, which I find marred by internal contradictions, because I will discuss it later in a review of White's most important book, *The Science of Culture*.

White's "Locus of Mathematical Reality" was first reprinted in *The Science of Culture* (1949) but it did not become widely known to mathematicians until James R. Newman reprinted it in his best-selling four-volume anthology, *The World of Mathematics* (1956). Although Newman included many pieces by mathematical realists (for example, a portion of G. H. Hardy's *A Mathematician's Apology,* with its vigorous defense of realism[4]), he was inclined to look favorably on White's cultural solipsism. I can still recall the shock I experienced when I first came upon the following passage in *Mathematics and the Imagination,* which Newman wrote with Edward Kasner: ". . . we have overcome the notion that mathematical truths have an existence independent and apart from our own minds. It is even strange to us that such a notion could have ever existed."

Kasner and Newman go on to admit that hundreds of great mathematicians held just such a view, but they are convinced that it was overthrown by (among other things) the discovery of non-Euclidean geometry. Twentieth-century mathematicians, they contend, now realize that mathematics "is man's own handiwork subject only to the limitations imposed by the laws of thought."

What the authors don't tell you is that even today the majority of great mathematicians still regard mathematical truths as independent of human thought. Nor do they remind you that relativity theory adopted non-Euclidean geometry (which of course was the work of human minds) because it best fitted what empirical investigations had discovered about the structure of spacetime, out there, in a universe not created by you and me.

Newman also included in *The World of Mathematics* a paper as muddled in its thinking as White's: "Mathematics and the World," by Douglas A.T. Gasking. It first appeared in 1940 in an Australian philosophical journal and has since been reprinted in several books. Gasking's thesis is that our choice of what mathematics to apply to the world is entirely a matter of convention, dictated by what we find convenient rather than by the structure of the outside world. To prove this, he introduces several "queer" multiplication tables, as he calls them, which he says work perfectly well in measuring a rectangular floor with integral sides, and then tiling it with unit squares. To make the queer multiplication work, we must do one of three things: (1) use a queer system of measuring the two sides of the rectangle we wish to tile, (2) use a queer system of counting tiles as we remove them from a bin, or (3) measure and count normally, but invoke queer laws of nature that change the length of our measuring rod while we use it or that change the area of each tile as we put it on the floor.

Consider Gasking's simplest example. Our strange multiplication table gives products that are twice what our familiar table gives: 1 times 1 = 2, 1 times 2 = 4, 2 times 2 = 8, 2 times 3 = 12, and so on. How do we make this work? When we take the tiles from the bin we simply count them by twos. Thus the first tile is called 2, the second is called 4, and so on. If our floor is 2 times 3 our strange arithmetic gives us an area of 12. Using our new way of counting, we count tiles until we reach 12. This gives us just the 6 we need. Clearly this reduces to the triviality that, instead of counting objects the ordinary way, we can get the same practical results if we counted by twos and then halve the final tally. Of course this is the same as doing ordinary arithmetic, except that we are doing it a more complicated way by giving different meanings to certain symbols.

I'll not spend time detailing the ambiguities, confusions, and contradictions in Gasking's paper. I know of no mathematician today who takes it seriously. If you are interested, check *Philosophy of Mathematics* (1964), edited by Paul Benacerraf and Hilary Putnam, where you'll find Gasking's eccentric essay followed by Hector-Neri Castañeda's paper, "Arithmetic and Reality," which thoroughly demolishes it. (For more on mathematics and cultural solipsism, see Part 2, Chapter 34.)

I find in my files a clipping from *Scientific American,* dated October 1964, about some studies that reinforce what I had to say about color perception as distinct from color language. Verne F. Ray, an anthropologist, writing in the *Transactions of the New York Academy of Sciences,* reports on his investigations of the color perception of a hundred Indian tribes. He found that no two of them divided the color spectrum exactly the same way. Some had only three color words in their language, others eight. One tribe had two words for two shades of yellow. A wave length on the dividing line between two color words in one language was sometimes in the middle of a color named in another language. Ray concluded that the language differences reflected no differences in color perception.

A vigorous defense of White's cultural solipsism is a paper by Raymond L. Wilder, "Mathematics: A Cultural Phenomenon," in *Essays in the Science of Culture: In Honor of Leslie A. White* (T.Y. Crowell, 1960), edited by Gertrude Dole and Robert Carneiro.[5] Wilder was a good friend of White, and one of his colleagues at the University of Michigan. I suspect that Wilder's philosophy of mathematics was a major influence on White's paper.

Wilder singles out my article as "one of the most bitter attacks on White's views" and then proceeds to take me to task for failing to understand modern mathematics. Now Wilder is of course a distinguished mathematician, and I am only a journalist; yet I must say that I find Wilder, like White, talking in a language both idiosyncratic and obfuscatory.

After quoting my remark that there is a sense in which the spiral form of a nebula is independent of human minds, Wilder adds: "I submit that if there were no human to *say* such things, the phenomena described would still be just phenomena and nothing more." Of course it would be just phenomena, leaving aside the possibility that the nebula could be observed by a nonhuman creature or by a god. Nobody can *say* a nebula has a spiral form unless there is somebody capable of saying it. The nontrivial question is whether it is meaningful to insist that the spiral form itself is mind dependent. If we refuse to say the form is "out there" in space, independent of you and me, do we have a right to say the *nebula* is out there?

Consider astronomy. Everything an astronomer says and writes is obviously cultural, because everything any human says and writes is part of culture. Moreover, astronomy is influenced in obvious ways by a culture's patterns of beliefs and interests. But who would want to say that the locus of astronomical reality is culture? In a sense it is, but since all science is cultural in the same sense, to say this is to say something vacuous. Astronomers and ordinary people talk in the language of Aristotelian realism. The locus of astronomy is the structure of the universe, not made by us, unless one believes that everything "out there" is a projection by our minds on some sort of unstructured fog.

To a realist, mathematical structure is mind independent in two senses. The universe is not shapeless, but patterned in ways that are described by mathematics. In addition, mathematicians investigate purely abstract structures, defined by formal systems, which may or may not have applications to the physical world. The proper attitude to take toward the ontological status of these abstract systems is, of course, one of the great unending controversies in metaphysics. Since I will discuss this in more detail in Part 2, Chapter 34, I will here say only that almost all mathematicians today agree with Hardy that a mathematician discovers truths that are independent of his culture and that those truths are qualitatively different from the conventions of traffic regulations or codes of etiquette.

There are two reasons for supposing that mathematical theorems are more than cultural conventions. One is that, whenever two cultures independently develop the same formal system, such as Euclidean geometry, they discover the same theorems. The second reason is that mathematics applies with eerie exactitude to the physical world. Any two cultures, isolated from each other, that develop a system for measuring the two sides of a right triangle and calculating the hypotenuse will discover the same Pythagorean rule, because that is how the world is structured. Of course, if they write down the rule or talk about it, their writing and talking will be mind dependent in the same way that writing and talking about the moon is mind dependent. But the moon itself, and the fact that it is spherical, is not mind dependent.

"If it should occur in the future," writes Wilder, "that contact is established with beings on another planet having highly developed cultures, and elements are found in these cultures isomorphic to mathematical elements in our own culture, would this make these elements any less *cultural*?" In a sense, of course not; but the sense is trivial. If extraterrestrial chemists discover that the hydrogen atom has only one electron (they would express this, of course, in their own set of symbols), all their talking and writing about chemistry will naturally be cultural. But who wants to say that culture is the locus of chemical reality? It is much simpler and clearer to say that matter is the locus of chemical reality. Trees are independent of the minds of woodchoppers. Woodchopping theory is cultural, but the theory rests on something that is not.

Of course it is mostly a matter of wordchopping, and Wilder would reply: sets of two things, like the two moons of Mars, do indeed exist "out there," but the number two does not. Like the good nominalist that he is, he regards all universals, such as numbers and circles and triangles, as mere symbols that are created by human minds. Therefore they are all part of culture. If all cultures in the cosmos were annihilated, the stars would continue to exist, and they would still exist in sets of two, three, four, and so on; but no one could *say* this, because there would be nobody around to say it. In this sense, all mathematics is cultural.

One may, of course, adopt any way of talking one likes, but the fact is that mathematicians do not talk like Wilder except for a few who are motivated by an intense desire to make humanity the measure of all things. I have known many mathematicians, some more eminent than Wilder. All of them, without exception, prefer to talk like Hardy. The notion that modern anthropology and the sociology of knowledge have rendered Hardy's way of talking obsolete is simply not true.

As I said in my original blast at White, if the cultural approach to mathematics is no more than a belief that everything that goes on inside human minds is something that goes on inside human minds, then who can disagree? No one wants to deny that "trees" are culture-bound in the sense that a mind is needed to isolate a certain portion of reality and give it the name "tree." The name is obviously mind dependent, but the structure of the tree is not. To adopt a language in which all the patterns of nature, and all the abstract patterns of formal mathematical systems, are as cultural dependent as marriage rituals or rules for how to use a knife and fork is to talk in a way so far removed from ordinary language, as well as the language of great scientists and mathematicians and even most philosophers, that in my layman's opinion it adds nothing to mathematical discourse except confusion.

NOTES

1. When I say the external world "exists" I mean nothing more than the simple, commonsense recognition of an ordered set of relations independent of human minds, which is somehow structurally similar to our subjective mathematical relations. It may be that this belief is merely a matter of convenience (i.e., it is simpler to assume it than to try to describe events in terms of shifting sense impressions); but, in any case, the controversy among empiricists over whether "realism" can be affirmed (as Russell and Reichenbach believe) or whether such an affirmation is meaningless (as Carnap and possibly Dewey think) is on a level irrelevant to the issue here under discussion. Even the most extreme anti-realists among the logical positivists would be appalled by the suggestion that logical and mathematical laws were culturally variable.

2. This was Kant's view, and even William James, in unguarded moments, defended it. (See James's footnote on page 428 of the Modern Library edition of *Varieties of Religious Experience.*) For a brief, clear exposition of the weakness of Kant's subjective mathematics, see Russell's *A History of Western Philosophy,* 1945, pp. 712 ff.

3. The demon's activity can, in fact, easily be shown to be self-contradictory and therefore meaningless, like the statement "Some odd numbers are even." For example, if we bring together two horses, two pigs, and two chipmunks, we have various combinations possible of two plus two. If we consider two horses and two pigs, then the fifth animal, created by the demon, must be either a horse or pig. Let us assume it is a horse. The grouping of two pigs and two chipmunks necessitates, say, a third chipmunk. But now we are unable to obtain five from the addition of two horses and two chipmunks because we already have three of each.

4. Hardy's words are often quoted (indeed, even White quotes them), but they are worth quoting again here: "I believe that mathematical reality lies outside us, that our function is to discover or *observe* it, and that the theorems which we prove, and which we describe grandiloquently as our 'creations,' are simply our notes of our observations." There is something amusing about an anthropologist, who knows little about mathematics, insisting that this view, held not only by most mathematicians today but also by most experts on the foundations of mathematics, has been rendered obsolete by the findings of cultural anthropology.

5. Wilder has defended his cultural approach to mathematics in two later books: *Evolution of Mathematical Concepts* (Wiley, 1968) and *Mathematics as a Cultural System* (Pergamon, 1981).

6

Mr. Smith Goes to Tulsa

In October 1947, Reverend Gerald Lyman Kenneth Smith moved his home to Tulsa. He's been there ever since, living with his wife and son in a rented house in a quiet residential district.

How has Tulsa reacted to the presence of this distinguished Disciples of Christ demagogue? American Communists and their stooges are forever warning us of the imminence of a native fascism. Here is Smith, our finest example of a clean-cut, Christian, homegrown fuehrer, operating in one of the nation's most right-wing cities (Gunther, in *Inside U.S.A.,* considers Tulsa second only to Houston as a center of conservatism), and at a time of unprecedented anti-Communist hubbub. Has Smith succeeded, under these seemingly ideal conditions, in arousing Tulsans to a pitch of Christian Nationalist frenzy?

The answer is that he has not. After two and one-half years of activity in Tulsa, consisting largely of meetings in fundamentalist churches with an occasional private gathering (admission by invitation only), he has succeded in attracting only a small, frowsy following of oldsters from the local Pentecostal churches, and perhaps a handful of neanderthal businessmen. Twice he has attempted giant mass meetings in Convention Hall. Both were dismal failures. I happened to have had the dubious privilege of attending both rallies.

The first mass meeting took place in the winter of 1947. Huge ads in the papers announced that Smith would speak on Henry Wallace and name key "Reds" in Oklahoma. Unfortunately Smith failed to appear. Rev. Jonathan E. Perkins, a white-haired preacher from Delavan, Wisconsin, at that time Smith's chief henchman, opened the rally. Perkins has since crossed swords with Smith and written a pamphlet called *Gerald L. K. Smith Unmasked.* After a rambling, uninspired address by "converted Communist" Kenneth Goff, the

This essay originally appeared in the *New Leader,* June 10, 1950, and is reprinted with permission.

Rev. W. T. McMullan, a tall cowboy evangelist in high boots and black ribbon tie, arose and said solemnly, "I have a feeling deep down in my heart that history is being made here tonight." A few grim-faced old ladies clapped weakly. When the collection was announced, half the audience got up and left.

Smith's second mass meeting, held last month, was somewhat livelier, though the audience was no better—little more than a thousand. A young Pentecostal minister, the Rev. M. W. Howard, introduced Smith, and for two hours Smith bellowed about the dangers of Zionism, racial mongrelization, world government, atheism, and the "Henry Wallaces and Eleanor Roosevelts" who are bringing the country to disaster.

Smith's oratorical technique has mellowed considerably since the volcanic days of his alliances with Francis Townsend, Father Coughlin, Huey Long, and Dudley Pelley's Silver Shirts. Mencken once described him as "the gustiest and goriest, the deadliest and damnedest orator ever heard on this or any other earth . . . the champion boob-bumper of all epochs." Though heavier and less vigorous, he is still an effective spellbinder, with a hypnotic habit of trembling an upraised hand or forefinger for thirty seconds or more while he enlarges a point, then slapping his palms together at a well-timed climax.

It is easy to forget that Smith comes from a long line of fundamentalist preachers. To regard him as merely an unscrupulous racketeer seeking money and power is to miss completely, in my opinion, the ambiguous character of his personality. Like his former employer, Huey Long, and like most political demagogues, he is a complex mixture of motives. What appears to be simple skulduggery is, in most cases, I think, the combined result of abysmal ignorance, religious bigotry, unconscious power drives, paranoia, and the familiar ability of such fanatics to rationalize dishonesty as a justifiable means to noble ends.

The literature currently distributed by Smith is unbelievably fantastic. On each seat at last month's rally was a forty-page booklet called *My Fight for the Right,* in which Smith discusses twenty-three "murderous attempts" to destroy his life and career. In the middle of this paranoid pamphlet is a two-page ad for the well-known *Protocols of the Elders of Zion,* obtainable for a dollar from Smith's St. Louis headquarters.

A widely distributed leaflet titled *The Jews Have Got the Atom Bomb!* begins as follows:

Whoever controls the atom bomb controls the world, except, of course, for the miraculous intervention of God Almighty. As of today, Jews are in control of the secrets involved in the manufacture and manipulation of this instrument . . . . Bernard Baruch, the enigmatic Jew who has been a secret and Rasputin-like power in the affairs of our government for forty years is the mysterious power behind the atom bomb throne. Baruch, whose wealth comes from mysterious sources closely related to the profiteering of two terrible wars, realizing he was growing very old, devised and designed a technique for shifting his power to newer and younger Jews. While America was preoccupied with the casualties of the last war, while millions of boys were limping home blind and halt, broke and disillusioned from a war which Herbert Hoover says could have been avoided, Bernard Baruch and his ilk were concentrating on the control of the atom bomb through the manipulation of un-named personalities and international rogues operating in close conjunction with the United Nations.

Another choice piece of Smith literature is a book by "Mr. X," given free with subscriptions to *The Cross and the Flag*. This scholarly work, *The Roosevelt Death, a Super Mystery*, hints darkly that Franklin Roosevelt is not really dead but somewhere in Israel hatching a fiendish Jewish plot. *The Cross and the Flag*, official periodical of Smith's Christian Nationalist Crusade, supplanted Father Coughlin's *Social Justice* in 1942. It is published in Fort Worth with funds from a foundation sponsored by eighty-five-year-old George W. Armstrong, Texas oil millionaire and reportedly Smith's chief financial backer.

Financially, of course, Smith is far from unsuccessful. He is what Arnold Forster, in his book, *A Measure of Freedom*, calls a "successful failure." According to Forster, Smith's income last year exceeded $150,000. Donations to his Christian Nationalist party, as reported by Smith himself totaled more than $90,000. His most successful fund-raising meetings in 1949 were in Los Angeles where attendance was often quite large.

But why has Smith failed so miserably to recruit followers in Tulsa? The answer seems to be twofold.

1. The "silent treatment." When Smith first came to Tulsa, the city's leaders, including representatives of Jewish and Negro groups, ministers, radio-station managers, and the editors of both daily papers, wisely agreed to combat Smith by the simple policy of ignoring him. No attempts have been made to denounce him from either press or pulpit. The papers accept his paid advertisements, but they do not print his handouts, nor do they report his activities. Solomon Fineberg's article, "Checkmate for Rabble-Rousers" (*Commentary*, September 1946), defends the silent treatment brilliantly, and there is little doubt that in Tulsa it has proved exceedingly effective. Smith is aware of this strategy, of course. At last month's meeting he blamed his poor press on the pressure against editors by the city's wealthy Jewish advertisers.

2. The absence of any radical or liberal opposition in Tulsa. There are probably no more than a dozen Communists in the city; possibly an equal number in Greenwood, the Negro area. I doubt if Smith has any more inkling of who they are than Senator McCarthy has of who in Washington is Red. The Tulsa organization farthest left is the League of Women Voters.

One is led to the curious conclusion that perhaps Smith *underestimated* Tulsa conservatism! Liberal and left-wing sentiment is so rare in the city that no one really understands or cares who Smith is; and so he is deprived of a valuable opposition that might raise a rumpus and thereby give him priceless publicity.

A measure of both the quality of Tulsa's political awareness and the failure of Smith's shabby crusade was a remark made by a prominent oilman when Smith's name came up.

"He's a Red, isn't he?" ventured the oilman.

POSTSCRIPT

A slightly different version of this piece appeared in *The Progressive,* December 1948.

In 1965 Smith and his wife, Elna, settled in Eureka Springs, Arkansas, a small town in the northwest corner of the state. At about that same time Eureka Springs became a haven for several hundred hippies, who, surprisingly, turned out to be as tolerant of Smith as he was of them. Smith's first project was a 70-foot-high white statue of Jesus on a mountain near the town. A local long-hair described it (*New York Times,* July 27, 1972) as "a milk carton with head and arms." Soon Smith followed with a Christ Only Art Gallery, a Bible Museum, a 167-acre model of the Holy Land, and several other tourist attractions. When he died in California in 1976, at seventy-eight, almost everyone outside of Eureka Springs had forgotten him.

Today, when our fundamentalist Moral Majority steers clear of racism, it is hard to believe how successful Smith became with his mix of Bible pounding, admiration for Hitler, and overt hatred of blacks, Jews, and Catholics. In 1944 he was the presidential candidate of the America First Party. He called F.D.R. "Franklin D. Jewsevelt," attacked Harry Truman's "Jewish brain trust," and tried to prove that Eisenhower was a "Swedish Jew" unfit to be president.

Smith was a major asset in Huey Long's rise to power. When Long was assassinated in 1935 by a young dentist, Smith was walking beside him. He preached at Long's graveside. Soon he was accusing Mississippi's Senator Theodore G. Bilbo of having participated in a conspiracy to murder Long. This prompted Bilbo, himself no mean rabble-rouser, to call Smith "a contemptible, dirty, vicious, pusillanimous, with-malice-aforethought, damnable, self-made liar."

Smith's greatest oratorical heights were probably reached at a 1946 rally in Cleveland for Townsend's National Recovery Plan. Father Coughlin was on the platform. Bathed in sweat, Smith ripped off his tie, threw his jacket on the floor (both old Billy Sunday tricks), waved a Bible in the air, and bellowed:

We must make our choice in the presence of atheistic Communistic influences. It is Tammany or Independence Hall! It is the Russian primer or the Holy Bible!

It is the Red Flag or the Stars and Stripes! It is Lenin or Lincoln! Stalin or Jefferson! James A. Farley or Francis E. Townsend!

Mencken was in the audience. This is how he described Smith's performance:

> His speech was a magnificent amalgam of each and every American species of rabble-rousing, with embellishments borrowed from the Algonquin Indians and the Cossacks of the Don. It ran the keyboard from the softest sobs and gurgles to the most ear-splitting whoops and howls, and when it was over the thousands of delegates simply lay back in their pews and yelled. Never in my life, in truth, have I heard a more effective speech.

The evangelists who dominate today's television are all pussycats compared to Smith. Let us hope we will never see the likes of him again.

7

Beyond Cultural Relativism

Some of the Ethiopians tattoo their children, but we do not; and while the Persians think it seemly to wear a brightly dyed dress reaching to the feet, we think it unseemly; and whereas the Indians have intercourse with their women in public, most other races regard this as shameful. . . .

The sentences above are not from a modern textbook on cultural anthropology. They are from the writings of Sextus Empiricus, the ancient Greek skeptic who flourished in the second and third centuries of the Christian Era. Sextus was one of the earliest, though by no means the first, of the apologists for the point of view anthropologists call "cultural relativism" — the view that there are no standards of "good" and "bad" other than the laws and customs of a given culture.

By numerous examples Sextus made clear that the laws and customs of the ancient world varied widely from one society to another. Since there are no universal standards to which one can appeal, he reasoned, it is impossible to decide which is "best" among conflicting customs. "No more" — a phrase meaning that one point of view is "no more" true than another — was the central axiom of the Greek skeptics. What course of action, then, should the wise man follow? Sextus Empiricus gave a clear and simple answer: Suspend judgment on ethical matters and conform to the customs of your country.

Since the time of Sextus a distinguished number of thinkers have shared his ethical views. In this paper, however, we shall be concerned only with the growth of "no more" in the social sciences, particularly in recent anthropology. The question will be raised of whether this growth, so necessary

This essay originally appeared in *Ethics,* October 1950, and is reprinted with permission.

and healthy at the outset, has not reached such bizarre extremes that it obscures from the cultural anthropologist what may well be his major scientific task.

In the late nineteenth century, under the influence of Darwin, sociologists and anthropologists were convinced that cultures followed an orderly development from low, brutelike forms to the refinements of modern civilization. Primitive societies were investigated, not to determine objectively what they were like, but to uncover facts that would fit previously conceived patterns of progress. The savage in Spencer's *Principles of Sociology* is only slightly above the gorilla in mental and moral attainments. At the opposite end of Spencer's scale, exemplifying the highest type of culture, was, of course, British middle-class society.

It was against this "genetic" approach that twentieth-century social scientists rebelled. As methods for investigating primitive societies grew more efficient and less biased, it soon became apparent that the savage was not nearly so stupid and immoral as Spencer had supposed. He was capable of quite complex reflection on practical problems posed by his environment, and he was caught in a matrix of moral restrictions fully as elaborate as those of Victorian England.

Of course it was true that if you went back far enough you could find a rough evolutionary development of man, marked by such discoveries as fire and iron; but, in the period of, say, the last ten thousand years, investigations disclosed only a bewildering and changing pattern of cultural traits that were impossible to force into schemes of orderly upward movement. To avoid the ethnocentrism of his predecessors, the modern cultural anthropologist leaned over backward to refrain from expressing a "value judgment" concerning any aspect of his data. To be rigidly objective, all expressions of "good" and "bad" dropped out of his vocabulary. His work became purely "descriptive." Different cultures were regarded as "incommensurable" because no external yardstick existed by which they could be compared.

In 1907 a Yale sociologist, William Graham Sumner, published his famous *Folkways*. The book was a somewhat haphazard compilation of variations in social customs, designed — like Sextus Empiricus's compilations of seventeen centuries previous — to impress the reader with the diversity of human behavior and the tendency of every culture to suppose its customs superior to all others. It was this book that introduced the word *mores* into the social sciences. "Folkways" was Sumner's generic term for all customs; "mores" are folkways that have acquired ethical value, so that violation of them is considered evil or immoral. A woman who went about Manhattan with her hair dyed green would be violating the folkways. She would be regarded as eccentric but not immoral. If, however, she walked up Broadway in the nude, this would violate the mores, and she would be promptly arrested.

Like Sextus, Sumner recognized the wisdom of conformity. He wrote:

It is vain to imagine that a "scientific man" can divest himself of prejudice or previous opinion, and put himself in an attitude of independence toward the mores. He might as well try to get out of gravity or the pressure of the atmosphere. The most learned scholar reveals all the philistinism and prejudice of the man-on-the-curbstone when mores are in discussion.

Sumner himself was an outstanding example of scholarly prejudice. He accepted without question, as did Spencer, the mores of the conservative businessman, devoting a good part of his energies to public agitation against trade-unions, child-labor laws, the eight-hour day, and all government measures that interrupted the "natural laws" of supply and demand. One of his essays was titled, significantly enough, "The Absurd Attempt to Make the World Over." Even his phrase "the forgotten man," which Franklin Roosevelt appropriated in 1932 for a different purpose, had reference to the forgotten citizen who Sumner believed was being injured by government welfare services and swollen union wages.

Impossible though it may be to escape the mores in daily life, it is not impossible to evade them in the practice of cultural anthropology. Stimulated by the extraordinary progress of twentieth-century investigations and still in reaction against the naïve moralizing of Victorian schools, modern anthropologists (with the exception of the Russians, who are still in the evolutionary phase) have come to regard a "value judgment" as the cardinal sin of their profession. Any expression of "better" or "worse" is looked upon with horror as a gross violation of scientific objectivity.

A moment's reflection and you will see that *as a scientist* the anthropologist holding this point of view cannot be concerned with progress. For progress assumes that, after a culture pattern has changed, the new is somehow superior to the old. But to admit this is to make a moral judgment in terms of standards outside the process of change. An "unscientific" group within the culture might propose a change, and the anthropologist could advise how to achieve it; but he cannot, as a scientist, suggest the change. Of course he may slip occasionally and make a passionate plea for some type of reform (for example, to eliminate racial prejudice). The following section from Ruth Benedict's well-known *Patterns of Culture* is typical:

Like the behavior of Puritan divines, their [American business tycoons] courses of action are often more asocial than those of the inmates of penitentiaries. In terms of the suffering and frustration that they spread about them there is probably no comparison. There is very possibly at least as great a degree of mental warping. Yet they are entrusted with positions of great influence and importance and are as a rule fathers of families. Their impress both upon their own children and upon the structure of our society is indelible. They are not described in our manuals of psychiatry because they are supported by every tenet of our civilization. They are sure of themselves in real life in a way that is possible only to those who are oriented to the points of the compass laid down in their own culture. Nevertheless a future psychiatry may well ransack our novels and letters and public records for illumination upon a type of abnormality to which it would not otherwise give credence.

This is excellent rhetoric, but one wonders how Dr. Benedict harmonized such emotions with the theme of her book, namely, that cultures cannot be compared on ethical grounds but must be viewed simply as different, but equally valid, patterns of life. Of course a future society may regard the American business tycoon as abnormal. But on what basis can we expect this judgment to be superior to the judgment of our own society, in which the getting of wealth and power is venerated?

In a more recent book, *Man and His Works: The Science of Cultural Anthropology,* Melville J. Herskovits writes: "Cultural relativism is a philosophy which, in recognizing the values set up by every society to guide its own life, lays stress on the dignity inherent in every body of custom, and on the need for tolerance." But, as a shrewd reviewer pointed out, "dignity" and "tolerance" are by no means universally recognized values even within our own culture. Herskovits concludes his 650-page book with the statement that cultural relativism is anthropology's "greatest contribution" and that it "puts man yet another step on his quest for what ought to be" — apparently oblivious to the patent fact that, if man "ought to be" anything other than he is, there must be standards of value with their loci outside individual cultures.

Since the time of Sumner, every aspect of human life has tumbled into the anthropologist's bag of folkways. Aesthetics was one of the first to go. No anthropologist would dare assert that the art or music of one tribe was better or worse than that of another. Of course it may be more "complex," but that is a different matter. Frazer's *Golden Bough* and the science of "comparative religion" long ago relegated sacred "projective systems" to the folkways. The work of Durkheim, Max Weber, and others gave rise to a new discipline — the "sociology of religion." A review of Joachim Wach's recent study in this field stated: "The volume is distinguished by its author's careful effort to refrain from explicit value judgments in a field in which normative evaluations have been traditional obstacles to scientific insight."

You might suppose that science and mathematics would lie beyond the folkways. But no — the "sociology of knowledge" is another well-established discipline, launched by the late Karl Mannheim, of the University of London. In Mannheim's view this science was simply an investigation of the interactions of all forms of knowledge with their sociological context. He was not so naïve an idealist as to suppose that there was no external world, of definite structure, which science sought to describe with greater and greater accuracy. The fact that tribes had different theories about the shape of the earth would not have led Mannheim to suspect that the earth had no shape at all. But later disciples of Mannheim have twisted his views into a subjective idealism that refuses to admit that science, or even the laws of mathematics,[1] are grounded in a reality independent of the cultural process.

Extreme proponents of the relativism of knowledge do not tell us how their view, which they find superior to all others, manages to escape the all-pervading relativity. It is a tricky criticism. Perhaps they would reply in the manner in which Sextus Empiricus replied when charged with the same inconsistency. The statement that all assertions are false, he writes, may be the one exception—just as we can say that Zeus is the father of all the gods but not the father of himself. Or, if this is not the case, he continues, why not admit frankly that skepticism *does* destroy itself? Fire may destroy fuel and, in so doing, destroy itself; or a laxative purge food from the stomach and itself be purged. A man may climb to a high place on a ladder, Sextus concludes, then overturn the ladder with his foot. But few cultural relativists, one suspects, would care to think of themselves as stranded on a summit from which they survey all forms of error, including their own.

The notion advanced by Comte, Durkheim, and Spencer of a "science of ethics," which would construct on an empirical, natural basis a set of standards for judging human conduct, is a notion that goes against the grain of modern cultural anthropology. Such a science would force value judgments into investigations that the anthropologist feels should be kept objective—free of all moral suppositions.

To contemporary naturalistic philosophers the phrase "value judgment" does not have so ominous a ring. Most anthropologists would be startled to learn that John Dewey, whose influence on the social sciences has been incalculable, has always been a firm opponent of cultural relativism and a vigorous champion of science-based morality.

In 1938, in a well-known essay, "Does Human Nature Change?"[2] Dewey wrote:

> The existence of almost every conceivable kind of social institution at some time and place in the history of the world is evidence of the plasticity of human nature. This fact does not prove that all these different social systems are of equal value materially, morally, and culturally. The slightest observation shows that such is not the case.

The basis on which Dewey is willing to make moral judgments is simply stated. It is on the basis of a common human nature possessed by all men, which finds expression in a common set of "needs." He continues thus:

> By "needs" I mean the inherent demands that men make because of their constitution. Needs for food and drink and for moving about, for example, are so much a part of our being that we cannot imagine any condition under which

they would cease to be. There are other things not so directly physical that seem to me equally engrained in human nature. I would mention as examples the need for some kind of companionship; the need for exhibiting energy, for bringing one's powers to bear upon surrounding conditions; the need for both cooperation with and emulation of one's fellows for mutual aid and combat alike; the need for some sort of aesthetic expression and satisfaction; the need to lead and to follow, etc.

Whether my particular examples are well chosen or not does not matter so much as does a recognition of the fact that there are some tendencies so integral a part of human nature that the latter would not be human nature if they changed. These tendencies used to be called instincts. Psychologists are now more chary of using that word than they used to be. But the word by which the tendencies are called does not matter much in comparison to the fact that human nature has its own constitution.

It is important to note that Dewey does not hesitate to include psychological needs in his list. Many modern anthropologists have been willing to grant that there are physical needs common to all cultures; but, for the most part, they are reluctant to admit universal psychological needs. This hesitancy is understandable in view of the diversity of psychological patterns, but at times the hesitancy becomes absurd.

A good example is the chapter "What Is Human Nature?" in Malinowski's *A Scientific Theory of Culture and Other Essays* (1944). The author grants that all humans belong to the same species and therefore have certain "minimum needs" in common, which he lists as follows: breathing, eating, drinking, sex, rest, activity, sleep, micturition, defecation, escape from danger, and avoidance of pain. There is nothing wrong with this list, of course, except Malinowski's insistence that the list provides an adequate description of human nature. Apparently, it did not occur to the author that on these terms a cow becomes a member of the human race.

Broadening the list to include psychological needs in no sense implies that such needs derive from inherited patterns of behavior. Exactly how much in the way of inheritance enters into these needs is still much in dispute among biological and social scientists; but, even should it prove true that nothing is inherited and that all our peculiarly human traits—for example, the creation and enjoyment of art and humor—are learned responses, it still remains that such socially conditioned needs are as characteristic of human cultures as the conditioned behavior traits of birds characterize bird nature. They are universal because they spring from the interaction of what is common in the mental and physical structures of all humans with what is common in the environment of all cultures. Walking is a cultural universal because all men have legs and because the laws of gravity, motion, and inertia do not vary from one locale to another.

Of course we know little as yet about these psychological needs and how they can best be satisfied. But it is clear that the work of the cultural anthropologist in combination with the work of the psychologist offers the most fruitful avenue for research. As this research proceeds, there is reason to hope that a new basis for moral judgments may emerge. Of course it is necessary, as Durkheim recognized, to make two wild assumptions: (1) it is better to be alive than dead; (2) it is better to be healthy and happy than sick and miserable. Such axioms are, it must be granted, "unscientific." They may even be "metaphysical." But in view of the fact that no one cares to dispute them, there seems to be no good reason why a social scientist should not, as an existing "person," affirm them without shame.

There are signs, it is gratifying to observe, that the American social scientist is beginning to develop this courage. One of the earliest indications was a book published several years ago by sociologist Robert S. Lynd. Titled *Knowledge for What?* the book aroused a storm of controversy in social-science circles by attacking vigorously the extreme relativism of the "detached" investigator who refuses to do more than describe. Lynd argues not only that the sociologist should have the right to make value judgments in terms of the degree to which the satisfactions of human needs (Lynd calls them "cravings") are maximized, but, more important, he feels that this should be the primary task of the social sciences.

A second piece of writing that had an equally upsetting effect was the "Methodological Note on Facts and Valuations" in the Appendix to Gunnar Myrdal's classic work on the Negro problem, *American Dilemma* (1944). Myrdal attacked what he called the laissez-faire or "do-nothing" view of the American sociologist. A "disinterested social science" is "pure nonsense," he argues, because every choice of a research project involves some sort of evaluation, even if only in terms of its worth in providing new knowledge. And the refusal to make a moral judgment concerning conflicting views is itself a judgment affirming the equality of the views, leading easily into a defense of the status quo and to stagnation of reform. Since it is impossible for the social scientist to operate in a completely objective fashion, Myrdal proposes that moral judgments be accepted frankly and be explicitly stated in all research reports.

But the American cultural anthropologist is a shy creature. Not one of any prominence has yet had the audacity to declare in a firm, unshaken voice that he has made, or intends to make, a value judgment. The men who have come closest to such revolutionary acts are Ralph Linton, professor of anthropology at Yale, and his associate, Abram Kardiner, clinical professor of psychiatry at Columbia and a practicing psychoanalyst.

Ruth Benedict had introduced into ethnology her concept of a psychological pattern that characterized a given culture. But the pattern was obtained by haphazard, intuitional methods. Her conclusions lacked verifiability and precision. In the last decade Kardiner and Linton have combined the research methods of cultural anthropology and psychoanalysis to develop a more fruitful technique for uncovering these configurations. Their methods revolve about the concept of the "BPT," or "basic personality type," first explained in 1939 in Kardiner's *The Individual and His Society* and more recently (1945) in a work by Kardiner, Linton, and others, called *The Psychological Frontiers of Society.*

The BPT is simply the personality equivalent of the "basic body type." Physical anthropologists have long been able to make a statistical survey of, say, an island tribe to determine characteristic body features. But the determination of characteristic personality traits presents problems of much greater difficulty. By employing techniques borrowed from psychoanalysis — detailed life-histories, personality tests of the Rorschach type, and dream material — Kardiner and Linton and their colleagues have achieved astonishing results.

Although Kardiner has made plain that we have no basis for deciding that the BPT of one culture is better or worse than that of another, he has suggested that we evaluate a culture in terms of how well it molds members to fit the BPT. *Psychological Frontiers* closes with a strong criticism of what Kardiner calls the "pattern of American Calvinism," a Protestant configuration characteristic of our rural areas and running counter to our BPT because it suppresses impulses that our culture as a whole regards as good and releases impulses that our culture, again as a whole, considers destructive. Thus it is possible to define "progress" within a culture as a movement that results in more and more people who resemble the BPT.

Passing over the disturbing implication that such "progress" would sacrifice variety to uniformity, the important point to make is that this view in no sense provides a genuine escape from relativism. For we have as yet no way of deciding when a BPT is good or bad. We know that in a stable society the BPT and the entire cultural heritage tend to reinforce each other. But, in spite of this, the BPT does change slowly. Kardiner cites as an example the effect that new methods of child-rearing in America may have on our BPT. This places the author in a curious dilemma. For, if the BPT changes, then perhaps a change of BPT is more desirable than working for a "progress" that merely strengthens and stabilizes the BPT. To decide this, however, would require a value judgment concerning the BPT itself. It is clearly impossible to advocate a change of BPT except on the basis of a set of standards by which conflicting BPT's can be judged.

That a BPT may be "bad" is strongly suggested by the section of *Psychological Frontiers* in which Dr. Cora Du Bois writes of the people of Alor, a small island in the Netherlands East Indies. The chief characteristic of the Alor culture is that everybody hates everybody else. The BPT is "anxious, suspicious, mistrustful." The natives have deep predatory and exploitive drives, mutual anxiety, violent and indiscriminate aggressions, and repressed hatreds. They engage in no constructive enterprises because their energies are absorbed in protecting themselves against the hostilities of one another. Cooperation is rarely achieved, and when it is, it is by a domination-submission pattern rather than by love and trust. Marriages are almost always discordant, and women are reduced to a role of "sheer vegetation." The men spend most of their time engaged in an elaborate, meaningless financial system in which everyone tries to cheat everyone else. There is no creative art. Religious myths are filled with parental hatreds and revenge. No attempt is made to idealize either parents or the tribal gods. There is late toilet-training, marked lack of cleanliness, and insensitivity to odors. Frustrations are so great that a typical Alorian, judged by our BPT, would be considered psychotic. It is difficult to tell whether the Alorese are unhappy, Dr. Du Bois writes, because they are unaware of their "wretchedness."

The author struggles desperately to evade the charge that she has made a moral judgment in criticizing Alor culture. Her condemnations rest solely, she declares, on "psychological grounds"—on the degree to which the island culture fails to meet basic psychological needs. This should not be interpreted, she insists, as "moralizing."

At this point a disciple of Dewey would be quick to make clear that moralizing, in any constructive modern sense, is precisely that—making a judgment of praise or blame in terms of human needs. And why should a cultural anthropologist hesitate?[3] The battle against the naïve ethnocentrism of earlier investigators has long ago been won. The relativism that dealt the death blow was a necessary corrective. What is urgently needed at the moment is a corrective of the corrective—the boldness to affirm that there is a common human nature on the basis of which valuations can be made and in terms of which real progress can be measured.

If such "moralizing" is impossible in principle, then consider the odd sort of mysticism that the ethnologist is forced to defend. He must believe in some sort of mysterious Emersonian law of compensation that operates among human societies—some "God of Relativism" who makes certain that all cultures are exactly and forever balanced in the degree to which they meet human needs. For every gain the culture makes, there must be a compensating loss (otherwise the culture would be "better" than it was before), and for every loss there must be a compensating gain (otherwise the culture would be "worse"). It is difficult to imagine a primitive projective system with superstitions more fantastic.

Perhaps it is not too presumptuous to hope that the groundwork laid by Kardiner and Linton will lead some brave ethnologist to propose a "BHPT," or "basic *healthy* personality type," in reference to which a set of standards might be found. Such standards would not be "absolutes" in the traditional metaphysical sense. They would be what some philosophers have called "relative absolutes." No perceptible changes in the biological foundations of human nature have occurred during the period of recorded history, nor will such changes take place in the foreseeable future. It is in terms of this relative stability of human needs that relatively permanent standards could be formulated.

If a concept of the BHPT develops, it seems not at all naïve to suppose it capable of giving genuine social directives, not merely for strengthening the BPT (as Kardiner already has proposed) but for altering the BPT when it clearly departs (as does the Alor) from mental health. Of course it may turn out that there are many different cultural configurations roughly equal in the degree to which they meet human needs. There may be no single best way, just as there often are alternative solutions to algebraic equations; or, as von Neumann has made clear in his exciting work on the *Theory of Games and Economic Behavior,* there may be equally successful strategies both for winning games and for solving economic problems.

The work of the Freudian ethnologists has already rescued cultural anthropology from its fixations on variations in the shapes of bows and spearheads and turned its attention toward more important issues. Let us hope it will soon outgrow its adolescent fear of moralizing and develop the courage to declare, without stammering, that health and happiness are preferable to sickness and misery and that it is better to be alive than dead. Then, at last, the cultural anthropologist will be ready to combine forces with the psychologist, perhaps even with the philosopher, in the great tasks of formulating a naturalistic ethics and drawing up the blueprints for the City in the Skies.

POSTSCRIPT

Since I wrote the foregoing paper there has been a rapid decline of cultural relativism as a philosophy, though not of course as methodology. At the same time, there has been little evidence that cultural anthropologists in the United States, except for a small minority, have developed much concern with the task of shaping a science of culture that would permit cross-cultural value-judgments and provide a foundation for a naturalistic ethics. Most of today's textbooks of anthropology give the problem only a passing glance. The current scene is best described as wildly eclectic, one of formless confusion with respect to basic philosophical issues.

The emphasis on basic personality types was all the rage when I wrote my essay. It generated weighty books on how the German BPT led to Hitler, how the Russian BPT led to Stalin (the practice of swaddling babies was supposed to condition Soviet citizens to accept an authoritarian leader), and similar nonsense. Ruth Benedict's *The Chrysanthemum and the Sword: Patterns of Japanese Culture* is the best known of these many studies of national character. Then around 1970 this whole approach mysteriously faded away. The work of Freudian-oriented anthropologists such as Kardiner and Linton, in whom I saw so much promise, turned out to be remarkably sterile.

A few anthropologists found time in the fifties to talk about a basic human nature, universal values, and what some called a "metacultural reality" that gave meaning to progress. George P. Murdock actually listed seventy-three cultural universals, running in alphabetical order from age-weaning, athletic sports, and bodily adornment, to visiting, weaning, and weather control.[4] Clyde Kluckholn called them "panhuman values." In his paper "Ethical Relativity: Sic Et Non," Kluckholn defended a position identical to my own. Extreme cultural relativism, he wrote, as typified by Benedict and Boas, is intolerable, because it forces a vindication of such cultural patterns as slavery, cannibalism, and Nazism. Luckily, there is a universal human nature. "Some needs and motives are so deep and so generic that they are beyond the reach of argument: panhuman morality expresses and supports them." No one can question the importance of exploring conflicting patterns of culture, said Kluckholn. Some human values obviously are relative, but anthropology's greater task, he insisted, is to search, in cooperation with behavioral scientists and philosophers, for panhuman values on which a naturalistic ethics can be based.[5]

There were other trends running counter to cultural relativism at the time I wrote my article. Evolutionary anthropologists in the Soviet Union, and Leslie White in the United States, found a basis for cross-cultural values in the laws by which cultures evolve. Soviet anthropologists, as we all know, seldom hesitate to declare Soviet culture superior in all respects to decadent capitalist cultures.

At the moment, at least in France, the strongest challenge to cultural relativism is the structural anthropology of Claude Lévi-Strauss. He agrees with Noam Chomsky that there is a universal human nature and that, because it is part of the universe, all human minds have the same deep structure, bound by laws of logic and mathematics—laws independent of cultural variations on shallower levels. In sharp contrast to the views of Lucien Lévy-Bruhl (and White), Lévi-Strauss is convinced that the most primitive savage reasons in exactly the same fundamental way as an Einstein. The task of anthropology is more than just endless description of different cultural patterns. It is a search for the infrastructure common to these patterns. On the basis of this structure we can develop a science of culture that will help solve humanity's problems. All cultures may be equal, but some are more equal than others.

Now that Sartre is dead, existentialism is almost dead, with structuralism replacing it as the latest French cultural fad. But as structuralism spreads outward into philosophy and the arts, producing such whimsies as structuralist painting and structuralist poetry, it has become as amorphous as existentialism became. Nobody quite knows anymore just what "structuralism" is supposed to mean. Since everybody recognizes the existence of biological structure, in a broad sense everybody is a structuralist, just as in a broad sense everybody is a pragmatist or an existentialist. It remains to be seen how soon the structuralist craze will give way to some new Gallic plaything, and what sort of lasting contributions it will make.

In spite of these colorful and confusing trends away from old-fashioned relativism, the central paradox remains. How can cultural anthropology preserve the undeniable advantages of an objective, value-free empirical approach to its subject matter and at the same time go beyond this to find a basis for moral judgments? Perhaps the task is in principle impossible for scientists acting as scientists. I have more to say about this in the chapter on ethical relativism in my *Whys of a Philosophical Scrivener*.

NOTES

1. For a detailed attack on the view that mathematical laws are grounded in cultural relations see "Mathematics and the Folkways," Part 1, Chapter 5.

2. *Rotarian*, February, 1938; reprinted in *Problems of Men* (New York: Philosophical Library, 1946), p. 184.

3. It may be that unconscious guilt feelings are no small factors in many anthropologists' fear of valuation. For, if there is an objective, real difference between right and wrong, then there is a sense in which "sin" and "guilt" are more than illusions created by our mores; and one is haunted (especially if reared in Christian orthodoxy) by childhood memories of the biblical God with his righteous anger and flames of hell. This is not to imply that anthropologists have special reasons for feeling guilty, but only to suggest that feelings of guilt may play a greater role than is realized in the attraction that moral relativism has exerted on post-Puritan thinking.

4. Murdock, "A Common Denominator of Culture," in *The Science of Man in the World Crisis* (Columbia University Press, 1945), edited by Ralph Linton.

5. Kluckholn's paper first appeared in the *Journal of Philosophy*, vol. 52, 1955, pp. 663-67. It was reprinted in *Culture and Behavior: Collected Essays of Clyde Kluckholn* (Free Press, 1964), ed. by Richard Kluckholn. See also Kluckholn's essay, "Education, Values, and Anthropological Relativity" in the same volume, and "Universal Categories of Culture," in *Anthropology Today* (University of Chicago Press, 1953), ed. by Alfred L. Kroeber.

8

H. G. Wells: "Premature" Anti-Communist

A welcome aspect of the American liberal's fast growing disenchantment with the Soviet myth is the rediscovery of early political writing by men and women who saw clearly, and almost from the beginning, the essential evils of Soviet ideology. The names of Rosa Luxemburg and Karl Kautsky are being mentioned with increasing frequency; and Bertrand Russell's *Practice and Theory of Bolshevism,* first published in 1920, was reprinted two years ago without alteration, so accurate was Russell's insight.

In view of this trend, it is astonishing so little attention has been called to H. G. Wells's long and vigorous opposition to communism. Perhaps it is because American critical opinion is still in a phase, temporary I believe, of depreciation of Wells's genius. Perhaps, also, Wells's distrust of Stalinism may have played a minor role throughout the thirties in the steady decline of his reputation. I can cite my own feelings as a case in point. During the days of my fellow-traveling, though I had unbounded admiration for Wells, I felt ashamed of his persistent and stubborn Soviet carping. Wells was jealous, I suspected, of the fact that the Bolsheviks had set about the task of constructing the Good Society without seeking his advice or paying tribute to him as one of their prophets. Today, when I reread Wells's discussions of Marx and Soviet communism, I am amazed at how balanced and restrained they were. If he erred at all, he erred in underestimating the forces of Soviet corruption.

Wells's first visit to post-revolutionary Russia, in 1920, is described in

This essay was originally published in the *New Leader,* October 7, 1950, and is reprinted with permission.

his *Russia in the Shadows*. The book pictures a giant nation in a state of almost total breakdown, held together by an emergency government essentially honest, but fanatical in its worship of Marxist dogma.

> It will be best if I write about Marx without any hypocritical deference. I have always regarded him as a Bore of the extremest sort. His vast unfinished work, *Das Kapital*, a cadence of wearisome volumes about such phantom unrealities as the *bourgeoisie* and the *proletariat*, a book forever maundering away into tedious secondary discussions impresses me as a monument of pretentious pedantry. . . .
>
> In Russia I must confess my passive objection to Marx has changed to a very active hostility. Wherever we went we encountered busts, portraits, and statues of Marx. About two-thirds of the face of Marx is beard, a vast solemn woolly uneventful beard that must have made all normal exercise impossible. It is not the sort of beard that happens to a man, it is a beard cultivated, cherished, and thrust patriarchally upon the world. It is exactly like *Das Kapital* in its inane abundance, and the human part of the face looks over it owlishly as if it looked to see how the growth impressed mankind. I found the omnipresent images of that beard more and more irritating. A gnawing desire grew upon me to see Karl Marx shaved. Some day, if I am spared, I will take up shears and a razor against *Das Kapital;* I will write *The Shaving of Karl Marx*.

In a brief interview with Lenin (who spoke excellent English) Wells was favorably impressed. He found him an energetic, straightforward, intelligent little man with "a pleasant, quick-changing brownish face . . . lively smile and a habit (due perhaps to some defect in focussing) of screwing up one eye as he pauses in his talk." They "parted warmly." In a later discussion of this visit, in his autobiography, Wells credits Lenin with a "more vigorous and finer brain" than Marx, capable of transforming the narrow creed of Marxism into a flexible, creative program. After the interview Lenin exclaimed (if we are to believe Trotsky), "What a bourgeois he is! He is a philistine! Ah, what a philistine!" The sympathetic picture of Lenin in *Russia in the Shadows,* and the recommendation that the Western world be patient with his attempts to bring order out of chaos, aroused bitter Tory attacks on Wells in the London papers.[1]

A section headed "Psychoanalysis of Karl Marx" in a remarkable novel of ideas, *The World of William Clissold* (1926), is Wells's liveliest expression of contempt for Marxist orthodoxy. The following quotation is typical.

> It is for the psychoanalyst to lay bare the subtler processes in the evolution of this dream of a Proletarian saviour. Everybody nowadays knows that giant, in May-day cartoons and Communist pamphlets and wherever romantic Communism expresses itself by pictures, presenting indeed no known sort of worker, but betraying very clearly in its vast biceps, its colossal proportions, its small head and the hammer of Thor in its mighty grip, the suppressed cravings of the restricted Intellectual for an immense virility . . .

The Work, Wealth, and Happiness of Mankind (1931), Wells's survey of the social sciences, contains excellent discussions of the emptiness and inexactitude of communist jargon, the overemphasis on economics in the interpretation of history, the sham erudition, and the increasingly reactionary character of an orthodoxy that bore an astonishing resemblance to a religious cult.

> For the edification of the weaker brethren there are now prophets and saints, Marx and Lenin to begin with, whose intelligence and character must no longer be questioned, whose every utterance was divine. And there is even a mystical communism affecting the art and literature of Moscow profoundly, whose aim is self-identification with "the Proletarian." "The Proletarian" is a superhuman entity with whom the devout Marxist seeks and attains spiritual communion. The individuality of the worshipper is merged therein. From the Proletarian springs "Prolet-art," for example, among the first fruits of the new spirit. It is art without individuality. Proletarian thought, proletarian science, proletarian conduct have, it is believed by the devout Communist, strange and novel superiorities of their own.

Yet, aware as he was of these fatal defects, Wells continued to hope that the Russian experiment might profit from its mistakes and somehow manage to muddle forward toward a more enlightened planned economy.

In 1934 Wells visited Russia again, and through an interpreter conversed for several hours with Stalin. The meeting is described in Wells's autobiography. He found Stalin shy and friendly, but with a less astute, more doctrinaire mind than Lenin. He spoke in dreary party formulas, his imagination "invincibly framed and set." Stenographic accounts of the interview were published in many forms by communist presses throughout the world.[2] To the faithful, of course, Stalin had played the role of Big Brother, explaining patiently but firmly to Wells some of the kindergarten principles of Marxian science. "His explanation," wrote a British communist editor, "made as much impression on Mr. Wells as an explanation of the working of an internal combustion engine would make on a kitten."

Wells left Russia this second time with a feeling of profound distress. Stalin had been unwilling to concede that an inch of political progress had been made by the New Deal, and Wells feared that Russia and America would continue to diverge with a "maximum of mutual misunderstanding . . . until there is a new type of intelligence dominating the intellectual life of Communism." "I had expected to find a new Russia stirring in its sleep and ready to awaken to Cosmopolis, and I found it sinking deeper into the dope-dream of Sovietic self-sufficiency."

Earlier in the autobiography, published in 1934, Wells had written:

> Marxism is in no sense creative or curative. Its relation to the inevitable reconstruction of human society which is now in progress, is parasitic. It is

an enfeebling mental epidemic of spite which mankind has encountered in its difficult and intricate struggle out of outworn social conditions towards a new world order. It is the malaria of the Russian effort to this day. There would have been creative revolution of a far finer type if Karl Marx had never lived.

Five years later, in *The Fate of Man,* Wells found Russia still stumbling forward, but "faltering and losing its imaginative appeal." In the great purges he saw:

> . . . the human reality of incompetent men trying to cover up the mess they are making of things, of wrongfully-appointed men holding on to their jobs by trick and subterfuge, of hates and jealousies, of elaborate misrepresentations to save the face of groups involved in a common failure, of the manufacture of countervailing evidence, counter-accusations, resort to influence in high quarters. . . . And at the last come the confessions, to put a consistent face on the untellable tale of fudging and muddle-headedness. Better persuade yourself you are a consistent conspirator than a self-protective fumbler, a snake rather than a worm.

In 1942 the *Labour Monthly,* a British Communist periodical, made the mistake of asking Wells to contribute a tribute to Russia for their November issue. His letter of refusal was published the following month. After reference to Russia's "omniscient disdain" for all other political movements, Wells wrote:

> It is difficult to over-estimate the mischief the Communist Party has done to mankind in the past third of a century. Its wildly irrational propaganda of extravagant menace has done enormous mischief in discrediting genuine radical and revolutionary thought in the Atlantic countries.

I quote this because, as far as I can determine, it was Wells's last significant pronouncement on communism. During the remaining war years he produced a number of magazine and newspaper pieces, some of them containing references to communism, but they are the repetitious, at times muddled and peevish, writings of a sick, aging man.

In this brief article I obviously have made no attempt to discuss the evolution of Wells's political views, or his important role in the history of English socialism. Nor have I endeavored to cover more than a fraction of his published utterances on communism. I have tried only to indicate, by a few highlights, the consistency of Wells's views on the Soviet experiment, from the days of its inception to his death in August 1946.

There is a tendency among recently disenchanted communists and fellow-travelers to rationalize their period of domination by the Soviet mystique. Not until the last few years, you hear them say, has the behavior of Russia forced upon us a realization of her corruption and tyranny. You would think, to listen to these pious justifications, it was some *defect* of vision that made "premature" anti-communists of such men as Russell and Wells. I think there is a more honest attitude. There were those who saw more clearly than we, and we did not listen to them.

NOTES

The two notes below accompanied my original article but were not used. When I asked Sol Levitas, then editor of the *New Leader,* why he dropped the note about the Hicks pamphlet, he told me he did so in deference to Hicks, who was then writing a literary column for the magazine.

1. For example, Winston Churchill's "Mr. Wells and Bolshevism," in the *Sunday Express,* December 5, 1920.

2. In America, the CP pamphlet carried an introduction by Granville Hicks in which Wells is branded a "petty-bourgeois intellectual," fearful of the role of the working class, and "hysterical" in his criticism of Marx. "If Stalin's share in the interview is an impressively clear and straightforward formulation of the theory and practice of Marxism," Hicks wrote, "Wells's contribution is an unconscious revelation of the hopeless confusion and intellectual emptiness of liberalism." This was written, of course, before Hicks's dramatic break with the Party in 1939.

9

Is Nature Ambidextrous?

"Next Boy!" said Alice, passing on to Tweedledee, though she felt quite certain he would only shout out, "Contrariwise!" and so he did.

"You've begun wrong!" cried Tweedledum. "The first thing in a visit is to say, 'How d'ye do?' and shake hands!" And here the two brothers gave each other a hug, and then they held out the two hands that were free, to shake hands with her.

—Through the Looking Glass

Bertrand Russell once pointed out that, just as the easiest objects to see are those neither too big nor too small, so the easiest conceptions in mathematics are those neither too complex nor too simple. "It must have required many ages," Russell wrote in a well-known passage, "to discover that a brace of pheasants and a couple of days were both instances of the number 2." In this article we will examine an equally elusive concept—the distinction between right and left—an examination that will lead us into many curious by-paths.

Let us begin our exploration, like Alice, by stepping for a moment through the looking glass. Assuming we ourselves are not reversed by this process, we will quickly discover that the room behind the mirror is both remarkably like and unlike the room we have left. Metric and topological properties will be unchanged; and yet not a single object (if we take into consideration minor blemishes), will be exactly like its counterpart. They all, as Alice put it, "go the other way."

In the idiom of the projective geometer, we have walked through a reflection plane from one "sense class" into another. The structures we examine have undergone the simplest type of projective transformation. They have been "reflected" in such a manner that all mathematical properties remain unchanged except for a reversal of left-right orientations. Certain shapes however, will appear unaltered. We will call these shapes "symmetrical" and

This article originally appeared in *Philosophy and Phenomenological Research,* December 1952, and is reprinted with permission.

assume that all such structures are "superposable" on their mirror images. Structures not superposable will be called "asymmetric."

The choice of the term "sense class" to distinguish one side of the mirror from the other arises from a simple fact that may be difficult to grasp fully at first, but should become clearer as we proceed. This fact is: There is no *formal* method of defining left or right. The distinction is entirely conventional, but because of our "sense" of left and right we find it convenient to apply those terms to asymmetric objects and their mirror images.[1] For example, we call one shoe a left shoe, the other a right; or we say a screw has a left- or right-handed thread. But there is no logical or mathematical way to describe what we mean by a left shoe.

In *Principles of Mathematics* Russell makes clear that the distinction between left and right is one form of an asymmetrical relation—and that, since such relations are necessary for any ordered series, they can be said to underlie most of mathematics. The difference between before and after, greater and less, left and right, and similar relations, cannot be reduced to mere linguistic difference. To say A is to the left of B is not identical with the assertion that B is to the right of A because there is a difference of meaning between left and right. The notion of the two senses, involved in all asymmetric relations, is regarded by Russell as an independent axiom "not explicable in terms of any other notions."

Apparently Kant was the first eminent philosopher to be puzzled by the odd fact that an asymmetric object and its mirror image can have identical metric properties and yet not be the same. Expressed another way, no amount of inspection or measurement of one in isolation will reveal a property not possessed by the other, and yet one cannot be substituted for the other without revealing a major difference. "What can more resemble my hand or my ear," Kant wrote in Section 13 of his *Prolegomena,* "and be in all points more like, than its image in the looking glass? And yet I cannot put such a hand as I see in the glass in the place of its original. . . ."

Kant considered this a paradox that could not be solved if spatial relations were regarded as external to the mind. It could be avoided only by adopting his transcendental idealism, in which all spatial (and temporal) relations are regarded as mental qualities projected upon the unknown *Ding-an-sich.* In Kant's words, "What then is the solution? These [mirror image] objects are not presentations of things as they are in themselves, and as the pure understanding would cognize them, but they are sensuous intuitions, i.e., phenomena, the possibility of which rests on the relations of certain unknown *things in themselves* to something else, namely our sensibility."

As a philosophical "realist," Russell rejects this view by making asymmetrical relations, like other spatial relations, a part of the external world.[2] He finds "nothing mysterious" about the asymmetry of three-dimensional figures, presumably because asymmetry can also exist in one and two dimensions. It is hard to see how the fact that left-right distinctions exist in all dimensions (including those above three) makes the duality less mysterious, but Russell is clearly right in the sense that it is no more mysterious than any other geometrical axiom that seems to hold true both in the imagination and in the structure of the world. Certainly there is no more reason to regard asymmetrical relations as nonobjective than similarly to regard any other geometrical axiom, and Kant was unquestionably at fault in considering their existence a *unique* argument for the subjectivity of geometry.

The lack of a formal definition for right and left is not as obvious as it might at first seem. The full implications can best be brought out, perhaps by considering the following unusual problem. Let us suppose we have established radio communication with the inhabitants of a planet in some totally unknown portion of the cosmos where the configuration of stars and planets in their sky would be meaningless to us. To focus the problem sharply we will assume that these beings are exactly like us, speaking the same language and inhabiting a similar world. What we do not know, however, is whether their world is, or is not, a mirror image of ours. We know they have hearts, for example, but we do not know which side of the body their heart is on.

The problem is this: Is there any way we can communicate to these people what we mean by left and right? Can we arrive at a common understanding, say, of the difference between right and left shoes so we can be certain which of our shoes corresponds to their left shoes?

The inclination at first is to suppose there might be some geometrical process we could describe to our distant twins which they could employ to reach an understanding of our "left." But if this were possible it would clearly contradict our former assertion that the distinction between left and right is incapable of definition by formal methods. The fact is, there is no way apart from reference to a commonly observed left-right structure by which we can communicate the meaning of left. We can agree on up and down, and forward and back, but we can never be sure that our sense of left and right corresponds with theirs. To express this another way, if the entire cosmos suddenly reversed all its left-right orientations (as though a god had rotated it through a fourth dimension, analogous to our turning over a sheet of paper), obviously no theorem in geometry would be affected. From our point of view the reversal would be meaningless; or, as Leibniz put it, to ask why God created the cosmos as it is, rather than its mirror image, is to ask "a quite inadmissible question."

We are now prepared to restate the problem in a slightly different, but more exasperating, manner. Instead of assuming that the entire world of our sister planet may or may not be reversed, we will assume only that living forms may be reversed. In other words, all substances and natural laws that may have left-right orientations can be assumed to be the same on both planets. We cannot, of course, permit an identity of geographic configurations (otherwise we could define left as the direction toward China when you stand in the United States and face Canada), nor can we assume a similar solar system.

We have seen there is no *geometrical* way to define the distinction between right and left. The question that now presents itself is: Can the distinction be conveyed by an *operational* method involving physics or chemistry?[3]
If a space ship, carrying a crew of scientists and a laboratory stocked with
any known substances and equipment, were to pass through a spacetime warp
that flipped the vessel over in the fourth dimension, and the vessel landed on
a strange planet in an unknown corner of the cosmos, is there any method
by which the scientists could prove to themselves they had been reversed?[4]
Or would they have to withhold opinion until they returned to earth, where
they would find everything in reflected form? In seeking to answer these questions we must first survey some of the asymmetric natural phenomena that
suggest themselves as possible means of solving our dilemma.

A number of rotational effects caused by the earth's spin have a clockwise
or counterclockwise character. The Foucault pendulum, precession of
gyroscopes, and Coriolis effects are typical. But, even though we may assume
our sister planet to be rotating on an axis parallel with ours and in the same
direction, these rotational phenomena are of no help to us in defining right
and left. The reason is that the rotations cannot be given unambiguous
description without agreement as to which is the Northern Hemisphere. The
turning of the Foucault pendulum, the gyroscopic precession, and the Coriolis effects are clockwise in one hemisphere, counterclockwise in the other.
But it is precisely the distinction between north and south that cannot be
communicated without an understanding of right and left. We can agree on
what it means to stand erect, facing the direction in which we are carried
forward by the earth's spin, but we cannot indicate on which side the North
Pole lies because we have not yet found a definition of left. As we shall see
later, even a magnet will not provide this information.

Stereochemistry seems to offer a more fruitful field. There are numerous
substances that are "optically active"; that is, they have the property of
rotating a plane of polarized light in either a clockwise or a counterclockwise
direction (as the observer faces the light source with the substance between
his eyes and the source). Could we not suggest to our twins that they procure an optically active substance, observe the way it rotates the plane of
light, then define left as the direction toward which the upper or lower part
of this rotation moved?

Unfortunately, every optically active substance exists in two forms, one
a mirror image of the other, and the two forms have identical properties in
all respects save properties of a right-left character, or properties resulting
from their reaction with other asymmetric substances. Such pairs of compounds are known as stereoisomers. Isomers are substances composed of
molecules that contain identical atoms, but with the atoms linked together
by topologically different structures. (A convenient way to think of this is
to regard the atoms as solid balls bound to each other in various ways by
connecting cords. Actually, of course, each atom may be merely a configura-

tion of electro-magnetic waves oscillating about a common center.) Stereoisomers, on the other hand, are isomers that are topologically identical, but one cannot be superposed on the other.[5] They are asymmetric (in the sense previously defined), or, to borrow a term from solid geometry, they are "enantiomorphic." It will be well to digress a moment to examine more precisely the meaning of enantiomorphic.

In all dimensions a figure is considered "reflexible" if it is superposable on its mirror image. Examples in three dimensions are a bottle, brick, shoe box, chair, and coffee cup. It is surprising, if you look about a room, how many man-created objects have reflexible shapes. All these shapes would seem unchanged to Alice on the other side of the looking glass. Objects *not* reflexible, that is, not superposable on their mirror images, are enantiomorphic. This includes all solids that do not have at least one "plane of symmetry," i.e., a plane that bisects the object in such a way that, if the plane is a mirror, half the object together with its reflection will restore the original shape. All asymmetrical solids lack this plane of symmetry and are therefore reversed by the looking glass. Many objects that might seem at first to be reflexible, prove on closer inspection to be enantiomorphic. For example, dice (when the spots are considered) and a pair of scissors. Such objects are always capable of existing in two forms, although one may be rarer than the other. Thus there are few pairs of left-handed scissors, and modern dice are now standardized so that when you hold a die with the 1 uppermost, the 2 will be found always to the left of the 3.

If a stereoisomer possessed a property that distinguished it from its enantiomorph, and the property was independent of our sense of left and right, then that substance could be used as a means of solving our problem. For example, if dextrose (right-handed sugar) weighed more than levulose (left-handed sugar), we could tell the inhabitants of our sister planet to procure the heavier sugar, then proceed to define left and right in terms of its effect on a plane of polarized light. To our chagrin, however, no such properties exist! All the observable differences between two stereoisomers are dependent on our sense of right and left, or on the left-right structures of other things.

We can make this clearer by considering the five most important distinguishing properties of stereoisomers. (1) Each will rotate a plane of polarized light. The rotations are opposite, but the degrees of twist are exactly equal. (2) The salts of each compound will form enantiomorphic crystals, but the crystals are identical except in respect to their left-right orientations. (3) They have different rates of reaction with other compounds, but only if the other substances likewise contain asymmetric molecules. A stereoisomer and its mirror image will have the same rates of reaction with a given symmetrical substance. Likewise, the reaction of two stereoisomers (of different substances) with each other will be identical with the reaction of their respective twins. (4) Certain molds and bacteria will attack one type and not the other, but this is due to asymmetry in the structures of the organisms, and we have stated our problem so as to exclude a known identity of left-right structure in the living forms on the two planets. (5) They have different effects on the body of living organisms, but again this is due to the asymmetric character of body enzymes.

To pursue this last statement further, if certain "racemic" compounds (optically inactive substances containing an equal mixture of right and left stereoisomers) are swallowed or injected, the organism may utilize only the molecules of one type and excrete the mirror images. Or it may utilize both types, but at different rates. Also, there are marked differences in the taste and smell of certain stereoisomers and their enantiomorphs, due to the asymmetric character of our sensory nerve endings. The toxicity of certain stereoisomeric poisons may also vary widely from one type to the other. Cigarettes contain levo-nicotine (in this sense we can say our cigarettes are left-handed!), which is twice as toxic as dextro-nicotine. Because all organic substances are asymmetric, any liquid containing organic compounds is likely to affect the body differently in its right and left forms, as well as taste differently. These facts give a meaning unsuspected by the author to Alice's remark, "Perhaps looking glass milk isn't good to drink"; or to the thoughts of the right-handed Irishman in W. H. Auden's *The Age of Anxiety* who contemplates his reflection in the mirror behind a New York bar and wonders:

> My deuce, my double, my dear image,
> .... What flavor has
> That liquor you lift with your left hand. . . . ?

It is an interesting fact that inorganic stereoisomers are invariably racemic, whereas organic stereoisomers (proteins, amino acids, enzymes, hormones, etc.) are always in either a pure right or left form. In photosynthesis, for instance, a plant will combine symmetrical water and carbon dioxide to produce asymmetric starches and sugars. This remarkable ability of cells to create asymmetric molecules has not yet been duplicated in the laboratory. It is, in fact, one of the basic (though often unmentioned) unique properties of life. Apparently, the asymmetric character of enzymes plays a major role. It is essential to all life processes, and it may well be that underlying molecular asymmetry is responsible for almost all the differences between the species of a given genus (since the various species are usually composed of identical mixtures of the same substances). Molecular asymmetry is therefore an essential element in an evolutionary process that depends for its operation on a large number of variations. It is hard to imagine such a proliferation of different living forms as we have on the earth resulting from the limited combinations possible among symmetric molecules.

In this connection it should be pointed out that complex organic compounds that have more than one asymmetric carbon atom (i.e., a carbon atom in the center of a cluster of asymmetrically linked atoms) may have more than two stereoisomeric forms. Thus, if there are two such atoms, each cluster has a mirror image; but, because the clusters can vary independent of each other, there are four possible forms of the compound. Three carbon atoms yield 8 varieties; 4 carbon atoms yield 16. To convey some idea of the structural complexity of organic compounds, 15 different amino acids, each asymmetric, may combine in various ways to form 32,768 different proteins.[6]

Laboratory-produced stereoisomers are always racemic, though several methods, originally worked out by Pasteur, enable the chemist to separate left and right forms. As might be expected, there is no method of doing this without (1) using the chemist's own sense of right and left in separating salt crystals of the substance, (2) the aid of organic asymmetrical compounds. If it were otherwise, our problem would be solved. We could obtain a substance in racemic form and apply a process that did not involve right and left; then if the result were a pure left-handed form we could send a plane of polarized light through it and thereby achieve a precise definition of left. Attempts have been made to effect the separation of mirror-image molecules by means of magnetic fields combined with polarized light, but so far without much success. Even if they succeeded, the use of the magnetic field introduces (as will be made clear shortly) a conventional right-left distinction.

We are now in position to see why our initial assumption that we cannot know the left-right orientations of living forms on our sister planet is a reasonable one. Considering biological laws alone, earth's evolutionary tree might easily have been a mirror image of the present one. This raises the interesting question of how the compounds in the first protoplasm acquired their left-right character. If we assume all life came from a single bit of protoplasmic material, we can imagine this material subject to many varieties of asymmetrical forces. Such forces would range all the way from local and accidental left-right phenomena, through the asymmetrical rotational effects arising in the two hemispheres, to broader and more basic asymmetries involving the earth's electric and magnetic fields. How any of these forces could have formed the first organic stereoisomers we do not, of course, know. It is not inconceivable, however, that if life had started in another hemisphere, or if the earth had been rotating in the opposite direction, our hearts might now be on the right side.

The field of inorganic crystallography also presents asymmetric phenomena; but, again, such crystals exist in both forms, which differ only in respect to their left-right properties. For example, many inorganic crystals are optically active because of their crystalline structure. Quartz and cinnabar are the two minerals with this property. But, like stereoisomers, quartz and cinnabar exist in both forms, each rotating the plane of polarized light an equal distance and in opposite directions.

All this is exceedingly aggravating. Before declaring the problem insoluble, however, we have one remaining field to investigate—the field of asymmetric magnetic and electrical phenomena.

The most familiar example of a left-right electromagnetic effect is the direction of magnetic lines of force surrounding a current. The "right-hand rule" tells us that if we grasp a wire with the right hand, thumb pointing in the direction the current is flowing (positive to negative), our fingers will indicate the rotation of magnetic lines of force circling the current. (The rule arose at a time when the current was believed to move from positive to negative. It is now known that the electrons flow the other way, calling for a "left-hand rule"; but the former rule has remained conventional.) Will not this rule provide us with a means of communicating right and left?

The answer is that it will not! Actually, the magnetic lines of force indicate nothing more than a circular field at right angles to the current, and it is entirely conventional whether we speak of this field in terms of a right- or left-hand rule. The right-hand rule is used because it indicates the direction in which the north pole of a compass will point when the compass is brought near the wire. Strictly speaking, nothing is "moving" around the wire, and all attempts to demonstrate a magnetic "current" have been failures. If the earth were to reverse its poles, this would reverse the compasses, and the right-hand rule would have to be replaced by a left-hand rule. As we have seen, there is no geometrical way to distinguish the earth's poles without an agreement as to right and left; consequently the orientation of a magnet in the magnetic field surrounding a current is of no help to us.[7]

Our problem could be solved, or course, if there were some means of defining the north pole of a magnet without reference to the earth. Unfortunately, no such means has been discovered. The strengths of the two poles are identical, and a magnet floating on water exhibits no tendency to float in either direction. Experiments in which a colloidal suspension of iron filings is deposited on a bar magnet have yielded some beautiful microscopic patterns resembling tweed cloth, but there is no asymmetry in the pattern along the polar axis. If this pattern contained, for example, triangles that pointed toward one pole, then we would have a neat solution to our dilemma. We could direct our twins to let a magnet orient itself beneath a wire in which the current moved toward them. If the magnet were coated with filings, the triangles would now point in a direction that would provide unambiguous definitions of right and left.

At this point the reader may wonder why an electromagnet could not be substituted for a compass. The difficulty is that although there is no ambiguity about the direction of the current in a helix surrounding an electromagnet, the position of the poles depends on whether the helix is clockwise or counterclockwise! And this, of course, cannot be communicated without an understanding of left and right.

Just as moving electrical charges create a field in which magnets orient themselves, so do magnets create fields in which currents take on a left-right character. A well-known experiment is one in which a freely moving vertical wire, the lower tip in mercury, is made to circle about the end of a magnet.

The same principle is involved in a primitive type of motor called "Barlow's wheel." But in these, and similar experiments, the direction of rotation depends on which pole of the magnet is employed.

A magnetic field also will twist a plane of polarized light. Again, the direction of twist is a function of the orientation of poles. The rotation of the earth's magnetic field gives a slight twist to polarized light reflected from horizontal surfaces; but, as might be anticipated, the rotation is opposite in the two hemispheres.

One final type of electromagnetic phenomena will now be considered briefly—the motion of charged particles as they pass through magnetic fields. When such a particle enters the field in a direction perpendicular to the lines of force, it is thrown into a circular movement the direction of which is a function of two factors—the orientation of magnetic poles and whether the particle is positively or negatively charged. The type of charge can, of course, be defined unambiguously. Thus in a cyclotron there is a spiral movement of charged particles through a magnetic field. But such circular asymmetries cannot be used to define left and right because of the ambiguity in defining magnetic poles.

Suppose, however, instead of using a magnet to produce the field, we make use of the field surrounding a current. We then permit a charged particle to enter this field at right angles to the lines of force and observe the direction of its revolution. Since the movements of both the current and the particle are unambiguous, would not this provide a precise definition of left and right? Alas, nature frustrates us once more; but we will have to consider the experiment in greater detail to see why this is so.

Imagine a current flowing toward you, magnetic lines of force circling the wire. A charged particle enters this field, we will assume, below the wire, moving at right angles to the lines of force. A moment's reflection and you will see that the particle must of necessity revolve on a vertical plane parallel to the wire. Since the wire points toward you, this means the revolution of the particle cannot have for you a left and right orientation unless you step to either the right or left of this plane. If the particle does not cut the lines of force exactly at right angles, its path will be a helix that can be observed without shifting your position, but unfortunately the helix will be clockwise or counterclockwise depending on whether the particle was moving diagonally to the right or left when it entered the field.

If a current is substituted for a charged particle in the experiment above, the same laws of deflection obtain and the same difficulties are encountered. There is, in fact, *no combination of currents, moving charged particles, and magnetic fields that will result in an unambiguous definition of left and right.* At some point in every such experiment either the right and left sense convention will enter, or the employment of magnetic poles, which in turn cannot be defined except in terms of a right-left convention.

Is there any reason to hope that, as more is learned about the nature of magnetism, a solution to our problem may be found? At present, this seems unlikely. The currently accepted theory of magnetism bases magnetic phenomena on what is called "electron spin." But a spinning electron is not enantiomorphic. The direction of spin depends on the position of the observer; a rotating sphere, spin and all, can be superposed on its mirror image. When a bar of iron is magnetized, the electrons (or submicroscopic "domains" of electrons) are oriented so that most of them are spinning in the same direction, with axes parallel to the polar axis of the bar. After the bar is magnetized it will always orient itself the same way in a magnetic field, but there is no underlying structural difference between the poles. As previously pointed out, the north and south poles of a magnet cannot be distinguished except conventionally in terms of their orientation relative to the earth's poles.

We are forced, therefore, to concede that our original problem is insoluble. There is neither a formal nor operational definition of left, no means by which it could be communicated to our sister planet. Another way of formulating this surprising conclusion is as follows: *Every known inorganic asymmetric structure or phenomenon exists in two mirror image forms identical in all respects except left-right orientations.* Mother Nature is ambidextrous. Apart from living organisms, she has no right- or left-handed habits; whatever she does asymmetrically, she does in mirror-image forms.

Logic and mathematics cannot, of course, dictate Nature's behavior. There is no a priori reason why science might not tomorrow discover some type of structure or natural law that throughout the cosmos would invariably possess a left-handed twist. It would be like discovering that cinnabar was unstable in its right-handed form, or that a certain type of ray had a wave component that always spiraled clockwise as the ray moved forward. But so far, outside of earth's living forms, no such single-handed habits have been found—a fact which strongly suggests that all natural laws reduce ultimately to the behavior of symmetrical waves and/or particles. The principle of symmetry, which Archimedes felt intuitively to be universal, remains unshaken. Like that famous pair of enantiomorphs, Tweedledum and Tweedledee, Nature extends her right and left hands simultaneously for a handshake.

POSTSCRIPT

I was prompted to write this essay after a brief conversation with Bob Hummer, a magician friend who never went to college but had a fine mind and a knack for inventing marvelous mathematical magic tricks. Hummer said one day: Have you ever thought about how hard it would be to explain to some intelligent creature on another planet what we mean by "left" without referring to something you both could see that had a left-right structure?

The more I thought about this the more puzzling it became. After some reading on the topic I concluded that the task would be impossible, because nature makes no fundamental distinction between right and left. I wrote a forgettable science-fiction story about it, and this paper. Five years later, to my vast surprise, physicists overturned the "law of parity," and in doing so disclosed that nature is *not* ambidextrous. Mirror-reflection symmetry is violated in what are called the weak interactions. Partly as penance for my bad guess, I wrote an entire book about it called *The Ambidextrous Universe*. A much revised edition, with new chapters about the asymmetry of time, was published in 1979 by Scribner's.

I have included here this out-of-date essay because it provides an easy-to-understand background that explains why in 1957, when parity was overthrown, the world's leading physicists were even more amazed than I. Abdus Salam, Pakistan's Nobel Prize-winning expert on quantum mechanics, said it was like discovering a race of giants who had only one eye, but instead of the eye being in the middle of the forehead, like on the Greek Cyclops, it was on one side of the face. The implications of this discovery are still far from fully understood. Nobody yet knows if nature's handedness is an accident of imbalance in the Big Bang or whether there is a level below quantum theory (as in the twistor theory of Roger Penrose) on which asymmetry is an irreducible property of the structure of the universe.

NOTES

1. It should be made clear at the outset that the duality explored in this paper is called a left-right duality, rather than up-down or front-back duality, only because our bodies have almost identical right and left sides and consequently we interpret our mirror image as a left-right reversal. Strictly speaking, it is only when we stand with a side to the mirror that it reverses the left-right axis. A mirror in front or in back of us reverses the front-back axis, and a mirror on the floor or ceiling reverses the up-down axis. It is entirely a matter of convenience that we speak of "left" and "right" asymmetrical forms—rather than up and down, or front and back, forms— and that the problems under discussion here have been traditionally formulated in left-right terms. The reader who thinks, "Why be so concerned with the left-right convention? Are not up and down, front and back, equally important and equally arbitrary?" has not yet grasped the heart of the matter. The basic duality explored here is much deeper—it is the duality of asymmetric figures in their two mirror-image forms.

2. For a recent and clear statement by Russell detailing his objections to Kant's geometrical views, see pp. 712-18 of his *History of Western Philosophy* (1945).

3. It must be stated at this point that the difficulty of communicating left and right, under the conditions described, is unique in the sense that a similar difficulty is not encountered in regard to other asymmetrical relations. Up and down can be defined in terms of toward the center of the planet or away from it; forward and back in terms of direction of vision; before and after, large and small, heavy and light, inside and outside, even true and false, can be given operational meanings that would be communicable to our sister planet.

4. The notion that a human being, if "turned over" in the fourth dimension, would

be transformed into his mirror image has been exploited in many science-fiction tales, the first of which was H. G. Wells's "The Plattner Story" (1896). Wells did not take into consideration the fact that a reversal of Plattner's enzymes and other body proteins would probably render all available food unfit to eat. Cf. also my story "Left or Right?" *Esquire* (February, 1951).

5. The first important treatise suggesting that molecules had this mirror-image character was published in 1875 by the Dutch chemist (and first Nobel Prize winner in chemistry), Jacobus H. van't Hoff. It was dismissed by his colleagues as "miserable speculative philosophy."

6. For this and other data relating to organic asymmetry I am indebted to Renee von Eulenburg-Wiener's excellent book, *Fearfully and Wonderfully Made* (1939).

7. This fact was completely misunderstood by Ernst Mach, who believed that the deflection of a magnetic needle by a current indicated a basic asymmetry in physical laws. See Hermann Weyl, *Philosophy of Mathematics and Natural Science* (revised English edition, 1949), p. 160.

10

The Royal Historian of Oz

> It is not down on any map; true places never are.
> —Melville, *Moby Dick*

America's greatest writer of children's fantasy was, as everyone knows except librarians and critics of juvenile literature, L. Frank Baum. His *Wonderful Wizard of Oz* has long been the nation's best-known, best-loved native fairy tale, but you will look in vain for any recognition of this fact in recent histories of children's books. Aside from an obscure booklet by Edward Wagenknecht and a brief magazine article by James Thurber, no one has felt it worth-while to inquire as to what merits the Oz books may have or what manner of man it was who first produced them. By and large, the critics have looked upon Baum's efforts as tawdry popular writing in a class with Tom Swift and Elsie Dinsmore; certainly not to be compared with such classic "children's" fantasies as *Pilgrim's Progress* and *Gulliver's Travels*.

Fortunately, children themselves seldom listen to such learned opinion. Nothing in the world could induce them to plod their way through Bunyan's dreary discourse on Protestant fundamentalism or Swift's impudent nose-thumbing at the human race. Even Lewis Carroll's Alice books, with their archaic British phrases, abrupt transitions, and nightmarish episodes, have lost almost all their appeal for a modern child unless he or she happens to be a prodigy who plays chess and dabbles in semantics and symbolic logic. Yet today, half a century after they were written, children still turn the pages of Baum's Oz books with passionate delight. Surely it is only a matter of time until the critics develop sufficient curiosity to read the books themselves. When they do, they will be startled to find them well written, rich in excite-

This essay originally appeared in *Fantasy and Science Fiction,* January and February 1955, and is reprinted with permission.

ment, humor, and philosophy, and with sustained imaginative invention of the highest order. In anticipation, therefore, of this event, it may be of interest to recount here for the first time the full story of Baum's remarkable career.

Lyman Frank Baum was born May 15, 1856, in the little town of Chittenango, near Syracuse, New York. His mother, Cynthia Stanton, was Scotch-Irish in descent and a devout Episcopalian. On his father's side his ancestors came from Germany, settling in central New York in 1748. His grandfather, the Reverend John Baum, was a circuit-riding Methodist minister. Benjamin Ward Baum, his father, was one of the nation's earliest oil producers, with extensive holdings in the Pennsylvania oil fields, and owner of a large estate near Syracuse in an area that is now the town of Mattydale.

Baum's childhood was spent in comparative luxury at Rose Lawn, the name of his father's estate. Here he was privately tutored except for a short period of attendance at Peekskill Military Academy. Young Frank did not take to military discipline, a fact that may explain the satire that pervades his descriptions of the Royal Army of Oz. (For a time it numbered twenty-seven officers and one private named Omby Amby, though on most occasions it consisted only of the Soldier with the Green Whiskers.)

When Baum was entering his teens, his father bought him a small printing press. For several years, during the summer months, Frank and his younger brother Harry wrote and printed a monthly newspaper that they called the *Rose Lawn Home Journal.* This may have aroused Frank's interest in a newspaper career. At any rate, at the age of seventeen he took a job in Manhattan as cub reporter on the *New York World.* Two years later we find him opening his own printing shop at Bradford, Pennsylvania, where he established the *New Era,* a paper still published today. But the work was dull and his spirit restless. For a while he managed a small chain of "opera houses" owned by his father in New York and Pennsylvania.

The theatrical world fascinated him more and more. Occasionally he acted with traveling stock companies, using a stage name because his family frowned on his associations with the theater. At one time he even tried to make a go of his own Shakespearean troupe. Finally he turned to play writing and in 1881 achieved his first literary success with an Irish musical comedy called *The Maid of Arran.* The play opened at his own opera house in Gilmour, Pennsylvania, then moved to Manhattan, where it enjoyed a profitable run. Baum wrote the book, music, and lyrics, produced and directed, and, under the name of Louis F. Baum, played the romantic lead! His acting was described in one review as "quiet and effective."[1]

Judging by early descriptions, young Baum must have made an impressive stage appearance. He was slightly over six feet, slender, and athletically proportioned, with brown hair, gray eyes, fair skin, and handsome angular features. His voice was low and well modulated and he sang in a rich baritone. In later years he always wore a large bicycle-handle mustache that was fashionable in his time. In photographs his eyes seem humorous, kindly, dreamy.

During the first year of his play's success, Baum married Maud Gage, of Fayetteville, New York, an attractive, spirited girl whose strong will and practical mind served to counterbalance her husband's reluctance to take money matters seriously. It proved to be a permanent, happy marriage. The play was on the road for several years, but when Maud became pregnant Baum dropped out of the cast and returned with her to Syracuse. There he set up a small company to manufacture and sell "Baum's Castorine," a crude-oil product used for greasing axles. This aspect of the oil business did not long hold his interest. He tried his hand at three more Irish melodramas — *Matches, Kilmourne,* and *The Queen of Killarney.* Only the first two were actually produced. They enjoyed brief runs but failed to achieve the popularity of his first play.

In 1887, with two small sons to support, Baum turned his face westward in search of greener pastures. His wife had a brother living in Aberdeen, a small prairie town in the region that was soon to become the state of South Dakota, and it was there that Baum took his family. At first he ran a variety store called Baum's Bazaar, but his generosity with credit made it difficult to keep the business solvent. He next bought a weekly paper, the *Aberdeen Saturday Pioneer,* and edited it for two years. "Our Landlady," his front-page column, poked good-natured fun at the local gentry but apparently made a few enemies. There were later rumors that he became involved in a pistol duel with one villager. The duel began with the two men standing back to back in the middle of the street. They were instructed to walk away from each other to the ends of the block, circle the block, and start shooting as they came together on the opposite side. Each man, as soon as he turned his first corner, reportedly ran up an alley and vanished from the scene.[2]

Two more sons were born in Aberdeen. The paper failed in 1891 and Baum moved his family to Chicago, where he first took a job as reporter on the *Chicago Post.* For a time he traveled through the Middle West selling china and glassware for a Chicago importing firm while his wife supplemented the family income by doing embroidery. His luck turned in 1897, when he tapped a hitherto unexploited magazine field by founding the *Show Window,* a monthly periodical for window trimmers. It was the official organ of the National Association of Window Trimmers of America, of which Baum was founder and first president.

For some time Baum had delighted his four sons by telling them ingenious tales that amplified the meaning of familiar Mother Goose rhymes. He began putting these stories on paper, and in 1897 a collection was published by the Chicago firm of Way and Williams in a handsome format with illustrations by Maxfield Parrish. *Mother Goose in Prose,* as it was called, was Baum's first book for children as well as Parrish's first job of book illustrating.[3] It must have sold well, because it soon appeared in a London printing and in several other American editions.

Baum's next book, *By the Candelabra's Glare,* is now extremely rare and much sought by collectors. He issued it himself in 1898, setting the type, printing it, and even binding it in his own workshop. It is a collection of sentimental, undistinguished verse. "My best friends have never called me a poet," he confesses in the foreword, "and I have been forced to admire their restraint." One poem, "La Reine Est Morte—Vive la Reine!," is an amusing attack on the type of woman then active in the feminist movement. The third stanza reads:

> And shout hurrah for the woman
>   new!
> With her necktie, shirt and tooth-
>   pick shoe,
> With tailor-made suit and mien
>   severe
>   She's here!

Baum's mother-in-law was a prominent feminist, a fact that may help explain his dislike of the New Woman. Even the Oz books contain many sly digs at the suffragettes, and one book, *The Land of Oz,* is one long satire on the movement. It chronicles the temporary overthrow of Oz by an army of comely young women.[4] The revolution is bloodless, owing to the fact that the Royal Army (i.e., the Soldier with the Green Whiskers) flees in terror when the girls brandish their knitting needles at him. Once the female dictatorship is established, the husbands of Oz are forced to take over all the former duties of their wives. This proves annoying to both wives and husbands, but luckily the throne is soon restored.

General Jinjur, the pretty farm girl who leads the revolt, is one of Baum's best "meat people" characterizations (in Oz "meat people" are sharply distinguished from such personages as the Scarecrow and Tin Woodman who have no flesh and blood). She is a shrewdly drawn portrait of the masculine protest type. Her face wears "an expression of discontent coupled to a shade of defiance or audacity." She walks with "swift strides" and there is about her "an air of decision and importance." In a later Oz book she blacks her husband's eye for milking a red cow when she wanted him to milk the white one. Whenever the Scarecrow's painted face becomes faded, it is Jinjur who enjoys retouching it. It is not her own face that she paints, but that of a straw man.

Baum's third hardcover work, published in 1899, was *Father Goose, His Book.* It is a collection of nonsense rhymes for children, illustrated by Baum's friend William Wallace ("Den") Denslow, a Chicago newspaper artist, and hand-lettered by another Chicago artist and friend, Ralph Fletcher Seymour.[5] To everyone's surprise the book was an immediate sell-out, requiring four reprintings in the three months that followed the first edition.

For several years Baum had been taking his family each summer to

Macatawa, a Michigan resort town on the shore of Lake Michigan. With the money earned by *Father Goose* he had a summer cottage built there, which he named "The Sign of the Goose." Most of the furniture was built by Baum himself. Since early manhood he had suffered from a bad heart and his doctor had advised him to do more of the manual craft work that he so much enjoyed. It was characteristic of Baum that he used the goose as the decorative motif of his cottage. A large rocking chair was in the shape of a goose. A frieze of green geese bordered the living room walls. A stained-glass window portrayed a goose in brilliant colors. Even the tiny brass heads of his upholstery tacks were specially made for him in the shape of geese![6]

Baum continued to edit his trade journal and in 1900 published *The Art of Decorating,* a mammoth handbook on the decoration of store windows and interiors. But his interest had now shifted to juvenile writing and his head was brimming with unusual ideas. During that year four children's books came from his pen. Two were unimpressive — *The Army Alphabet* and *The Navy Alphabet,* oversize books of mediocre verse telling the reader that A stands for Admiral, B for Bulwark, and so on. The other two books were fantasies, each concerned with adventures in a mythical land of enchantment. *A New Wonderland* had as its setting the Beautiful Valley of Phunnyland, where it snows popcorn, rains lemonade, and "the thunder is usually a chorus from the opera of Tannhauser." The other book — the book destined to make him immortal — was *The Wonderful Wizard of Oz.*

A New Wonderland (later retitled *The Magical Monarch of Mo)* is a collection of short, hilarious tales. It was written for an eastern firm and published by them at about the same time that *The Wonderful Wizard of Oz* was issued by George M. Hill, the small Chicago house that had published *Father Goose. The Wonderful Wizard* almost failed to find a publisher. It was turned down by every house to which it was submitted, Mrs. Baum later recalled in a letter,[7] because it was "too different, too radical — out of the general line." Mr. Hill finally consented to act as the book's distributor only after Baum and his illustrator, Denslow, agreed to shoulder all printing expenses. The book was not actually distributed to stores until the fall, but before the end of the year it had become the fastest-selling children's book in America. In 1955 a first edition sold at auction in Manhattan for six hundred dollars.

The book's story, as everyone knows, is about a plain-spoken little orphan girl who suddenly finds herself, like Lewis Carroll's Alice, in a magic land. Alice fell into Wonderland by way of a rabbit hole. Dorothy Gale is blown into Oz by a Kansas cyclone. And behind her strange adventures, as in all of Baum's fantasies, there lurks many an intended level of higher meaning. The Cowardly Lion, Scarecrow, and Tin Woodman illustrate delightfully the human tendency to confuse a real virtue with its valueless outer symbols. The Lion wants the Wizard to give him courage, the Scarecrow wants brains, and the Tin Woodman desires, beneath the coldness of his metal exterior, a warm heart. All three possess, of course, the things they seek. The Lion quakes with fear but meets all danger bravely. The Scarecrow thinks better than anyone in the party, and the Tin Woodman is so concerned over his lack of heart that his "reverence for life" exceeds that of a Schweitzer. On one occasion when he accidentally steps on a beetle he weeps so copiously that his tears rust and lock his jaws.

Even the ancient philosophic question of which is superior, the head or the heart, is explicitly raised. "I shall ask for brains instead of a heart," remarks the straw man, "for a fool would not know what to do with a heart if he had one." To which the tin man replies, "I shall take the heart, for brains do not make one happy, and happiness is the best thing in the world."

Baum wisely adds: "Dorothy did not say anything, for she was puzzled to know which of her two friends was right."

After the success of *The Wonderful Wizard,* Baum handed his trade journal over to a new editor and began work in earnest on other books for children. Three were published in 1901, none about Oz. *Dot and Tot of Merryland* is a full-length fantasy for very young readers. *The Master Key,* for older boys, is a science-fiction story about the wonders of electricity. The third volume, *Baum's American Fairy Tales,* deserves special mention because it marks the first appearance in American letters of fairy tales of merit that have the United States as a setting.

In 1902 Baum published *The Life and Adventures of Santa Claus,* a warm, moving story told in almost biblical prose and involving an elaborate Dunsany-like mythology. Its appearance, however, was completely overshadowed by the success in Chicago of a musical extravaganza based on *The Wizard.* Baum wrote both book and lyrics, Paul Tietjens composed the music, and Denslow designed the costumes.[8] The final script had been so heavily revised by Julian Mitchell, the producer, that it bore little resemblance to the original. Oz fans are usually shocked to learn that in the stage version Dorothy's pet is not a little black dog named Toto, but a huge cow called Imogene. There is a Lady Lunatic, very much out of place in Oz, and even a Poet Prince, with whom Dorothy falls in love!

Baum first reacted to many of these changes with amazement and indignation, but after the musical had become a smashing success, playing eighteen months on Broadway, he decided that Mitchell knew his audiences. In concluding a letter to the *Chicago Tribune* (Sunday, June 26, 1904, Part 4, p. 1) he expressed his views as follows:

> I confess, after two years of success for the extravaganza, that I now regard Mr. Mitchell's views in a different light. The people will have what pleases them, and not what the author happens to favor, and I believe that one of the reasons why Julian Mitchell is recognized as a great producer is that he faithfully tries to serve the great mass of playgoers — and usually succeeds.
>
> My chief business is, of course, the writing of fairy tales, but should I ever

attempt another extravaganza, or dramatize another of my books, I mean to profit by the lesson Mr. Mitchell has taught me, and sacrifice personal preference to the demands of those I shall expect to purchase admission tickets.

Two vaudeville comedians who worked as a team, Fred Stone and Dave Montgomery, were catapulted to stardom by the stage success of *The Wizard.* Stone played the Scarecrow and Montgomery the Tin Woodman. (The role of Dorothy, it is interesting to note, was taken by Anna Laughlin, mother of today's "star-spangled soprano," Lucy Monroe.) The two comics were in England when Mitchell wired them to return for parts in the musical. New York papers reported that Mitchell met Stone with the comment, "Fred, you are a perfect scarecrow." To which Stone indignantly replied that his clothes had been made by one of the finest tailors in England. A chapter of Fred Stone's autobiography, *Rolling Stone,* published in 1945, is devoted to the musical. It is interesting to learn from this that Fred's brother, Edwin, took the role of Dorothy's pet cow, and that Fred fell in love with and married the girl who played the Lady Lunatic.

Flushed with the success of his musical, Baum and his wife sailed for Europe in January of 1906 for a six-month vacation abroad. The trip took them through Egypt, Greece, Italy, North Africa, Switzerland, and France. Baum's heart condition prevented him from climbing to the top of the Great Pyramid, a challenge that his robust wife was unable to resist. "The steps are from three to four feet in height," Maud wrote in a letter home, "and the ascent so strenuous that I rested several times on the way up."[9] A dramatic eruption of Mt. Vesuvius, witnessed by the Baums, prompted Baum to write a friend that the crater was the only thing he had seen on the trip that smoked more than he did.

Paul Tietjens, who wrote *The Wizard's* musical score, also took a vacation abroad, spending it in Paris with Denslow. There he met and married the American girl who later became the poet Eunice Tietjens. In her autobiography, *The World at My Shoulder,* she describes Denslow as "a delightful old reprobate who looked like a walrus." Back in the States, she and her husband called on Baum at his Michigan cottage, "The Sign of the Goose." She wrote:

L. Frank Baum was a character. He was tall and rangy, with an imagination and a vitality which constantly ran away with him. He never wrote fewer than four books a year. . . . Constantly exercising his imagination as he did, he had come to the place where he could honestly not tell the difference between what he had done and what he had imagined. Everything he said had to be taken with at least a half-pound of salt.[10] But he was a fascinating companion.

He was never without a cigar in his mouth, but it was always unlit. His doctor had forbidden him to smoke, so he chewed up six cigars a day instead. There was one exception to this. Before he took his swim in the lake in the afternoon he would light a cigar and walk immediately into the water. He would solemnly wade out till the water was up to his neck and there walk parallel with the shore, moving his arms to give the impression that he was swimming. When a wave splashed on the cigar and put it out he at once came in and dressed.

His house was full of the most remarkable mementos of the time when it had been necessary for him "to rest his brain," following a stroke of facial paralysis. He had painted the walls with stencilled designs; he had made a sign of wrought iron and painted wood for the dooryard, "At the Sign of Father Goose"; he had made furniture; he had written a small book of poems(!), had set it up in type himself, printed and bound it by hand. Last of all, because all this had not yet rested his brain enough, he had made an elaborate piano arrangement of Paul's music for *The Wizard of Oz*—though he was no musician it was pretty good—had then figured out the system by which pianola records were made, and had cut a full-length record of this arrangement out of wrapping paper! This seems to have done the trick, and he was presently back at work.

Surviving friends of Baum all remember him as a modest, dignified gentleman who enjoyed meeting people, talking, and telling funny stories. "He was a very kindly man," Mrs. Baum states in a letter, "never angry, pleasant to everyone, but when his mind was active with some story he would meet his best friend and not see him."[11]

Throughout his adult life Baum did not affiliate with any church organization save for a brief period of membership in an Episcopalian church in Aberdeen. But he was always a "religious" man in the sense that he believed in both God and immortality. For a time he was intrigued by theosophy, and although he rejected most of the preposterous doctrines of this cult he seems to have retained a belief in reincarnation and the law of Karma. His eldest son, Frank, now a retired Army colonel in Los Angeles, tells me in a letter that his father always believed that he and his wife had been together in previous incarnations and would be together again in future lives. (In Baum's fantasies I can recall only two places where he touches on the question of soul survival. *Sea Fairies* has a satirical section in which a school of "holy" mackerel express their conviction that, when they are jerked out of their element by a hook, they "go to glory"—to an "unknown, but beautiful sea." And in *Sky Island,* when inhabitants of the blue region reach the close of their life, they walk through the Arch of Phinis into the Great Blue Grotto, but what happens to them on the other side is not known.)

Aside from marching in a few torchlight parades for William Jennings Bryan, Baum was as inactive in politics as in church affairs. He consistently voted as a Democrat, however, and his sympathies seem always to have been on the side of the laboring classes. (In *Sea Fairies* an octopus expresses great indignation at having been likened to the Standard Oil monopoly!) I do not know whether Baum ever read William James, but he certainly shared James's love of variety and his democratic tolerance for ways of life alien to his own. There is a remarkable scene in *The Lost Princess of Oz* (p. 148) in which a group of animals, meat and meatless, argue about who among them is superior. The matter is finally settled by the Cowardly Lion who says quietly:

> Were we all like the Sawhorse we would all be Sawhorses, which would be too many of the kind; were we all like Hank, we would be a herd of mules; if like Toto, we would be a pack of dogs; should we all become the shape of the Woozy, he would no longer be remarkable for his unusual appearance. Finally, were you all like me, I would consider you so common that I would not care to associate with you. To be individual, my friends, to be different from others, is the only way to become distinguished from the common herd. Let us be glad, therefore, that we differ from one another in form and in disposition. Variety is the spice of life and we are various enough to enjoy one another's society; so let us be content.

This theme of tolerance runs through all of Baum's writings, with many episodes that poke fun at narrow nationalism and ethnocentrism. In *John Dough and the Cherub*, for example, we encounter the Hilanders, who are tall and thin, their country separated by a stone wall from the Lolanders, who are short and fat. A law observed in both regions forbids anyone to ask questions of strangers or of inhabitants on the opposite side of the wall. As a consequence, neither country knows anything about the other, regarding its own area as a paradise and inhabitants on the other side as barbarians.

Like William Morris, whom he read and admired, Baum had a constitutional dislike of the mass-produced item, whether a piece of furniture or a man. "After all," says the Scarecrow to Tommy Kwikstep (a boy with twenty legs), "you have the pleasure of knowing you are unusual, and therefore remarkable among the people of Oz. To be just like other persons is small credit to one, while to be unlike others is a mark of distinction." I can think of only one spot outside of Oz where individuals of eccentric appearance do not suffer because of their deviation from the norm, and that is in the world of the carnival and circus sideshow. Perhaps it was his circus-background that enabled the Wizard to adjust so easily to life in Oz.

Eccentric as Baum's "meatless" characters are, they have a consistency of personality and behavior that makes them very real to the mind of a child. On one occasion when Baum had not written for weeks, Maud asked him what the trouble was. "They won't do what I want them to," he replied. When he began writing again and she asked how the matter had been settled, his answer was, "By letting them do what they wanted to."[12] It is a believable answer. Baum was a natural storyteller and even his most outlandish characters seem always to move about with a life of their own.

In spite of the fact that he continued to receive hundreds of letters (a mere trickle of the deluge to come!) from children who wanted to hear more about Oz, Baum's interests still lay in fairy tales of other sorts. His *Enchanted Island of Yew* (1903) is not a bad story (the chapter on Twi, a land where everything exists in double form, is an amazing *tour de force*) but it did not sell well, and it is marred by unpleasant psychological undertones.

Finally, in 1904, Baum yielded to the persistent demands of his readers. He wrote *The Marvelous Land of Oz* (later retitled *The Land of Oz*), dedicating it to Montgomery and Stone. It is his only Oz book in which Dorothy does not appear. The central character, a small boy named Tip, is later revealed to be Princess Ozma in enchanted form. For many years the Baums had longed for a daughter, and the book's dramatic climax may well have been an expression of such a desire.

Many new and entertaining "meatless" characters are introduced in the story. Jack Pumpkinhead is an awkward, wooden figure whose head is a pumpkin carved in an eternal grin. A wooden sawhorse is brought to life, much to its own astonishment. And of course we must not fail to mention Professor H. M. Woggle-Bug, T.E.

The Woggle-Bug is Baum's caricature of the overeducated pedant. He had originally been an ordinary woggle-bug, living in the hearth of a country schoolhouse. There he had become extremely learned by listening to the lectures of Professor Nowitall. One day the professor discovered him in the room, and to show his pupils what a woggle-bug looked like, put him in a magic lantern that projected his magnified image on the screen. At a moment when the attention of the class was distracted, the Woggle-Bug stepped down from the screen and made an escape in his greatly puffed-up condition. "H.M." stands for "Highly Magnified," and "T.E." for "Thoroughly Educated." The Woggle-Bug is addicted to using big words and has to be rebuked occasionally for his tendency to indulge in bad puns. This is partly a satire on Baum himself, for the Oz books abound in puns. They reach a crescendo in a later book when Dorothy visits the Kingdom of Utensia, where all the citizens are pieces of kitchenware. In eight pages of text Baum manages to introduce no less than fifty puns!

The Woggle-Bug eventually becomes the President of the College of Art and Athletic Perfection. His great contribution to the higher learning is the invention of a pill that gives a student all the knowledge he needs simply by swallowing it. This frees students from the burden of attending classes and permits them to spend all their time on college sports.

The Woggle-Bug, an operetta that Baum based on *The Land of Oz*, was produced in Chicago in 1905, but its run was short. *The Woggle-Bug Book*, issued the same year to publicize the play, is now a rare collector's item. It is a large picture book in paper covers, telling of the Woggle-Bug's adventures in an American city.

In addition to his summer home at Macatawa, Baum now began spending part of each winter in a cottage at Coronado, on the California coast. In 1905 he purchased Pedloe Island, eighty miles off the coast, and announced to the press his plans to convert the island into a miniature land of Oz that would serve as a playground for youngsters. An eleven-year-old San Francisco girl was appointed Princess of Oz. A palace and statues of leading Oz personages were to be erected, and a monument to Jack Pumpkinhead built on Wizard's Point. The project never got beyond the planning stage and may have been little more than a publicity stunt to promote the sale of the second Oz book.

Queen Zixi of Ix, Baum's effort to write an old-fashioned European-type fairy tale, appeared in 1905. That same year Baum tried his hand at an adult novel. *The Fate of a Crown,* a romantic tale about Brazil, was published under the pseudonym of Schuyler Staunton. Another romance by Staunton, *Daughters of Destiny,* came out the following year. His final attempt along these lines was *The Last Egyptian,* issued anonymously in 1908. The three novels are well-written adventure tales, but otherwise have little to recommend them.

Six other pseudonyms were used by Baum. Captain Hugh Fitzgerald was his *nom de plume* for two boys' books about the adventures of one Sam Steele. Six novels about the Boy Fortune Hunters (two were reprints of the Sam Steele books) came out under the name of Floyd Akers. John Estes Cooke (not to be confused with John Esten Cooke, a Virginia historian whom Baum may have admired) was the name he used for a privately printed edition of *Tamawaca Folks.* Tamawaca is an anagram for Macatawa. The novel is about Baum's friends in the resort area.

Under the name of Edith Van Dyne, Baum wrote seventeen novels for teen-age girls. Ten of them are about Aunt Jane's nieces, five about Mary Louise, and two about Orissa Kane, a girl aviator. After Baum's death, books by Edith Van Dyne continued to appear but were the product of other hands. *Annabel,* a love story about a red-haired lass, was written under the pseudonym of Suzanne Metcalf. As Laura Bancroft, he published six small books of fantasy (subsequently issued as a single volume called *Twinkle and Chubbins*) and *Policeman Bluejay,* a longer fantasy (later issued as *Babes in Birdland*). With the possible exception of the Bancroft books, none of these pseudonymous works are of lasting value. But the potboilers for older boys and girls, including two published under his own name (*The Daring Twins* and *Phoebe Daring*), brought him a steady and considerable income.

On one occasion, Mrs. Baum recalls,[13] an eastern publisher visiting in Chicago expressed to Baum's publisher a strong desire to meet Mrs. Van Dyne. He was so persistent that the firm finally arranged a tea at which the visitor was introduced to a lady who had been carefully coached to play the role. The publisher was charmed and edified. Baum and his wife attended the tea, enjoying the hoax immensely.

In 1907 Baum returned to his role of Father Goose by publishing *Father Goose's Year Book,* a kind of diary with blank pages on the right and humorous poems and aphorisms (such as "Rolling billiard balls gather no salary") on the left. But Baum's readers were no longer interested in Father Goose; they wanted to hear more about Oz. The second Oz book had not

concerned Dorothy—in fact no one from the "outside world" appeared in
the story. But readers remembered Dorothy with fondness, and yielding to
their entreaties Baum reintroduced her as the protagonist of *Ozma of Oz,*
the third volume in the series.

Dorothy's companion on this second adventure is a proud yellow hen called
Billina. Other "Ozzy" characters also introduced for the first time include
Tik-Tok, a mechanical copper man; the Hungry Tiger, who longs to eat little babies but whose conscience never permits him to do so (the *id* versus
the *super-ego*!); and the Nome King, a whimsical mixture of evil and the
comic, who appears in many later Oz books as the sworn enemy of Dorothy
and Ozma.

Tik-Tok is one of the earliest robots in American fantasy. As his directions for winding read, he "thinks, speaks, acts, and does everything but live."
Parts of his mechanism are always running down at crucial moments. Once
in a later book he lapses into double talk when his thought mechanism, but
not his speech, ceases to function.

The remaining Oz books, all excellent, though some have sections of
careless writing, contain scores of outrageous personages. There is the Woozy,
a blue, square-shaped animal of wood whose eyes dart fire whenever anyone
says "Krizzle-Kroo" (the Woozy does not understand what this means and
it is this that makes him so furious). There is the Patchwork Girl, a cotton-
stuffed, but far from stuffy figure whose meeting with the Scarecrow is one
of the highlights of the book in which she first appears. Nor does one easily
forget such minor characters as Johnny Dooit, with the long gray whiskers
and copper tool chest, who can build anything in just a few seconds; the
Braided Man, who sells boxes of assorted rustles for ladies' skirts and flut-
ters for flags; the Fuddles, a race of 3-D jigsaw people who "scatter" when
disturbed, thereby giving befuddled visitors the fun of putting them together
again.

The two most important cats in Oz deserve a paragraph. Both behave
exactly as you would expect cats to behave if they could talk. Eureka,
Dorothy's meat cat, permits herself to undergo a long court trial to determine if she has eaten one of the Wizard's piglets before she informs the court
where the little pig can be found. Bungles, a glass cat with a cold ruby heart,
is so reluctant to show her emotions that once, when she leaves to obtain
help for friends in distress, she moves very slowly to give the impression she
is indifferent to their fate. As soon as she is out of sight, however, she runs
like a streak of crystal.

At the close of *The Emerald City of Oz*, sixth in the series, Baum tried
to drop the series altogether. Glinda, the most powerful sorceress in Oz, casts
a spell over the country that makes it impossible for the Royal Historian
to find out what is happening inside its borders. You can imagine, of course,
the flood of letters from heartbroken youngsters! Fortunately Baum was able
to reestablish communication with the Shaggy Man, by wireless, and thus

continue the series. Before writing the seventh Oz book, however, he managed to finish two superbly written fantasies, *Sea Fairies* and *Sky Island*. They tell of the adventures of Mayre Griffiths, better known as Trot, and her peg-legged sailor companion, Cap'n Bill. Both Trot and Cap'n Bill later become honored citizens of Oz.

Certainly one reason for the immense popularity of the Oz books is the fact that they are told with such a wealth of detail that a strong sense of reality is created. These details range from such trifling observations as the fact that the Scarecrow has difficulty picking up small objects with his padded fingers, to important data about the history, geography, and customs of Oz. There is even a map of Oz, drawn by Professor Woggle-Bug. It formed the front end-paper of early editions of *Tik-Tok of Oz* and also was issued separately as a book insert.

No Oz reader need be told that Oz is roughly rectangular and divided into four regions, each with a characteristic color. The first edition of *The Road to Oz* was actually printed on tinted paper that changed color each time the scene shifted to another region! In the center of Oz is the Emerald City (a reflection of Baum's love of Ireland), where Princess Ozma rules in a palace of glittering gems. Surrounding Oz on all four sides is the Deadly Desert. Anyone setting foot on the desert turns instantly to dust.

Many social and economic details about Oz are known. Its population is more than half a million. The Emerald City, at the time it was almost conquered by the Nome King, had 9,654 buildings, 57,318 inhabitants. There is no sickness or disease in Oz. No one grows older and death occurs only rarely.[14] All animals talk in Oz and they are treated with as much respect as humans. In many ways Oz resembles the anarchist utopia of William Morris's *News from Nowhere*.[15] There is virtually no police force because all Ozites are happy, unselfish, and law-abiding. They work half the time, play half the time. There is no money, no rich, no poor. "Each person," the Royal Historian tells us, "was given freely by his neighbors whatever he required for his use, which is as much as anyone may reasonably desire."

Fortunately, not all parts of Oz are this orderly—especially the wild, unsettled areas of the Gillikin and Quadling regions, where many queer and unruly races flourish. Otherwise there would be no dangers and consequently no adventures.

Dangers yes, but horrors no. It is a rare occasion when Baum describes a scene that might frighten a sensitive child. Only a morbid adult could object to a wicked witch melting away or Jack Pumpkinhead carving a new head for himself to replace a former one that has spoiled. Baum's intention, stated in the preface of *The Wizard*, to leave out the "heartaches and nightmares" was amply fulfilled. You have only to glance through Grimm and Andersen, *Pinocchio*, or many another classic fairy tale to realize how skillfully Baum managed, in contrast with these works, to retain the excitement and avoid the violence and tears. Perrault's original story of Red Riding

Hood, still the version told to French children, ends with the wolf eating both the little girl and her grandmother. I am told that youngsters in France find this highly amusing. A respectable case can even be made for the view that violent images provide a healthy purging of a child's sadistic emotions as well as a valuable early introduction to the reality of evil. "Children love a lot of nightmare and at least a little heartache in their books," writes Thurber; and he for one is glad that Baum did not succeed completely in keeping these elements out of his work.[16] It is true that Baum occasionally forgot his promise, especially in *Dorothy and the Wizard in Oz,* where an atmosphere of violence and gloom hangs over a large part of the tale, and in the macabre episode (in a later book) of the Tin Woodman's conversation with his former head. But on the whole his books are singularly free of shocking scenes and the spirit of Oz is a happy, sunny one. There are only two references in all of Baum's Royal History to its having rained in Oz.

Literary masterpieces are often written with astonishing carelessness of detail. Cervantes completely forgot that Sancho Panza's ass had been stolen; with no word of explanation we find Sancho riding him again. Robinson Crusoe strips off his clothes, swims out to the wreckage of a ship, and a moment later we find him filling his pockets with biscuits from the ship's bread room. Like the Baker Street Irregulars, who delight in inventing plausible explanations for Watson's memory lapses, a group of Oz enthusiasts can spend many pleasant hours suggesting ways for harmonizing similar contradictions in the Royal History.

The Land of Ev, for example, lies just across the Deadly Desert. But in what direction? You can find a basis for placing it to the north, south, east, or west of Oz. The early history of Oz, before the Wizard arrived in his balloon, is riddled with difficulties. There is reason to believe that grass takes on the color of each region in Oz and equally good reason to think it doesn't. Exactly what happens when a Nome touches an egg? Does he wither away or turn into a mortal? Why do the Shaggy Man and Polychrome, the Rainbow's daughter, act like strangers when they meet (in *Tik-Tok of Oz*) for the second time? These are only a fraction of the tantalizing problems that face the student of Oz.

An equally fascinating pastime is to speculate on how Baum arrived at the names of various characters and countries. In many instances the basis is obvious. For example, Princess Langwidere is a haughty woman with a "languid air." General Jinjur is a girl with lots of "ginger." But what about Woot the Wanderer, protagonist of *The Tin Woodman of Oz*? Did Baum take the initials of the tin man's title then switch the "T" from front to back?

The word Oz itself has been the subject of much speculation. The most popular theory is that Baum, searching for a name, looked up at a filing cabinet and saw the words "From O to Z." Another is that it came from "Boz," the nickname of Charles Dickens, one of Baum's favorite authors. And someone has pointed out that Job lived in the land of Uz. The late Jack

Snow advanced a captivating theory in the preface of his monumental *Who's Who in Oz*. Baum once wrote that he had always enjoyed stories that cause the reader to exclaim with "Ohs" and "Ahs" of wonder, and Mr. Snow points out that Oz can be pronounced either "Ohs" or "Ahs."

The Baums moved to Los Angeles in 1909. Baum constructed an enormous circular birdcage in the garden of his home and stocked it with a large variety of songbirds. This love of wildlife is reflected in all of Baum's writings, and one has the feeling that when the Tin Woodman expresses horror at the thought of injuring a butterfly, he is expressing the sentiments of the author. Baum never cared for hunting and fishing. In early life his favorite outdoor sports seem to have been swimming, archery, and motorboating, though as he approached his sixties he turned more to golf and gardening. When the Baums moved to Hollywood in 1910, a large garden surrounded Ozcot, Baum's name for the house he built there. Baum won many cups in state flower competitions and even became known locally as "The Chrysanthemum King of Southern California."

At the time Ozcot was built, Hollywood was still a small suburban town. The infant movie industry then centered in New York. But as Jack Snow has observed, Baum was unable to escape from fairyland. The motion picture empire grew up around him. Mrs. Baum remained at Ozcot, on Cherokee Avenue near Sunset Boulevard, until her death in 1953 at the age of 91. The house has since been torn down to make room for a modern apartment building.

As one would have expected, Baum was early fascinated by the artistic potential of the cinema. In 1908, while still living in Chicago, he had invested heavily in the production of a series of short, hand-colored movies depicting stories from his books. He called them "Radio Plays." They were presented in Chicago and later in New York with Baum standing by the screen to narrate the tales. He lost so heavily in this venture that in 1911 he found it necessary to file a bankruptcy petition in California, listing his debts as $12,600 and his assets as two suits of clothes and a typewriter.[17]

Baum made another attempt to repeat the stage success of *The Wizard*. His musical *The Tik-Tok Man of Oz* opened in Los Angeles in 1913, then went on tour after profitable runs in San Francisco and Chicago. The comedy team of James Morton and Frank Moore took the roles of Tik-Tok and Shaggy Man, respectively. Queen Ann Soforth was played by Charlotte Greenwood. The play opened, like *The Wizard*, with the impressive sound and lighting effects of a violent storm; in this case the storm at sea that washes Betsy Bobbin of Oklahoma and Hank the mule to the shores of the Rose Kingdom. The book was written after the play, and dedicated to Louis F. Gottschalk, who provided the play's musical score.

Although this was Baum's last stage success, his enthusiasm for the theater never left him. In later years he wrote and acted in musicals produced by the Uplifters, a Los Angeles social club that he helped found. The names of the officers were invented by him: Grand Muscle (president), Elevator (vice president), Royal Hoister (secretary), Lord High Raiser (treasurer), and the Excelsiors (directors). Will Rogers, George Arliss, and many other Hollywood notables later became members. Let us hope that someday someone will uplift the manuscript of *The Uplift of Lucifer*, one of the plays Baum wrote for this club.

In 1914 Baum turned his attention once more to motion pictures, forming the Oz Film Manufacturing Company to produce screen versions of his tales. In a press interview he explained that because of their many color plates his books had to sell at a price that kept them from millions of youngsters. Through the movies he hoped to make his stories available to every American boy and girl for the cost of admission to the theater — five cents. Like so many smaller film companies that were trying to get started at the time, Baum's company was soon backed against the wall by the competition of larger studios. Only five films were completed: *The Patchwork Girl of Oz* (played by Pierre Coudere, a French acrobat), *His Majesty the Scarecrow of Oz* (later retitled *The New Wizard of Oz*), *The Magic Cloak*, *The Last Egyptian*, and *The Gray Nun of Belgium.*

The Wizard of Oz was filmed as a one-reeler by Selig Pictures in 1910. Another silent version was issued in 1925 by Chadwick Pictures, starring the comedian Larry Semon as the Scarecrow. Oliver Hardy took the role of the tin man. And of course everyone has seen MGM's lavish technicolor spectacle, first released in 1939, with Judy Garland in the role of a singing Dorothy. Ray Bolger played the capering straw man, Jack Haley the Tin Woodman, and Bert Lahr an outrageously funny Cowardly Lion. Other roles included Billie Burke, badly miscast as Glinda, Frank Morgan as the Wizard, and the Singer Midgets as the Munchkins. The picture featured some excellent tunes ("Over the Rainbow" and "We're Off to See the Wizard") and had several inspired touches, such as running the farm scenes in black and white to contrast them with the brilliant colors of Oz. But to my taste the picture was marred by sentimentality toward the close and the inexcusable final revelation that the whole thing was a dream.

Baum's generous heart, unlike the fine velvet heart of the Tin Woodman, was not replaceable. Angina attacks and a gall-bladder operation kept him in bed during the last year and a half of his life. *The Tin Woodman of Oz, The Magic of Oz,* and a rough draft of *Glinda of Oz* were written during this period. The last book is almost devoid of humor. I have often fancied that the sunken island on which Dorothy was trapped beneath a lake was an unconscious expression of Baum's own sinking emotions. The island was raised when Dorothy thought of the proper magic words. There were no magic words for Baum's failing heart, and on May 6, 1919, at his home in Hollywood, it finally gave way. He was buried in Forest Lawn Memorial Park, at Glendale, where a simple monument bearing his name and dates of birth and death marks his resting place.

Glinda of Oz, edited by one of Baum's sons, was published posthumously. The next book in the series, *The Royal Book of Oz,* carries Baum's name on the cover and a statement inside by Mrs. Baum that her husband had left some unfinished notes for another Oz book. These notes, she says, were turned over to Ruth Plumly Thompson, then a twenty-year-old Philadelphia journalist and children's author who had loved the Oz books as a child. All this seems to have been merely a device on the part of the publisher for easing the transition to a new author. The book was written entirely by Miss Thompson. She has since published eighteen additional Oz books, writing them with a zest and humor that has won her an ardent following.

John Rea Neill, who illustrated all of Baum's Oz books except the first one, also tried his hand at writing three Oz books. He was not a skillful writer, but as the Royal Painter of Oz his pictures are as indissolubly linked with the Oz books as Tenniel's drawings are linked with Alice. Whatever one may think of Neill's pictures as works of art, there is no denying that he caught the full flavor of Baum's text, and his illustrations have exactly the sort of color and realism that Oz books require. Denslow's drawings for *The Wizard* possess a quaint wooden charm, but I have yet to meet an Oz enthusiast who regrets that Denslow did not carry on with the series.

Much can be said in praise of Miss Thompson's books and also of the most recent Oz book, written by Rachel Cosgrove; but in the opinion of many Oz fans the mantle of Royal Historian best fitted the shoulders of the late Jack Snow. His two Oz books are remarkable in capturing the mood and style of Baum. I have already mentioned his *Who's Who in Oz,* which contains lively biographies of every Oz character who ever appeared in an Oz book, as well as biographical sketches of each Oz author and illustrator, and plot summaries of all the Oz books.[18]

Ray Bradbury has spoken many times of the influence of Oz on his career as a popular author of fantasy and science fiction. His story "The Exiles" pictures a future in which the psychologists have succeeded at last in destroying all books of fantasy. The narrative closes with the collapse of the Emerald City as the last Oz book goes up in flames.

But I do not think the Emerald City will collapse for a long, long time. A child's love of fantasy is too healthy a love. "Perhaps some of those big, grown-up people will poke fun at us," Baum wrote in his introduction to *A New Wonderland,* "—at you for reading these nonsense tales . . . . and at me for writing them. Never mind. Many of the big folk are still children— even as you and I. We can not measure a child by a standard of size or age. The big folk who are children will be our comrades; the others we need not consider at all, for they are self-exiled from our domain."

POSTSCRIPT

The books of L. Frank Baum gave me so much pleasure as a child that I have enjoyed few chores more than writing the foregoing tribute. It first ap-

Illustrations by John Rea Neill from *The Road to Oz*

peared as a two-part article in *Fantasy and Science Fiction* (1955), then edited by Anthony Boucher, an ardent Oz buff. A corrected and expanded version appeared in an edition of *The Wizard,* titled *The Wizard of Oz and Who He Was,* published by Michigan State University Press in 1957. This volume, long out of print, also contained an essay on Baum by Russell B. Nye, my original bibliography (not here included), and some trivial annotations I added to Baum's text.

In 1956 Roland Baughman, head of the special-collections department of Columbia University's library, sponsored a major exhibit of Baum's writings. (Its 50-page catalog is now a collector's item.) This exhibit, my article, and an essay by Baughman in *Columbia Library Columns* (May 1955) were opening volleys in a battle against the librarians who until then had regarded all Oz books with contempt. As a result of our attack, Oz fans and collectors around the country suddenly discovered they were not alone and began to contact one another. Justin Schiller, then thirteen (he is now the nation's top rare-books dealer specializing in children's literature), founded the Wizard of Oz Club and began issuing a periodical he called *The Baum Bugle.* The first issue, four mimeographed pages, went to sixteen subscribers. I am on the masthead as "Chairman, Board of Directors."

The Baum Bugle is today a lively, colorful periodical devoted to every aspect of Oz. It comes out three times a year for the more than a thousand members of the International Wizard of Oz Club. The society holds annual conventions in different parts of the country. If you are an Ozmopolitan and care to join the fun, write to the club's secretary, Fred Meyer, 220 N. Eleventh Street, Escanaba, MI 49829.

The fight for Baum's recognition has now been so decisively won that many younger librarians are amazed to learn that opposition to Baum's books ever existed in library circles. The literature on Baum and his successor, Ruth Plumly Thompson, and on Oz illustrators Denslow and Neill, is now so large that I will note only a few highlights.

Russell P. MacFall, working with a manuscript left by Baum's son Frank, wrote *To Please a Child* (1961), a biography of Baum that I regret to say is out of print. Michael Patrick Hearn's fabulous *Annotated Wizard of Oz* was published by Clarkson Potter in 1973. In 1974 Bowling Green University issued Raylyn Moore's monograph, *Wonderful Wizard, Marvelous Land,* with a preface by Ray Bradbury. Hearn and Douglas Greene collaborated on a biography of Denslow titled *W. W. Denslow* (1976), and Hearn is currently working on a new biography of Baum that has been authorized by the Baum estate. Random House published *The Oz Scrapbook,* a lavishly illustrated work by Greene and Dick Martin, in 1977. A 103-page *Bibliographia Oziana,* by various hands, was produced in 1976 by the Oz society.

Dover Publications has issued paperback facsimiles of Baum's first two Oz books and five of his non-Oz fantasies, for each of which I wrote an introduction. All of Baum's Oz books are now available in inexpensive Ballantine paperbacks, and they may soon be followed by Miss Thompson's Oz books. Many of Baum's short stories, never in book form, have appeared and continue to appear in *The Baum Bugle*. Several book collections of some of these stories have also been published. Essays about Baum and Oz, too numerous to list, have been written by distinguished critics for various academic journals.

The all-black version of *The Wiz* was a big success on Broadway in 1975, and later was made into a movie. Walt Disney Productions, which long ago acquired movie rights to all of Baum's Oz books except *The Wizard,* is planning a new musical, *The Return to Oz.* It is safe to say that at long last, some fifty years after his death, the genius of Baum is finally being recognized.

In my article on Baum I expressed the hope that someone would uplift the manuscript of *The Uplift of Lucifer.* Manuel Weltman of Los Angeles succeeded in uplifting it and privately publishing it as a booklet in 1963. The musical was first produced by the Uplifters in Santa Barbara, California, October 23, 1915, with original music by Louis F. Gottschalk. After Baum's death, the Uplifters staged it again on January 27, 1920, on the annual "Frank Baum Night," with Hal Roach taking the role of Demon Rum, Satan's bartender.

The file-cabinet story about how Oz got its name seems to have been first published in an interview with Baum in the *New York Mirror,* January 27, 1904. "I have a little cabinet file on the desk just before me," said Baum. "I was thinking and wondering about a title and had settled on 'Wizard' as part of it. My gaze was caught by the gilt letters on the three drawers of the cabinet. The first was A-G, the second H-N, and the last were O-Z. My eyes rested on the last drawer and Oz furnished the missing link for my title."

Good reasons for doubting this story are given by Daniel Mannix in his "Off to See the Wizard—1903," Part 2, in *The Baum Bugle,* Spring 1969. See also Jay Delkin's article, "The Meaning of 'Oz,' " ibid., Autumn 1971.

In the fifth of my footnotes for *The Wizard of Oz and Who He Was* I wondered what had happened to the key to Dorothy's house. Baum tells us in Chapter 3 that when Dorothy left the house she "closed the door, locked it, and put the key carefully in the pocket of her dress." "Dorothy may still have this key," I speculated. "It would be interesting to know if the old farmhouse is still standing at the spot where the cyclone left it."

Philip José Farmer answered these questions in his 1982 novel, *A Barnstormer in Oz.* The house became a state monument, often visited by the Munchkins. For what happened to the key, and the role it played in saving the lives of Glinda and Dorothy's son, and repelling an insurrection led by an evil witch called Erakna the Uneatable, you must read Farmer's amusing, ingenious fantasy. Most Oz buffs won't like to be told that only Baum's first Oz book is based on facts (the others were all made up), but Farmer's book is fun to read anyway.

NOTES

1. From the *New York Mirror* (theatrical paper), June 24, 1882.

2. This story is told in a letter to me from Ralph Fletcher Seymour, a Chicago artist who knew Baum during his Chicago days. How much of the story is true? No one knows. In *Aunt Jane's Nieces on Vacation* (1912) Baum devotes Chapter 13 to an account of just such a duel.

3. One of Baum's most moving inscriptions is to be found in a presentation copy of this book to his sister, Mary Louise Baum Brewster:

> My dear Mary: When I was young I longed to write a great novel that should win me fame. Now that I am getting old my first book is written to amuse children. For, aside from my evident inability to do anything "great," I have learned to regard fame as a will-o-the-wisp which, when caught, is not worth the possession; but to please a child is a sweet and lovely thing that warms one's heart and brings its own reward. I hope my book will succeed in that way—that the children will like it. You and I have inherited much the same temperament and literary taste and I know you will not despise these simple tales, but will understand me and accord me your full sympathy. Lovingly your brother Frank.

4. "We are revolting!" exclaims the leader of the Revolution to the Guardian of the Gates. To which he understandably replies, "You don't look it."

5. Seymour tells the story of this book's preparation in his privately printed autobiography, *Some Went This Way,* Chicago, 1945, p. 46.

6. A lengthy interview with Baum at his "Sign of the Goose" appeared in the *Grand Rapids Herald,* August 18, 1907. There is a picture of Baum sitting in his goose chair, as well as photographs of the interior of the cottage.

7. A lengthy letter to Jack Snow in 1943, replying to seventy-five questions about her husband that Mr. Snow had asked in a previous letter.

8. This was not Baum's first attempt to collaborate with Tietjens and Denslow on a musical comedy. In 1901, at Tietjens's urging, he wrote the book of a comic opera titled *The Octopus* or *The Title Trust.* In Tietjens's unpublished diary, now in possession of his daughter, he describes their unsuccessful attempts to find a producer. Baum was particularly fond of the song "I Am a Great Promoter," to be sung by Gripem Harde. There are references to other songs, but unfortunately no intimations of the plot. The diary also contains many details about the wrangling of the three men over the contract for their second effort, *The Wizard,* and speaks of "much friction" between Baum and the producer, Julian Mitchell. Nothing came of later comic opera projects—*Father Goose, Prince Silver Wings,* and *The Pagan Potentate*—on which Tietjens and Baum planned to work jointly.

9. From *In Other Lands than Ours,* a collection of Mrs. Baum's letters from abroad, privately printed by her husband in 1907.

10. Cf. the following paragraph of a letter dated June 7, 1943, from Baum's nephew, Henry B. Brewster, of Syracuse, N.Y., to Jack Snow: "Mr. Baum always liked to tell wild tales, with a perfectly straight face, and earnestly, as though he really believed them himself. . . . His mother was very religious . . . and felt she knew her Bible very well. Frank Baum seemed to take particular delight in teasing her and I recall, not once but many times, how he would pretend to quote from the Bible,

with which he definitely was not familiar. For example, once she said, 'Frank, you are telling a story,' and he said, 'Well, Mother, as you know, in St. Paul's epistle to the Ephesians he said, "All men are liars." ' Whereupon his mother said, 'Why, Frank, you are wrong, I do not recall that,' and irrespective of the fact that she had been fooled so many times she would look up her Bible to see if she were wrong, and he right. Frank Baum was one of the most imaginative of men. There was nothing wrong, but he did love to 'Fairytale,' or as you might say, tell 'white lies.' "

11. From her letter to Jack Snow, op. cit.

12. Ibid.

13. Ibid.

14. "It is possible for beasts—or even people—to be destroyed, but the task is so difficult that it is seldom attempted. Because it is free from sickness and death is one reason why Oz is a fairyland, but it is doubtful whether those who come to Oz from the outside world . . . will live forever or cannot be injured. Even Ozma is not sure about this, and so the guests of Ozma from other lands are always carefully protected from any danger, so as to be on the safe side."—*The Magic of Oz,* p. 83.

15. The ultimate ideal of Marxian socialism, after the state has withered away, is of course an anarchist society. This explains an article in *New Masses,* October 4, 1938, titled "The Red Wizard of Oz." Stewart Robb, the author, had just discovered that Oz books had been banned from all New York City libraries and he satirically suggests that the reason may be a political one. Another letter of Robb's, in the *New York Post,* October 9, 1938, compares the late Frank ("I am the law") Hague, then mayor and political boss of Jersey City, to the Supreme Dictator of the Flatheads (*Glinda of Oz*). The Supreme Dictator keeps getting reelected because of a law that gives himself the authority to count the votes. Both letters appear in Robb's privately published book *Letters on Nostradamus,* New York, no date.

16. "The Wizard of Chittenango," by James Thurber, the *New Republic,* December 12, 1934.

17. *Chicago Tribune,* August 16, 1911.

18. With one exception, *The Laughing Dragon of Oz,* by Baum's son, Frank Joslyn. This was issued by Whitman Publishing Company in 1934, as one of their "Big Little Book Series," and sold in the dime stores for ten cents. His second book, *The Enchanted Princess of Oz,* was purchased by Whitman but never published. No characters from previous Oz books appear in either work.

Mention also should be made of two "Oz" books published by Denslow. He and Baum parted company over a disagreement as to how much the illustrations had contributed to the success of the first Oz book and its musical. Feeling that he was in part a creator of Oz, and legally in possession of a copyright on his illustrations, Denslow wrote and illustrated a picture book titled *Scarecrow and the Tin Man* (New York: G. W. Dillingham, 1904), telling how the two men escape from a New York theater in which they are appearing, and of the mishaps that befall them before the police send them back to the theater. Denslow also issued a 43-page booklet of color plates from the first Oz book. It was called *Pictures from the Wonderful Wizard of Oz* (Chicago: George W. Ogilvie, no date) and carried his own name on the title page but no mention of Baum. Accompanying the pictures is a story by Thomas H. Russell about the adventures of a "Little Girl" with the Scarecrow and the Tin Man. Neither of these books contains the word Oz.

11

Librarians in Oz

The distinguished Public Educator of Oz and President of the Royal College of Art and Athletic Perfection is Professor H. M. Woggle-Bug, T.E. As all students of Oz know, the initials stand for Highly Magnified and Thoroughly Educated. "I am in reality a very big bug," the professor said on one occasion, "and doubtless the most intelligent being in all this broad domain."

In the United States there is a peculiar species of librarian, the members of which have much in common with Professor Woggle-Bug. No longer content to be mere custodians of books, they have taken upon themselves the additional burden of deciding what the less thoroughly educated public should and should not read. Their motto: "Wake up and read what *we* think you should read."

In the field of children's books these librarians have developed a chronic allergy to fantasy, and to Oz books in particular. Last February the State Librarian of Florida, Miss Dorothy Dodd, included *The Wizard of Oz* on a list of books that she urged all public libraries in her state to withdraw from circulation. "Kids don't like that fanciful stuff anymore," agreed Dr. Frank B. Sessa, chairman of the Miami Public Library. "They want books about missiles and atomic submarines." According to Miss Dodd, the books on her list are "poorly written, untrue to life, sensational, foolishly sentimental and consequently unwholesome for the children in your community."

Librarians have been saying this about Oz books for half a century, but in recent years their voices have become more strident. In 1957, Ralph Ulveling, Director of Libraries in Detroit, admitted that for thirty years *The Wizard of Oz* had not been permitted in the children's room of the Detroit Public Library or any of its branches. Three copies were available in the stack col-

This essay originally appeared in the *Saturday Review*, April 11, 1959.

lection. "This is not banning," he wrote in the *American Library Association Bulletin* (October 1957). "It is selection."

The *Detroit Times* failed to appreciate such a fine distinction. They published *The Wizard of Oz* serially, introducing each installment with a statement saying that this was the book that the city's library had banned. Most libraries make similar "selections." The New York Public Library is a bit more tolerant. *The Wizard* can be found in the children's room, but if a child wants to read any of L. Frank Baum's thirteen other Oz books he must go to the main reading room, or to one of the rare book rooms, where valuable first editions of Oz books are guarded under lock and key.

Is there any doubt that today's youngsters want to read about Oz? At present at least seven different editions of *The Wizard* are in print, and all of them sell briskly. Reilly and Lee, the small Chicago house that published all the Oz books except *The Wizard,* is now having Baum's books re-illustrated, one by one, because the plates for the old illustrations have finally worn out. Two years ago, a Milwaukee librarian (Milwaukee is one of the few cities where Oz books are not banned from circulating libraries) reported that the children had worn out 135 copies of *The Wizard* in eight years, were rapidly wearing out the fifty remaining copies, and that twenty-five more were on order.

In 1956, the *New York Times* conducted a poll of teenagers in the Greater New York area, asking them, "Which books did you like best when you were young?" The Oz books topped the list. "As a child, I did not particularly like to read," declared one girl, "but in the fourth grade I found a book which stimulated me so that I wanted to go on reading as much as I could. The book was *The Land of Oz.* It was filled with the rarest and most absurd images; I had never encountered such make-believe. The fantastic creatures I met overwhelmed and delighted me . . ."

Granting that children do like the Oz books, one can hear Miss Dodd murmur, that doesn't mean that we shouldn't make valiant efforts to persuade them to read better books. Well, I deny that there are better books; at least not better fairy tales for an American child. I am not alone in this opinion. In fact it is the opinion of almost everybody who isn't a librarian or self-styled authority on juvenile literature and, I am happy to add, of many librarians as well. Roland Baughman, head of the special-collections department of Columbia University Libraries, wrote a splendid and moving appreciation of Baum in the *Columbia Library Columns,* May 1955. The following year Columbia sponsored a magnificent exhibit of Baum's writings.

In 1957, the Michigan State University Press brought out an edition of *The Wizard,* with the original Denslow illustrations. This volume contains another excellent critical evaluation of Baum, written by Russell B. Nye, chairman of the university's English department and a Pulitzer Prize winner. The new Reilly and Lee edition of *The Wizard* carries an afterword by still another English professor, Edward Wagenknecht, of Boston University. He calls the book "the greatest wonder tale ever written in this country."

"Come, then," he urges, "and follow the road of yellow brick to the Emerald City. For life itself is a quest, and you too are a pilgrim. And you will not make your own journey less wisely for having followed Dorothy in hers."

First editions of Baum's books are now heavily collected. Mrs. Robert G. Ford, a rare-book dealer in Lake Worth, Florida (in *Florida,* Miss Dodd!), specializes in Baum, and issues elaborate price lists of items relating to Baum and Oz. A first edition of *The Wizard* sold recently at the Parke-Bernet Galleries in Manhattan for $600. And who, Miss Dodd, do you suppose owns the world's finest Baum collection? He is C. Beecher Hogan, lecturer in English at Yale and a leading authority on Oz.

It would be hard to extract a harsh word about Baum from the many creative writers who loved the Oz books as children. James Thurber, Phyllis McGinley, Philip Wylie, Ray Bradbury, Ellery Queen, John Dickson Carr — this is only a sampling of writers whose admiration for Baum happens to be on record. "What a curious thing to be questing for — a human heart," wrote Paul Gallico (*Esquire,* February 1957) in ironic reference to the Tin Woodman. "One sets out to seek a vast treasure or conquer new lands, worlds or planets, but to wish and search for nothing more than a dear and tender heart that can beat for others and be filled both with love and compassion, what kind of stuff is this to set before the child of today?"

Anthony Boucher, reviewing the Michigan State University Press edition of *The Wizard* for his magazine *Fantasy and Science Fiction* (August 1957), reread Baum's tale carefully just to make sure his memory wasn't playing him false. "I hasten to assure you — " he writes, "in case you feel that so many librarians can't *all* be wrong and that your immature taste may have misled you — that *The Wizard* seems every whit as wonderful to me today as it did forty years ago. Here is genuine fantasy, creative, funny, tender, exciting, surprising, delightful; and beside it the bulk of today's 'authorized' juveniles in our field seems more sterile than ever."

How can one account for the violent prejudice against Oz on the part of a small but highly vocal group of thoroughly educated librarians? One reason has already been suggested: the enormous popularity of the Oz books. If a circulating library has one, the children clamor for more. The books soon fall apart at the seams and new copies have to be ordered.

Another reason, perhaps, is that the Oz books have never been illustrated in the current mode. Children themselves enjoy John R. Neill's realistic pictures, but progressive parents who hang mobiles in the nursery naturally find Neill old-fashioned. It is an open secret in publishing circles that books for today's youngsters are designed (and often written) for adults. The looser, more distorted the illustrations, sometimes to the extent of being unintelligible to a child, the more sophisticated it makes Mother feel when she buys the book. It doesn't matter, because her children seldom read the book anyway. They prefer to watch Popeye and the Three Stooges.

POSTSCRIPT

The odd Dr. Dodd's remarks about Oz received a lot of publicity, including an AP wire story and an editorial in *Life* (February 16, 1959) headed "Dorothy the Librarian." Among letters about the *Life* editorial, published later, Mary Louise Rheay, of the Atlanta Public Library, declared herself wholeheartedly in agreement with Dodd, but a Florida reader, Doris Lankton, disagreed:

> As a newly elected member of the Delray Beach Public Library Board, I should like to state to the entire universe that I am, forever, on the side of Dorothy of Kansas (not to mention Aunt Em, Uncle Henry, Toto, Glinda, Ozma, the Wizard—and even the Munchkins) as opposed to Dorothy, the Florida Librarian.

When I wrote my piece, abstract expressionism was dominating the art world. At the moment, there is a big swing back to realism, and as always the publishers of children's books are falling in step. Any day now you may see an article on John R. Neill in one of the graphic-arts journals.

12

Why Librarians Dislike Oz

Long-time admirers of L. Frank Baum have the satisfaction these days of watching the librarians and critics develop a slow, creeping awareness of the fact that a Hans Christian Andersen once lived in the United States. Children, of course, have known this since 1900. But among librarians and self-styled experts on juvenile literature, a strange myth has developed: Baum was just another hack author of series books and the sooner the youngsters forget about him the better. In 1953, Cornelia L. Meigs edited for Macmillan a 624-page *Critical History of Children's Literature;* not a single mention in it of Baum. To this day there are thousands of children's librarians around the nation—kindly, bespectacled, gray-minded ladies—who will tell you with pride that they do not permit a single Oz book to sully their shelves.

Now here indeed is a most curious paradox. At the moment there are a dozen or so editions of *The Wizard of Oz* in print. It obviously is the best-loved fairy tale ever written by an American author. "I can still read *The Wizard of Oz* with as much enjoyment as I found in it fifty years ago," writes Edward Wagenknecht in his afterword to a new Reilly and Lee edition. (Professor Wagenknecht is a distinguished author who teaches English literature at Boston University. His booklet *Utopia Americana,* 1929, was the first critical appreciation of Baum and is now much prized by collectors.) MGM's musical extravaganza, starring Judy Garland as Dorothy, has become a staple television feature of the Christmas season. Articles on Baum are turning up in the literary quarterlies (e.g., "The Utopia of Oz" by S. J. Sackett, *The Georgia Review,* Fall 1960; "The Oddness of Oz," by Osmond Beckwith, *Kulchur 4,* 1961).

This essay originally appeared in the *American Book Collector,* December 1962. © 1962 by William Thorsen. Reprinted with permission.

"I have never known a child," writes Clifton Fadiman in a new Macmillan edition of *The Wizard*, "who didn't scoot through it at supersonic speed, enjoying every word and making fast friends at once with those Three Musketeers of Oz—the Cowardly Lion, the Scarecrow and the Tin Woodman . . . I can remember reading them [Oz books] aloud, hour after hour after hour, to our two children Anne and Kim . . . our ancient, dog-eared, thumb-marked tattered Oz volumes still occupy a place of honor on the shelf."

On Mr. Fadiman's shelf, yes; but not on the shelves of the children's section in thousands of public libraries. Nevertheless, the growing popularity of Oz is having its impact on the librarians. Ten years ago they reacted to any mention of Oz with cold, blank stares. Today they will tell you that *The Wizard* is not really a bad book, but of course everybody knows (by "everybody" they mean all the other librarians) that it is the only good book Baum ever wrote.

Well, Baum wrote a lot of other good books; in fact many of his other fantasies are better than *The Wizard*. But why this curious, persistent resistance to Baum? Why this allergy to Oz? After giving the matter some thought I have concluded that seven principal factors are involved.

1. Baum's Oz books, with the exception of *The Wizard*, were published by Reilly and Britton (later Reilly and Lee), a small Chicago firm that lacked the prestige of the large eastern houses. To make matters worse, Reilly and Britton specialized in series books by hacks: the Boy Scouts of the Air series, the Boys Big Game series, the Airship Boys series, and so on. Baum himself, using the pseudonym of Edith Van Dyne, wrote ten novels in the Aunt Jane's Nieces series, five in the Mary Louise series, and two books about Orissa Kane, girl aviator. (Ten years ago one could still find Edith Van Dyne books on 25-cent tables; now the dealers are wised up and likely to ask several dollars per volume.) Without exception, these nonfantasy series books issued by Reilly and Britton are undistinguished. It was easy to suppose that the Oz books, also issued in series, were equally poor; as poor as, say, the Raggedy Ann fantasy series, which became popular in the decade following Baum's death in 1919.

2. Even if series books *have* a certain merit, they annoy librarians. A child reads one book, his interest is hooked, he demands another. Stock one, you must stock them all. Librarians found it expedient to avoid series books altogether, and of course this included the Oz books.

3. Baum's books were oversize volumes, lacking the side-stitching and reinforced hinges necessary to withstand strenuous handling. And strenuous handling they got. Librarians do not like to keep replacing shaky volumes or going to the expense of rebinding.

4. The illustrations in Baum's books (with the exception of Maxfield Parrish's pictures for *Mother Goose in Prose*) are not first rate; certainly not to compare with Tenniel's illustrations for *Alice*, Ernest Shepard's drawings for the *Pooh* books and *Wind in the Willows*, Garth Williams's drawings

for *Charlotte's Web* or Arthur Rackham's many superb illustrations for various children's classics. William Wallace Denslow, who illustratred *The Wizard of Oz* and one other Baum fantasy, *Dot and Tot of Merryland,* was a Chicago newspaper cartoonist of no great shakes. John R. Neill, who illustrated all of Baum's other Oz books and most of his non-Oz fantasies, was a Pennsylvania artist of so-so talents.

Not that Neill's pictures are not just right for a child! They have color, detail, realism; they enter happily into the spirit of Baum's imagination. But adult taste (and adults, remember, buy the books) has moved steadily in the modern direction, toward semi-abstract, distorted pictures, beside which Neill's art has a quaint, old-fashioned look. I have not the slightest doubt that if a careful test were made to determine what sort of pictures young children, free of parental nudging, do in fact prefer, they would choose Neill over most of the modern illustrators who win prizes for their work. (I once showed a prize-winning illustration — it purported to be a picture of a cat — to a small child. He turned it upside down trying to puzzle it out.) But the trend in art has moved steadily away from Neill, who was not great to begin with. Surely this has been another factor in the development of the Oz allergy.

5. Baum's books received little editing. Even the best of writers often need heavy editing (witness Thomas Wolfe!), but Reilly and Britton simply did not have the staff for it. I have no direct proof of this, but I suspect that Baum's copy was printed pretty much in the form received. As a result, there is a carelessness and roughness in many of his paragraphs that could have been polished out by a skillful editor.

It is tiresome to hear critics of Baum call attention to these spots of careless writing: the overall worth of a work of fiction is seldom affected by such trivia. Especially its worth for a child. You can give a child a book written with great stylistic elegance and drenched with poetic phrasing, but if the child is not interested in what happens to the characters in the next chapter he will quite sensibly put down the book and turn on the television. Baum was a great storyteller; he was not a great stylist. This too has played a role in prejudicing the librarians.

6. Many later Oz books, by writers other than Baum, are not up to the level of Baum's books. The best, in my opinion, are some of the Oz books by Ruth Plumly Thompson, who has done nineteen of them, and the two Oz books by Jack Snow. But three Oz books by Neill, the artist, are very poor. Many critics of Oz fail to distinguish between Baum and the various authors who carried on after his death; indeed, I am sure that many of them never read an Oz book by Baum other than *The Wizard.*

7. Fantasy is not for everybody. Even at the eight-to-ten age level, an ideal age for starting on Oz, there is no question that children divide rather sharply into two classes: those who enjoy far-out fantasy and those who don't. It is a division that tends to last throughout their lives. I know of no studies by professional psychologists on this matter, but I hazard the guess that an

eight-year-old's liking for fantasy reflects the strength of his imagination; his ability to call up familiar images from daily life and put them together in strange, unexpected, Ozzy ways. I suspect also that it is from the ranks of such children, when grown, that come our most creative individuals. Frank D. Drake, the radio astronomer who named and now directs Project Ozma, the program of listening in on radio waves from outer space in the hope of hearing messages from other planets, is (not unexpectedly) an Ozmapolitan. I have yet to meet an American writer of fantasy or science fiction, from Ray Bradbury down, who did not enjoy the Oz books as a child. And I know of many professional philosophers, scientists, artists and professors of English literature who will not hesitate to pay tribute to Baum's genius.

Consider, now, the poor librarian. What sort of mind is most attracted to such a profession? You see at once that for the most part (there are of course exceptions) it would attract a prosaic, matter-of-fact mind. An individual with a soaring imagination is not likely to be happy shuffling file cards and carrying on a librarian's routine chores. As a result, a strong selective factor establishes a built-in prejudice among librarians against wilder forms of fantasy. I sometimes suspect that all children's librarians come from Abilone, Arizona; admirers of *The Circus of Dr. Lao* will know what I mean. The good citizens of Abilone attended Dr. Lao's circus, but its colossal marvels left them unimpressed. The man with the long neck and green necktie, in G. K. Chesterton's essay "The Dragon's Grandmother," surely was a librarian. This essay is the greatest defense ever written of the fairy tale; it can be found in *Tremendous Trifles,* and every children's librarian should be forced to read it.

Lord Dunsany wrote a poem called "A Word in Season" that I cannot read without thinking of Baum and his critics. I will quote only the middle stanza:

> Their watchers looked for a wind to blow;
>   And the new wind sang, and they could not hear it.
> It slipped at dusk by the mean dull row
> Of their narrow houses, from fields of snow
>   In a magical land: they were very near it
> For wonderful moments, and did not know.
> The new wind sang and they could not hear it.

But there are happy signs that at last the librarians are beginning to take the cotton out of their ears. Perhaps the age of space, with its Ozzy prospect of finding intelligent life elsewhere in the universe, has something to do with it. Perhaps it is the great need for creative, bold, imaginative thought in the sciences, especially in the social and political fields. Whatever it is, fantasy for children seems to be coming back into its own. Coming back, that is, among the parents who buy the books. The youngsters have never changed.

POSTSCRIPT

A number of librarians sent me indignant letters after my article was reprinted in *School Library Journal* (February 1963). One woman apparently confused my adjective "gray-minded" with gray-haired. At any rate, she wrote to tell me that she was young and pretty, with dark hair, and loved the Oz books. I also received several letters from librarians in small towns who reported that *their* libraries carried Oz books, and that the books were enormously popular. The *Chicago Tribune* (February 23, 1963) carried an editorial headed "The Wizard of Oz" that strongly upheld my views.

Since then, articles praising Baum have appeared so often in library journals and related periodicals that one of these days I wouldn't be surprised to read an article claiming that it was the librarians who rediscovered Oz. Richard Paul Smyers, of the South Bend (Indiana) public library, wrote a delightful piece, "A Librarian Looks at Oz," for the state's *Library Occurrent* (December 1964). He chided me for perpetuating the stereotype of the maiden lady librarian "who delights in routine card shuffling to the exclusion of anything extraordinary," but he admitted that the type was still all too prevalent. He closed by advising all librarians "who shudder at the mention of the word Oz" to sit down and read an Oz book for fun. "It won't hurt a bit and there's an even chance you will like it."

When Smyers sent me a copy of his article, his letter opened with such a pleasant parody of a Lewis Carroll stanza that I must reproduce it:

> "The time has come," the Walrus said,
>   "To talk of many things:
> Of lands of Ev, and Mo, and Oz,
>   And all their queens and kings,
> And why librarians, it seems,
>   Hate nearly all these things."

Two recent instances of how respectable Oz has become are provided by two excellent articles by Michael Hearn: "L. Frank Baum and the 'Modernized Fairy Tale,' " in *Children's Literature in Education,* vol. 10, no. 2, 1979; and "Discovering Oz (the Great and Terrible) at the Library of Congress," in the *Quarterly Journal of the Library of Congress,* Spring 1982.

13

When You Were a Tadpole and I Was a Fish

In 1941, T. S. Eliot startled the literary world by editing an anthology called *A Choice of Kipling's Verse.* Graduate students of English literature, who had been ashamed to admit that they could recite whole chunks from "Mandalay," "Boots," "Gunga Din," "Danny Deever," suddenly found the courage to transfer their copies of Kipling from that dark, inaccessible corner of the bookcase to a shelf where they could be seen by visitors.

In the introduction to his anthology, Eliot proposed a useful distinction between "poetry" and "verse." Verse, he said in effect, has a simple, metrical beat; it expresses clear, unambiguous ideas. Content and form can be grasped completely, or almost completely, on first reading. Poetry differs in degree. Its sound patterns and ideas are subtler, less lucid, impossible to understand fully on first reading. The poem's richness grows with rereadings.

Eliot did not intend the distinction to be invidious. Poetry and verse are two different things, they express different intentions. Kipling did not *try* to write poetry. What he wanted to do he did, and did magnificently. When he wrote (in "Danny Deever"), "What's that that whimpers over'ead?" the word "whimpers," said Eliot, is "exactly right." (Perhaps Eliot had Kipling's use of this word in mind when he used it himself, at the close of *The Hollow Men,* to describe the way the world ends.)

In short, Eliot thought Kipling wrote great verse.

In my opinion, Langdon Smith's "Evolution" is great verse. Not as good as Kipling's, perhaps, but good enough to merit critical attention. As to its popularity, there is not the slightest doubt. It has been reprinted in dozens

This essay originally appeared in the *Antioch Review,* Fall 1962. © 1962 by The Antioch Review, Inc. Reprinted with permission of the Editors.

of anthologies of "best loved" poems, usually—as is often the fate of poems of this sort—with badly garbled lines. (In Hazel Felleman's *Best Loved Poems of the American People*, for example, there are at least six flagrant errors.) It would be hard to find a geologist or biologist who had never read the poem; moreover, all sorts of unlikely people fall under its spell. Fifteen years ago I sat at a table, in a Thompson's restaurant in Chicago, with a group of magicians attending a magic convention in the city. It was three A.M. Somehow the word *evolution* was mentioned. Harry Blackstone, one of the world's great stage conjurors, put down the deck of cards in his hand, cleared his throat, and recited Langdon Smith's poem from beginning to end. There was no special reason he had memorized it. The poem had simply caught his fancy when he was a young man.

Literary critics are seldom interested in "verse" unless the author is a famous writer (e.g., Edgar Allan Poe), so it is not surprising that they have nothing at all to say about Langdon Smith. No one, so far as I can discover, has ever written an article about him. In fact, the most remarkable thing one can say about Smith is that almost nothing has been said about him.

He was a newspaper reporter for the Hearst papers in New York City. There are two meager sources of biographical information: a short entry in *Who's Who in America, 1906-07*, and an obituary in the *New York American*, April 9, 1908, page 6.

The *Who's Who* sketch is tantalizingly vague. Smith was born in Kentucky (no town is mentioned) on January 4, 1858, had a common school education at Louisville (1864-72), and was married on February 12, 1894, to Marie Antoinette Wright. (His obituary speaks of her as a Louisville girl.) During his boyhood he served in the Comanche and Apache wars; later he was a correspondent in the Sioux war. He went to Cuba for the *New York Herald* when war broke out in 1895. When the United States declared war on Spain, he was a correspondent in Cuba for the *New York Journal*. He was (the sketch continues) at the bombardment of Santiago, on the hill with the Marines at Guantanamo, and present at the battles of El Caney and San Juan. The sketch closes: "Author: *On the Panhandle*; also short stories. Address: 154 Nassau Street, New York."

No book called *On the Panhandle* was ever published. Was it an unprinted manuscript? Novel or nonfiction? Is the title a hoax? Were his short stories ever published? I have been unable to find the answer to any of these questions.

Smith's obituary in the *New York American* adds little except a photograph and some details about his illness and death. The picture is that of a handsome, dark-mustached man. He is called "one of the best known of newspaper writers in the country." For ten years he had been on the newspaper's staff. His last signed articles of importance had been on the second trial of Harry K. Thaw and the departure of the U.S. naval fleet on its first round-the-world cruise. His interview with the then Secretary of War, William Howard Taft, had appeared on March 23.

Biographical details in this obituary are obviously copied from *Who's Who*, though the writer has embroidered some of them. Thus: "His best known work was entitled *On the Panhandle*, but he had also written many short stories which had a considerable vogue." In addition to his poem, "Evolution," Smith had also written (so the obituary reads) a "familiar" poem entitled "Bessie McCall." (This poem is not listed in *Granger's Index to Poetry*; I have been unable to discover when or where it was printed.) Friends called him Denver Smith, a nickname alluding to his earlier days as a telegraph operator in Denver. His death on April 8 occurred at his home, 148 Midwood Street, Brooklyn. He was 50. There is no mention of children or other survivors.

On the following day the *American* reprinted the entire poem "Evolution" on its editorial page, followed by a tribute to Smith. "He had no mannerisms, no affectations, no sentimentalities. Keenly enjoying life, whether of the plains or the city, he invested it with enjoyment for those who knew him and for those who read what he wrote." Of his poem, the tribute says: "Mr. Smith wrote and rewrote it many times before he was satisfied with it."

A check through the clippings on Smith that are on file in the reference room of the *New York Journal-American* turned up little of interest. Two thin folders on him contained only his obituary, a sampling of a sports column that he wrote, and a column about him, by Hype Igoe, dated April 21, 1939. Mr. Igoe, who had known Smith, recalls a purple passage from Smith's celebrated account of the testimony of Evelyn Thaw on the witness stand to defend her husband; he writes about Smith's friendship with Jim Corbett in the days before Corbett defeated John L. Sullivan for the world's heavyweight boxing crown. Apparently Smith was at one time sports editor of the paper. Igoe mentions Smith's other poem, giving it a fuller title and one that suggests it has been deservedly unremembered: "Bessie McCall of Suicide Hall."

The first appearance in print of "Evolution" as a complete poem was on a page of classified advertisements in the morning Hearst paper, then called the *New York Journal and Advertiser*. The exact date is not known. A paragraph heading a reprint of the poem (in a magazine called *The Scrap Book*, April 1906, pp. 257-59) reads:

History records that in 1895 Mr. Langdon Smith, at that time connected with the Sunday edition of the New York *Herald*, wrote the first few stanzas of the following poem. They were printed in the *Herald*. Four years later, having joined the staff of the New York *Journal* in the interim, Mr. Smith came across the verses among his papers, and, reading them over, was struck with a sense of their incompleteness.

He added a stanza or two and laid the pen aside. Later he wrote more stanzas, and finally completed it and sent it in to Mr. Arthur Brisbane, editor of
the *Evening Journal*. Mr. Brisbane, being unable to use it, turned it over to
Mr. C. E. Russell of the *Morning Journal*. It appeared in the *Morning Journal*—in the middle of a page of want "ads"! How it came to be buried thus
some compositor may know. Perhaps a "make-up" man was inspired with a
glimmer of editorial intelligence to "lighten up" the page.

But even a deep border of "ads" could not smother the poem. Mr. Smith
received letters of congratulations from all parts of the world, along with re-
quests for copies. The poem has been in constant demand; and it has been almost
unobtainable . . .

Two years later the poem was printed again in a quarterly magazine, *The
Speaker* (September 1908, pp. 394-97). Since then it has been reprinted
countless times in anthologies. So far as I know, the first anthology to include it was Edwin Markham's two-volume *Book of Poetry* (vol. 1, p. 352).
"Strange to say," Markham comments, "this is the only poem of distinction
that he is known (to me) to have written."

Strange also is the fact that Markham's version of "Evolution" supplies
four lines missing from all other versions of the poem I have seen. The lines
precede the poem's final four-line stanza and are as follows:

> For we know that the clod, by the grace of God,
> Will quicken with voice and breath;
> And we know that Love, with gentle hand,
> Will beckon from death to death,

It is unlikely that Markham would have added these inferior lines just
to make the last stanza conform in length to the others. More likely they
were in the first printed version. One wonders if Smith himself later blue-
penciled them.

"Evolution" has been printed as a book or pamphlet at least four times.
A hand-lettered booklet, with line drawings by an anonymous artist, bears
neither date nor publisher's imprint. In 1909 a 51-page hard-cover version
was issued by John W. Luce and Company, with an introduction by Lewis
Allen Browne. (Browne is best known as the author of a popular book on
religion, *This Believing World*.) Unsigned notes on the various geological
terms mentioned in the poem are placed on pages opposite the stanzas.
Browne's introduction gives the impression that he knew Smith, but obviously
he did not. His "facts," from the sources already mentioned, add little of
interest. In 1911 another hardcover edition was published by W. A. Wilde
and Company, with decorative page borders by Fred S. Bertsch. This edition apparently enjoyed a wide sale, because copies of it, until a few years
ago, were common in second-hand bookstores. A Danish translation by Jens
Christian Bay (no illustrations) was privately printed in Holstebro, Denmark,
in 1930.

How can one explain the poem's continuing popular appeal? First of all, there is the strong jungle beat that makes the poem so easy to memorize, so effective to recite. Its stanzas are constructed skillfully, and there are passages (as Eliot noted of Kipling's verse) that reach the intensity of poetry. Second, the poem conveys what Darwin had in mind when he wrote, at the close of his *Origin of Species,* "There is grandeur in this view of life." The epic surge of evolution, from its humble beginning in the dark sea to the mellow light of Delmonico's, is caught in this poem as it has not been caught in any other poem before or since.

Finally, Smith has given evolution a strong religious cast. Did he himself believe in transmigration? It would be interesting to know. The theme of lovers reuniting in successive reincarnations, throughout the earth's long geological history, was a common one in popular fantasy novels of the late nineteenth century. Smith handles the theme so playfully, however, that it is hard to tell how serious he is. It is precisely his ambiguous touch here that makes it possible for the poem to be enjoyed by any reader, regardless of his beliefs about the soul's existence before birth or after death. Lewis Browne, for example, was a thoroughgoing naturalist, yet he thought the poem had "the ring of genius," and that its "crowning glory" was the way in which Smith "interwove throughout his masterpiece of imagination the golden thread of romance."

Browne closes his introduction by noting that Smith's wife died within five weeks after her husband's death, a fact that his friends took to indicate the strong bond between them. I have not been able to verify this. It may be truth, it may be a myth inspired by the poem. It is one of the many curious mysteries that continue to surround the poem and its author.

There is, at least for me, something haunting and sad about the lives of "one-poem men," as Burton Stevenson calls them in his book on *Famous Single Poems,* individuals who achieve immortality by writing one great piece of popular verse and nothing else. Because of the "nothing else" they almost literally vanish from history. "Casey at the Bat" was first published in the *San Francisco Examiner* (another Hearst paper, by the way) in 1888. The author, Ernest Lawrence Thayer, was, like Smith, a journalist. It is this country's best-known humorous poem. What sort of man was Thayer? What else did he write? "A Visit from St. Nicholas," another immortal poem, appeared anonymously in 1823 in the *Sentinel,* a newspaper in Troy, New York. The author was Clement Clarke Moore, professor of Oriental languages at the General Theological Seminary of New York. He is remembered today only because he scribbled down these lines to read to his children on Christmas Eve. He considered them so trivial that for twenty years he refused to admit he had written them.

Robert Graves, writing about "one-poem men" in his book, *On English Poetry*, divides them into two types: the born poets, so frustrated by environment that only once in their lives are they able to break through and create a poem, and those who are not poets at all, but who "write to express a sudden intolerable clamour in their brain." Having once expressed themselves, they have no further need of poetry. The first type is not hard to understand. The second type, if such there be, is not so easy to understand. I should think that there is a field here for investigation by those psychologists concerned with "creativity."

Scholars have done their work on Moore and Thayer (both are included in Burton Stevenson's book); Smith is still wrapped in undeserved anonymity. Even his name is appropriately anonymous. Smith. But smiths are artisans, and Langdon Smith was a credit to his clan. He fashioned for himself what must have been a colorful life, and on at least one occasion he hammered out a colorful ballad. It will probably be chanted long after the efforts of many contemporary poets, with enormous reputations, are forgotten by everybody except the historians of literature.

Evolution
Langdon Smith

I

When you were a tadpole and I was a fish,
In the Paleozoic time,
And side by side on the ebbing tide
We sprawled through the ooze and slime,
Or skittered with many a caudal flip
Through the depths of the Cambrian fen,
My heart was rife with the joy of life,
For I loved you even then.

II

Mindless we lived and mindless we loved,
And mindless at last we died;
And deep in a rift of the Caradoc drift
We slumbered side by side.
The world turned on in the lathe of time,
The hot lands heaved amain,
Till we caught our breath from the womb of death,
And crept into light again.

III

We were Amphibians, scaled and tailed,
And drab as a dead man's hand;
We coiled at ease 'neath the dripping trees,
Or trailed through the mud and sand,

Croaking and blind, with our three-clawed feet
Writing a language dumb,
With never a spark in the empty dark
To hint at a life to come.

IV

Yet happy we lived, and happy we loved,
And happy we died once more;
Our forms were rolled in the clinging mold
Of a Neocomian shore.
The eons came, and the eons fled,
And the sleep that wrapped us fast
Was riven away in a newer day,
And the night of death was past.

V

Then light and swift through the jungle trees
We swung in our airy flights,
Or breathed in the balms of the fronded palms,
In the hush of the moonless nights.
And oh! what beautiful years were these,
When our hearts clung each to each;
When life was filled, and our senses thrilled
In the first faint dawn of speech.

VI

Thus life by life, and love by love,
We passed through the cycles strange,
And breath by breath, and death by death,
We followed the chain of change.
Till there came a time in the law of life
When over the nursing sod
The shadows broke, and the soul awoke
In a strange, dim dream of God.

VII

I was thewed like an Auroch bull,
And tusked like the great Cave Bear;
And you, my sweet, from head to feet,
Were gowned in your glorious hair.
Deep in the gloom of a fireless cave,
When the night fell o'er the plain,
And the moon hung red o'er the river bed,
We mumbled the bones of the slain.

VIII

I flaked a flint to a cutting edge,
And shaped it with brutish craft;
I broke a shank from the woodland dank,
And fitted it, head and haft.
Then I hid me close to the reedy tarn,
Where the Mammoth came to drink; —
Through brawn and bone I drave the stone,
And slew him upon the brink.

IX

Loud I howled through the moonlit wastes,
Loud answered our kith and kin;
From west and east to the crimson feast
The clan came trooping in.
O'er joint and gristle and padded hoof,
We fought, and clawed and tore,
And cheek by jowl, with many a growl,
We talked the marvel o'er.

X

I carved that fight on a reindeer bone,
With rude and hairy hand,
I pictured his fall on the cavern wall
That men might understand.
For we lived by blood, and the right of might,
Ere human laws were drawn,
And the Age of Sin did not begin
Till our brutal tusks were gone.

XI

And that was a million years ago,
In a time that no man knows;
Yet here tonight in the mellow light,
We sit at Delmonico's;
Your eyes are deep as the Devon springs,
Your hair is as dark as jet,
Your years are few, your life is new,
Your soul untried, and yet —

XII

Our trail is on the Kimmeridge clay,
And the scarp of the Purbeck flags,

We have left our bones in the Bagshot stones,
And deep in the Coraline crags;
Our love is old, our lives are old,
And death shall come amain;
Should it come today, what man may say
We shall not live again?

XIII

God wrought our souls from the Tremadoc beds
And furnished them wings to fly;
He sowed our spawn in the world's dim dawn,
And I know that it shall not die;
Though cities have sprung above the graves
Where the crook-boned men made war,
And the ox-wain creaks o'er the buried caves
Where the mummied mammoths are.

XIV

Then as we linger at luncheon here,
O'er many a dainty dish,
Let us drink anew to the time when you
Were a Tadpole and I was a Fish.

POSTSCRIPT

As far as I know, my tribute to Smith continues to be the only article ever written about him or his poem. I had intended to do a series of essays on "one-poem poets," with an eventual book in mind, but I wrote only three more. My paean to Ernest Thayer and "Casey at the Bat" first appeared in *Sports Illustrated*, then later was expanded to make the introduction to my book, *The Annotated Casey at the Bat* (1967). The story of Clement Moore's Christmas poem will be found in the introduction I wrote for the Dover reprint of L. Frank Baum's fantasy, *The Life and Adventures of Santa Claus* (1976). My essay on the now deservedly forgotten "Speak Gently," a once popular poem that Lewis Carroll parodied, is reprinted here as Chapter 17 of Part 1. Someday I may get around to "The Lost Chord," "The Old Oaken Bucket," "The House by the Side of the Road," "Out Where the West Begins," and other examples of great doggerel by one-poem rhymsters.

At the time Smith wrote his ballad, the theme of couples having been lovers in past incarnations was common in both poetry and fiction. A notable verse example is Kipling's "The Sack of the Gods." It has exactly the same stanza form as Smith's ballad, and contains such lines as, "I was Lord of the Inca race, and she was Queen of the Sea." W. E. Henley's poem, "To W.A.," which closes with the lines, "When I was a king in Babylon, and you were a virgin slave," was also widely quoted in Smith's day. A listing of novels with reincarnation love themes, which were best sellers in the early 1890s, would run to dozens of titles. Smith's originality was in combining reincarnation with evolution. If there are earlier examples of this in English fiction or poetry, I have not come across them. Nor do I know of any memorable examples that came later. There must have been several comic parodies of Smith's ballad, but I know of only one, a mediocre baseball parody included in Grantland Rice's *Only the Brave* (1941).

I was tempted to annotate the geological terms in Smith's poem, but decided this would add nothing to the poem. Delmonico's, in stanza 11, is of course the famous Manhattan restaurant where fashionable people once dined. In Smith's day it was at the corner of Fifth Avenue and Forty-fourth Street, where it remained until it expired in 1923. An entire book about it, *Delmonico's: A Century of Splendor*, by Lately Thomas, was published in the late sixties.

The date of the *New York Morning Journal*, in which "Evolution" first appeared, is still unknown. If any reader can run this down and photocopy the page for me, I will be deeply grateful.

14

Logic Paradoxes

Philip Quarles, a character in Aldous Huxley's novel, *Point Counter Point*, is a novelist who is planning a "musicalized" novel of contrapuntal themes. "Put a novelist into the novel," reads one of Quarles's notes. "But why draw the line at one novelist inside your novel? Why not a second inside his? And a third inside the novel of the second? And so on to infinity, like those advertisements of Quaker Oats where there's a Quaker holding a box of oats, on which is a picture of another Quaker holding another box of oats, on which etc., etc. At about the tenth remove you might have a novelist telling your story in algebraic symbols or in terms of variations in blood pressure, pulse, secretion of ductless glands, and reaction times."

There are many examples of similar literary whimsies. Edouard, the novelist in Andre Gide's *The Counterfeiters*, is writing a novel called *The Counterfeiters* into which he plans to put himself as a character. E. E. Cummings' play *Him* is about a playwright who is writing a play about a playwright who is . . . "The Notebook," a short story by Norman Mailer, recounts an argument between a young writer and his girlfriend. She accuses him of being an observer of life, not a participant. As they argue, he gets an idea for a story, which he jots down in his notebook. The idea, of course, is to write a story about a young writer who is arguing with his girlfriend when he gets an idea . . . And there is Max Beerbohm's devilish tale "Enoch Soames" (reprinted in the Vintage paperback, *Seven Men*), in which "reflexiveness flickers delicately in and out," as the English mathematician J. E. Littlewood once described it.[1]

It is the reflexiveness or self-reference that distinguishes these examples from more familiar forms of the infinite regress, such as the hierarchy of

This essay originally appeared in the *Antioch Review,* Summer 1963. © 1963 by The Antioch Review, Inc. Reprinted with permission of the Editors.

fleas in Dean Swift's oft-quoted jingle. There is something fascinating and disturbing about a combination of self-reference and infinity, and no one has been disturbed and fascinated more than the logician. The reason: in formal logic this sort of thing often results in flat contradictions that lie like ugly blots on otherwise elegant deductive systems.

The oldest and simplest of the logic paradoxes is known as the Liar: "All Cretans are liars," said Epimenides the Cretan. (Epimenides was a semi-legendary Cretan prophet of the sixth century B.C. and the original Rip Van Winkle; he was said to have once slept for fifty-seven years.) The Liar was much debated by the ancients. The Stoic philosopher Chrysippus wrote six treatises about it, none surviving. A Greek poet, Philetas of Cos (he was so thin, contemporaries claimed, that he carried lead in his shoes to keep from being blown away), is said to have worried himself into an early grave because of it. Saint Paul repeats the paradox solemnly in his epistle to Titus 1:12-13.[2]

The simplest phrasing of the Liar is: "This sentence is false." It is easy to see the difficulty. If the sentence is false, it must be true. But if it is true, it must be false, and so on deeper into the whirlpool. There are endless variants. "All rules have exceptions." "All knowledge is doubtful." Bertrand Russell has expressed his belief that the philosopher George Edward Moore lied only once in his life. When asked, "Do you always tell the truth?" Moore thought a moment and replied, "No."

Gordon Dickson's story, "The Monkey Wrench" (*Astounding Science Fiction*, August 1951), tells of the disastrous effect of informing a giant electronic computer: "You must reject the statement I am now making to you, because all the statements I make are incorrect." Such a statement was actually fed to a computer a few years before Dickson wrote his story. William Burkhart and Theodore Kalin, then undergraduates at Harvard where they were studying logic under Willard Van Orman Quine, had built the world's first electrical machine for symbolic logic. When given a form of the Liar paradox, the computer went into an oscillating phase, alternating true with false and making, as Kalin described it, "a hell of a racket." (Incidentally, all statements in this article may be considered completely trustworthy except the last sentence of the sixth paragraph.)

One is tempted to think that if self-reference is forbidden, paradoxes of the Liar type are prevented, but this is not the case. Proof is provided by this medieval paradox:

Socrates: "What Plato is about to say is false."

Plato: "Socrates has just spoken truly."

The English mathematician, P. E. B. Jourdain, in 1913, suggested the following way to present the same paradox. On one side of a blank card print:

THE SENTENCE ON THE OTHER SIDE OF THIS CARD IS TRUE

On the opposite side of the same card print:

THE SENTENCE ON THE OTHER SIDE OF THIS CARD IS FALSE

There is no self-reference in either form of the paradox. Each sentence refers to the other, like a pair of Keystone cops chasing one another around a house. In addition to the vicious circularity, there is a kind of double infinite regress such as you see in opposite mirrors of a barber shop, in the story of Alice who is dreaming of the Red King who is dreaming of Alice who is dreaming of the Red King, and in Miguel de Unamuno's plaintive cry: "Dream us, O God of our dream!"

Forms of the Liar paradox lead us into situations that effectively freeze human action. How can a witness reply to a lawyer who says: "Please answer *yes* or *no* to the following question: Will the next word that you speak be *no*?"[3] The Greeks liked to debate about the crocodile that snatched a baby from its mother and offered to return it if the mother could correctly answer the question: "Will I eat your baby?" If the mother had said, "No," there would have been no difficulty, but she was clever enough to say, "Yes." This threw the poor reptile into a quandary. Another Greek paradox tells of a young lawyer who had the following agreement with his teacher, Protagoras: If he won his first case he would pay for his instruction; if he lost, he would not pay. The youth kept refusing to accept cases until Protagoras forced the issue by suing him. Naturally the young man defended himself. Whatever the court decides, the situation is cloudy.

In Chapter 51 of the second book of *Don Quixote*, Sancho Panza is confronted by a similar paradox. The owner of a large manor, on the island of Barataria, requires every man who enters his estate to announce the purpose of his visit. If the man tells the truth he is unmolested; if he lies he is hanged. A whimsical joker has answered the question by saying that he intends to be hanged on the gallows he sees ahead of him. As governor of the island, Sancho has sworn to uphold the local laws. In this case, if he permits the hanging, the man will be hanged unjustly because he told the truth, but if he lets the man go free, the man deserves to hang. With his usual common sense Sancho decides: there is no more reason to hang the man than not to hang him, and since it is better to show mercy than to kill, the man should be set free.

Groucho Marx once said that he refused to join any club that would have him for a member, a policy certainly not conducive to action.[4] There are people, one suspects, who for similar reasons never marry. These cases, however, are less like the Liar than like a famous self-reference paradox of set theory that was discovered by Bertrand Russell. Some sets are members of themselves. For example, the set of all things that are not apples is obviously not an apple. Consider the set of all sets that are *not* members of themselves. Is it a member of itself? However you answer, you are sure to contradict yourself.

One of the saddest, most dramatic turning points in the history of logic involves this paradox. Bertrand Russell and Alfred North Whitehead were collaborating on their great work *Principia Mathematica* when Russell discovered his paradox. "I communicated the misfortune to Whitehead," he wrote later, "who failed to console me by quoting, 'never glad confident morning again.' " In Germany, Gottlob Frege was finishing the second volume of his life's work, *The Fundamental Laws of Arithmetic*, convinced that at long last, by means of set theory, he had placed mathematics on a firm logical basis. The volume was at the printers when Russell's letter arrived, in 1902, telling him of the paradox. Frege had only time to insert a brief appendix that begins: "A scientist can hardly encounter anything more undesirable than to have the foundation collapse just as the work is finished. I was put in this position by a letter from Mr. Bertrand Russell . . ."

Behind this "dry statement," writes Rudolf Carnap (in his *Logical Syntax of Language*), "one senses a deep emotion." It has been said that Frege's use of the word *undesirable* is the greatest understatement in the history of science.

Like the Liar, Russell's paradox can be given endless disguises. Russell himself once explained it by describing a village barber who put up a sign saying: "I shave all those and only those men in town who do not shave themselves." Who, Russell wanted to know, shaves this barber? Apparently he shaves himself if and only if he doesn't. A librarian is asked to catalog all catalogs that do not mention themselves. Should this new catalog list its own title? In all such paradoxes, a member of a set S is given a certain relation R to all and only those members of S that are not in relation R to themselves. By choosing different relations, it is easy to invent new paradoxes. For example, who repairs the robot that repairs all and only those robots that are not self-repairing?

Grelling's paradox (after the German mathematician Kurt Grelling) divides all adjectives into two classes: self-descriptive and non-self-descriptive. Words such as *English*, *polysyllabic*, *short* are self-descriptive. *German*, *monosyllabic*, *long* are non-self-descriptive. To which class belongs the adjective *non-self-descriptive*? Placing it in either class produces a contradiction. In similar fashion we can divide all integers into two classes: those that can be expressed in English with twelve words or less, and those that require thirteen words or more. Consider "the smallest integer that cannot be expressed in less than thirteen words." Since we just expressed it in twelve words, to which class does this integer belong? Max Black of Cornell University came up with this one. Various integers are mentioned in this chapter. Fix your attention on the smallest integer that is *not* referred to in any way in this chapter. Is there such an integer?

Russell thought all these paradoxes, including his own, similar in some way to the Liar. In 1903 he began an earnest attempt to find a solution for them. "I would, if necessary," he writes in *My Philosophical Development*, "have spent the whole of the rest of my life in an attempt to meet [this challenge]. But for two reasons I found this exceedingly disagreeable. In the first place, the whole problem struck me as trivial and I hated having to concentrate attention upon something that did not seem intrinsically interesting. In the second place, try as I would, I could make no progress. Throughout 1903 and 1904, my work was almost wholly devoted to this matter, but without any vestige of success."

Eventually Russell found a solution in what he called the doctrine of types. It is now called the "simple theory of types" because later mathematicians have greatly simplified Russell's early complicated formulations. The theory arranges sets in a hierarchy of types in such a way that no set is permitted to be a member of itself. Apples belong to the set of all apples, but this set can be an element only in a set of second order, such as the set of all fruits. Sets of second order can be elements only in sets of third order, and so on to infinity. In this way, self-contradictory sets are eliminated. There is no class that contains all and only those classes that do not contain themselves, no adjective that refers to all and only those adjectives that do not refer to themselves. The barber paradox, as Quine puts it, "need not shake our faith in logic but only in the barber. There *is* no barber of the kind described."[5]

The so-called "semantic paradoxes" such as the Liar, which involve "true" and "false," are eliminated by a similar hierarchy; this time a hierarchy of languages. Alfred Tarski, the Polish logician, was the first to make this clear. His position is now accepted by almost all logicians, though they may differ on details in the construction of the language ladder. From this point of view the assertion, "This statement is false," is meaningless, or, as Carnap prefers to say, not a sentence. The meaninglessness derives not from the self-reference but from the confusion of language levels. On the lowest level is the "object language" in which statements are made about physical objects: e.g., "Mars has two moons." It is the basement language that Huxley speaks of (in the quotation that begins this article) as the language of "tenth remove." Words such as "true" and "false" cannot occur in this language. They occur only in what Tarski calls a metalanguage. Statements in this second-order language can in turn be talked about, called true or false, only in a third-order metalanguage. As Russell once expressed it: the man who says "I am telling a lie of order n" *is* telling a lie, but a lie of order $n + 1$.[6]

This hierarchy of metalanguages, like the hierarchy of types, is infinite. The picture within the picture, the play within the play, is still with us; but the vicious circle has been cut and opened up into a straight line, extending upward into infinity.

POSTSCRIPT

The literature on logic paradoxes is, of course, immense. Basic references include the sections on paradoxes in *Principia Mathematica*, by Russell and Whitehead; *Foundations of Set Theory*, by Abraham Fraenkel and Yohoshua

Bar-Hillel; and *The Foundations of Mathematics*, by Evert Beth. An excellent nontechnical essay, "Paradox," by Willard Van Orman Quine, appeared in *Scientific American*, October 1962.

My *Scientific American* column on infinite regresses can be found in my *Sixth Book of Mathematical Games*; and the first section of my *Aha, Gotcha!* (W. H. Freeman, 1982) concerns logical paradoxes of all types. My successor at *Scientific American*, Douglas Hofstadter, has written three columns on self-reference, filled with amusing instances, in the issues of January 1981 and January and June 1982.

I have left my *Antioch Review* article unaltered except for adding the footnotes.

NOTES

1. Jorge Luis Borges, in an essay on Don Quixote (in *Other Inquisitions*), calls attention to several instances of self-reference in Cervantes's novel. In Book 1, Chapter 6, a priest and a barber discuss Cervantes's writings. In Book 2 we learn that the Don and Sancho Panza have read Book 1. Borges mentions other examples of self-reference in fiction, such as one of the stories in the *Arabian Nights*, in which the Sultana tells the story of her telling the 1,001 tales.

Alfred Appel, Jr., in his *Annotated Lolita* (McGraw-Hill, 1970), discusses self-reference in Nabokov's fiction (one character, Krug, in *Bend Sinister*, goes insane when he learns that he is an imaginary person invented by Nabokov). Appel cites other instances in works by Samuel Beckett, Raymond Queneau, James Joyce, and in a Dick Tracy comic strip. At one point in Molly Bloom's famous soliloquy she asks Joyce to stop writing it!

2. An entire book is devoted to papers on the liar paradox: *The Paradox of the Liar*, edited by Robert L. Martin (Yale University Press, 1970). It has an extensive bibliography.

3. Prediction paradoxes of this sort arise when the method of predicting is part of the event being predicted. Many years ago I amused myself by thinking of examples. Here is one similar to Jourdain's liar card. On the back of the card is a picture of, say, a lady. On the front is printed: "If you expect the picture on the back of this card to be right-side up, indicate your guess by turning over the card from side to side. If you expect the picture to be upside down, turn the card end for end." The picture is of course oriented so that a successful prediction is logically impossible.

4. Among other logic paradoxes involving organizations there are: The Procrastination Society that nobody joins because they keep delaying it; the Apathy Society which has no members because anyone wanting to join is disqualified for not being apathetic enough; and the polling firm that conducted a survey to find out how honest people were when they answered questions. The survey showed that over half lied when they were polled.

5. As I carelessly stated the paradox, with typical male chauvinism, there is a simple answer. The barber is a woman.

6. Without the metalanguage restriction, the propositional calculus can be used

to prove anything whatever: God exists, Satan exists, God does not exist, and so on. The proof takes many forms. Charles Peirce's proof that black is white (in his *Collected Papers*, vol. 4, p. 54) is one of the simplest. I will give it here as a proof that God exists.

Consider the sentence: "Either this entire statement is false or God exists."

The entire statement must be either true or false. If false, then the entire statement must be true. Assume then that the entire statement is true. If so, one of its alternatives must be true. The first alternative (on our assumption) is false. Therefore the second alternative, "God exists," must be true.

The way out, of course, is to recognize that the sentence, "Either this entire statement is false or God exists," is a meaningless sentence.

15

Carroll versus Baum

It was just a century ago this month that Macmillan in London published its first edition—two thousand copies—of *Alice's Adventures in Wonderland*. Lewis Carroll himself had arranged this date. It had been on July 4, three years earlier, that he and a friend had taken Alice Liddell and her two sisters on a boating trip up the Isis. "On which occasion," Carroll later noted in his diary, "I told them the fairy tale of Alice's adventures underground. . . ." *Through the Looking-Glass* appeared six years later, and the two dreams soon coalesced to become England's greatest fantasy tale.

If anyone had suggested to a Victorian critic that Alice was great literature, he would have been met with an incredulous snort. Clever and amusing, perhaps, but great literature? Reviews of the first *Alice* book were mixed. *The Athenaeum* called it a "stiff, overwrought story" with "square, and grim, and uncouth" illustrations. "Too extravagantly absurd to produce more diversion than disappointment and irritation," said the *Illustrated Times*.

But children and adults loved it, both in England and here, and before twenty years had passed, a hundred thousand copies had been printed. Warren Weaver, in his recent book *Alice in Many Tongues*, lists more than forty languages into which *Alice's Adventures* are now translated. There are several Russian versions, including one written by Vladimir Nabokov when he was a young man living in Germany. ("Not the first Russian translation," he once told a reporter, "but the best.") How can one explain the persistent popularity of this strange, outlandish dream and its even stranger sequel?

My own view is—though it arouses some Carrollians to a pitch of frenzy—that *Alice* is no longer a children's book. I do not deny that here and there a few unusual children, more in England than here, are still capable of enjoying it, but I believe their number is steadily diminishing. Like *Gulliver's*

This essay originally appeared in the *Saturday Review,* July 17, 1965.

Travels, *Robinson Crusoe*, and *Huckleberry Finn*, *Alice* has joined that curious list of books that librarians call "children's classics" but which are read and relished mostly by grown-ups. I myself have never met a child who said that *Alice* was one of his or her favorite books, and I have met only two U.S. adults who said they had enjoyed it as a small child. (Please don't write me an angry letter saying you have just read *Alice* to your five-year-old and she *loved* it. Try reading to her *A Midsummer Night's Dream* or Norman Mailer's *American Dream*; you'll find she loves them, too.)

The truth is that, from a modern child's point of view, the *Alice* books are plotless, pointless, unfunny and more frightening than a monster movie. Let me summon a few distinguished witnesses. Katherine Anne Porter, in a radio panel discussion of *Alice* in 1942, confessed that the book had badly frightened her as a little girl. All those household things going mad and reminding her of the uncertainty and insecurity she felt in an adult world she couldn't understand! Bertrand Russell agreed. *Alice*, he declared flatly, is unsuitable for any child younger than fifteen. "There are many objections to it as a children's book. In fact, I should like to label it 'For Adults Only.' "

"I wonder," said Mark Van Doren, "if the young these days actually do like it as much as children used to like it."

"My experience," replied Lord Russell, "is that they don't, and I think this is because there are so many more children's books now and because, when I was young, it was the only children's book that hadn't got a moral. We all got very tired of the morals in books."

Another great mathematician, Norbert Wiener, tells in his autobiography how Alice's metamorphoses terrified him as a boy, and how it was not until many years later that he learned to value the book. H. L. Mencken, in his autobiography, writes: "I was a grown man, and far gone in sin, before I ever brought myself to tackle *Alice in Wonderland*, and even then I made some big skips."

For intelligent children over fifteen and adults who, unlike Mencken, are not bored by fantasy, the *Alice* books are rich in subtle humor, social satire, and philosophical depth. Both books, especially the second, are crammed with paradoxical nonsense of exactly the sort that mathematicians and logicians revel in. It is no accident that you are likely to find more references to *Alice* in a book by a modern philosopher of science than in a book by a literary critic. The central symbol in Edward Albee's Broadway enigma, *Tiny Alice*—the infinite regress of the castle in the castle in the castle—is straight out of the looking glass. Alice dreams about the Red King but the Red King, too, is dreaming, and Alice is only a "thing" in *his* dream. This double regress of Alices and kings, into infinitely more dreamlike levels nested in the skulls of each, is a delicious thought to philosophers concerned with separating reality from illusion. But, if a small child understands it at all, he is more likely to be upset than amused.

Moreover, *Alice* swarms with jokes that no American child will catch (e.g., the Ugly Duchess's clever double pun on the proverb "Take care of the pence and the pounds will take care of themselves"). And there are jokes not even an English child today can understand (e.g., the parodies on poems, now forgotten, that Victorian children memorized). There are even jokes that a child in Carroll's time would not understand unless he was part of the Oxford community (e.g., the three Liddell-little puns in the first verse of the prefatory poem—the last name of Henry Liddell, dean of Christ Church and the father of Alice, rhymed with "middle"). It is all this, from the obscure word plays to the philosophical and mathematical paradoxes, that keeps the *Alice* books alive among adults long after they have ceased to delight the average child.

It is instructive to compare Carroll with our own greatest writer of fairy tales, L. Frank Baum. On the surface, the two men seem remarkably unalike: Carroll the shy, withdrawn, stammering, prim, devout, celibate teacher of mathematics; Baum, the friendly, outgoing father of four boys, a man who acted and sang in his own Broadway shows, published a newspaper in North Dakota before that area became a state, started his own movie company in Hollywood. But underneath their differences they shared a deep love for children (though on Carroll's side, only for little girls), and a genius for entertaining them with brilliantly imagined stories of outrageous comic fantasy.

Baum's first juvenile book, *Mother Goose in Prose*, weaves stories around nursery rhymes in a manner comparable to Carroll's episodes about the Tweedle brothers, Humpty Dumpty, the Knave of Hearts, and the Lion and the Unicorn. The title of Baum's book, *A New Wonderland*, published in 1900, is an obvious reference to *Alice*. *The Wonderful Wizard of Oz*, issued the same year, parallels *Alice* in many ways. Like Alice, Dorothy Gale is a healthy, bright, attractive, outspoken, unaffected, supremely self-confident and courageous little girl who suddenly finds herself in a mad world where animals talk and nature behaves in a thousand unexpected ways. Alice drops into wonderland through a rabbit hole. Dorothy is blown to Oz by a cyclone. Mother and Father are conveniently absent from both stories. (Dorothy is an orphan, Alice never thinks about her parents.)

Of course there are also profound differences between the two classics, both in style and content. Baum is less interested in mathematical and word play, more in telling a straightforward adventure story. No one would expect to meet that eminent Oxford linguistic philosopher Humpty Dumpty in Baum's Oz; though we do meet a Humpty in *Mother Goose in Prose*, and I suppose Baum's Woggle-Bug and Carroll's egg have much pride and pedantry in common. (The White Knight, wearing yellow armor, turns up as Sir Hocus of Pokes in Ruth Plumly Thompson's *Royal Book of Oz*.) No one would expect to find the Scarecrow or Tin Woodman behind the looking glass. You can no more imagine the Cheshire Cat in Oz than you can imagine Bungles, the glass cat, or Dorothy's cat Eureka in Carroll's wonderland, although the White Rabbit might have strayed from Bunnybury, in the Quadling Country of Oz. This is not the place to detail differences, but surely one outstanding difference is that Baum's characters are, for the most part, as lovable as they are outlandish. They are "Ozzy," but seldom cruel or mad. Oz is a happy Utopia. Indeed, it is so attractive to Dorothy that she finally settled there permanently with Uncle Henry and Aunt Em. Both of Alice's dreams turned into nightmares.

It is a funny little irony of our culture that there are still librarians around who keep *Alice* on the children's shelves and *The Wizard* off. As recently as 1957 Ralph Ulveling, director of the Detroit Public Library, explained in a letter to the *American Library Association Bulletin* (October issue) why his library kept *The Wizard* in its adult stacks only and did not permit it in the children's room. "More than thirty years ago," he wrote, "the decision was made that with so many far better books available for children than was the case when *The Wizard* was first published, the library would simply let the old copies wear out and not replace them. . . . This is not banning, it is selection."

Well, as Humpty said, words can mean whatever we want them to mean. Personally, I find it easier to believe in the Scarecrow than in Mr. Ulveling. My advice is: Give *The Wizard* (in its handsome Dover paperback edition, with its bibliography of Baum's other books) to that ten-year-old; send *Alice* (*The Annotated Alice*, of course) to anyone over fifteen who is bored with reading novels about psychotics in a real world.

Fantasy, said G. K. Chesterton (in his marvelous essay "The Dragon's Grandmother"), reminds us that the soul is sane "but that the universe is wild and full of marvels. Realism means that the world is dull and full of routine, but that the soul is sick and screaming . . . In the fairy tales the cosmos goes mad; but the hero does not go mad. In the modern novels the hero is mad before the book begins, and suffers from the harsh steadiness and cruel sanity of the cosmos." It is a good bet that both *Alice* and *The Wizard* will be around for many centuries after *Tiny Alice* and *The American Dream*—even that monstrous, million-punned labyrinthine dream of H. C. Earwicker's—have been forgotten by everybody except the collectors and students of twentieth-century curiosa.

POSTSCRIPT

Many Oz enthusiasts responded to my little essay with cheering letters, two of which appeared in the *Saturday Review* (August 14, 1965, pp. 26 and 39) along with one unfavorable letter. To give Oz detractors their due, here is how Jeannette C. Nolan, of Indianapolis, came to Ulveling's defense:

> As a confirmed "Alice" fan, I must protest Martin Gardner's article, "A Child's Garden of Bewilderment." I challenge Mr. Gardner's statement that "It is in-structive to compare Carroll with our own greatest writer of fairy tales, L. Frank

Baum." Greatest? Well, well! I maintain that any comparison of the sort is patently ridiculous. The "Alice" books are unique, a manifestation of sheer genius. They cannot be classified, contrasted, or lumped with other books, nor do they need to be. Neither do they need to be annotated. The reader, child or adult, who does not at first exposure take Alice to his heart will be no fonder after she is explained to him.

But, since Mr. Gardner has posed the question, let me speak for those readers who rate the Oz books as entirely commonplace, pedestrian in style, characterization, concept, and story line. They were written for children, yes; also, and unfortunately, they were written *down* to children; they seldom rise above the level of the television fare viewed so constantly by present-day American youth—with what ultimate effect only time will tell. Ralph Ulveling, director of the Detroit Public Library, is to be commended for his judgment in not replacing on his shelves the old copies of the Oz books as they wear out. There are, indeed, hundreds of books now available for children that are not written down to them.

I find it most intriguing that Katherine Anne Porter and Lord Bertrand Russell have said that, as children, they were badly frightened by Alice's adventures. One may perhaps believe that Miss Porter drew upon this experience in creating the grisly characters in her *Ship of Fools*. But Lord Bertrand Russell? Surely there has been nothing in his adult attitudes or utterances to suggest an early traumatic timidity. Or am I wrong?

Yes. Russell *was* a shy, awkward, lonely child. In his autobiography he tells of walking in the fields, watching sunsets, and contemplating suicide. "I did not, however, commit suicide, because I wanted to know more of mathematics." Of course Jeannette Nolan is wrong about Baum, too.

16

Santa Claus

Our native mythology is largely derivative. We do have a few homegrown legends (Johnny Appleseed, Paul Bunyan, . . .) and some tall tales about George Washington, but most of our great myths are borrowed from Europe.

With one exception! There is a single towering personality, as immortal as Pan, whose character was almost wholly shaped by residents of New York. I speak of course of Santa Claus.

Let us not confuse him with pale predecessors and curious counterparts. Saint Nicholas, the much-venerated fourth-century bishop of Myra, was tall and lean. By the twelfth century his feast day (December 6) had become a church holiday, but after the Reformation he fell into disrepute, and it was not long until St. Nicholas Day merged with December 25, the official day for celebrating the birth of Jesus.

Holland is the only Protestant country where the saint has survived as a legendary gift-giver. For six hundred years, on the Eve of St. Nicholas, Dutch children have been putting their shoes by the fireplace. During the night, Sintirklass and his Moorish assistant, Zwarte Piet (Black Peter), arrive by ship from, of all places, Spain. The saint mounts a white horse that gallops from roof to roof. The Moor pops down chimneys to leave gifts, but Sinterklass, not wishing to soil his white robe and red cassock, does no more than drop candy down the chimney.

The histories of winter gift-bringers in other lands are colorful and confusing. There is Father Christmas in England, and Père Noel in France. Germany's Kriss Kringle, or Christ Child, is a fairy, not the infant Jesus. (Curiously, the Pennsylvania Dutch appropriated the name for Santa Claus.) In Italy, on Twelfth Night, it is the good witch Befana who slides down the

This essay originally appeared in the *New York Times Book Review*, December 7, 1975.

chimney. The legend is that she was sweeping her house when the Three Wise Men asked her to accompany them to Bethlehem. Befana was too busy. Later she regretted her decision and has been wandering around ever since, looking for the Holy Child.[1] Her counterpart in old Russia was an evil old woman, Baba Yaga, who intentionally misdirected the Wise Men. In new Russia the tinseled tree is now decorated on New Year's Eve and it is Grandfather Frost, looking exactly like Santa, who arrives in the night. In Spain the Wise Men bring the gifts.

The first Dutch settlers of New Amsterdam brought St. Nick with them, and Washington Irving was the first to write about the Americanized saint. Exactly what he then looked like is not clear, but Irving tells us that the Dutch children hung their stockings by the fire, and the saint would come "riding over the tops of trees" in a "wagon" to rattle toys and candy down the chimney.

Now comes the most amazing part of the story. Dr. Clement Clarke Moore was a professor at an Episcopalian seminary near his home in what is now Manhattan's Chelsea section. One snowy Christmas Eve, in 1822, Moore read his children a poem he had scribbled for them. It found its way to the editor of a newspaper in Troy, New York, who published it anonymously on December 23, 1823, as "An Account of a Visit from St. Nicholas."

Moore did not admit his authorship until the poem appeared in a collection of New York verse in 1837. He wrote lots of "serious" poetry, all of it undistinguished, but the "Visit," which he dashed off so carelessly, became the most popular Christmas poem in English.[2]

The idea of Santa himself descending the chimney seems to be original with Moore. It was probably also Moore who gave St. Nick his twinkling eyes, rosy cheeks, cherry nose and the pack of toys, but the pipe and the finger-on-nose gesture came from Irving.[3] It was long assumed that Moore invented the sleigh and reindeer, but now we know that these, too, were not original. A rare little book of verse, *The Children's Friend*, published a year before Moore wrote his poem, has a picture of Santa in a sled drawn by one reindeer. Beneath it are these lines:

Old Santeclaus with much delight
His reindeer drives the frosty night.
O'er chimney tops, and track of snow,
To bring his yearly gifts to you.

Thomas Nast, a German-born newspaper cartoonist, was the next major influence on Santa. Nast, too, was a New Yorker, best known today for his attacks on the Tammany Tiger. He made scores of drawings of Santa, mostly in the 1880s, for Christmas issues of *Harper's Weekly*. The saint was enlarged to a fat man of normal height (Moore's Santa was a tiny elf), and the fur that covered Moore's St. Nick was replaced with a red satin suit trimmed with white ermine.[4]

L. Frank Baum, another New Yorker (he was born near Syracuse and began his career by starring in a Broadway melodrama written by himself), wrote the best of many novels about Santa Claus. In 1902, after the huge success of his *Wonderful Wizard of Oz*, Baum published *The Life and Adventures of Santa Claus*. How did Santa come to be what he is? It is this enormous gap in our knowledge that Baum filled by creating an elaborate background mythology. Next year, when Dover reprints this unjustly forgotten book, you can read about how Claus was abandoned as a baby, hundreds of years ago, in the Forest of Burzee, just south of Oz. You will learn how Claus was raised by Necile, the lovely wood nymph who found him, how he settled in Laughing Valley, where he learned to make toys. When he was old and fat and about to die, Ak, the Master Woodsman, called a council of the immortals. They conferred upon good Claus the Mantle of Immortality.[5]

In *The Road to Oz*, Santa is the most distinguished guest at Ozma's birthday party. He chats with Dorothy, the Scarecrow, the Tin Woodman. At the royal banquet it is Santa who leads the toast to Ozma. It is Santa, riding the Saw-Horse, who heads a great parade through the Emerald City.

The Ozzy old fellow was certainly at home in Oz. Most Americans, who have not yet heard of the Laughing Valley, still suppose that the saint lives at the North Pole. It is a quaint superstition. Ozmapolitans know better.

NOTES

1. See *The Legend of Old Befana*, retold and illustrated by Tomie de Paola (Harcourt, Brace, Jovanovich, 1980).

2. Doubts have been raised over whether Moore is the sole author of the poem. There is a tradition in a Livingston family, originally from Dutchess County, New York, that their ancestor, Henry Livingston, wrote the poem. The claim is that the poem found its way anonymously to Moore, who polished it, perhaps added to it, and so thought of it as essentially his own. Details of the controversy are given by Burton Stevenson in his *Famous Single Poems* (1935), and by Tristram P. Coffin in his *Book of Christmas Folklore* (Seabury, 1973). Stevenson discounts the Livingston claim; Coffin supports it.

3. Irving's remarks about St. Nick are scattered throughout *The History of New York*, which he wrote under the pseudonym of Diedrich Knickerbocker. The paragraph that most influenced Moore's poem (from Book 2, Chapter 5) is worth quoting in full:

And the sage Oloffe dreamed a dream, and lo, the good St. Nicholas came riding over the tops of the trees in that self-same wagon wherein he brings his yearly presents to children, and he descended hard by where the heroes of Communipaw had made their late repast. And he lit his pipe by the fire and sat himself down and smoked, and as he smoked the smoke from his pipe ascended into the air and spread like a cloud overhead. And Oloffe bethought him, and he hastened and climbed up to the top of one of the tallest trees, and saw that the smoke spread over a great extent of country; and as he considered it more attentively he fancied that the great volume of smoke assumed a variety of marvelous forms, where in dim obscurity he saw shadowed out palaces and domes and lofty spires, all of which lasted but a moment and then faded away, until the whole rolled off and nothing but the green woods were left. And when St. Nicholas had smoked his pipe he twisted it in his hat-band, and, laying his finger beside his nose, gave the astonished Van Kortlandt a very significant look, then mounting his wagon he returned over the tree-tops and disappeared.

4. In Victorian England the most popular drawings of Father Christmas were by John Tenniel, illustrator of Lewis Carroll's *Alice* books, for Christmas issues of *Punch*. See vol. 69: p. 267; 75:295; 79:295; 85:307; 95:307; 97:307.

5. You'll find more about Santa in my introduction to the Dover reprint of Baum's fantasy. Of course I only scratched the surface of a large literature on the history of Santa Claus. A colorful anthology could be assembled of sequels to the poem (both comic and serious), of which the most famous, of course, introduced Rudolph of the red nose, now a permanent part of the happy mythology.

17

Speak Roughly

Aside from the couplet:

> . . . feeling sure that they must be
> Tweedledum and Tweedledee,

which links the uncompleted last sentence of Chapter 3 of *Through the Looking-Glass* to the title of Chapter 4, there are exactly one dozen poems in the first *Alice* book and one dozen in the second. Considering his love of mathematical order, Lewis Carroll may have intended it that way.

Of the twenty-four poems, ten are undisputed parodies of poems or songs known to contemporary readers. In all but one—"I'll tell thee everything I can . . ."—the original rhyme and meter are copied. In most cases the first line of the original is parodied. An eleventh poem, "They told me you had been to her . . .," is based on an earlier poem by Carroll that spoofs the opening line of a popular song. Four poems are unaltered nursery rhymes. Five surely are not parodies: the prefatory poem to each book, the terminal poem of the second book, the riddle poem ("First the fish must be caught . . ."), and the Mouse's tail. This leaves four poems that could be parodies:

1. "I passed by his garden . . ."
2. "Jabberwocky"
3. "The sun was shining on the sea . . ."
4. "In winter when the fields are white . . ."

It was thought in Carroll's time that the third was intended to resemble a poem by Thomas Hood, but Carroll is on record as having denied it. John Mackay Shaw, in his monograph on *The Parodies of Lewis Carroll* (Florida

This essay originally appeared in *Lewis Carroll Observed*, ed. by Edward Guiliano (New York: Clarkson Potter, 1976), and is reprinted with permission.

State University Library, 1960), has suggested poems that 1, 2, and 4 somewhat resemble in tone, and Roger Green has argued that "Jabberwocky" was intended to copy the feeling and atmosphere of a German ballad that had been translated by one of Carroll's cousins. In all four cases, the resemblance seems to me insufficient to justify the belief that Carroll had a specific poem in mind as the basis for a parody.

None of the nonsense poems in the *Alice* books are literary parodies in the sense of an attempt to copy the style of a poet. As Dwight Macdonald emphasizes in his splendid anthology, *Parodies* (Random House, 1960), they are better described as burlesques. "He [Carroll] simply injected an absurd content into the original form with no intention of literary criticism. When he did parody serious poets, he was not very good, tending to be either too broad (as in "Hiawatha's Photographing" and his Swinburne parody, "Atalanta in Camden Town") or too fantastic (as in his parody of Tennyson's "The Two Voices"). But these qualities were just what he needed for the *Alice* poems, since the originals were both crude and fantastic."

It is sometimes said that many of Carroll's burlesque poems — especially "Father William," "The Crocodile," and "Speak Roughly" — were intended to deflate the pious, pompous, and hypocritical morality of Victorian times. I do not believe this. It is true that the *Alice* books are happily free of such moralizing, and that this contributed in no small way to their great and continuing popularity. But Carroll was not free of that morality. On the contrary, his moralizing exceeded that of the leading writers of his time.

For example, Carroll was so offended by the slightest impropriety in language or action on the stage that he constantly wrote to newspapers about it. He even considered editing an edition of Shakespeare for girls in which he would bowdlerize Bowdler by omitting lines that Bowdler considered inoffensive.

Exactly what did Carroll object to in the theater? In his article on "The Stage and the Spirit of Reverence," he spells it out in detail. "O God, sir, here's a dish I love not," says Benedick in *Much Ado*. When Carroll heard this line, toned down to "O Lord," he was so upset that he thought the phrase should have been left out entirely. In *Pinafore* the Captain says, "Damn me!" and little girls in the chorus echo it by singing, "He said 'Damn me!' " "I cannot find words," wrote Carroll, "to convey to the reader the pain I felt in seeing those dear children taught to utter such words to amuse ears grown callous to their ghastly meaning. Put the two ideas side by side — Hell (no matter whether *you* believe in it or not: millions do), and those pure young lips thus sporting with its horrors — and then find what *fun* in it you can! How Mr. Gilbert could have stooped to write, or Sir Arthur Sullivan could have prostituted his noble art to set to music such vile trash, it passes my skill to understand."

The slightest jesting reference to the Devil (in whom Carroll firmly believed), whether on stage or in society, also caused Carroll much pain. "The whole subject," he declared, "is too closely bound up with the deepest sorrows of life to be fit matter for jesting."

And what did Carroll find admirable on the stage? In a melodrama called *Silver King*, a scoundrel turns out of doors a poor mother whose child is dying. "It was good," wrote Carroll, "to hear the low fierce hiss that ran through the audience . . . " In another play, *The Golden Ladder*, a greengrocer explains why he named his child Victoria Alexandra. "And I guv her them two names because they're the best two names as is!" When Carroll saw the play, a ripple of applause greeted the line. "Yes," Carroll observes, "the very sound of those names — names which recall a Queen whose spotless life has for many long years been a blessing to the people, and a Princess who will worthily follow in her steps—is sweet music to English ears!''

Nor did Carroll confine his moralizing to articles, letters, and privately published tracts. His long novel, *Sylvie and Bruno*, is saturated with Victorian piety and rhetoric. It even contains a poem on love as preposterous as any poem by Robert Southey or Isaac Watts. When the original manuscript of *Alice's Adventures Under Ground* was published, Carroll added a preface and an "Easter Greeting to Every Child Who Loves 'Alice.' " Both are so filled with sentimental moralizing that even Victorian readers must have winced when they read them.

No, I do not think Carroll intended to puncture the *sentiments* of any of the pious poems burlesqued in his *Alice* books. He was in total agreement with their sentiments. His intent was more obvious. He chose poems so well known to Alice Liddell, and to his other readers, that they would catch at once the fun of his burlesques, and he chose poems so close to doggerel that the fun was inoffensive and even heightened. In the case of "Speak Roughly," the only additional intent is the expression of Carroll's dislike of little boys. Change the sex of the child in these verses and one cannot conceive of Carroll having written them. As they stand, they express a hostility so deeply buried in Carroll's psyche that even he did not fully understand it.

Now for a capital little mystery, although it is hard to imagine a literary question more trivial. Solving it would contribute nothing to our understanding of Carroll or his writing; indeed, it would make little contribution of any sort to literary scholarship. Nevertheless, the question is *there*, like the mountain to be scaled, and whoever solves it will earn a permanent footnote in the literature of peripheral Carrolliana.

The question: Who wrote the poem that "Speak roughly . . ." parodies?

As all Carrollians know, "Speak Roughly" is the lullaby the Duchess sings to her baby before it turns into a pig. Its two stanzas, each followed by a chorus of "Wow, wow, wow!" are:

> Speak roughly to your little boy,
> And beat him when he sneezes:

> He only does it to annoy,
>> Because he knows it teases.
>
> I speak severely to my boy,
>> And beat him when he sneezes:
> For he can thoroughly enjoy
>> The pepper when he pleases!

Before tackling the question of *who* wrote the poem that this parodies, we must consider the question of *what* poem it parodies. When Florence Milner wrote "The Poems in 'Alice in Wonderland' " (*The Bookman*, September 1903), she took for granted that "Speak Roughly" poked fun at a sentimental poem, "Speak Gently," enormously popular in Victorian England and also in the United States. "There is evidently some uncertainty as to the author of this poem," she writes, "for it occasionally appears as anonymous, but is generally credited as below." She then quotes eight stanzas (omitting the next-to-last stanza, a common practice in reprintings of "Speak Gently"), followed by the by-line G. W. Langford.

The editors of *The Lewis Carroll Handbook* (1931), and John F. McDermott in his introduction to *The Collected Poems of Lewis Carroll* (1929), also credit the poem to Langford. It seems likely they merely echoed Milner. I, too, accepted Milner's creditation in a note on "Speak Roughly" for the first edition of my *Annotated Alice*.

However, when John Shaw was writing a monograph on the parodies, he was puzzled by his inability to find a printed version of the poem, earlier than Milner's, which bore Langford's name; indeed, he was unable to find Langford. Contrariwise, *Granger's Index to Poetry* and *Bartlett's Familiar Quotations* both credited "Speak Gently" to one David Bates. Further research led Shaw to two books in which "Speak Gently" appears.

The Eolian by David Bates (Philadelphia, 1849) is a collection of poems privately published by the author. "Speak Gently," with nine stanzas, appears on page 15. *The Poetical Works of David Bates*, edited by his son, Stockton, was privately published in Philadelphia in 1870, the year the elder Bates died. "Speak Gently" is on page 18.

A brief entry in *Appleton's Cyclopedia of American Biography* (Appleton, 1888) reads:

> **BATES, David,** author, b. in Philadelphia, Pa., about 1810; d. there, 25 Jan., 1870. He was the author of numerous meritorious poems, many of which were published in book form under the title "The Eolian." . . . He was the author of the well-known poem "Speak Gently," about which, shortly after its publication, there was a notable controversy and counterclaims as to its authorship. "Childhood" is another of his best-known pieces. A complete edition of his poems was edited by his son (Philadelphia, 1870).

Obituary notices were found by Shaw in the *Philadelphia Public Ledger* and the *Philadelphia Inquirer,* January 27, 1870. The second is the more informative:

> Mr. David Bates, a well-known Philadelphia broker and poet, died in this city on Thursday in the 61st year of his age. He was a native of Ohio, and came to this city many years ago, where he started in business as a banker, and was of the firm of Boyd and Bates. He was well known in literary circles. He was the author of many well-known poems, some of which are now standard literature, among these one, "Speak Gently," has a world-wide reputation — it was written for this paper. He was a contributor to *Sartain's Magazine, Godey's Lady's Book, Van Court's Magazine,* and other prominent periodicals of the day. He was a member of the Board of Brokers, in which association he was known by the familiar name of "Old Mortality." A wife and family are left to mourn his loss.

To this information, Stockton Bates, in the introduction to his father's poetical works, adds the following information.

David Bates was born at Indian Hill, Hamilton County, Ohio, March 6, 1809. He lived on a farm until he was fourteen, when he set out to seek his fortune. He had learned to play the flute, and apparently tramped about on foot, playing the flute on street corners and taking odd jobs here and there. For a short time in Buffalo he was befriended by a man he had known in Ohio. The unnamed friend sent young Bates to school for a few months, then died. Bates walked from Buffalo to Indianapolis, where he got a job with a mercantile firm and eventually rose to the post of buyer. His job required frequent visits to the East, where he "became acquainted in Philadelphia and subsequently made it his home."

Stockton goes on to state that his father "wrote for most of the prominent magazines and periodicals, and enjoyed the confidence and appreciation of men of letters." But no mention is made of where a single poem in *The Eolian* was first published. "Speak Gently" is singled out as the book's best-known poem, and "Childhood" is cited as the only other poem to have attained a "world-wide reputation." Because of its translation into other languages, Stockton adds, "Speak Gently" has become "almost a universal hymn." He praises his father as a man with "high regard for the beautiful and good," whose prose was never marred by "a single impure or profane word," and who "sought not fame, but wrote for the pleasure it gave him, and for the good he hoped to do."

When I learned of David Bates, from Shaw's monograph, it seemed to me that the matter had been laid to rest. In the second printing of my *Annotated Alice* I credited the poem to Bates and reproduced the nine stanzas as they appear in *The Eolian.* Roger Green, who had discovered Bates on his own, attributes "Speak Gently" to Bates in his 1962 revision of *The Handbook.*

Then, suddenly, information about Langford surfaced. In 1969 Shaw received a letter from Frederick Langford of Pasadena, California, informing him that his great-grandfather was a brother of George Washington Langford, none other than the second claimant to "Speak Gently." Shaw's correspondence with Langford threw enough doubt on Bates's authorship to prompt Shaw to write an amusing paper on the matter, "Who Wrote 'Speak Gently'?"[1]

G. W. Langford, Shaw tells us, was born in Carlow County, Ireland, in 1824. After being brought to the United States in 1835, he lived with his family in Huron, Erie County, Ohio, until sometime between 1841 and 1843. From then until his death in 1849 at age twenty-five, he was with his uncle in Schuyler County, Illinois, except for a visit to Ireland in 1845. He never married. His only other known poem, "The Absent One," has an Irish locale. There is a strong tradition in the Langford family that he wrote both this poem and "Speak Gently" during his visit to Ireland.

Florence Milner's remarks about "Speak Gently" suggest many pre-1900 references to Langford as the author, but so far only three early printings of the poem have been found with Langford's by-line.[2] The British Museum has a piece of sheet music bearing all nine stanzas (music by Mrs. Mounsey Bartholomew), with the lyrics attributed to George Washington Longford *[sic]*. The sheet is undated, but the museum acquired it in 1862. Five stanzas of the poem are in J. E. Carpenter's *Songs: Sacred and Devotional* (London: Frederick Warne, 1865), credited to "G. W. Langford." The book refers to music by "Miss Lindsay," published by R. Cocks and Company, but no date is given. McGuffey's *Third Eclectic Reader* (New York, 1879) contains the poem, with the by-line "G. W. Hangford" *[sic]*. At the time Shaw wrote his *Jabberwocky* article, only one printing of the poem, earlier than *The Eolian*, was known. All nine stanzas appear on page 256 of *Sharpe's London Magazine*, February 1848, but no author is named.

My interest in the matter was minimal until a few years ago when I found on sale in a flea market a tiny book (4½ by 2½ inches) of temperance verse called *The Temperance Token, or Crystal Drops from the Old Oaken Bucket.* It had been edited by Kate Barclay and published by George H. Derby & Co., Geneva, N.Y., 1847. The nine stanzas of "Speak Gently" appear anonymously on pages 78-79. The book's copyright was entered in 1846. This is the earliest known book printing of the entire poem.

I was unable to find the poem in any previous anthology of temperance verse, although I had access to a very limited number of such books. Kate Barclay had earlier edited an anthology of Odd Fellows verse. It does not include "Speak Gently," but it occurred to me that Kate may have found the poem either in a temperance or an Odd Fellows periodical. A spotty search of temperance magazines failed to unearth it, but in leafing through *The Golden Rule*, an Odd Fellows weekly published in New York City, I hit the jackpot. "Speak Gently," with no by-line, is on page 120 of volume 2 (August 16, 1845). The volume's index lists it under "Poetry—original," so it could be a first printing. The stanzas are as follows:[3]

Speak gently!—it is better far
 To rule by love, than fear—
Speak gently—let not harsh words mar
 The good we might do here!

Speak gently!—Love doth whisper low
 The vows that true hearts bind;
And gently Friendship's accents flow;
 Affection's voice is kind.

Speak gently to the little child!
 Its love be sure to gain;
Teach it in accents soft and mild:—
 It may not long remain.

Speak gently to the young, for they
 Will have enough to bear—
Pass through this life as best they may,
 'Tis full of anxious care!

Speak gently to the aged one,
 Grieve not the care-worn heart,
The sands of life are nearly run,
 Let such in peace depart!

Speak gently, kindly to the poor;
 Let no harsh tone be heard;
They have enough they must endure,
 Without an unkind word!

Speak gently to the erring—know,
 They may have toiled in vain;
Perchance unkindness made them so;
 Oh, win them back again!

Speak gently!—He who gave us life
 To bend man's stubborn will,
When elements were in fierce strife,
 Said to them, "Peace, be still."

Speak gently!—'tis a little thing
 Dropped in the heart's deep well;
The good, the joy which it may bring,
 Eternity shall tell.

  While Shaw was searching for early printings of "Speak Gently," he was struck by the number of poems he came across that had exactly the same rhyme and meter, and with opening lines that could have served just as well as the basis for Carroll's parody. For example, *The Children's Magazine* (New York, 1848) printed an anonymous poem "from the *Warder* (Irish)" called "Little Children."[4] It begins:

Speak gently to the little child,
  So guileless and so free,
Who with a trustful, loving heart,
  Puts confidence in thee.

Note that the line in the Bates-Langford poem closest to Carroll's open-ing line is the first line of the third stanza, whereas here the identical line opens the poem. Is it possible that *this* is the poem Carroll had in mind? To make matters worse, Shaw found dozens of other poems by English and American authors, all with appropriate opening lines, similar subject mat-ter, and written in quatrains with the same structure as "Speak Roughly." No less than ten poems, by ten different authors, begin "Speak gently . . .," eight start "Speak kindly . . .," and others open with "Speak softly . . .," "Speak not harshly . . .," and similar phrases.

"To so perceptive a person as Lewis Carroll," Shaw concludes his article, "this deluge of didactic verse must have been apparent, and the impression grew upon me that, just as each of these variants of a common theme seems but an echo of all the others, his parody may well be an echo of all of them rather than any one of them. It is true that the Bates-Langford version shows up more frequently in this list than any other, but this may be due to the fact that this is the poem for which both Frederick Langford and I have been searching."

In the absence of evidence that may turn up in letters or missing portions of Carroll's diary, we cannot be certain that Carroll specifically had the Bates-Langford poem in mind. However, I believe it can be said with confidence this poem did exceed all the others in popularity on both sides of the Atlan-tic. So far, no poem on Shaw's list has been traced to earlier than 1845. It seems reasonable to suppose that the great success of the Bates-Langford poem sparked the numerous later imitations, and that contemporary readers of the first *Alice* book would have taken "Speak Roughly" to be a parody of the Bates-Langford version.[5]

The strongest evidence for the enormous popularity of "Speak Gently" is the number of times it was set to music as a popular song, or included in a hymnal. I found two musical versions published in Boston in 1846, and one in Philadelphia in 1856.[6] All nine stanzas appear on each piece of sheet music, but no one is credited for the lyrics. Frederick Langford found ten different musical versions in the British Museum, all issued in England be-tween 1849 and 1864.

The poem's first appearance as a hymn, so far as I can discover, was in *A Book of Hymns*, compiled by Samuel Longfellow and Samuel Johnson, published in Cambridge, Massachusetts (Metcalf and Co., 1846).[7] This is the first known book publication of "Speak Gently," although only five stan-zas are given. There is no music and no by-line. The same five stanzas, credited to "Bates," are in Henry Ward Beecher's *Plymouth Collection of Hymns and*

Tunes (A. S. Barnes, 1855). I have already mentioned the inclusion of the five stanzas in Carpenter's 1865 anthology, published in London, where they are credited to Langford. In 1871, stanzas 1, 3, 5, 6 appeared anonymously as hymn 33 in *Pure Gold for the Sunday School*, edited by Robert Lowry and W. Howard Doane (Biglow and Main). Three of the five stanzas entered the first *Christian Science Hymnal* (1892) and have been in the church's hymnal ever since, although the musical setting has varied.[8]

Why has the poem so completely vanished from the pop culture of English-speaking lands?[9] Is it because our age is not one that admires gentleness? Do we prefer to speak roughly, not just to babies when they sneeze but to everybody the poem asks us to treat with gentleness? Is it because medical science has rendered quaint the line "it may not long remain" and that references to the "good we may do here" and the rewards awaiting us in eternity have become equally anachronistic? The poem is obviously doggerel, but that is not the point. We have to ask why millions of people were emotionally stirred by the poem a hundred years ago, whereas today the poem is remembered only because Lewis Carroll probably parodied it.

Let's go back to the question of who wrote "Speak Gently." Langford's case suffers from a failure to find his name linked to any printing of the poem earlier than Bates's 1849 book. On the other hand, Langford's death in 1849 (assuming he did indeed write the poem) could explain why Bates's authorship was not immediately contested. The efforts of Langford's relatives to establish his claim seem to have developed much later. Although *Appleton's Cyclopedia* speaks of controversy and counterclaims, I have been unable to find any published record of such controversy. Is it buried in old newspaper files? Did it exist only in private letters?

The chief evidence favoring Bates is, of course, that the poem is in two of his books. But there are suspicious aspects. We know that by 1849 the poem was already famous. It had been set to music at least twice in America, it was being sung in churches, it had appeared in at least two book collections, and it had been published as early as 1845 in an Odd Fellows journal.[10] In view of the poem's popularity, one would have expected Bates to have indicated when he wrote it and where it was first published. There is not a line in his book about where *any* of his poems had earlier appeared. His son is equally uninformative. By 1870, when Stockton Bates edited his father's poems, there surely had been controversy of some sort over the authorship of "Speak Gently." Stockton makes no mention of such controversy, nor as mentioned before does he divulge when and where the poem had first been published.

One obituary of the elder Bates states that the poem had been written for the *Philadelphia Inquirer*. If the poem could be found in this paper prior to August 16, 1845 (the date of its publication in *The Golden Rule*) with Bates's by-line, his claim would be enormously strengthened. If it cannot be found in the *Inquirer*, or if it appeared there after the date of *The Golden Rule*, his case would be enormously weakened.

A check should also be made of the periodicals mentioned in Bates's obituary to see if any of his other poems actually did appear in them. And are there surviving descendants of Bates who may own family letters or other documents bearing on the question?[11]

The odds, it seems to me, still favor Bates. But we should not forget that a respectable man, well liked in his community, is capable, under certain circumstances, of falsely claiming the authorship of a popular poem. A classic instance is provided by George Whitefield D'Vys, of Cambridge, Massachusetts, who claimed to be the author of "Casey at the Bat." The poem had been written by Ernest Lawrence Thayer and published in 1888 in a humor column Thayer was then writing for the *San Francisco Examiner*. The column was signed "Phin," Thayer's nickname.

Nobody knew who Phin was, so no name was attached to the poem when it was widely reprinted. The actor De Wolf Hopper began reciting it, and for five years even he did not know who wrote the poem. It was during this period that D'Vys proclaimed himself the author. I own a copy of a rare little booklet, *Casey at the Bat and Other Mudville Ballads*, which D'Vys had printed in Cambridge. It opens with Thayer's poem, followed by ten other ballads about Casey, all worthless. I have some letters written by D'Vys, shortly before his death, in which he speaks so convincingly of his authorship of "Casey" that one suspects the poor fellow actually believed it.

It is not hard to understand how such a deception can come about. An anonymous piece of doggerel, for reasons poorly understood and beneath the dignity of critics to investigate, suddenly becomes enormously popular. It is widely reprinted. It is set to music, almost everybody quotes it, many people memorize it, no one knows who wrote it. A humble versifier, Mr. X, who has been churning out his own doggerel and failing to get it printed, is having a few snorts in a local saloon. Someone quotes the famous poem. In a boozy moment of ego-boosting, Mr. X allows that it was *he* who penned those immortal lines. The rumor spreads. Soon the community is convinced that their local bard is indeed the author. It is too late to deny it. Mr. X is stuck with his story.

A few years later the situation has grown uncomfortable. There are doubters. Counterclaims are in the air, but no hard evidence. Finally, to bolster his shaky claim, Mr. X publishes his own book of verse for the primary purpose of including the famous poem that he did not write, and whose author he still may not know.

Is it possible that Bates was such a claimant? It is. It is also possible that neither he *nor* Langford wrote "Speak Gently." It is possible we will never know who did. On the other hand, somewhere in the dusty stacks of libraries, or recorded on the microfilm of old newspapers, there may be statements that will solve the mystery.

I would like to thank John Shaw for his great help in preparing this article. Needless to add, we would be pleased to hear from anyone who comes upon the slightest scrap of information that sheds light on this frivolous but nagging question.

POSTSCRIPT

The riddle of who wrote "Speak Gently" remains unanswered, but some fascinating new details have come to light.

Although for more than two decades I wrote a column on mathematics for *Scientific American*, it was the last magazine I would have thought to check for an early publication of the poem. A few years ago the magazine reprinted the four pages of its first issue, vol. 1, no. 1, August 28, 1845. To my amazement, all nine stanzas of "Speak Gently," without a by-line, are on page 3. The issue's date is only twelve days later than *The Golden Rule*'s. Both journals probably picked up the poem from an earlier source.

The Pierpont Morgan Library, in Manhattan, owns an undated autograph album that had belonged to Mrs. James T. Fields, probably the wife of James Thomas Fields of Ticknor and Fields, a house that published all the major poets of the day. In it is a handwritten "Speak Gently," signed by "Your friend, David Bates." The nine stanzas are identical, including every punctuation mark, with the poem as it appeared in *The Golden Rule*.

The poem that most resembles "Speak Gently" is "Think Gently," by Julia A. Fletcher. Its first book publication is believed to be *The Juvenile Gem* (New York, 1846). I quote below the poem as I found it in an anonymous, undated book (an owner of the book dated it 1895), *Christian Lyrics* (London: Frederick Warne). The book also contains an anonymous "Speak Gently."

> Think gently of the erring:
>   Ye know not of the power
> With which the dark temptation came
>   In some unguarded hour.
>
> Ye may not know how earnestly
>   They struggled, or how well,
> Until the hour of weakness came
>   And sadly thus they fell.
>
> Think gently of the erring:
>   Oh! do not thou forget,
> However darkly stained by sin,
>   He is thy brother yet;
>
> Heir of the selfsame heritage,
>   Child of the selfsame God,

He has but stumbled in the path
    Thou hast in weakness trod.

Speak gently to the erring:
    For is it not enough
That innocence and peace have gone,
    Without thy censure rough?

It sure must be a weary lot,
    That sin-stained heart to bear,
And those who share a happier fate
    Their chidings well may spare.

Speak gently to the erring:
    Thou yet may'st lead them back
With holy words and tones of love,
    From misery's thorny track:

Forget not thou hast often sinned,
    And sinful yet must be;
Deal gently with the erring, then,
    As God has dealt with thee.

A few years ago John Shaw and his assistant James Birchfield discovered that Julia's poem appeared in the *Pennsylvania Inquirer and National Gazeter*, February 7, 1845, page 1, column 9. This is six months before the earliest known printing of "Speak Gently," but which poem was published first is anybody's guess. To add to the confusion, A. Leonard reported in *Jabberwocky* (official organ of England's Lewis Carroll Society), Winter, 1975, that Julia's poem is hymn number 674 in *The Hymn Book for Primitive Methodist Sunday Schools* (London: 1899), where it is credited to G. W. Hangford!

Frederick Langford informed me that G. W. Langford's poem "The Absent One," was set in type in Ireland, the galleys dated 1845, but it is not known if it was actually printed. The long poem expresses Langford's disappointment at arriving in Ireland, expecting to see his younger brother, Benjamin Franklin Langford, and finding that he had gone to India. The brother had two books of poems printed in India before he returned to London.

David Bates's son, Stockton, who edited his father's posthumous collection of verse, also was a poet. I first learned this when I acquired a bound volume of three books in a series titled *100 Choice Selections*, published in Philadelphia by P. Garrett and Company. It contains numbers 28, 29, and 30. I bought it because "Speak Gently," credited to David Bates, is in No. 29 (dated 1890) headed by: "This beautiful and well known poem, was published in Philadelphia in 1845." Each of the three issues contains two poems by Stockton Bates, suggesting he may have had a hand in editing the volumes. The National Union Catalog lists two books of poetry by Stockton Bates: *Dream Life and Other Poems*, and *Introspective Thoughts on Birth, Life and Death,* both published in 1872. The books must be extremely rare. He was, by the way, a better poet than his father.

Now for a few more curious odds and ends:

A poem called "Words of Kindness" (it begins: "Oh speak unto the erring in words of kindness only . . . ") appeared in *Eliza Cook's Journal* (February 25, 1853) with the by-line John Alfred Langford. This was discovered by Shaw, who could find no connection between the author and G. W. Langford.

An undated scrapbook that I bought at an antiques fair is filled with poems clipped from undated newspapers. One poem is "Speak Gently" (first stanza omitted). The author is given as Thomas Sutherland, and a note at the end says "New York 1854." The scrapbook contains two other poems by Sutherland, one with the same "New York 1854" entry, the other, "Baltimore 1854." The newspaper may have used this as a fake name when they pirated anonymous verse. At any rate, neither Shaw nor I could find any records of a poet with that name.

Hillard's Fourth Reader, New Series, edited by G. S. Hillard (Boston: Brewer and Tileston, 1863) contains six stanzas of "Speak Gently" with eleven footnotes explaining the meaning of certain words.

A Milwaukee quarterly I ran across, *Christmas Ideals* (vol. 16, October 1859), devotes a page to six stanzas of "Speak Gently." It is credited to David Bates and surrounded by an illustration in color. A note at the bottom says: "Our sincere thanks to the author whose address we were unable to discover."

Frederick Langford, who has done extensive research on early printings of "Speak Gently" in England, and to whom I am indebted for many details, tells me that he has never found the name of David Bates on any published form of the poem in England. In books, magazines, and sheet music it is either credited to Langford or left anonymous.

Both Langford and Shaw have searched through the *Philadelphia Inquirer* for 1843-1845 without finding the poem, or any other poem signed by David Bates. Langford did find a long poem in 1845 credited to "D.B."

NOTES

1. Shaw's paper, which first circulated among his friends in 1971, was printed in *Jabberwocky,* no. 11 (Summer 1972).

2. *The Cyclopedia of Practical Quotations,* J. K. Hoyt (Funk and Wagnalls, 1896), credits a stanza of "Speak Gently" to G. W. Langford. The 1948 edition of *Bartlett's* names Langford as the author of a quotation from the poem, but this was the result of letters from the Langford family after a previous edition had credited the line to Bates. Later editions revert to Bates.

3. All nine of these stanzas are reprinted word for word in *The Eolian,* with identical punctuation except for a comma after "kindly" (stanza 6), and after "joy" (stanza 9). Ms. Barclay's version contains many punctuation changes. The third line of stanza 8 is altered to: "When elements were fierce with strife."

4. This poem is included in Mary J. Reed's *The Rosemary: A Collection of Sacred and Religious Poetry* (1848), and in many later anthologies such as Caroline May's *The American Female Poets* (1849), Thomas Buchanan Read's *The Female American Poets* (1852), and the anonymously edited *Home Scenes, or Lights and Shadows of the Christian Home* (1865).

5. In searching for book printings of "Speak Gently," not on Shaw's list, I found the following volumes of special interest:

Heavenly Thoughts for Morning Hours, selected by Lady Catherine Long (London: James Nisbet, 1851). All nine stanzas are given anonymously. The book I checked was a twelfth edition.

Analytical Fourth Reader, ed. Richard Edwards (New York: Taintor, 1867). "It requires soft tones and medium pitch," Edwards writes in introducing the anonymous selection, "and must be spoken slowly. . . . You also need to use clear tones, of pure quality, in reading this piece because the sentiments expressed are beautiful and good."

The Household Treasury of Christian Knowledge and Gems of Sacred Poetry. This is a massive, anonymously edited volume of more than five hundred pages, published in Philadelphia by Carson and Simpson, 1890. "Speak Gently," with no by-line, is on p. 40.

Heart Throbs, compiled by Joe Mitchell Chapple (Boston: Chapple, 1905). This anthology of sentimental verse was so well received that it ran through endless editions, not to mention its sequel, *More Heart Throbs*. Six stanzas of "Speak Gently," credited to Bates, are in *Heart Throbs* on p. 432.

6. One 1846 version, published by Oliver Ditson, sets the poem to previously published music by Irish violinist and composer William Vincent Wallace, with a special arrangement for guitar by E. B. Bohuszewicz. The other 1846 version has music arranged for pianoforte by Joseph Bird. The 1856 version, published by John March, has music by G. A. Morse.

7. Samuel Longfellow, brother of Henry Wadsworth Longfellow, was a Unitarian minister. An enlarged collection of *A Book of Hymns* (Ticknor, Reed and Fields, 1848) was so well received that by 1866 it was in its fifteenth edition. "Speak Gently" (stanzas 1, 4, 5, 7, 9) is Hymn 285 in all editions.

8. In the 1892 hymnal, stanzas 1, 7, 9 of "Speak Gently" are set to the tune "Evan" by William H. Havergal. No author is credited. In 1910 the same stanzas appear, set to "Sawley," a melody by James Walch, with lyrics credited to G. W. Langford. The present hymnal, first published in 1932, contains the hymn with two settings: one is the "Sawley" tune, the other "The Sarum Gradual" of 1527, arranged by Sir H. Walford Davies. Lyrics are credited to David Bates.

Hymnal Notes (1933), a companion to the 1932 *Christian Science Hymnal*, has an informative note on "Speak Gently." After stating that the poem had appeared unsigned in *Sharpe's London Magazine*, 1848, the note goes on to say: "It has been attributed to George Washington Hangford, misspelled Langford in the 1910 Hymnal. But it was written by an American poet, David Bates." (I am indebted to A. W. Phinney, of the committee on publication, First Church of Christ, Scientist, Boston, for this information.)

9. Not entirely. The poem turns up in A. L. Alexander's *Poems That Touch the Heart* (Garden City, N.Y., 1941), where it is credited to G. W. Langford; and in Michael R. Turner's *Parlour Poetry: A Casquet of Gems* (New York: Viking, 1969).

10. A short story by Timothy Shay Arthur, a prolific American writer of mid-nineteenth-century pious Christian fiction, provides another indication of how well the poem was known in 1849. A story called "Speak Gently," in Arthur's *Sketches of Life and Character* (J. W. Bradley, 1850), is based on the poem and is headed by the poem's first stanza. No poet is credited. In his 1849 introduction, Arthur states that every piece in the book had appeared earlier in a magazine or newspaper, many of them anonymously, but I was unable to run down the story's earlier printing.

11. It is probably sheer coincidence, but Langford lived in Huron, Ohio, from 1835 until 1843, and Stockton Bates writes that his father, when a young man, once lived in Sandusky, a town very close to Huron, an industrial suburb of Sandusky. It was in Sandusky that Bates met the unnamed friend who later paid for his schooling in Buffalo. Did young Bates also meet a youth, then in his teens, named George Washington Langford?

18

Kickshaws: A Miscellany of Word Play

Major Minor

John Train's *Remarkable Names of Real People* (Clarkson Potter, 1977) lists Major Minor, of the United States Army. The name is odd enough, but is it particularly rare? I think not; the surname Minor appears a little more often than once in every ten thousand names in Social Security files, and surely there are (or have been in the past two hundred years) considerably more than ten thousand majors in the United States Army. In fact, restricting attention to West Point graduates before 1959, Minors were in the classes of 1937, 1945, and 1946.

A stranger story surfaced in the *New York Times* of September 18, 1972 — it reported a man named Minor W. Major among the guests at a conference of corporation presidents. How did he get his name? "Before the Civil War, a young woman named Minor married a young man named Major and became Mrs. Major. He was a Confederate agent and he sank Union shipments on the Mississippi. He had a Yankee uniform for use at certain times, and in those circumstances Minor Major, the Confederate agent, became Major Minor, a Union officer. I'm a great-grandson of the Major who married Miss Minor," Minor W. Major said.

P. G. Wodehouse created a delightful bit of nonsense using these words in *Uncle Dynamite* (Didier, New York, 1948). In order to gain entrance to a country estate, Lord Ickenham passed himself off as Major Brabazon-Plank, an old school chum. When challenged by Constable Potter, who knew

---

This article originally appeared in *Word Ways*, February, 1981, and is reprinted with permission.

the real Brabazon-Plank quite well, Ickenham quickly shifted ground and claimed to be an elder brother instead:

> Potter: He (Bill Oakshott) give me your suitcase to take to the house, and he said "This here belongs to Major Brabazon-Plank."
>
> Ickenham: Just a slip of the tongue, such as so often occurs. He meant Brabazon-Plank, *major*. As opposed to my brother, who, being younger than me, is, of course, Brabazon-Plank, *minor*. I can understand you being confused, and what renders it all the more complex is that, as I myself am a mining engineer by profession, anyone who wants to get straight on the Brabazon-Plank situation has got to keep steadily before him the fact that the major is a miner and the minor a major. I have known strong men to break down on realizing this. So you know my minor, the major, do you? Most interesting. It's a small world, I often say . . . Why are you looking like a stuck pig, Bill Oakshott?

Quickie Puzzles

Ten students enrolled for a class in number theory. To aid in remembering their names, the professor seated them in the following order. Can you determine the basis of his ordering?

Don Edwards
Robert Worden
Edith Reed
Rolf Oursler
Jeff Ives
Jessi Xander
Rose Ventnor
Leigh Thompson
Toni Nesbit
Pete Norris

In his little book, *Puzzling Posers* (London, 1952), J. Travers gives the five-by-five letter square reproduced below. The puzzle is to imagine a chess king placed on any letter and moved (by king moves) to spell out a familiar motto. Starting at the center T, the solution is TOO MANY COOKS SPOIL THE BROTH. Note that there are just sixteen different letters in this sentence. Is it possible to construct a four-by-four letter square that will do the same job? We assume that S and O may be counted twice in a row to produce the doublings in the motto.

```
Y  N  E  B  H
A  C  H  T  R
M  O  T  T  O
O  O  O  P  L
K  S  S  I  O
```

Alphabetical Pie

Several years ago, James Davis of Auburn, Washington, sent me the following logological curiosity. Write the letters of the alphabet in a circle, with Z followed by A. Cross out all letters that possess left-right symmetry. The remaining letters, starting with J and moving clockwise, fall into five distinct groups, containing 3, 1, 4, 1, and 6 letters — these are the first five digits in the representation of pi!

Anagrams

John Donne's poem, "The Anagram," contains the following couplet:

> Though all her parts be not in th' usuall place,
> She hath yet an anagram of a good face.

Norman Mailer, in his 1973 book about Marilyn Monroe, went out of his way to point out that if the A in Marilyn is used twice, the O in Monroe used just once, and the Y omitted, the remaining letters can be arranged to spell Norman Mailer. No one can deny that Norman and Marilyn were very close.

The Wall Street Journal reported on September 6, 1978, that a Florida-based company called Xonex, which makes motor oil, was being sued by Exxon for using the letters of its name in anagram form. Patrick J. McEnary, president of Xonex, said it never occurred to him that the two names were anagrams until he received a letter from an Exxon attorney; in fact, he thought the letter was a hoax.

Economical Signs

<pre>
        I
    T H I N K
    T H I N
        I N
        I N K
</pre>

The business card of Peer Clahsen, a Swiss artist and toy designer, is reproduced above. Words such as THINK are rich enough in shorter words spelled out in the same order to make sensible messages possible. What, in fact, is the most fecund word of this type? Obviously, it depends upon the length of the word and the dictionaries allowed. In the April 22, 1979, *Philadelphia Inquirer*, Theodore Bernstein quoted Leo G. Staley of Columbus, Ohio, as finding ten common words in SCAPEGOAT: scape, cap, cape, ape, peg, ego, go, goat, oat, at. Ralph Beaman added five more: ca', pe, and goa from

Webster's Third, and scap and eg from *Webster's Second*; subsequently, he discovered that FIRESTONE was an even better nine-letter choice. In similar vein, Boris Randolph of Los Angeles discovered twenty-two words in MISIN-FORMATION: Mi, mis, misinform, sin, is, in, inform, information, for, form, forma, format, formation, ma, mat, a, at, ati, ti, I, ion, on. Puckishly, he noted "The letter M IS IN FORMATION."

I have been in tall buildings in which each men's room was indicated by a large brass M on the door, and each ladies' room by the same fixture installed upside down. Has anyone ever used a similar inversion device next to the buttons of an elevator: up and dn?

Carrollian Wordplay

Many readers are at least moderately familiar with Lewis Carroll's word-play—his word-games (Doublets, Mischmasch, and Syzygies, all explained in detail in John Fisher's *The Magic of Lewis Carroll* [Simon and Schuster, 1973]), his anagramming (William Ewart Gladstone = Wilt tear down all images?), and his acrostic poems. Here are a couple of less well known examples. In a letter that Lewis Carroll wrote in about 1862 to a little girl named Annie Rogers, he said he was enclosing

> A picture, which I hope will
> Be one that you will like to
> See. If your Mamma should
> Desire one like it, I could
> Easily get her one.

What is unusual about the construction above?

The following poem by Lewis Carroll turned up in an obscure publication called *The Lewis Carroll Circular*, No. 2, November 1974:

> I often wondered when I cursed,
> Often feared where I would be—
> Wondered where she'd yield her love,
> When I yield, so will she.
> I would her will be pitied!
> Cursed be love! She pitied me . . .

Why is this poem so remarkable?

Lewis Carroll's real name was Charles Lutwidge Dodgson. He was fond of using pseudonyms on letters and poems that he sent to various periodicals. Once he used the initials R.W.G. Can you see why? Answers to all three problems can be found at the end of this chapter.

I think Lewis Carroll would have been intrigued by the following collo-quy generated by Roberto J. Pick of Manhattan:

> Where are you going?
> To the movies.
> What are you going to see?
> Quo Vadis.
> What does that mean?
> Where are you going?
> To the movies.
> What are you going to see? . . .

and so on ad infinitum, with questioner and answerer alternating roles.

And Other Authors . . .

It is widely assumed that Rex Stout based his character of Nero Wolfe on Sherlock Holmes's stout brother, Mycroft, and there has even been speculation by Baker Street Irregulars that Nero was Mycroft's illegitimate son. The critic Leon Edel has noted that Rex means "king" in Latin, and Nero is the name of a Roman emperor. Both Nero and Wolfe, said Edel, "throw off ripples of evil" and is it a coincidence that Wolfe's assistant is named *Good*-win? Did Stout, as his *New York Times* obituary suggested, derive the name Nero Wolfe from Sherlock Holmes in the manner indicated below?

S H E R L O C K   H O L M E S
(N)   E R O   (W) O L (F) E

Someone should pull together all the wordplay in the writings of Poe. In the story "King Pest," a man with the initials H. T. (Hugh Tarpaulin) gets the best of T. H. (Tim Hurlygurly). In "A Tale of the Ragged Mountains," a man named Bedlo dreams of the death of a man named Oldeb. Poe was fond of such letter reversals, and there are other instances in both his fiction and his poe-etry.

In *Finnegans Wake* there are ten great thunderclap words, each 100 letters long, except for the last one, which has 101 letters. There are ten letters in the name James Joyce, and I suppose the 1,001 letters of the thunderclaps may have something to do with the Thousand and One Tales of the *Arabian Nights*. Is it possible that Joyce's thunderclaps conceal a coded message of some sort? Probably not, but Joyce had an interest in ciphers; J. F. Byrne, an intimate of Joyce's who devised the still-unsolved Chaocipher, was a model for Cranly in *Portrait of the Artist as a Young Man*, and his Dublin address, 7 Eccles Street, was the home of Leopold and Molly Bloom in *Ulysses*. It might be worthwhile for logophiles to investigate the thunderclaps in depth. Years ago, I wrote the ten words in order, each below the earlier one, to make a 10 × 1000 rectangle (omitting the final letter). The longest word I could find by reading vertically, top down, was NUDES, but I assume this is accidental. There are lots of concealed horizontal words that obviously are not accidental.

F. Scott Fitzgerald also enjoyed wordplay. The italicized purple passages in *This Side of Paradise* are poems concealed as prose, and I think it is no accident that the novel begins "Amory Blaine . . ." The initials A.B. signify, I suspect, both the A.B. degree Amory Blaine obtained at Princeton, and the fact that after graduation he starts to learn his ABCs. In one of Fitzgerald's novels, for no apparent reason, we read about "A man named Biloxi. 'Blocks' Biloxi, and he made boxes—that's a fact—and he was from Biloxi, Mississippi." The wordplay is rather feeble compared, say, to that in Nabokov, but can you guess the novel in which Mr. Biloxi from Biloxi appears?

The Oz books by L. Frank Baum are a happy hunting ground for word-play enthusiasts because of their many invented names for persons and places and things. For instance, in *The Magic of Oz*, the all-consonant word PYRZQXGL, if pronounced correctly, enables one to change oneself into any animal desired. I once tried to guess how Baum arrived at this word. Note that the consecutive-letter sequence PQR occupies the first, fifth and third positions of the word, and the consecutive-letter sequence XYZ the sixth, second and fourth positions—a mirror image. The last two letters do not partake of this symmetry, but GL might stand for GLinda, one of the good witches of Oz. It would be easy to write an entire book about Baum's wordplay, not to mention the later Oz books written by Ruth Plumly Thompson and others.

Frank Harary, a well-known mathematician at the University of Michigan, is coauthor of a book titled *Graphical Enumeration*. In the book, he discusses some results by mathematicians Ronald Read and E. M. Wright. A footnote states, however, that Read and Wright are both wrong. John Simon, writing about movie critic Rex Reed in his book *Paradigms Lost*, has a chapter titled "Why Reed Can't Write."

Acronymania

P. Howard Lyons of Toronto tells me he is the manager and treasurer of the Association of Creators of Really Original Names Yielding Meaning. The members, he says, are trying to devise an appropriate acronym for their organization, but haven't yet found one. This reminds me of Ruth Eisendrath's remark to me years ago that she was writing a satire on James Stephens's novel *The Crock of Gold* but couldn't think of a good title for it. And *that* in turn reminds me of Tom Wicker's May 14, 1978, newspaper column, where, in reply to various feminist proposals for single words that combine *he* and *she,* he suggested a one-word contraction for *she, he,* and *it.*

Floridians tell me that CALIF stands for Come And Live In Florida, and FLA means Flee Los Angeles.

Russell Baker, in his newspaper column of April 23, 1977, pointed out that the acronym of Moral Equivalent Of War is MEOW.

Answers

Quickie Puzzles: The names contain the integers from one through ten: dON Edwards, roberT WOrden, ediTH REEd, rolF OURsler, jeff IVEs, jesSI Xander, roSE VENtnor, lEIGH Thompson, toNI NEsbit, and peTE Norris.

A four-by-four square in which "too many cooks spoil the broth" can be spelled out is given below. No doubt others can be found.

```
L  T  K  S
H  I  O  P
E  R  M  C
B  A  N  Y
```

Carrollian Wordplay: The initial sounds of each line are phonetically equivalent to a, b, c, d, and e. The poem is a 6-by-6 word square in which the individual elements are words instead of letters. R W G are the fourth letters in Charles Lutwidge Dodgson.

And Other Authors: Mr. Biloxi can be found in Chapter 7 of *The Great Gatsby*.

POSTSCRIPT

Although the major emphasis in my Mathematical Games column, which ran for twenty-five years in *Scientific American*, was on recreational mathematics, I devoted many columns to word pastimes, not to mention the linguistic play that entered into columns about the numerologist Dr. Matrix. I edited the Dover edition of C. C. Bombaugh's classic *Oddities and Curiosities of Words and Literature*, adding lots of new material in my notes at the back of the book. And I wrote an introduction to H. E. Dudeney's only book of word play when it was reprinted by Scribner's in 1968 as *300 Word Puzzles*.

"Kickshaws" is the heading of a feature that appears in each issue of *Word Ways*, a quarterly journal devoted to recreational linguistics. The feature serves as a catch-all for unrelated short items. When Ross Eckler, the editor, asked me to write the feature for the February, 1981, issue, I pulled from my files the foregoing material, which had not found suitable places in my *Scientific American* columns.

Dmitri Borgmann is the author of two indispensable references for wordplay buffs, *Language on Vacation* (1965) and *Beyond Language* (1967), both published by Scribner's. Willard Espy followed with *The Game of Words* (Grosset and Dunlap, 1971), *An Almanac of Words at Play* (Clarkson Potter, 1975), and *Another Almanac of Words at Play* (Clarkson Potter, 1980). If you would like to subscribe to *Word Ways*, write to Ross Eckler, editor and publisher, Spring Valley Road, Morristown, NJ 07960.

19

Quantum Weirdness

Some is balls and some is strikes, but until I calls 'em, they ain't nothin'.
—Remark attributed to various big-league umpires

In the early eighteenth century the Anglican bishop George Berkeley (for whom, by the way, Berkeley, California, was named) startled the philosophical world by arguing, with great subtlety, that nothing can exist unless it is perceived by a mind. To be is to be perceived. Why, then, does a tree seem to keep existing when no one looks at it? Monsignor Ronald Knox expressed it this way:

> There once was a man who said: "God
> Must think it exceedingly odd
>   If he finds that this tree
>   Continues to be
> When there's no one about in the Quad."

The answer was supplied by an anonymous author in an equally famous limerick:

> Dear Sir, your astonishment's odd.
> *I* am always about in the Quad.
>   And that's why the tree
>   Will continue to be
> Since observed by yours faithfully, GOD.

This esssay originally appeared in *Discover*, October, 1982, and is reprinted with permission.

Berkeley restored the objective universe, in all its rich variety, by redefining matter as part of the mind of God. Indeed, he thought his philosophy provided a new proof of God's existence. Modern physicists hesitate to make this metaphysical jump, but in recent years a number of experts on quantum mechanics, notably the Nobel Prize-winner Eugene Wigner and John Wheeler of the University of Texas, have been defending a point of view curiously close to Berkeley's. Their position, which some physicists have called "quantum solipsism," has had a strong influence (much to Wheeler's dismay) on younger physicists and science writers who have dipped into Eastern religions and parapsychology. It has produced a spate of eccentric but popular books such as Fritjof Capra's *The Tao of Physics*, Gary Zukov's *The Dancing Wu Li Masters*, Michael Talbot's *Mysticism and the New Physics*, and (the worst of the lot) *Space-Time and Beyond,* by Bob Toben and Fred Alan Wolf.[1]

Quantum solipsism is a response to the fact that quantum mechanics (QM)—a universally accepted mathematical theory that describes and predicts the properties and behavior of matter—is saturated with dazzling paradoxes that seem to suggest that the external world has no well-defined structure until minds observe it. It was quantum theory that established, for example, the dual nature of light, which can be described either as an energy wave or as a stream of quanta (tiny packets of energy). QM replaced the strict causal determinism of classical physics with statistical laws about events in which randomness is so fundamental that Einstein was forced to protest that he could not believe that God plays dice with the universe. Although the laws of QM have been confirmed with great accuracy, they also display what physicist Heinz Pagels, in his marvelous new book, *The Cosmic Code*, calls "quantum weirdness." It is a weirdness that springs from the dark mystery of what happens when the wave function of a quantum system is "reduced" or "collapsed" by the act of measurement.

In QM, the wave function is a mathematical expression that describes a particle (an electron or a photon, for example) or a system of particles (a molecule or a tree or a solar system) and how it changes in time. The function gives the probabilities that when the system is measured certain variables—such as position, velocity, momentum, energy, and spin—will acquire certain values. The probabilities are not the same as in, say, flipping a penny; it is only our ignorance of the many forces operating on the penny that makes it impossible to predict heads or tails with better than 50 percent accuracy. In the case of the particle there are no forces in or near the particle, no local "hidden variables," that cause it to acquire definite properties when it is measured. It is as if nature makes no decision about these properties until the instant of measurement, and then the decision is made by pure chance.

Unfortunately, QM also tells us that as soon as a wave function is reduced to definite values by measurement, the entire system, which now includes the measuring apparatus, acquires a new wave function that gives only probabilities for the properties that will be found if the entire system is measured. This leads directly to a notorious thought experiment known as the paradox of Schrödinger's cat (after Erwin Schrödinger, one of the giant architects of QM, who first proposed it).

Imagine a cat inside a closed opaque box. The box contains a radioactive substance that has a 50 percent chance of emitting an electron within a given time interval. The electron will produce a click in a Geiger counter, which in turn will trigger a mechanism that will kill the cat. Because the entire system has a wave function that gives only probabilities until the system is observed, QM seems to say that at the end of the time interval the cat is neither alive nor dead until someone looks into the box. This observation then collapses the wave function, and at that instant the cat acquires the definite property of being dead or alive. Before observation, aliveness and deadness are somehow, in a way nobody understands, fused with equal probability in the wave function that describes the cat-box system.

Suppose the box is opened by a friend of Wigner's, who sees whether the cat is alive or dead. The box, cat, and friend now form a larger quantum system with a more complex wave function in which the state of the cat and the state of the friend's mind are indefinite until observed by Wigner or someone else. Physicists call this the paradox of Wigner's friend. It leads to an infinite regress. If Wigner observes a friend who observes the cat, the total system of box-cat-friend-Wigner remains indefinite (the cat still not alive or dead) until observed by a third person, and so on. The regress is sometimes called the von Neumann catastrophe, because it seems to follow from a classic formalization of QM by the great Hungarian mathematician John von Neumann.

In his collection of essays, *Symmetries and Reflections* (1967), Wigner argues that the regress is *not* infinite. It ends as soon as a conscious mind interrupts the chain of wave-function reductions. Only a mind, so goes his reasoning, has the faculty of introspection that allows it to *know* that "I am in such and such a state." To be "even more painfully precise," Wigner adds, it is "my own consciousness, since I am the only observer, all other people being the object of my observations." A friend who observes the cat will know if the animal is alive or dead, but until Wigner observes his friend, the cat *for Wigner* is still in an indefinite state.

Wigner confesses that he finds even the permanence of such things as trees "profoundly baffling." Because a tree is a quantum system, it too seems to have no definite properties until its wave function is reduced by observation. Since for Wigner his own consciousness is the fundamental reality, objects that seem to be "out there" are little more than useful constructs inferred from the regularities of his experience. He quotes with approval a statement by Schrödinger: "Would it [the world] otherwise [without conscious observers] have remained a play before empty benches, not existing for anybody, thus quite properly not existing?"

Most physicists do not buy this collective solipsism. They believe there are final reductions of wave functions whenever a macro event (an event above the subatomic level) occurs that cannot be time-reversed, such as the death of a cat, the registering of a particle's bubble-chamber track on film, the sound recording of a Geiger-counter click. Although Wigner seldom invokes Berkeley, or any other philosopher who wrestled with similar problems, his views seem to force him to say that a tree has no definite properties, and therefore only a vague existence, until a conscious mind perceives it.

Wheeler, in numerous papers, has taken a similar though less extreme tack. QM does indeed force us to deny, he says, that on the micro (or subatomic) level there is an external world of precise structure, independent of minds. "No elementary phenomenon is a phenomenon until it is an observed phenomenon." In some strange sense the universe is what Wheeler calls a "participatory universe." We are not observing something out there, behind a thick glass wall, Wheeler says. We must shatter the glass and influence the state of what we see.

In Wheeler's stupendous cosmological vision, there is an infinity of oscillating universes continually being born in big bangs and eventually dying in big crunches. Each universe has its own set of physical constants that arise by chance from its fireball. These constants must be finely tuned to allow the formation of suns and planets, and even more carefully tuned to permit life. Indeed, Wheeler believes, life is so unlikely that we are probably the only intelligent life anywhere in the entire cosmos. Moreover, unless a universe is so finely tuned as to allow conscious minds to evolve, it cannot be observed and so is not really real in any strong sense. An unobserved photon has a vague kind of reality, yes; but for Wheeler it is of a "paler and more theoretic hue" than the reality of an observed photon.

The last quotation is from Wheeler's book *Frontiers of Time* (1978). In this book and elsewhere he proposes a fantastic new thought experiment known as the delayed-choice test. It is a variation of the famous experiment involving a screen with two slits. A photon comes through one slit (like a particle) if measured by one kind of detector, or through both (like a wave) if measured by another detector—an experiment that demonstrates the dual nature of light. Suppose, says Wheeler, we wait until the photon has gone through the screen, then quickly decide which detector to use. Will not our decision determine which of two events (passage through one or two slits) took place in the past?

There is no alteration of the past, Wheeler makes clear, but rather a bringing of the past into existence. Our choice of measuring instrument determines whether the photon has penetrated the screen like a particle going through one slit or like a wave going through two. But this, says Wheeler, is a misleading way to put it. The photon *has* no precise past until we measure it! Perhaps the entire universe is like a delayed-choice experiment. It starts with the singularity of the Big Bang, then grows larger and more complex until finally it creates a giant eye (our consciousness) by which it observes itself, and in this way "imparts tangible reality to even the earliest days of the universe."[2]

In the past few years Wheeler has stated his belief that "observation" in QM need not involve a mind. It can be made by instruments, such as a Geiger counter, a bubble chamber, a grain of silver bromide, the retina of an eye, and so on. Records left by such measurements are macro structures as unalterable by minds as rocks and trees. Only on the micro level does an unobserved structure have a reality of paler and more theoretic hue. Like Niels Bohr before him, Wheeler does not push his solipsism to the Wignerian point at which one is puzzled by the persistence of rocks and trees. Nevertheless, on the quantum level, which underlies everything else, reality for both Bohr and Wheeler remains rather formless until it interacts with macro objects that ultimately will be observed by minds.

No physicist denies that a quantum particle is a ghostly thing for which it is impossible to build consistent models using the spacetime of classical Einsteinian physics. There is a sense in which an electron does not "exist" until it is measured. Nobody knows if its wave function is linked to waves as real as water or sound waves, or whether the function is as fictitious as the probability function that tells us a die will show any face with equal probability when it is tossed, or whether the function describes some third kind of thing that nobody yet understands. But from the ghostliness of an electron it does not follow, at least for most physicists, that a stone or a tree is equally ghostly.

The notion of both Wheeler and Wigner that a universe without conscious observers cannot be said to exist in a strong sense, on its fundamental level, is surely laced with difficulties. Does a chimpanzee have enough consciousness to give full reality to a universe? And if a chimp does, why not a bird or a fish? As Einstein remarked at one of Wheeler's Princeton seminars, "It is difficult to believe that such a description [QM] is complete. It seems to make the world quite nebulous unless someone, like a mouse, is looking at it."

Suppose the mechanism in Schrödinger's box does not kill the cat but only chops off an ear. Is the cat's consciousness strong enough to cut the chain of wave-function reductions, or is a human mind needed to make definite what happened to the cat? Must we say that the universe was only partly real before life appeared, and is slowly becoming more real as life evolves higher forms of consciousness?

In recent years, as a result of new experiments, there has been a marked revival of interest in another famous paradox of QM. It is known as the EPR paradox, after the initials of Einstein and two younger friends, Boris Podolsky and Nathan Rosen, who collaborated on a paper about it in 1935.

The EPR paradox has many variants. One of the simplest involves two photons that speed off in opposite directions when an electron and its antimatter equivalent, a positron, annihilate each other. No matter how far apart they get—it could be millions of light-years—they remain "correlated" in the sense that certain of their properties have opposite values. If, for example, photon A is measured for its spin and the result is +1, the spin of photon B must be −1. Recall that a particle does not have a definite spin before it is measured. According to QM, the photon's wave function dictates that at the moment of measurement nature decides to give it a plus or minus spin with equal probability. Thus if you measure a stream of photons, you get a sequence of plus and minus spins that are as randomly distributed as the heads-tails sequence obtained by flipping a coin.

Now we are in a terrible predicament. How can measuring photon A collapse the wave function of B (thus giving it a spin opposite that of A's), which may be millions of light-years away and is connected in no known causal way with its twin? Many physicists hoped and believed that the two particles remain correlated because of hidden variables inside or near them, like the correlation between two spinning Frisbees that are simultaneously tossed in opposite directions, one with each hand. Alas, experiments that violate a beautiful but highly complex theorem discovered in 1965 by John Bell have ruled out all hidden variables as an explanation for particle correlation.

Bell's theorem provided a way of testing the EPR paradox in a laboratory, and since 1965 many such tests have confirmed the paradox. One of them was a sophisticated new experiment by French scientists reported in the July 30 issue of *Science*.[3] It is no longer a thought experiment. Somehow one particle "knows" instantly (or almost instantly) the outcome of a measurement of the other particle. In no way does this violate relativity's rule that energy and signals cannot go faster than light. You can no more send a coded message by correlated photons than you can send a message by transmitting a sequence of heads and tails generated by flipping a coin. If there were some way to force a photon to acquire a desired spin when it is measured, it would be easy to use photon correlations to send coded messages faster than light. But QM forbids such forcing because it would destroy the irreducible randomness that is at the heart of quantum theory.

Nevertheless, the EPR paradox does suggest that distant parts of the universe are connected in some peculiar way not yet understood, a way that permits quantum information to travel faster than light. The strangest explanation put forth so far comes from Costa de Beauregard, a respected French physicist who shares with Brian Josephson (the Welsh Nobel Prize-winner who abandoned physics many years ago to investigate Transcendental Meditation and the paranormal) the belief that QM is the key to the claimed phenomena of parapsychology.[4] Quantum information, says Beauregard, travels backward in time from photon A, when it is measured, to the instant the two particles were created. Then it goes forward in time to photon B, arriving there at the precise moment it left A!

The EPR paradox disturbed Einstein profoundly. That measuring a particle could collapse the wave function of another particle many miles away seemed to him as absurd as the collapse of a person in Paris when a witch doctor in Haiti stabs a doll. And there were other aspects of QM that troubled him. As a disciple of Spinoza, who believed that every event in nature is completely determined by prior causes, Einstein could not abide the absolute chance at the heart of QM. But most of all he objected to QM because it seems to imply that on its most fundamental level the universe does not have a structure independent of human minds.

During the last decades of Einstein's life, his misgivings about QM isolated him from colleagues, who spoke with sadness about their "lost leader." Today, now that the EPR paradox is being dramatically confirmed around the world, some phsyicists are beginning to worry about it as much as Einstein did. Is it possible that the old maestro's intuitions were not so foolish after all? At any rate, many young physicists are now working on ingenious theories designed to replace QM with a deeper theory in which QM becomes a limiting case, a kind of first approximation, somewhat as Newton's theory of gravity became a limiting case of general relativity. Newton's laws work well for the ordinary velocities and masses on earth. But they are not accurate enough to account for phenomena that involve massive stars and velocities close to the speed of light.

In several recent papers Wheeler has likened the measurement problem in QM to a game of Twenty Questions he once played with a group of prankish friends. Unknown to Wheeler, they had agreed to have no word in mind when he began questioning. They answered yes or no at random, but with the proviso each would have at least one word in mind that fitted all the previous answers. Eventually Wheeler and the group narrowed the word down to "cloud." The point is that, in terms of the game, the word did not exist until it was created by Wheeler's interaction with his friends.

It seems to me that the Twenty Questions analogy applies only to properties of particles, not to the reality behind those properties. A particle may indeed have no precise position or momentum until it is measured. It may not even have an exact path in the past. But unless one is an extreme solipsist, one must believe in some kind of structured reality supporting the properties that is as mind-independent as the tree no one observes.

Consider a rainbow. It is as observer-dependent as an electron. Nothing is "out there" that deserves to be called *the* rainbow. Each person sees a different bow, a bow that has no position in space until it is observed. In a sense the bow has no reality apart from its observation. On the other hand, the bow is mind-independent in the sense that it can be photographed. It is a pattern that rests firmly on a structure of relations between falling raindrops, light from the sun, and an eye or a camera lens. Even the green of a leaf depends on a set of relations between leaf, light, and an observer. In no way does this justify a solipsism that insists a leaf has no reality until it is observed, or that quantum waves and particles have no reality until observed.

Here is how Einstein, in an essay on "Physics and Reality," looked at the way scientists choose their words when they play the question game with nature: "The liberty of choice, however, is of a special kind; it is not in any way similar to the liberty of a writer of fiction. Rather, it is similar to that of a man engaged in solving a well designed word puzzle. He may, it is true, propose any word as the solution; but, there is only *one* word which really solves the puzzle in all its forms. It is an outcome of faith that nature—as she is perceptible to our five senses—takes the character of such a well formulated puzzle. The successes reaped up to now by science do, it is true, give a certain encouragement for this faith."

No physicist doubts that the micro level swarms with quantum weirdness. It springs from the fact that the waves of QM are mathematical fictions, abstract waves of probability in multidimensional spaces constructed solely to describe quantum systems. What sort of reality is behind those waves, and how it is structured, nobody knows. But most physicists agree with Pagels that only the micro world is weird. "Once information about the quantum world is irreversibly in the macroscopic world," he writes, "we can safely attribute objective significance to it—it can't slip back into the quantum never-never land."

I count myself among those who are unable to believe, as Einstein could not and most philosophers and physicists today cannot, that the universe, or a stupendous event like the explosion of a supernova, is dependent for its existence on being observed by such paltry creatures as you and me.

POSTSCRIPT

To see how a solipsistic interpretation of QM leads to backward causality, consider the following thought experiment.

Imagine that a counter records whether an electron is emitted by a radioactive substance within a certain time interval. Automatic machinery then withdraws the substance and takes a photograph, *A*, of the counter reading. Ten minutes later another photograph, *B*, is taken of the same reading. Picture *A* is automatically conveyed to one room, *B* to another. From Wigner's point of view the wave functions of both photographs remain indefinite until a conscious mind observes them. Suppose Wigner looks first at *B* and sees that an electron has been emitted. A week later Wigner's friend enters the other room and looks at *A*. Picture *A* must, of course, show the same reading. Somehow, when Wigner looked at *B* it collapsed the wave function of *A*, giving it a definite state even though *B* did not exist when *A* was taken!

Among paraphysicists who are basing experiments on the possibility that psychics can influence past events, the most notable is Helmut Schmidt. He uses electronic randomizers (based on radioactive decay) to generate random numbers. A recording is stored without being observed. At a later date, a copy of the original recording is played for a psychic who tries to influence it by PK (psychokinesis). Schmidt reports that significant deviations from chance are then found on both the original recording and the copy (they are, of course, identical). Presumably, if the original had been examined before the PK experiment, it would have shown no deviations from randomness. But because it was not observed, both the original and the copy remain in a vague state, though correlated with one another, until the psychic alters them by his observation.

"The implication seems to be that the effect can work backward in time," Schmidt told the *New York Times* (January 27, 1980), "and that is an outrageous idea from a conventional standpoint. But it may be that some quantum effects not yet understood could account for just such an outcome."

Schmidt works at the Mind Science Foundation, San Antonio, Texas, a foundation funded by Texas oilman William Thomas Slick, Jr. For my views on recent attempts to base psychic forces on QM see "Parapsychology and Quantum Mechanics" in *Science and the Paranormal*, edited by George O. Abell and Barry Singer (Scribner's, 1981).

A word more about the EPR paradox. It is customary for physicists who have little interest in philosophical interpretations of QM to "resolve" the paradox by pointing out that the two correlated particles should be thought of as a single quantum system. Measuring one particle collapses the entire system's wave function (or "rotates its state vector" if one adopts the language of Hilbert space), thereby providing information about both particles. But this merely restates the paradox. The mystery remains in the sense that only sheer magic seems available to explain how two particles, separated by millions of light-years and not causally connected, can remain correlated as part of a single system.

NOTES

1. The first edition of this large paperback (Dutton, 1975) was written by Bob Toben "in conversation with physicists Jack Sarfatti and Fred Wolf." Sarfatti refused to allow his name on the revised edition issued by Dutton in 1982. The cover says it is by Bob Toben and Fred Alan Wolf "in conversation with theoretical physicists." Wolf's *Taking the Quantum Leap,* published a year earlier by Harper & Row, is relatively sober, but in the new edition of Toben's monstrosity he is back again with the usual hogwash about how QM can explain spoon bending, levitation, thoughtography, and other specialties of today's psychic quacks.

2. Bishop Berkeley knew nothing, of course, about the theory of evolution. But the Genesis account of creation, which he accepted as accurate history, presents for Berkeley a problem similar to the one faced by Wheeler. Are we not told that God created nonliving things before he created animals and Adam? And would the creation of material things not give them some sort of reality distinct from God's thoughts and from the observations of created finite minds?

In the third of his *Three Dialogues Between Hylas and Philonous*, Berkeley argues that, although material objects preexisted in the Divine Mind, they acquired a stronger reality when they were "created" and a still stronger reality when they became perceived by finite minds. The material universe had, writes Berkeley, only a "relative or hypothetical existence if you please" until it "became perceptible to intelligent creatures." Berkeley does not say whether "intelligent creatures" means only Adam and Eve, or whether it includes the beasts who also have eyes and finite minds.

Most philosophers of science today agree with Hume that Berkeley's arguments "admit of no answer and produce no conviction." Nevertheless, Berkeley deals with many fundamental problems that are being debated all over again by philosophers of QM.

3. Arthur L. Robinson, "Quantum Mechanics Passes Another Test," *Science*, July 30, 1982, pp. 435-36.

4. See John Gliedman's sad interview with Josephson in *Omni,* July 1982, pp. 87 ff.

20

The Curious Case of Paul Feyerabend

How to formalize the rules by which science operates, and why those rules work, are deep questions in the philosophy of science. There is little agreement among experts, but almost without exception they regard scientific method as a rational procedure. Science, they are persuaded, makes authentic progress. Not only does it discover new "facts" about nature; it also formulates laws and theories that provide increasingly better explanations for observed facts, and increasingly better predictions about what will be observed in the future.

The most notorious dissenter from these commonplace views is Paul Karl Feyerabend (pronounced fire-a-bend with the accent on a long *a*). He was born in Vienna in 1924, and received the Iron Cross for his service in the German Army during World War II. After studying science in Vienna and London (it was in London that he and Imre Lakatos, an influential Hungarian philosopher who died in 1974, became good friends), he settled in California, where he has been teaching philosophy at the University of California, Berkeley, since 1958.

In recent years Feyerabend has become the guru for a vague, scattered group of admirers. Some are counterculture physicists who are involved in Eastern religions and parapsychology. Others are sociologists who are down on scientific "orthodoxy" and so reluctant to take strong stands on scientific controversies that they constantly berate the scientific community for not taking time to engage in serious debate with promoters of astrology, the cosmology of Velikovsy, and similar nonsense. In what follows I will use

This essay originally appeared in *Free Inquiry*, Winter 1982-83, and is reprinted with permission.

AM to identify page references in Feyerabend's first book, *Against Method* (1975), and SFS for its sequel, *Science in a Free Society* (1978). For several years Feyerabend has been working on *The Rise of Western Rationalism*, but a publication date for this eagerly awaited treatise has not yet been set.

Feyerabend likes to call himself an "epistemological anarchist," or, better, a "flippant Dadaist" (AM, p. 21). His rallying cry, put forth partly as a joke, is "Anything goes!" By this he means that any scientific procedure, no matter how foolish it seems, can lead to progress, and any procedure, no matter how sound and rational it seems, can impede progress (SFS, pp. 165-66, 179, 188-89). There are no methodological rules, including rules of logic, that have not been violated, and rightly so, in the actual practice of science (SFS, pp. 13-15, 98-100, 212-13).

Nowhere in either book does Feyerabend mention any of the leaders of pragmatism: Peirce, James, Schiller, or Dewey. Nevertheless, he calls his basic approach a "pragmatic philosophy" (SFS, p. 19), and it is difficult to distinguish it from John Dewey's "instrumentalism." Science cannot, of course, operate without temporary rules, but the rules are constantly being transformed by the research process. Feyerabend leaves open the possibility that if the universe has a finite structure, and the human race lasts long enough, scientific method may eventually congeal into precise, permanent rules, but this seems unlikely. In any case, there are no signs of it happening. The history of science will continue to be careless, sloppy, and fundamentally irrational (AM, p. 179) in the sense that both its claims and its procedures are corrigible, perpetually being altered by experience (SFS, p. 99).

If Feyerabend were content to leave it at that, seeing science as a tool that is constantly improving as it enlarges our understanding of nature, few philosophers of science would object. But Feyerabend doesn't leave it at that. He pushes his tolerance for pseudoscience, and for eccentric ways of getting useful information about nature, into such an extreme relativism that science ceases to be a rational enterprise superior to the visions of mystics. The search for better and better knowledge becomes such a foggy process that it is almost impossible to distinguish good science from bad.

Feyerabend does not deny that science keeps improving its instruments of observation and its engineering technology. We obviously build faster spaceships and smaller and more powerful computers, learn more about the moons of Saturn, and so on. But when it comes to theories, such as relativity, quantum mechanics, quark theory, and evolution, we enter a subjective realm where choices depend less on reason than on metaphysical and religious beliefs, cultural pressures, and personal aesthetic tastes (AM, pp. 175, 285; SFS, pp. 8, 28). Feyerabend sees theories the way he sees moral systems. Competing theories and rival ethical systems are "incommensurable" in the sense that we can apply to them no objective yardstick (AM, pp. 171 ff; SFS, pp. 65 ff). In AM (pp. 226 ff.) he reproduces several optical illusions of the shifting gestalt type to model our constantly shifting visions of both nature and morality (AM, pp. 226 ff.). " 'Objectively' there is not much to choose between anti-semitism and humanitarianism. But racism will appear vicious to a humanitarian while humanitarianism will appear vapid to a racist" (SFS, pp. 9, 27).

For Feyerabend, science is more like a church than a rational undertaking, and its theories no closer to final truth than myths and fairy tales (AM, pp. 295-309; SFS, pp. 73-76). Science is only one tradition among many for seeking truth, perhaps not even the best (SFS, pp. 106-07). For this reason, Feyerabend recommends a free society (the "immortal Mill" is one of his heroes) in which there are open debates, and all traditions, including old and discarded ones, are allowed to proliferate (SFS, pp. 9, 29, 134). We do not have such a society because science has hardened into a dogma as rigid as Catholicism. It dominates the democracies and is supported by them.

To allow freedom for all traditions, Feyerabend wants as sharp a separation between science and state as we now have in the United States between church and state (SFS, pp. 31, 106-07). If the government funds science, it should also fund churches. If taxpayers believe in such things as astrology, Chinese herbal medicine, Hopi cosmology, parapsychology, faith healing, acupuncture, creationism, voodoo, or ceremonial rain-dances, then those theories must be taught in state-supported schools (AM, pp. 299-301; SFS, pp. 87, 134). "Three cheers to the fundamentalists in California who succeeded in having a dogmatic formulation of the theory of evolution removed from the textbooks and an account of Genesis included" ("How to Defend Society Against Science," a 1974 talk by Feyerabend that is reprinted in *Introductory Readings in the Philosophy of Science*, 1980, ed. by E. D. Klemke, Robert Hollinger, and A. David Kline).

Feyerabend repeatedly expresses admiration for Chairman Mao's decree that revived the teaching of ancient Chinese medicine (AM, pp. 50-51, 220, 305-06; SFS, pp. 88, 102-05). He favors similar action in the United States (though by democratic legislation rather than government fiat) to force state-supported schools to teach all traditions, not just orthodox science (AM, pp. 52, 216; SFS, pp. 107, 178). Science must be cut down to size, given a more modest role (AM, p. 204). A committee of laymen should be set up to determine if evolution is really as well established as biologists claim, and to decide whether rival theories of life should be taught in government-funded schools (AM, pp. 307-09; SFS, p. 96).

Feyerabend's extreme distrust of orthodox medicine pervades all his writings. In SFS (pp. 136-37) he goes into embarrassing details about a twenty-year illness that caused him to lose twenty-five pounds and to endure double vision, stomach cramps, and other symptoms so severe that he once fainted on a London street. Orthodox doctors in England made him more miserable with their standard tests, but could find nothing wrong. Finally he located a "quack" who massaged the acupuncture points for his liver and stomach. The treatment stopped his long-lasting dysentery and cleared up his urine.

Now in Berkeley, where he says he regularly sees an acupuncturist and a faith healer, he is slowly recovering.

This agonizing experience convinced Feyerabend that there is valuable medical knowledge around that establishment doctors treat with contempt. He is firmly persuaded that traditional Chinese medicine is superior to Western, both in diagnosis and in therapy (SFS, pp. 103, 175-76).[1] Thousands of women, he declares, have lost their breasts when they could have been cured by massage, diet, acupuncture, and herbs (SFS, pp. 175, 206). Children have been cured of leukemia by similar treatments (SFS, p. 206). Since his personal experience with Western medicine, he has avoided all scientific doctors "like the plague" (SFS, p. 194). Asked whether, if he had a child with leukemia, he would take it to a witch doctor or to Sloan Kettering, Feyerabend opted for the witch doctor. So, too, he adds, would many people he knows in California (SFS, pp. 205-06). Even voodoo has a firm material basis, and a study of it would enrich science.

So would the study of astrology. Feyerabend does not think much of astrology as now practiced, but he believes it has made genuine progress, just like other sciences. It contains profound ideas, and should be taken seriously by philosophers (AM, p. 100; SFS, pp. 91-96, 194). Under Feyerabend's photograph on the jacket flap of SFS is not a biographical sketch but a reproduction of his astrological chart. Even the efficacy of rain dances should not be dismissed out of hand. "Who," he asks, "has examined that matter?" (SFS, pp. 78, 138).

Anything goes! "The epistemological anarchist has no compunction to defend the most trite, or the most outrageous statement . . . he has no everlasting loyalty to, and no everlasting aversion against, any institution or any ideology" (AM, p. 189). He is against all programs, including his own. The rhapsody continues:

> His aims remain stable, or change as a result of argument, or of boredom, or of a conversion experience, or to impress a mistress, and so on. Given some aim, he may try to approach it with the help of organized groups, or alone; he may use reason, emotion, ridicule, an "attitude of serious concern" and whatever other means have been invented by humans to get the better of their fellow men. His favourite pastime is to confuse rationalists by inventing compelling reasons for unreasonable doctrines. There is no view, however "absurd" or "immoral," he refuses to consider or to act upon, and no method is regarded as indispensable. The one thing he opposes positively and absolutely are universal standards, universal laws, universal ideas such as "Truth," "Reason," "Justice," "Love" and the behaviour they bring along, though he does not deny that it is often good policy to act as if such laws (such standards, such ideas) existed, and as if he believed in them. He may approach the religious anarchist in his opposition to science and the material world, he may outdo any Nobel Prize winner in his vigorous defence of scientific purity. He has no objection to regarding the fabric of the world as described by science and revealed by

his senses as a chimera that either conceals a deeper and, perhaps, spiritual reality, or as a mere web of dreams that reveals, and conceals, nothing. He takes great interest in procedures, phenomena and experiences such as those reported by Carlos Castaneda, which indicate that perceptions can be arranged in highly unusual ways and that the choice of a particular arrangement as "corresponding to reality," while not arbitrary (it almost always depends on traditions), is certainly not more "rational" or more "objective" than the choice of another arrangement: Rabbi Akiba, who in ecstatic trance rises from one celestial sphere to the next and still higher and who finally comes face to face with God in all his Splendour, makes genuine observations once we decide to accept his way of life as a measure of reality, and his mind is as independent of his body as the chosen observations tell him.

Asked why he takes airplanes instead of brooms, Feyerabend's reply is: "I know how to use planes but don't know how to use brooms, and can't be bothered to learn" (SFS, p. 190). Lakatos wanted to know why Feyerabend, if he doesn't believe in objective standards of truth, never jumps out of fifty-story windows. Because, he answered, he has an innate fear of death, not because he can give rational reasons for such a fear (AM, pp. 221-22).

"People who genuinely have fears which they also sincerely consider irrational," writes Ernest Gellner (in an essay I will cite later in this article), "have no objection to being cured of those fears, if a painless cure is available. In fact, certain drugs are said to induce fearlessness in people in such circumstances. I am, however, convinced (not irrationally, I believe) that the reluctant anarchist, when offered the appropriate drug on the fiftieth floor, will also firmly refuse it."

As I have said, if Feyerabend's views are taken as no more than idiosyncratic distortions of Deweyan instrumentalism, they make a certain amount of sense. And who doubts that science often makes revolutionary leaps by shifting paradigms, to use Thomas Kuhn's language, in a way that sometimes resembles the changing of religious systems? But Feyerabend's relativism and his attacks on all rules are so extreme that not even Kuhn can buy them. "Vaguely obscene" was what he called them in a contribution to *Criticism and the Growth of Knowledge* (1970), edited by Lakatos and Alan Musgrave. To most philosophers Feyerabend is a brilliant but tiresome, self-centered, repetitious buffoon whose reputation rests mainly on the noise and confusion he generates, and the savagery with which he pummels everybody who disagrees with him.

Karl Popper, for instance, is a "mere propagandist" (SFS, p. 114), who likes to express "simple matters in pompous language" (SFS, p. 166). "Popperism is not a court but at most a tiny outhouse" (SFS, p. 208). And these epithets are mild compared to what Feyerabend has to say about lesser philosophers: "intellectual fascists" (SFS, p. 207), "intellectual midgets" (SFS, p. 217), blind men, liars, illiterates, incompetents, and so on. Feyerabend's attitude toward modern philosophers of science can be summed up crisply:

They are all crazy except himself and Lakatos, and he thinks Lakatos was slightly crazy. A great admirer of comic plays (he once attended an actor's school), Feyerabend writes that he has seriously considered a career as an entertainer preferable to teaching philosophy. George S. Kaufman, he adds, rates higher on his scale of values than "Kant, Einstein and their anaemic imitators" (SFS, p. 122).

For a restrained attack on Feyerabend's views see Ernest Nagel's latest collection of papers, *Teleology Revisited* (1979). A less inhibited attack is Ernest Gellner's essay, "Beyond Truth and Falsehood, or No Method in My Madness," in his *Spectacles & Predicaments* (1979). Gellner has no objection to good-natured clowning when it is combined with humanity and humility, but he finds Feyerabend's buffoonery

> persistently rasping, boastful, derisive and arrogant; its attitude to what is rejected is aggressive and holier-than-thou, and opponents are not allowed to benefit from the all-permissive anarchism; the frivolity contains a markedly sadistic streak, visible in the evident pleasure taken in trying (without success) to confuse and browbeat the "rationalists," i.e., people who ask questions about knowledge in good faith. This is why what might otherwise seem a harmless piece of Californian-Viennese Schmalz leaves such a disagreeable taste in the mouth.

NOTE

1. David Joravsky, reviewing Feyerabend's two books *(New York Review of Books,* June 28, 1979), makes a telling point about Feyerabend's obsessive praise of Mao's attempt to place traditional Chinese medicine on an equal footing with Western medical science. Nowhere does Feyerabend consider the hilarious effort by the Chinese government to persuade women that an effective means of birth control is to swallow a live tadpole. The result of this campaign was the discovery that the method doesn't work. If anything goes, and if the tadpole theory persists (as it does) in Chinese folklore, why should the government now persuade its women to use other methods? There must be some reason why so many folk medical practices (blood-letting, for instance) have been abandoned by modern medical science. "I'm not sure I know," writes Joravsky, "when he [Feyerabend] is clowning or crying or philosophizing. I'm not sure it matters."

Feyerabend's angry reply ("One might as well," he says, "talk to a Barbie doll") appeared in the October 11 issue, with a rejoinder by Jarovsky. For an excellent report on Mao's vast effort to revive Chinese folk remedies, see "Medicine in China," by Peggy Durdin, *New York Times Magazine,* February 28, 1960. Mao's effort was the greatest attempt by a government to promote pseudoscience since Hitler's support of Aryan anthropology and Stalin's support of Lysenkoism.

21

CSICOP: Who and Why?

Nobody knows just why Americans, since World War II, have become so increasingly obsessed by pseudoscience and the paranormal. Decay of traditional religions? Anxiety over how science is shaping the future? Deterioration of science teaching? Whatever the causes, science fiction has been strongly influenced by the trend, and to some extent has reinforced it.

Before proceeding, we must make an all-important distinction. Believing in a pseudoscience is not the same as enjoying imaginary science in science fiction. *The Time Machine* is a classic, but don't imagine for a moment that H. G. Wells took time travel seriously. Yes, all things may be possible in some far-off millennium, but the great science fiction writers who use such devices as time travel, parallel worlds, space warps, inertial drives, popping in and out of black and white holes, levitation, anti-gravity, matter transmission machines, extraterrestrial UFOs, mind swaps, reincarnation, and assorted powers of psi have seldom confused these marvels with serious science. I can assure you that the good doctor Isaac Asimov does not believe in the psychohistory so essential to his *Foundation* series, that Lester Del Rey does not believe in the ESP and precognition so essential to his entertaining novel *Pstalemate.* Commenting on his many stories involving ESP, Larry Niven once had this to say: "The fact is that I wrote them in the belief that no such thing existed. I wrote stories of magic for the same reason: I found the ideas interesting."

The same goes for intelligent readers of science fiction and fantasy. You don't have to believe in "the force" to enjoy *Star Wars,* or in extraterrestrial visitors to enjoy *E. T.* You don't have to believe in parallel worlds or telepathy to enjoy Wells's greatest science fiction novel, *Men Like Gods.*

This essay originally appeared in *Isaac Asimov's Science Fiction Magazine,* July 1983, and is reprinted with permission.

But there is a dark side to the use of pseudoscience in science fiction. I refer to those few writers, and not-so-few readers, who lack the training to distinguish good science from bad and who have been caught up in the current occult mania.

Consider the sad story of John Campbell, Jr. After his friend L. Ron Hubbard reportedly cured his sinusitis, Campbell launched in *Astounding Science Fiction* the astounding discovery of Dianetics. As we all know, it became the flourishing cult of Scientology. Soon Campbell was just as enthusiastically promoting such idiocies as the Hieronymous psionic machine and the Dean space-drive. These were more than just circulation-boosting gimmicks. Campbell truly believed. He may have been a great editor, but his knowledge of hard science was as minimal as his gullibility was unbounded. He became a passionate devotee of the paranormal. During the fifties it was not easy to sell him a story unless it concerned super psi-powers.

Campbell's friend A. E. van Vogt was equally naive. Count Alfred Korzybski's once popular cult of General Semantics underpinned his two null-*A* novels. *Siege of the Unseen* exploited the useless Bates system of curing visual ailments by wiggling your eyeballs. After his conversion to Dianetics, van Vogt abandoned writing to become one of Hubbard's top Hollywood auditors. When I attacked Dianetics in my *Fads and Fallacies* book, van Vogt wrote to warn me that my hostilities would soon cause serious heart disease and crippling arthritis and that only Dianetic therapy could avert such disasters. Now thirty years later my heart and joints are in fine shape, thank you, but van Vogt's mind and career were seriously crippled by Hubbard's nonsense.

Second only to Campbell in his baleful influence on science fiction was Ray Palmer, the strange little gnome who edited *Amazing Stories.* Although Palmer, unlike Campbell, knew he was promoting garbage, he convinced thousands of adolescent fans that evil "deros" actually live underground in vast corridors reachable by secret elevators. Palmer played a major role, still largely unrecognized, in starting the flying saucer mania. He founded *Fate* magazine. The first article ever published about modern UFOs ("I Did See the Flying Disks," by Kenneth Arnold, who began it all) appeared in volume 1, number 1, of *Fate,* Spring 1948. *Fate* still thrives as the country's leading purveyor of paranormal hogwash.

It is hard to believe, but not until 1976 did a periodical spring into existence that would survey contemporary pseudoscience from a scientifically literate point of view. Here is how it came about. Paul Kurtz, a philosopher at the State University of New York at Buffalo, was the moving force. Polls had shown that about one-fourth of the American people believe that the stars influence their lives. Kurtz thought it might be worthwhile to draft a manifesto condemning astrology and to have it signed by leading scientists. The overwhelmingly favorable response to the publication of this document in the *Humanist,* then edited by Kurtz, suggested that a great hunger existed for informed, skeptical evaluations of the surging irrationalisms.

At this time, psychologist Ray Hyman, magician James Randi, and I (we three are old friends) had been toying with the notion of starting an organization that would provide the media with useful information counter to the occult trend. But we had no funds. Somehow Kurtz found out about us, and about some thirty others of like mind. In 1976 we all met in Buffalo, at a meeting sponsored by the American Humanist Assocation, and so was born the notorious group known as CSICOP (we pronounce it "Sigh-cop"). The letters stand for the Committee for the Scientific Investigation of Claims of the Paranormal.

The premier issue of our official journal, called the *Zetetic,* after the Greek word for "skeptic," appeared in the fall of 1976. After the first three issues, edited by sociologist Marcello Truzzi, it became apparent that deep philosophical differences separated what Truzzi wanted the magazine to be from the desires of the other committee members. We wanted a magazine of open advocacy, one that would take a firm stand against the more preposterous forms of modern pseudoscience. Truzzi believed that even extreme cranks like Velikovsky should be treated with respect. He wanted the magazine to establish dialogues between skeptics and true believers, to present both sides of current controversies. In brief, he wanted a magazine with an objective, neutral tone, in contrast to what he derided as mere "debunking."

The rest of us did not regard *debunking* as such a negative word. We felt that when pseudoscience is far enough out on the fringes of irrationalism, it is fair game for humor, and at times even ridicule. Now we must pause for another important distinction. Unorthodox theories, obviously essential to the health and progress of science, are qualitatively different from theories so contrary to accepted science, so unsupported by adequate evidence, that the probability of their being true is practically zero. This is not to deny that pseudoscience fades along spectrums that lead to reputable science. Day fades into night, but there is a difference between day and night.

When, for example, a dentist claims he can put silver and gold fillings into teeth by paranormal means, without drilling, or a journalist of the occult writes a book about how the dead communicate with the living by telephone, we feel no obligation to treat such outlandish claims with solemn respect. On the other hand, when unorthodox claims are less extreme, we treat them seriously and try to present the evidence against them without ridicule.

The fact is that crazy, outlandish speculations by reputable scientists are constantly published in "establishment" journals. This is particularly the case in cosmology and subatomic physics, where theories almost have to be far out to be fruitful. At the moment the outstanding unorthodoxy in evolution theory is the "punctuated equilibrium" approach advocated by

Stephen J. Gould and others. We would never dream of trying to "debunk" this theory. Indeed, Gould is one of our Committee's active Fellows. On the other hand, we do not hesitate to oppose the flood theory of fossils advocated by today's leading creationists, because their arguments are in a different ball park, revealing an almost total ignorance of the most elementary levels of modern geology.

Truzzi has a more Fortean mind-set. He resigned as editor, and later resigned from the Committee to publish his own journal, the *Zetetic Scholar*. To avoid confusion we changed the name of our magazine to the *Skeptical Inquirer*. Twenty-two issues have now appeared, the magazine runs to 80 or more pages, and circulation is steadily rising. The editor, Kendrick Frazier, is an experienced science-writer who formerly edited *Science News*.

Kurtz continues to be the committee's energetic chairman, and Lee Nisbet is executive director. The "Fellows" are too numerous to list, but include many eminent philosophers, scientists, and writers. Among science-fiction writers, Isaac Asimov and L. Sprague de Camp are Fellows. Many other experts serve as scientific consultants.

To convey the *Skeptical Inquirer's* flavor, let me give a rundown on the Winter 1982-83 issue. The news section opens with a light-hearted report by our Amsterdam correspondent, Piet Hein Hoebens, on last August's international conference of the Society for Psychical Research, at Cambridge. British parapsychologist Susan Blackmore, Hoebens writes, "dropped a little bombshell" by announcing her conversion to skepticism. For years, she told a startled audience, she had tried to catch a glimpse of the occult, but "whenever I started to look into psi seriously, the evidence started to disappear." Ray Hyman delivered a ringing critique of the work of parapsychologist Charles Honorton, which prodded Honorton into a furious rebuttal. A Jerusalem psi-researcher showed a film about a new psychic metal-bender in Israel. It was so embarrassing that parapsychologist John Palmer called it "rubbish." To the even greater horror of the more serious scientists present, two metal-bending parties were arranged at which guests held spoons and forks in their hands, applied force, and were amazed to see the cutlery twist. The applied force, you must understand, was said to account only *in part* for the bending! One guest fainted after twisting his spoon. When our correspondent bent a spoon effortlessly, a believer hopped up and down in excitement over the fact that it worked even for skeptics!

Perhaps I should add that most cutlery bends much more easily than people realize. After all, how often have you tried to bend a spoon? One of Uri Geller's basic secrets is that he or one of his unknown assistants gets access in advance to the test spoons and secretly bends one back and forth many times until the metal is weakened and just about to snap. Later, Uri will pick out the prepared spoon, and of course it bends like putty when he strokes it with one finger.

Another news item in this issue reports the revival in China last year of what was called "dermo-optical perception" in the early 1960s, when there was a rash of claims that some female psychics in the Soviet Union could "see" without using their eyes. In China it took the form of children who claimed that while blindfolded they could read with their hands, feet, nose, ears, and even their armpits. There are many different ways of cheating at this. The simplest is based on the fact that it is almost impossible to blindfold someone, even by putting tape over the eyes, that wouldn't allow a clever charlatan to obtain a tiny aperture that would permit a peek down the side of the nose. A nose peek of what is written on a piece of paper is obtained under cover of misdirection, then the paper is wadded into a ball, tucked into an ear or under an armpit, and the message "read" with the skin. The late Rosa Kuleshova, who started it all in Russia, liked to read messages by sitting on them, thus proving that her behind was also optically perceptive. If you are interested in more details, read the chapter on dermo-optical perception in my *Science: Good, Bad and Bogus*.

There is also a report about newspapers, radio, and television having had a field day last August when a woman in Chicago was said to have burst into flames while walking down a sidewalk. Paul Harvey, especially excited by this event, described other cases of "spontaneous human combustion" alleged to have occurred in the past. It later turned out, as the *Skeptical Inquirer* reveals (you probably didn't see this in any newspaper), that the poor woman had been dead for about twelve hours before her scorched body was found, and her clothing had been doused with gasoline. There are no authenticated cases of human spontaneous combustion, and any chemist can tell you why. In fact, human bodies are extremely difficult to burn even with the aid of flammable liquids and a match, as many murderers have discovered to their dismay when they tried to hide the identity of their victims.

Another item pulls together outstanding instances of famous psychics' earthquake predictions that totally fizzled. Jeane Dixon, to give one, told the *National Enquirer* in 1964 that there would be a great California quake in 1965 or 1966. It didn't happen, but like all psychic prophets Dixon knows that, no matter how rare, only the hits are remembered. In 1968 she tried again. "A mammoth earthquake," she said, would occur on the West Coast in "about seven years." Edgar Cayce had an even worse record of failed quake predictions. Of course, with psychics predicting big quakes every year, eventually one of them is certain to make a sensational hit. For the record, I here predict a major quake along the San Andreas Fault in the fall of this year. If it doesn't happen, who will recall what I said?

In the same issue of our magazine there are five major articles. An anthropologist gives a scholarly history of palmistry. A Scottish architect presents strong evidence that recent photos of the Loch Ness monster are no more than pictures of floating logs. A psychologist speculates about why skeptics are skeptical. Author-editor Philip Klass, who heads our subcommittee on UFOlogy, tells a wild tale about his efforts to track down an alleged color photograph of a UFO. And there is an article by me about "How Not to Test a Psychic." It goes into unpublished details about a famous test of Uri Geller at Stanford Research International in which he reportedly guessed correctly, eight times out of ten, the number on a die shaken in a file box.

Two new books are reviewed at length, nine others get brief reviews, and seventeen recent articles of special interest from other publications are referenced with comments. There are letters from readers, cartoons, and other things intended to amuse and inform.

Are you fed up with the flood of paranormal sewage that oozes out of your television set and from the movie screens and the pages of irresponsible newspapers and magazines? Are you bored by the shabby science that never stops coming from cynical book-publishers who would rather make a fast buck than ask experts to evaluate a manuscript and then heed their advice? If so, come join our ranks. The cost of the *Skeptical Inquirer* is $16.50 for a year's four issues, and the address is Box 229, Central Park Station, Buffalo, NY 14215.

If you care to learn more about the views of those on the *Skeptical Inquirer*'s editorial board, here is a selected reading list.

Paul Kurtz has written and edited many books of philosophy, the latest being *Sidney Hook: Philosopher of Democracy and Humanism,* an anthology of essays published this year by Prometheus Books. Ray Hyman is the author of *The Nature of Psychological Inquiry* (Prentice-Hall) and coauthor of the only sensible book on dowsing, *Water Witching, USA* (University of Chicago Press). James Randi has written two attacks on fraudulent psychics: *The Truth About Uri Geller* and *Flim-Flam!* (both from Prometheus). My *Science: Good, Bad and Bogus* (Prometheus) was reprinted this year as an Avon paperback.

Philip Klass is the world's leading skeptical expert on UFOs. His *UFOs Explained* (Random House) and *UFOs: The Public Deceived* (Prometheus) should be read by everyone who still takes UFOs seriously. George Abell is the author of several astronomy textbooks and coeditor of *Science and the Paranormal* (Scribner), in which you will find many essays by Fellows of CSICOP. Kendrick Frazier wrote *Our Turbulent Sun* (Morrow) and edited *Paranormal Borderlands of Science* (Prometheus), a selection of articles from the *Skeptical Inquirer.*

Books by CSICOP Fellows run to many hundreds, about half of them written, of course, by Isaac Asimov. Of special relevance are: *Parapsychology: Science or Magic,* by Canadian psychologist James Alcock; *UFOs: A Scientific Debate* (Cornell University Press), coedited by Carl Sagan; *The UFO Verdict* (Prometheus) by Robert Sheaffer; *The Fringe of the Unknown* (Prometheus), by L. Sprague de Camp; and several books on psychic fraud by magician Milbourne Christopher.

Part II

1

Maritain Looks at Jews

In 1920 Gilbert Chesterton produced a travel book called *The New Jerusalem*, the last chapter of which dealt in some detail with what Christians often call "The Jewish Question." Two years later his colleague, Hilaire Belloc, wrote a three-hundred-page work, *The Jews*, which elaborated on Chesterton's thesis—i.e., that the Jews should be recognized openly as an alien body in Europe and segregated into autonomous communities. To the present time these two books have remained the only widely read analyses of the Jewish problem written in English by reputable Catholic authors. Both books carried an atmosphere of patronage and submerged anti-Semitism; and both books, in terms of what they stressed and did not stress, were felt by many to contain extremely inopportune rhetoric. The recent increase of anti-Jewish activity in Europe and the distortion of Catholic thought in America by the Coughlin movement made even more pressing the need for an intelligent and charitable Catholic analysis of the Jewish problem. For these reasons Catholic and non-Catholic liberals alike looked forward to the publication of Jacques Maritain's lecture, *A Christian Looks at the Jewish Question* (Longmans, Green, 1939).

Their hopes have been only partially fulfilled. It is true that the author places a timely stress on the evils of racism, that he reveals an acquaintance with modern anthropology, and that his writing is free of the patronizing tone that characterized the works of Chesterton and Belloc. But apart from these welcomed changes of tone and emphasis, the book says little that has not been amply and more clearly said before.

The author's discussion of the secular aspects of the topic is largely a recitation of matters familiar to any informed reader, or too trivial to be worth

This review originally appeared in *Ethics*, January 1940. © 1940 by the University of Chicago Press. Reprinted with permission.

considering. On page 8 we are told, "Evil is done not by 'the Jews,' but by *some* Jews, and also by *some* non-Jews." Maritain adds that if all the Jews of the earth were exterminated such evils as usury, financial monopoly, white slavery, and publication of pornographic literature would continue to exist! We are told in all seriousness that violent anti-Semitism makes a rational solution of the problem more difficult; that the masses of Jews are not wealthy but poor; that the Protocols of Zion are forgeries; that the myth of Aryan superiority is biologically unfounded; and that racism is an insult to Christianity, which affirms the common brotherhood of all men!

Maritain's solution, like that of Belloc and Chesterton, is to "accept the state of tension" between Jews and Gentiles and to seek the establishment of a political pluralism in which Jews would be segregated into self-governing districts. The Zionist movement is encouraged. It is suggested that nations widen their immigration laws and permit Jews to maintain communities within the nation or to enter sparsely populated colonial possessions (such as French Madagascar or Guiana). But—more important still—behind the evils of racism are the evils of our economic order, which, in turn, spring from the faithlessness of modernity. A spiritual rebirth is requisite for any significant solution.

However, even a solution engendered by an enlightened social order would be only a provisional one, for in the last analysis the dispersion of Israel is a sacred mystery. Like the church, Israel is in the world but not of the world, "shall not be, and never can be." The sacred mission of the Jews is to witness to biblical prophecy and to act as an irritant upon the world, stimulating and exasperating it as long as it remains heretical. The problem, therefore, "is an *insoluble* problem, that is, one without *definitive* solution until the great reconciliation foretold by the apostle [St. Paul in his Epistle to the Romans], which will resemble a resurrection from among the dead" (p. 25). A fuller treatment of the mystery of Israel may be found in the author's book, *Questions de conscience,* published in 1939.

The emphasis Maritain places upon biblical eschatology in dealing with the Jewish question will, of course, startle no Catholic. But to the reader outside of Rome, the book will read at times like a pamphlet from the press of a fundamentalist Bible institute.

2

Kafka: Problem and Prayer

The writings of Franz Kafka are of interest to students of ethics as remarkable literary expressions of an ancient ethical point of view — the point of view that sees human behavior as tragic and absurd and the quest for moral certainty as hopeless even though there may be, behind the madness, a true way.

For readers not yet acquainted with Kafka, it might be well to summarize, all too briefly, the highlights of his life and work.

He was born in 1883, the first child of a middle-class Jewish family in Prague. His father was physically large, strong, and domineering in contrast to Franz, who was thin, shy, neurotic. The child early developed an intense father complex that later so influenced his writing that he once described all his work as "an attempt to get away from my father."

After taking a law degree, he became a civil servant in a worker's accident insurance office, where he had firsthand contact with the endless red tape of a decadent Austrian bureaucracy, and where the insane, slapstick quality of the accidents formed a lasting impression.

Following an unhappy love affair (which he recognized as similar to Kierkegaard's) he contracted tuberculosis and died in 1924, at the age of forty-one, in a sanitorium near Vienna. Before his death he left written instructions for his friend, Max Brod, to burn his unpublished manuscripts. (During his lifetime he had permitted to be published only a small number of stories.) Among the manuscripts were three unfinished novels. For excellent reasons Brod disregarded his friend's request, editing the novels for publication under the titles of *Amerika*, *The Trial*, and *The Castle*.

Each of these novels is exceedingly complex, employing strange dreamlike symbols that have been variously interpreted, each dealing with a single pro-

This review originally appeared in *Ethics,* January 1948. ©1948 by the University of Chicago Press. Reprinted with permission.

tagonist who finds himself trapped in a maze of frustrating, inexplicable circumstances.

In *Amerika* the central character is a European refugee thrust suddenly into the alien culture of a caricatured America. In *The Trial* Joseph K. awakes to find himself under arrest. As the trial progresses, in the hands of a hierarchy of mysterious and fumbling courts, Joseph K. tries vainly to discover what crime he committed, by what law he is being tried, and who are the judges. When his execution finally occurs, the questions are still unanswered.

The Castle concerns a man called "K" who enters a village dominated by a shabby bureaucracy of officials living in a nearby castle. Through several hundred pages of weird and sordid episodes, K tries desperately to reach proper castle authorities for legal permission to remain in the village as a "land surveyor." His efforts fail. Finally, exhausted and sleepy, he dies. On his deathbed, word comes from the castle that he will be permitted to stay because of "certain auxiliary circumstances."

Edwin Muir, the English translator of *The Castle*, has called the novel a modern *Pilgrim's Progress*, but with these important differences: The hero has no plan of salvation. He moves in darkness. He is not sure what the goal is or whether he is on the right path. And all the signs on the road, advice of people he meets, even his own intuition, may be false.

The Kafka Problem (New Directions, 1946) is a collection of forty critical essays, by different authors, written about Kafka since his death. The book was edited by Angel Flores. There are many points of dispute, but basically the critics divide into two broad groups—the mystics and the naturalists.

To the mystics, Kafka is a kind of Hebrew Kierkegaard who either believed in God (or something like God) or at least nourished the hope that God (or something like God) existed. Under the influence of Kierkegaard's *Fear and Trembling*, which he read often, Kafka was obsessed (so the mystics feel) with the comic, irrational, even cruel and immoral, character of God's will as seen through man's finite eyes. The novels become modern versions of the Book of Job.

The extreme example of this approach is John Kelly's essay, *"The Trial and the Theology of Crisis,"* in which the victim of *The Trial* is made to assume the curious role of a Protestant convert. The execution is taken by Kelly to be the death of the "natural man" as the soul of Joseph K. reaches the limits of despair (the Barthian "crisis") and turns to God for salvation. As Kelly bluntly puts it, "He evolves into a Pauline Christian" (p. 159). It would be interesting indeed to have in *The Trial* a novel "as firmly grounded in the rigid and elaborate theology of crisis, as was *The Divine Comedy* in the Scholastic theology" (quoting Kelly, p. 170), but unfortunately there are insuperable difficulties in this view.

Closer to the truth of Kafka is the naturalist approach of Charles Neider, whose essay, "The Cabalists," is the most important contribution in the collection. His thesis is simple: Kafka may or may not have believed in God, but, in either case, his novels are intended as satires on religious "cabalas" — i.e., institutions, such as Christianity and Judaism, that society ignorantly supposes to be in touch with God. ("I have not been led into life by the—it is true—now heavily sinking hand of Christianity like Kierkegaard, nor have I, like the Zionists, snatched the last corner of the disappearing prayer shawl of the Jews," Kafka wrote in his diary.)

"The mystical school," Neider asserts, "is blinded, by its obsession with the Castle as the divine, into as ready an acceptance of the Castle cabalism as the villagers themselves. The mystical interpreters, in short, manage to adjust themselves very nicely to the village; and it is they who find the state of grace, not K" (p. 429).

Paul Goodman's book *Kafka's Prayer* (Vanguard, 1947), the first full-volume study of Kafka in English, is an invaluable contribution to the naturalist school of Kafka criticism as well as a lyrical expression of Goodman's own philosophy.

"When we look at that [Kafka's] thought, the religious thought," Goodman writes, "there is no God, no moral code, no punishment, nor anything else that Freud would teach us to find in a late Super-ego religion" (p. ix). Kafka is considered a "far superior theologian to Kierkegaard" (p. 36) precisely because of his refusal to regard the "courts" as transcendant. Kierkegaard's view that the highest way is a solitary one, concerning only the individual in his relation to God, is branded "uncharitable and presumptuous" (p. 36): "In heaven's name, you Dane, to whom is one to give his neighbor-love, as is bidden?" Goodman asks (p. 37). Even Kafka's sense of infinity is not "sublime" but rather an expression of "anxiety" over two "incompatible constructions" (p. 265).

On the assumption that Kafka was agnostic, and by implication a naturalist, Goodman turns to the question of why Kafka was compelled to write of the world as an endless labyrinth of blind alleys — an "infinite regress" of frustrations. The immediate answer lies, of course, in Kafka's neurotic, almost psychotic, personality. With an amazing grasp of Freudian techniques, as modified by Wilhelm Reich and others, Goodman probes the nature of Kafka's father complex, with its associated feelings of guilt, inferiority, self-contempt, narcissism, sadism, masochism, and homosexuality. One of Goodman's most startling suggestions is the hypothesis that Kafka's guilt neurosis was bound up with a childhood fear that he had caused the death of two younger brothers. *The Trial* is analyzed in detail as a novel of "persecutory paranoia" with repressed homosexuality and delusions of reference. *The Castle* is dissected as a novel of "constructive will," in which the hero exhausts his will in futile attempts to overcome obstacles partly of his own creation.

But, in addition to the diseases of the mind, there are the diseases of society — sick social institutions (the courts and the castle!) that are bolstered by neurotic urges and in turn help create the neuroses. A good part of Goodman's book is a critique of society from the standpoint of the new anarchist trend, based on Kropotkin, which seems to be gaining an increasing number of adherents among writers here and abroad (for example, Aldous Huxley and Henry Miller).

Perhaps the best summary of Goodman's views is on page 220: "In principle the dilemma of the shut-in will and ego is not natural and inevitable; it is not man's fate as certain new theologians of the absurd declare it. I, for my part, believe that it is a disease of our personalities and our institutions. (Yes, this I *know*.) Kafka himself believed so, I have tried to show. But I believe there is a therapy for this disease, and even a politics."

And Goodman adds in parentheses, with a Kafkan touch of sadness and irony, "If indeed I believe it, and this belief is not my own castle."

3

Thomas Wolfe and the Unfound Door

Herbert J. Muller begins his book *Thomas Wolfe* (New Directions, 1947) with a discussion of "myth"—a fashionable term among critics for the symbolic story that orders and gives meaning to human experience. From the outset, Muller states, Wolfe regarded himself as "mythmaker" with the central theme of a search for a father and a home; as Wolfe expressed it, for "the image of a strength and wisdom external to his need and superior to his hunger, to which the belief and power of his own life could be united." To Muller, Wolfe's great literary achievement was "the gradual widening and deepening of the implication of his theme, the transformation of a private legend into a public myth . . ." (p. 6). And although he did not achieve a "complete imaginative organization of our situation, an adequate symbolic expression of our faith and hope," Muller concludes, he was nonetheless our "closest approach to a Homer"; considering the complexity of the nation "his life work was perhaps as close as we can expect to come to an American epic" (p. 189).

There is no need to dwell here on more than the barest outline of Wolfe's pilgrimage, which provides the content of his four novels. *Look Homeward, Angel* is the story of his boyhood, adolescence, and young manhood—tormented by a sense of a lost Paradise, of men "forever strangers to one another," seeking in vain for "the great forgotten language, the lost lane-end into heaven, a stone, a leaf, an unfound door." *Of Time and the River* carries Wolfe through graduate study at Harvard and launches him on a frenzied search for knowledge and experience—a search described by Muller as

This review originally appeared in *Ethics*, July 1948. ©1948 by University of Chicago Press. Reprinted with permission.

"an insane passion to walk a million streets, read a million books, make love to a million women—to eat, see, know, feel everything under the sun" (p. 1).

In *The Web and the Rock*, Wolfe continues his Faustian quest. Living on the rock of Manhattan, enmeshed in the web of life, he finds his "Helen"—but not the secret door. Wolfe wrote: "He thought that he could twist his hand a certain way, or turn his wrist, or make a certain simple movement of rotation into space . . . and that by making this rotation with his hand, he would find the lost dimension of that secret world, and instantly step through the door that he had opened."

Although Muller recognizes Wolfe's incapacity for a permanent, satisfying love and correctly ties this up with his insatiable passion to know a million people, it seems to me he underplays the extent to which Wolfe's neurotic behavior exhibited a Casanova pattern, resting in part at least on a sense of inferiority concerning his gigantic size. It is significant that the one overwhelming love affair of his legend is with a woman he cannot possibly marry.

You Can't Go Home Again, the final novel, covers the period of Wolfe's sudden success with his first book, his tragic attempt to return to his home town, the coming of America's Great Depression, and his final discovery (like Goethe's Faust) of life's meaning in the brotherhood of man and the common task of building the good society.

It was the depression, Muller feels, that shook Wolfe out of his earlier belief that an artist was a privileged genius free of all social obligations. "Wolfe was deeply impressed by the fortitude of the people. He came to feel a solidarity with them in their suffering and their ability to survive. He came to realize that he was not actually singular, that his prized individuality was not the sum of his differences from others, and that even the qualities that distinguished him were valuable chiefly because of all that united him with his fellows" (p. 9).

The novel closes with a remarkable letter that Wolfe writes to his publisher outlining his new-found faith. The letter tells of his hunger for love and fame, how he has found both and realized they are not enough. It tells of the effect upon him of the depression, and his growing conviction that America was sick with an ailment "akin to Germany's—a dread world-sickness of the soul." The attitude his publisher has toward this downward trend of history is the resignation of *Ecclesiastes*—a fatalism that accepts the tragedy of man's fate. Wolfe writes that he cannot share this resignation, and Muller quotes him: "In everlasting terms—those of eternity—you and the preacher may be right; for there is no greater wisdom than the wisdom of *Ecclesiastes*, no acceptance finally so true as the stern fatalism of the rock. Man was born to live, to suffer, and to die, and what befalls him is a tragic lot. There is no denying this is the final end. *But we must, dear Fox, deny it all along the way*" (italics in original).

Wolfe goes on to affirm his faith in a naturalistic humanism—a conviction that evil can be conquered, that progress is more than an illusion. "To believe that new monsters will arise as vicious as the old, to believe that the great Pandora's box of human frailty, once opened, will never show a diminution of its ugly swarm, is to help, by just that much, to make it so forever," he writes.

And then the famous passage: "I believe that we are lost here in America, but I believe we shall be found. . . . I think the true discovery of America is before us. I think the true fulfilment of our spirit, of our people, of our mighty and immortal land, is yet to come. I think the true discovery of our democracy is still before us. And I think that all these things are certain as the morning, as inevitable as noon."

Thus, as Muller makes clear, Wolfe brings his legend to a close with a ringing declaration of faith in human progress that places him within the tradition of James and Dewey and Justice Holmes—a faith that "regarded the good life as an adventure in an evolving, unfinished world, an experiment that is more hopeful as well as more dangerous because its conditions are not absolute and unalterable. . . . American democracy . . . is one of the great historic adventures of the human spirit" (Muller, p. 188).

And, yet, true and fine as these sentiments are, is there not about them a kind of whistling in the dark? Muller voices the opinion of most critics when he says that the earlier novels, recording the agony of Wolfe's search, are "more memorable than the announcement of his arrival" (p. 183). Somehow the conclusion seems lame and colorless after the titanic struggles that went before.

A door was found, but was it the door he sought?

4

Orwell's Nineteen Eighty-four

Like Huxley's *Brave New World* and H. G. Wells's earlier romance *When the Sleeper Awakes*, Orwell's skillfully constructed nightmare belongs to that variant of satirical fantasy that portrays a future society for the purpose of attacking what the author regards as evil contemporary trends. But Huxley's novel takes place in 632 A.F (After Ford), and Wells's in 2100 A.D.; and although their messages are similar to Orwell's, their heightened fantasy makes it possible to read them with detached amusement. *Nineteen Eighty-four* (Harcourt, Brace, 1949), on the other hand, is but thirty-five years away, and even passages of high humor cannot be read without a shuddering sense of familiarity.

Although Oceana — the grim superstate in which the novel's protagonist, Winston Smith, is a minor bureaucrat — comprises the Americas, England, Australia, and South Africa, it is clearly a caricature of present-day Russia. The rulers are the "Inner Party" members, fully aware that their basic motive is the exercise and preservation of power. An "Outer Party," under the constant surveillance of "Thought Police," constitutes the middle class. The remaining 85 percent of the population is composed of "Proles," a shabby slave class kept in such ignorance by state-controlled education and propaganda that they cannot revolt or even conceive of Oceana being other than it is.

To provide a personalized image for love and loyalty, the Party hierarchy culminates in "Big Brother," who may or may not exist but whose mustached countenance stares from posters, banners, coins, stamps, and book jackets. He is Oceana's substitute for God. Hate is directed toward Emmanuel Goldstein, semimythical leader of "The Brotherhood," a subversive movement plotting to overthrow the government.

Reprinted with permission from *Ethics*, January 1950. ©1950 by the University of Chicago Press.

Oceana is permanently at war with either Eurasia or Eastasia, two rival superstates, but it is merely a token war. All three have atom bombs and know that one state cannot, at present, be conquered even by the other two combined. The war serves the purpose of keeping the population in a constant state of hysteria and deprivation, as well as of draining away surplus goods and labor.

At any moment the war may shift from one superstate to the other. This requires not only a shift of the propaganda line but also a complete revision of all historical documents — newspapers, books, films, and photographs — to show that the current enemy has *always* been the enemy. A magnificent scene describes a Party orator who is whipping a crowd into a frenzy of hatred for Eurasia. A messenger slips into his hand a piece of paper informing him that Eurasia has become an ally and Oceana is now at war with Eastasia. The speaker transposes enemies in midsentence, without breaking the syntax.

Nothing altered in his voice or manner, or in the content of what he was saying, but suddenly the names were different. Without words said, a wave of understanding rippled through the crowd. Oceana was at war with Eastasia! The next moment there was a tremendous commotion. The banners and posters with which the square was decorated were all wrong! Quite half of them had the wrong faces on them. It was sabotage! The agents of Goldstein had been at work! There was a riotous interlude while posters were ripped from the walls, banners torn to shreds and trampled underfoot. The Spies performed prodigies of activity in clambering over the rooftops and cutting the streamers that fluttered from the chimneys. But within two or three minutes it was all over. The orator, still gripping the neck of the microphone, his shoulders hunched forward, his free hand clawing at the air, had gone straight on with his speech. One minute more, and the feral roars of rage were again bursting from the crowd . . .

Although members of the Communist party usually consider themselves free of the sexual mores that characterize Western cultures, Orwell has correctly perceived the sense in which communism is the Puritanism of the twentieth century. For every aspect of the life of a devoted Communist, including sex, is oriented toward Party ends. In Oceana only the Proles are permitted sexual freedom. Among Party members, promiscuity is unforgivable. "Sexual intercourse was . . . a slightly disgusting operation, like having an enema." An organization called the "Junior Anti-Sex League" advocates celibacy, with *artsem* (artificial insemination) as the most efficient means of producing children. "It was not merely that the sex instinct created a world of its own which was outside the Party's control and which therefore had to be destroyed if possible. What was more important was that sexual privation induced hysteria, which was desirable because it could be transformed into war fever and leader worship." Party neurologists are at work on methods for abolishing the orgasm.

The early part of the novel concerns a surreptitious love affair involving Winston Smith and Julia, a freckle-faced machinist who operates a novel-writing machine in the Fiction Department of Minitrue (Ministry of Truth). Sharing a common hatred of the government, they go to O'Brien, an Inner Party member whom they believe to be a leader of the Brotherhood, and offer their services to the underground. But O'Brien (by a hoary plot device) proves to be engaged in counterintelligence and is, in fact, one of the coauthors (no book is produced individually) of *The Book*, a supposed work of Goldstein. Winston and Julia are arrested. The rest of the novel deals with the remorseless, sickening torture of Smith by O'Brien, not merely to extract absurd confessions, but to get inside Smith's mind—to convert him to orthodoxy and a genuine love of Big Brother.

The official language of Oceana, "Newspeak," is a compressed English from which all words for expressing heresy are slowly being dropped. Such terms as *honor*, *justice*, *morality*, *internationalism*, *democracy*, *science*, and *religion* have already ceased to exist. Closely allied with Newspeak is the doctrine of "doublethink," Oceana's dialectical materialism.

> *Doublethink* means the power of holding two contradictory beliefs in one's mind simultaneously, and accepting both of them. The Party intellectual knows in which direction his memories must be altered; he therefore knows that he is playing tricks with reality; but by the exercise of *doublethink* he also satisfies himself that reality is not violated. The process has to be conscious, or it would not be carried out with sufficient precision, but it also has to be unconscious, or it would bring with it a feeling of falsity and hence of guilt. *Doublethink* lies at the very heart of Ingsoc [English socialism], since the essential act of the Party is to use conscious deception while retaining the firmness of purpose that goes with complete honesty. To tell deliberate lies while genuinely believing in them, to forget any fact that has become inconvenient, and then, when it becomes necessary again, to draw it back from oblivion for just so long as it is needed, to deny the existence of objective reality and all the while to take account of the reality which one denies—all this is indispensably necessary. Even in using the word *doublethink* it is necessary to exercise *doublethink*. For by using the word one admits that one is tampering with reality; by a fresh act of *doublethink* one erases this knowledge; and so on indefinitely, with the lie always one leap ahead of the truth . . .

Doublethink rests on an epistemology described by O'Brien as "collective solipsism." It is the degraded form of pragmatism that opponents of Dewey are forever accusing him of holding. The external world, with its real past, ordered parts, and natural laws, is merely a projection of minds. "Reality exists in the human mind," says O'Brien, "and nowhere else. Not in the individual mind, which can make mistakes, and in any case soon perishes; only in the mind of the Party, which is collective and immortal. Whatever the Party holds to be truth *is* truth." One of the most harrowing episodes of

Smith's inquisition is the process by which he is finally persuaded that two plus two is sometimes five.

It is important to understand that Orwell is not attacking democratic socialism. In a letter to an American labor leader he wrote: "My recent novel is *not* intended as an attack on socialism or on the British Labour Party (of which I am a supporter) but as a show-up of the perversions to which a centralized economy is liable and which have already been partly realized in Communism and fascism" (quoted on p. 8 of the *New York Times Book Review*, July 31, 1949).

Orwell's tale of terror was written from a political point of view that probably differs in no basic respect from that of, say, H. G. Wells's beautiful and moving Utopia novel, *Men Like Gods*. The new world of Wells is a City in the Skies to which humanity might rise with the aid of science, sanity, and intelligent planning. Orwell's Oceana is the City in the Sea to which mankind might sink — to which a large segment of mankind has already almost sunk — with the aid of perverted science, mental sickness, and careless planning.

Nineteen Eighty-four is unlikely to have the permanence of such masterpieces of cultural satire as *Gulliver's Travels* or Butler's two books on Erewhon; but as a well-timed political document it may prove singularly effective in helping us understand, and profit from, the tragic failure of Russian socialism.

POSTSCRIPT

As I assemble this anthology, in 1983, Irving Howe, one of the nation's most influential democratic socialists, and Norman Podhoretz, an equally influential neoconservative, have just published essays in which they reconsider Orwell's novel. If Orwell were alive today, age 82, would he still be a democratic socialist? Both writers recognize the futility of such a question, but give their opinions anyway. Writing in the *New Republic* (1982 year-end issue), Howe has little doubt that Orwell would still be on the side of democratic socialism. Podhoretz, also to nobody's surprise, is convinced (*Harper's*, January 1983) that Orwell "would be taking his stand with the neoconservatives."

I agree with Howe. Of course Orwell would take his stand with the neoconservatives in his intense opposition to Soviet socialism, but Orwell never lost sight of the gulf that separates democratic socialism from a socialism backed by bullets instead of free votes. It is a distinction neoconservatives do their best to blur, and Podhoretz, in his tribute to Orwell, does his usual job of blurring.

5

Can God Be Proved?

Contemporary Protestant theology has become a battleground for a renewed clash between the age-old adversaries, faith and reason. L. Harold DeWolf, professor of systematic theology at Boston University, has attempted in his book *The Religious Revolt Against Reason* (Harper, 1949) a survey and critical evaluation of the new irrationalism, which has its origin in Kierkegaard, and its leading exponents in Karl Barth, Emil Brunner, and Reinhold Niebuhr. DeWolf recognizes the important differences between these three, but finds them in substantial agreement in their distrust of reason as a method of obtaining religious truth.

A major criticism of this book, it seems to me, is that the author simply hasn't worked hard enough on his material. His quotations from the irrationalists, for example, are seldom the strongest that can be culled from their writings. "There is no way from us to God," declares Barth in a neglected passage, "not even a *via negativa*—not even a *via dialectica*—nor *paradoxica*. The God who stood at the end of some human way—even of this way— would not be God." Again: "That is the mystery of the message of the Bible— that here we are told of God whom we do not find in the glow of twilight, or in the blossoming tree that we admire, or in a creation of art, or even in the voice of conscience—no, not there." And one misses Barth's famous rhetorical question that so powerfully sums up his "marginal note" to theology, "What manner of God is he who can be proved?"

There is no mention of Barth's historic battle with the Czech Jesuit, Father Enrich Przywara, whose book *Analogia Entis* defended the Thomist view that God could not be spoken of by analogy with the human mind if there were not a natural image of deity in our consciousness. "I hold the *analogia*

This review originally appeared in the *New Leader,* March 18, 1950, and is reprinted with permission.

entis to be the discovery of the antichrist and consider that on that ground alone one cannot be a Roman Catholic," Barth writes in his *Dogmatics*.

DeWolf's book is a curious blend of overemphases and omissions. Many references are made to the "finite God" theology of the author's friend and former teacher, Edgar S. Brightman, although Brightman's views have had little influence on the conflict under discussion. And there is no mention at all of Unamuno, the passionate Spanish mystic who was neither Catholic nor Protestant, but certainly one of the greatest of modern Christian irrationalists. Surely there was a place for Unamuno's agonized cry, "I do not know, I do not know, I do not know."

After making a case for each side, DeWolf seeks to harmonize them by preserving all he believes of value in both points of view. But he is clearly on the side of the rationalists, believing that human reason, operating on data obtained by experience, can arrive at the conclusion that God's existence is highly probable. For example, the emergence of creative novelties in the evolution of the cosmos, and even "the very existence of a causal system may be taken as an evidence of a cosmic purpose and hence of God" (p. 191). Moral and aesthetic values also constitute "data" upon which reason can construct proofs of God.

Unfortunately, DeWolf does not give the steps in the rational "proofs" that he believes can be based on experiential data, and so the reader is unable to determine the strength or weakness of his case. One wonders how he would account for, say, Dewey's failure to believe in God, considering the fact that Dewey is a stout champion of moral and aesthetic values. Apparently he would insist that Dewey is deficient in the ability to reason.

It all sounds thin and squeaky beside the Barthian evangelistic thunder. If Protestant rationalism cannot make a stronger defense than this against the Continental revolutionaries, then Protestant rationalism is indeed dying, if not already dead.

6

A Failed God and the Vital Center

The corruption of the Soviet experiment, from the great vision that inspired Lenin to the monstrous, hope-abandoned state it is today, is the great political tragedy of our time. In the twenties, millions found in Russia an incarnation of the age-old dream of a just republic. In the thirties (Koestler calls it the "Pink Decade"), fellow-traveling among Western scholars and writers became so fashionable that expressing criticism of Russia was considered bad taste — like criticizing a woman's hat. Not until the late forties did it become clear, beyond every reasonable doubt, that the Russian god-man had grown into a paranoid, feeble-minded giant.

The God That Failed (Harper, 1949) is part of the rapidly growing literature of disenchantment. It was the happy idea of Richard Crossman, British socialist and assistant editor of the *New Statesman and Nation*, to assemble in one volume the personal confessions of six prominent writers, each telling why he entered and later abandoned the Communist cause. Of the six, Arthur Koestler, Ignazio Silone, and Richard Wright were active in the party. André Gide, Louis Fischer, and Stephen Spender were fellow-travelers but were close enough to the party to have shared with the others the same euphoria of conversion. Koestler describes this experience as follows:

> To say that one had "seen the light" is a poor description of the mental rapture which only the convert knows (regardless of what faith he has been converted to). The new light seems to pour from all directions across the skull; the whole universe falls into pattern like the stray pieces of a jigsaw puzzle

This review originally appeared in *Ethics,* July 1950. ©1950 by the University of Chicago Press. Reprinted with permission.

assembled by magic at one stroke. There is now an answer to every question, doubts and conflicts are a matter of the tortured past — a past already remote, when one had lived in dismal ignorance in the tasteless, colorless world of those who *don't know*.

To all six, leaving the movement brought the same bitter sense of desolation. "I headed home alone, really alone now," says Richard Wright, after describing the events that precipitated his final break. Silone writes:

> The truth is this: the day I left the Communist Party was a very sad one for me, it was like a day of deep mourning for my lost youth. . . . It is not easy to free oneself from an experience as intense as that of the underground organization of the Communist Party. Something of it remains and leaves a mark on the character which lasts all one's life. One can, in fact, notice how recognizable the ex-Communists are. They constitute a category apart, like ex-priests and ex-regular officers. The number of ex-Communists is legion today. "The final struggle," I said jokingly to Togliatti recently, "will be between the Communists and ex-Communists."

It is important to understand that not one of the six broke with communism because of a change in what he regarded as the ends of social justice. They broke because of a conviction that Russia had betrayed those ends. The same loyalties led them out that led them in, and in this double movement they acquired a new insight into the strength of the democratic means. Their former impatience had led them to believe it necessary to abandon democratic values for temporary fascist expedients. It is the recognition of the fatal character of this strategy that forms the underlying ethical theme of all six essays — the recognition that, except for rare occasions, an evil means corrupts both those who use it and the final end itself. It was a truth that had been vigorously expressed by nineteenth-century philosophers but which had to be rediscovered in a twentieth-century setting. Koestler phrases it effectively:

> The lesson . . . that man is a reality, mankind an abstraction; that men cannot be treated as units in operations of political arithmetic because they behave like the symbols for zero and the infinite, which dislocate all mathematical operations; that the end justifies the means only within very narrow limits; that ethics is not a function of social utility, and charity not a petty-bourgeois sentiment but the gravitational force which keeps civilization in its orbit.

In looking back over the political writing of the twenties, it is remarkable how few leading thinkers perceived the fatal flaws in the head of the newborn Russian giant. And it is doubly remarkable, when one turns to the warnings of the neglected few who did see clearly, to find their criticism so just and penetrating. Crossman calls attention to Bertrand Russell's *Bolshevism: Practice and Theory*, written in 1920 and recently republished without alterations. And we should not forget such sharp-eyed prophets as Karl Kautsky and Rosa Luxemburg, or even H. G. Wells. It was easy to dismiss Wells's attacks on Bolshevism as the sour grapes of a utopian, disappointed because he had not been consulted in the formation of the brave new world. And yet how sane and balanced and contemporary his criticisms sound when reread today!

In America postwar disenchantment has dispelled forever the delusion of the Popular Front period that cooperation for common objectives is possible between liberal and Communist groups. One result has been the growth of Americans for Democratic Action, the first important liberal political action organization to exclude Communists from membership.

Arthur Schlesinger, Jr., professor of history at Harvard, is a founder of ADA and one of the leading intellectual pilots of America's expanding "non-Communist left." His book, *The Vital Center* (Houghton Mifflin, 1949), is the first major attempt to summarize ADA's hitherto somewhat misty views.

But the book is more than just the affirmative side of the nation's disenchanted liberalism. It is a passionate, witty, brilliantly executed examination and defense of the liberal-democratic faith. By necessity, liberalism must tolerate conflicting views and so appear weak and vacillating beside a robust authoritarianism. It is the great merit of *The Vital Center* that it presents liberalism as a "fighting faith" without sacrificing those virtues of tolerance and skepticism that lie at the heart of the liberal tradition.

In the chapter "The Failure of the Right," Schlesinger makes clear that we cannot look to the businessman for political leadership. His views are seldom more than rationalizations of business interests, and, when confronted with a political evil, such as Hitler, his response is always one of timidity and compromise. "Tear away the veil of Rotarian self-congratulation or of Marxist demonology, and you are likely to find the irresolute and hesitating figure of George F. Babbitt."

A similar chapter, "The Failure of the Left," is a slashing attack on the fellow-traveling mentality. Like the Doughfaces of the Civil War, "northern men with southern principles," the modern Doughfaces are "democratic men with totalitarian principles." In times of crisis, the fellow-travelers turn to communism, while the extreme Right turns to fascism. Both groups are capable of delivering a free society to a totalitarian enemy.

Chapters on Russia and the Communist movement draw a merciless picture of the "corruption of the Soviet vision," which the author finds anticipated in Dostoevski's parable of the Grand Inquisitor. Compared with modern Soviet terror, czarist persecutions take on an *opéra bouffe* quality. Schlesinger discusses Soviet regimentation over the arts and sciences, the nauseating worship of Stalin, the incredible labor camps, which "play no rational role in a system of justice nor even in a system of labor," existing only to carry to an ultimate the obliteration of individual freedom. The American Communist party and its shameless control of the Henry Wallace movement is described with accuracy, understanding, and humor.

Other chapters deal with civil rights, foreign policy, world government ("In the long run, the supporters of world government are right; but in the short run, their efforts too often serve to distract men of good will from the urgent tasks of the moment"), and the liberals' great dilemma of choice between harassing monopoly or permitting it to take firmer root so that it can more easily be nationalized. Schlesinger defends a mixed economy in which federal ownership is extended in certain areas (in the form of independent public corporations similar to TVA), the cooperative movement is expanded, and private ownership continues to play an indispensable role.

In the vanguard of American progress, Schlesinger sees the emergence of a "new radicalism" that "need not invoke Marx at every turn in the road, or point its prayer-rug every morning to Moscow." Accepting conflict without anxiety, recognizing the fallibility and weaknesses of men, drawing strength from both the "non-Communist left" and the "non-Fascist right," the new radicalism becomes a "vital center," tugging society forward against the backward pulls of the totalitarian Left and Right.

> The spirit of the new radicalism is the spirit of the center — the spirit of human decency, opposing the extremes of tyranny. Yet, in a more fundamental sense, does not the center itself represent one extreme? while at the other, are grouped the forces of corruption — men transformed by pride and power into enemies of humanity.

> The commitment is complex and rigorous. When has it not been so?

7

The Culturology
of Leslie White

Leslie Alvin White, professor of anthropology at the University of Michigan, has brought together a collection of published and unpublished papers into a volume titled *The Science of Culture: A Study of Man and Civilization* (Farrar, Straus, 1949). On the dust jacket A. L. Kroeber calls it "a gauntlet-flinging book. With unswerving ruthlessness it holds the recognition of culture to be a Copernican act that necessarily revolutionizes all our thinking if only we are consistent and unafraid . . . White's basic position, his philosophy, is both sound and modern." Huntington Cairns calls it "the first thorough analysis of the new field of culturology . . . a brilliant and authoritative contribution to social theory." In my opinion the book's interior, a jumble of private peeves and prejudices, offers little to justify such encomiums.

White's central thesis is that a great revolution took place in human thought when "culture" was first recognized as a unique subject-matter, with its own laws and principles, but that modern anthropologists are not sufficiently aware of this fact. One reason for their obtuseness is a semantic one. The science that studies culture is usually called "cultural anthropology" or "science of culture." White is allergic to these terms. He proposes instead the singularly inept word *culturology*. "If 'museology' [art of museum management] can become respectable, why not 'culturology' . . . ?" he asks. Adoption of this label, he strongly feels, will have consequences comparable to the substitution of "temperature" for "heat" in the history of physics. *Culturology* is a "creative" word. It "establishes and defines a new science."[1]

The first to outline the scope of this new discipline, White tells us, was

This review originally appeared in the *New Leader*, January 14, 1950, and is reprinted with permission.

E. B. Tylor. His great insight was expanded by Morgan, Durkheim, Kroeber, Lowie, Wissler, and Murdock. But, alas, most modern anthropologists have been backsliding. Sapir, Goldenweiser, Boas, Benedict, Radcliffe-Brown, Linton, Herskovits, and Hooton are soundly drubbed for their opposition to the True Tradition. The Freudian anthropologists (White does not deign to name them) are rudely waved aside as having "sold their culturological birthright for a mess of psychiatric pottage."

"In line with this emphasis upon the individual, we note that the most popular trend in American anthropology today is the study of personality. 'Depth psychology,' ink-blot tests, psychiatry, etc., are almost *de rigueur* these days for the up-to-date anthropologist. Thus we see that much of anthropology today has regressed to a level even below that of most sociologists and some social psychologists."

The chief sin of these misguided moderns, Freudian or otherwise, is the belief that the human will is capable of directing cultural progress. White is a determinist with a vengeance. Cultural history can be predicted, but never changed. His diatribes against free will betray such flimsy knowledge of classical analyses of this troublesome topic that they read like clichés in a philosophy 101 term paper. Sample:

> When one set of causative factors outweighs another, we call it "choice" or "decision": I decide to play golf. "Free will and choice" is merely the way in which we experience the preponderance of one factor or set of factors over another. Not realizing what lies back of this experience we can believe that it is our doing and hence call it choice and Free Will.[2]

Emphasis on the uniqueness of culturology, as distinct from other sciences, makes it necessary for White to lay great stress on the gap between animal and human minds. A qualitative difference has emerged in human thinking, he insists, which can be defined in terms of man's ability to employ symbols. Animals respond only to signs. The difference between sign and symbol is that symbols have meanings assigned to the users; animals cannot create the meanings of signs. (Charles Morris in his *Signs, Language, and Behavior* [1946] draws the same distinction with a more precise terminology. Animal signs are called "signals"; both signals and symbols are sub-classes of signs.[3])

It is a man's ability to deal with symbols that makes "culture" a peculiarly human product. "Cultural reality" is the vast, intricate network of relations between human minds. One is amused to find the author taking pains to show that this was Karl Marx's view. I do not know what sort of Marxist White fancies himself,[4] but it is alarming to find the usual defense of Soviet religious policy: "Under the Soviets there was more religious freedom—freedom for all faiths, freedom to believe and to worship as one pleased—than there ever had been under the old regime.

White's attempt to make cultural reality stand alone, without support from other realms of being, reaches unbelievable extremes in his chapter "The Locus of Mathematical Reality." In it he argues that mathematical truths are "wholly dependent upon the mind of the species." "Mathematics in its entirety, its 'truths' and its 'realities,' is a part of human culture, nothing more." "The locus of mathematical reality is cultural tradition." "Its [mathematical] reality is cultural; the sort of reality possessed by a code of etiquette, traffic regulations, the rules of baseball, the English language or rules of grammar."

The fact that different tribes use different number bases for counting, and that physicists no longer find Euclidean laws logically necessary, misleads White into support of a position that means, if it means anything, that there might be cultures in which two pebbles added to two pebbles would yield something other than four pebbles. The resemblance between this view and the "collective solipsism" satirized in Orwell's *Nineteen Eighty-four* is astonishing. Compare, for example, the following two quotations:

White: "Mathematical concepts are independent of the individual mind but lie wholly within the mind of the species. . . ."

O'Brien: "Reality exists in the human mind, and nowhere else. Not in the individual mind, which can make mistakes, and in any case soon perishes: only in the mind of the Party, which is collective and immortal."

Readers of the novel will recall the agonizing scene in which the protagonist is tortured by O'Brien into the conviction that two plus two is sometimes five.[5]

In his less fantastic papers White simply belabors the commonplace. The chapter "Mind is Minding" defends the Aristotelian view that mind is a function of the brain, without independent existence. In light of the fact that no important psychologist or anthropologist since William James has regarded mind as otherwise, one wonders why White bothered to devote an entire chapter to it. Equally fusty are his attacks on the Great Man theory of history (with the inevitable quotes from William F. Ogburn on how inventions are made simultaneously by different people), and his arguments to prove there is no instinctive aversion to incest. Has anyone lately, outside of the Freudian fundamentalists, said there was?[6]

The book closes with an impassioned plea for recognizing man's impotence to do more than observe and predict the course of history; but fortunately White's oracle tells him the path is probably upward (if the atomic bomb doesn't, etc.) and makes possible this noble flourish: "The science of culture is young but full of promise. It is destined to do great things — if only the subject of its study will continue its age-old course: onward and upward."

POSTSCRIPT

I have let this review stand as originally written except for restoring the opening paragraph, which the editors had dropped, and adding all the notes. Let

me add that in this review, as well as in my paper on White's philosophy
of mathematics, I might have hesitated to use such strong language had it
not been for White's habit of using even stronger language when he was skull-
cracking those who disagreed with him.

NOTES

1. White told Robert Carneiro (see note 3) that on the day he discovered that
William Ostwald, a German chemist, had in 1909 anticipated his coinage of
"culturology" by using the term *kulturologie*, he was so excited "that he was unable
to sleep and had to take a long walk through the streets of Ann Arbor to calm himself
down." White devotes seven pages of his book to a defense of this word, replying
to H. L. Mencken and others who found the term unusually ugly and clumsy.

2. The vehemence with which White attacked Free Will (he liked to capitalize it)
exceeds even that of psychologist B. F. Skinner. White was particularly incensed by
the way in which a belief in free will seemed to him to cripple and enfeeble the writings
of leading anthropologists. As examples of this crippling he quotes such statements
as "Man should democratically take control of his own destiny and build himself
a world that is fit to live in" (Margaret Mead), and "There are none of our current
problems which cannot be solved if people will put their minds to them" (Ralph Linton).

To White, such sentiments were infantile hogwash. "It is not 'we' who control
our culture, but our culture that controls us." In White's vision, culture has a life
of its own, so self-sufficient that the environment (the external world) and even individual human beings play only trivial roles in its evolution. "We no longer think
of culture as designed to serve the needs of man," he wrote, "culture goes its own
way in accordance with laws of its own." It evolves "as if human beings did not exist."

Will knowledge of cultural laws enable us to control the evolution of human
societies? No. "Understanding culture will not . . . alter its course or change the 'fate'
that it has in store for us, any more than understanding the weather or the tides will
change them." Even the question of whether a person believes in free will or determinism is determined. "His philosophy is merely the response of his neuro-sensory-
muscular-glandular system to the streams of cultural stimuli impinging on him from
the outside. What is called 'philosophizing' is merely the interaction of these cultural
elements within his organism. His 'choice' of philosophic beliefs is merely a neurological
expression of the superior strength of some of these extra-somatic cultural forces."

This reasoning applies, of course, to White's own belief in determinism, thereby
undercutting any objective ground for regarding it as superior to a belief in free will.
White here touches on a paradox as basic to Marxism as to culturologism. If cultures
evolve by their own fully deterministic laws, if free will is an illusion, if we can only
predict the future, not alter it, why dispel energy trying to persuade people of anything?
Why did White waste time exhorting his colleagues to adopt his own brand of evolutionary anthropology? The only answer he could give is that the forces of nature,
operating through his culture, compelled him.

3. White would have been suspicious of the claims of today's talking-ape researchers. On this point I think he was mostly right (see Part 2, Chapter 44). His view
of human beings as symbol-manipulating mammals was so fundamental to him that
he could write: "Culture is merely the name we give to matter-and-energy in symbolic form." (White, "Ethnological Theory," in *Philosophy of the Future: The Quest*

of Modern Materialism, ed. by Roy Wood Sellars, V. J. McGill, and Marvin Farber, Macmillan, 1949.)

4. I have no personal knowledge of White's evolving views about the Soviets. Robert Carneiro, in his tribute to White (in *Totems and Teachers*, ed. by Sydel Silverman, Columbia University Press, 1981), tells us that White's acceptance of evolutionism was strongly influenced by his visit to Russia in 1929. It introduced him to the writings of Marx and Engels, who had found in the work of Lewis Morgan support for their program of abolishing capitalism.

According to Carneiro, White became convinced in 1929 that communism was the wave of the future. At the annual meeting of the American Association for the Advancement of Science, in 1930, he delivered a paper, "An Anthropological Appraisal of the Russian Revolution," in which (I quote Carneiro) "he predicted the collapse of the capitalist system and the eventual triumph of socialism." This rousing lecture received front-page coverage in both *Pravda* and the *New York Times*. Maxim Gorky praised White for his courage. Of course our native reds were overjoyed, and the University of Michigan was flooded with demands for White's resignation.

After that, White was more discreet about voicing his political opinions. However, according to Carneiro, he never abandoned the belief "that major cultural changes occur through the accumulation of small, quantitative increments that lead, once a certain point is reached, to a qualitative transformation." In plain language, to a revolution. Nor did White ever abandon the Marxist dogma that economic change (especially in the production of energy) underlies cultural change. Carneiro quotes White: ". . . the type of social organization, art, and philosophy of a given cultural system will be determined in form and content by the underlying technology." White liked to tell his classes: "The locomotive always precedes the Brotherhood of Railway Trainmen." He once said to Carneiro that he had read the first chapter of *Das Kapital* sixteen times and each time learned something new.

Marx and Engels had good reason to admire Morgan, a Rochester, New York, lawyer turned anthropologist, though he never held an academic post. Morgan's central thesis is that culture evolves through well-marked stages, each closely tied to technology. Modern capitalism, he was convinced, would self-destruct, to be superseded by democratic socialism. Morgan's views are strongly reflected in *Origin of the Family, Private Property, and the State*, by Marx and Engels.

British and U.S. anthropologists in the Boas tradition of cultural relativism, and understandably suspicious of all universal laws of cultural change, vigorously denounced Morgan and his admirers. Morgan's masterpiece, *Ancient Society, or Researches into the Lines of Human Progress from Savagery, through Barbarism, to Civilization* (1877), was reissued by Harvard University Press in 1964 in a handsome edition edited and annotated by White.

5. I have let these paragraphs stand even though they overlap my attack (see Part 1, Chapter 5) on White's mathematical philosophy. In my opinion, had White grounded mathematics in a reality independent of human minds, it would have strengthened rather than weakened his philosophy of culture.

6. This statement is no longer true. Sociobiologists believe that incest taboos have a genetic component that extends beyond close relatives to any person with whom one had been close-bonded as a child. See the section on incest taboos in Chapter 2 of Edward O. Wilson's, *On Human Nature* (1978), and its footnote 37, which gives some basic references.

8

Relativity and Truth

Philipp Frank was a charter member of that small but influential group of logical empiricists including Carnap, Neurath, Schlick, and others, which came to be known as the "Vienna Circle." His little book *Relativity—a Richer Truth* (Beacon, 1950) is a defense, on a popular level, of the ethical views of this group. Einstein, whose post at the University of Prague was assumed by Frank in 1912, has contributed a brief foreword.

Frank's thesis is that relativity in modern physics does not lead, as critics of science often suggest, to a denial of moral and political values. On the contrary, he feels, the application of the relativistic spirit to ethics leads to a "richer" formulation of truth. "Truth" is used in a pragmatic sense, and Frank does not hesitate to state his essential agreement with the ethical views of American pragmatists.

To repeat Frank's simple illustration, the discovery that the earth was round made it necessary to redefine "up" and "down" as relative to the center of the earth. "Would it be correct, now," he asks, "to say that . . . an element of uncertainty or doubt had slipped into our statements . . . ?" To say this, he continues, "would be a grave misrepresentation of the role of 'relativization' in science . . . by using this more complex type of statement, by employing this richer language, our assertions remain as definite, as 'objective,' as 'absolute,' as the statements of the simpler type, which we used to describe our former poorer experience."

Similarly, our recognition that there are no ethical absolutes permits us to draw upon new knowledge in psychology and the social sciences for the formulation of truer ethical and political principles. A chapter attacks the view that higher education can be unified by adopting a metaphysical creed

This review originally appeared in the *New Leader*, August 12, 1950, and is reprinted with permission.

such as Thomism or dialectical materialism. The wiser method, he argues, is to permit common principles to "emerge as a natural product of the tendencies toward integration that are inherent in the sciences themselves." Although Dewey is not mentioned in this section, Frank is defending the view to which Dewey has devoted a lifetime of educational activity.

An excellent chapter calls attention to the compatibility of pragmatism and democracy. and the inability of totalitarianisms, such as Nazi Germany and Stalinist Russia, to accept scientific objectivity. A final section casts a mystical tinge over the scientist's faith in the rationality of nature—the Spinozistic "cosmic religion" about which Einstein has elsewhere written so eloquently.

At the level on which this book is written, it is difficult to find areas of disagreement. But there are deeper issues that Frank does not touch. For example, it is one thing to recognize that science never gives us final truth, and quite another to deny that the term "final truth" has meaning. Our knowledge of the center of the earth may alter constantly as investigation proceeds, but this does not mean that the nature of the earth's core is constantly changing. Members of the Vienna Circle have a distressing habit of talking as though the cosmos had no definite structure, or, more precisely, that it is meaningless to say it has; and about this point there now rages a bitter controversy among empiricists.

Again, in the field of ethics it is one thing to recognize that our moral principles derive from a cultural pattern; quite another to argue that all patterns are equally effective in meeting basic human needs. This is anthropology's problem of "cultural relativism," about which another vigorous battle is under way, and concerning which Dr. Frank is also silent.

Finally, there is the question of whether belief or nonbelief in some type of metaphysical ground for moral values has a significant influence on a person's mental health or behavior. It may be, as Freud himself once suggested, that mankind is so constituted it cannot escape widespread neuroses without faith in God. It may prove, as psychology advances, that men lack intensity in seeking the good life unless they believe "goodness" to have a more stable meaning than the pragmatic one. Or it may prove otherwise.

These are some of the questions concerning metaphysical and ethical relativism that still plague us. Perhaps Frank did not have space in his little book to discuss them, but the fact that there are no hints about them gives one the uneasy feeling that the author has already dismissed them as "pseudo problems."

9

Einstein as Philosopher

To anyone interested in theoretical physics, epistemology, or philosophy of science, *Albert Einstein: Philosopher-Scientist*, edited by Paul Schilpp (Library of Living Philosophers, 1949), is a book of highest importance. Twenty-five authorities—philosophers, physicists and mathematicians—contribute essays, followed by an article in which Einstein comments critically on the essays. In addition, the book contains an informative, delightfully mellow autobiography (Einstein calls it his "obituary") and an excellent bibliography of Einstein's writings.

From a philosophic standpoint, the essay that impressed me as most significant was Reichenbach's, dealing with the philosophic implications of relativity. It clarifies many confusing issues, such as the precise sense in which the non-Euclidean language of relativity is a convention chosen solely for its simplicity, although future developments may give it a firm footing in external reality. (For example, if more powerful telescopes someday reveal that wherever the telescope is pointed it will be possible to see our own galaxy, this will confirm the "closed" character of space—a topological property unexplainable in Euclidean terms.)

More important from the standpoint of technical physics are essays by Bohr and others that examine Einstein's rejection of what has come to be the accepted attitude toward quantum phenomena. Most physicists today regard certain "random" aspects of the behavior of the electron as basic in the sense that no laws exist that would make possible exact prediction. Only when large numbers of electrons are involved do statistical laws emerge. Einstein, with his Spinozistic faith in a completely ordered and deterministic Nature, looks upon this as a temporary state of ignorance, believing that

This review originally appeared in the *New Leader*, February 5, 1951, and is reprinted with permission.

as physics advances all haphazardry in quantum theory will be removed. As he expresses it in a letter to Max Born, "You believe in God playing dice and I in perfect laws. . . ."

It is interesting to note that two distinguished contributors reject the general theory of relativity in favor of a view closer to that of Ernst Mach, one of Einstein's eminent predecessors. Mach suggested that the total mass of the cosmos (or galaxy) might form an "inertial system" that provides a fixed frame of reference for the definition of accelerated motion. Bridgman's essay accuses Einstein of departing too far from "operationally defined" concepts and is, I believe, fully answered by Einstein. Nevertheless, it is now widely recognized that, on the basis of the special theory (firmly grounded in the Michelson-Morley experiment), it is possible to devise numerous theories of gravitation and inertia, all more or less capable of explaining known empirical data. At present, the chief rival to Einstein's general theory is the "kinematic" relativity of the late E. A. Milne, an Oxford physicist. Milne sides with Bridgman in favoring Mach's approach, but his contribution to the book is so technical that I would not presume to guess whether his curt dismissal by Einstein is or is not deserved.

The book is rich throughout in historical explication and in suggesting exciting contemporary trends. For example, Karl Menger proposes "a geometry of lumps—that is, a theory in which lumps are undefined concepts, whereas points appear as the result of limiting or intersecting processes applied to these lumps." This approach was anticipated by the Philosopher of *The Crock of Gold,* who announced, "Finality is death. Perfection is finality. Nothing is perfect. There are lumps in it."

Only one essay deals with Einstein's political thinking. It does little more than summarize his views—his pacifism and its suspension during World War II, Zionism, faith in world government, the conviction that the USSR is significantly less a threat to peace than was Nazi Germany, and the belief that because of America's greater military potential we must assume a lion's share of guilt in the current drift toward war. It is these latter beliefs that have made Einstein an easy prey for cynical exploitation by the "Progressive" party and other Stalinist fronts.

The most charitable view of Einstein's Soviet sympathies is that they spring from a sincere desire for peace but operate on hopelessly inadequate information and are perhaps strongly influenced by several of his close associates.[1] Our admiration for his genius and greatness of heart must, alas, be tempered by awareness that his political faith, as Morris Cohen once wrote, "needs to be supplemented by a more realistic vision of the brute actualities of existence."

NOTE

1. For documentation on Einstein's inability to understand the nature of Stalinism, see the postscript to Chapter 2 of my *Science: Good, Bad and Bogus* (1981), and "My Running Debate with Einstein," by Sidney Hook, in *Commentary*, July 1982.

10

Hans Reichenbach

Professor Hans Reichenbach (formerly leader of a group of logical empiricists in Berlin, now on the faculty of the University of California) looks upon traditional philosophy as consisting almost entirely of poetic speculation. The great philosophers asked important questions, but they lacked the means for answering, and their grandiose systems—though presented as products of reason—are little more than rationalizations of nonrational beliefs, of more interest to the psychologist than the philosopher.

By "philosopher" Reichenbach means the modern empiricist who has dismissed metaphysics as meaningless and recognizes as knowledge only the truths obtained by science. This is the central theme of his new book, *The Rise of Scientific Philosophy* (University of California, 1951). After a brief discussion of Plato, Aristotle, Kant, Spinoza, Hegel, and Marx—all of whose views are considered disguised emotional preferences—the author turns his attention to the empirical tradition. Less emphasis is placed on the contributions of individual philosophers than on the influence of modern physics and non-Euclidean geometry, and the development of symbolic logic as a tool for precision in philosophic analysis.

Two original contributions to scientific philosophy, for which the author is well known, are briefly touched upon. They are his "three-valued logic" (for application to quantum theory, adding the value of "indeterminate" to those of "true" and "false") and his "multivalued logic" (in which true and false are the polar terms of a continuum of values representing all degrees of probability from 0 to 1).

The book closes with a discussion of ethical matters in the light of the new orientation. Reichenbach argues that moral laws cannot be considered true or false, since they are expressions of personal desires and directives for

This review was originally published in the *New Leader*, June 11, 1951, and is reprinted with permission.

the behavior of others. "Science tells us what is, but not what should be." The question of whether there is a common human nature underlying all cultures, which might provide the basis for a standard of values, is left open, but he feels that the answer is not important. His reason for thinking this is that most ethical debates are over means, rather than ends, and in this realm science can give us genuine answers.

"Political decisions are virtually all of this type. For instance, whether the government should control prices is a question to be answered by economic analysis; the ethical aim of producing [needed] goods . . . for as low a price as possible is not under discussion. . . . Those who ask the philosopher for guidance in life should be grateful when he sends them to the psychologist, or the social scientist. . . ."

It is in this discussion that I think Reichenbach's otherwise excellent book takes on a flimsiness. On page 299, he mentions in passing that the nobility in feudal states, capitalists, and political aristocrats of totalitarianisms find satisfaction in their superiority over others not in their class. How then can we reply to a Nietzsche who proposes, quite frankly, that a master class enjoy its superior satisfactions through exploitation of a slave class? Reichenbach does not think this a significant question, and as a consequence his discussion of ethics does not seem to me to touch fundamentals. It is true that, within a culture such as the United States, there is rough agreement on ends and arguments chiefly over means. But, when a democratic society is in conflict with a fascist society, how would Reichenbach arbitrate the dispute?

Apart from this animadversion, I know of no book since Ayer's *Language, Truth, and Logic* (1936) that is a better layman's introduction to the spirit of the new empiricism. I once took a course with Professor Carnap that was held in a classroom occupied during the previous hour by a Great Books class. The blackboard would often be covered with charts of Platonic or Aristotelian metaphysical terms. When Carnap wished to use the blackboard, he would erase everything written thereon, and I have always remembered this as a pleasant symbol of the movement in which he, Russell, and Reichenbach have played such major roles.

Those who feel an exultation in the cleansing sweep of Carnap's arm will find that same emotion in these words of Reichenbach:

> There is no compromise between science and speculative philosophy. Let us not attempt to reconcile the two in the hope of a higher synthesis. Not all historical developments follow the dialectical law: one line of thought may die out and leave its place to another that springs from different roots—like a biological species that survives only in fossil form, once another species, better equipped, has taken over. Speculative philosophy . . . is decaying. A different philosophy is in the ascendant. . . .

11

The Spoor of Spooks

Scientific and scholarly nonsense, always good for lurid copy in the *American Weekly*, has in recent years won footholds in surprisingly respectable quarters. In view of this trend it is refreshing to find a leading publisher resisting the temptation to make a fast buck with another book on flying saucers and publishing Bergen Evans's second hilarious blast at human gullibility: *The Spoor of Spooks and Other Nonsense* (Knopf, 1954). Like his earlier work *The Natural History of Nonsense*, Evans tackles his topics with impudent gusto. Followers of J. B. Rhine will not be amused by the chapter heading "Psi-ing in the Carolines," but then no believer in Psi phenomena would be amused or impressed by any unfavorable treatment of the subject, so what does it matter? Like Bertrand Russell, whose *Outline of Intellectual Rubbish* is a classic of similar genre, Evans delights in the sly quip and the flippant footnote. One of his footnotes is simply "Hmm!"

The book is not, however, primarily a book on pseudoscience, but a witty compendium of mistaken beliefs, scientific and otherwise. Professor Evans's range is wide—the overestimated piety of the Middle Ages, the exaggerated villainy of the Renaissance; historical myths like the story of William Tell or the Dutch boy who put his finger in the dike; great sayings of famous people that were not said at all or said by someone else ("Go west, young man," "Let 'em eat cake," "I disapprove of what you say, . . ."); the myth of Fascist efficiency—Evans was in Italy in 1930 and the trains did *not* run on time; Theresa Neumann and other women who claim to live without adequate food or drink; the alleged ability of such pundits as Clifton Fadiman and Robert Hutchins to read entire pages at a glance. Scores of popular misconceptions about sex, love, marriage, child rearing, longevity, crime,

This review originally appeared in the *Saturday Review*, November 13, 1954.

dope addiction, and the nation's laws are examined in the cold light of available evidence.

One amusing chapter, though somewhat out of place in the context of the book, concerns the average American's "autointoxication" or love affair with his car. "It is his romance, upholstered and on springs. It is his magic carpet, complete with radio and heater. It is his solace: he may be henpecked at home and browbeaten at work, but in the sweet intervals of coming and going he is a god at whose slightest bidding a hundred horses spring forward. He has achieved divinity with a down payment." Evans thinks that the "symbiosis" of the American and his car is a social phenomenon to be ranked with the tulip mania or the dancing mania.

It is difficult to imagine how any reader could fail to find exploded in these pages at least a dozen of his own cherished beliefs. I did not know, for example, that clothes moths have no objection whatever to the smell of cedar, that gumdrops are superior to cheese as bait for mousetraps, that Churchill's phrase "blood, sweat, and tears" was first used by John Donne and later by Byron, or that the story of the Black Hole of Calcutta rests on the flimsiest of historical evidence.

There are a few spots where one might quibble about a point of view or have doubts about the soundness of a statistic, but on the whole there is a feeling that the author has researched his material carefully. The book is a mine of off-trail but worthwhile information, a delight to read, and a welcome antidote to the sensational but wildly inaccurate articles that boost the circulation of so many popular magazines.

12

Fermat's Last Theorem

Who but Eric Temple Bell would have thought of writing such a book? The atomic bomb was, he confesses, the source of his inspiration. If atomic energy finally obliterates humanity, what great mathematical problems, Bell asked himself, are likely to be still unsolved when the darkness falls? One problem comes immediately to mind: Fermat's last theorem.

Pierre Fermat, by profession a jurist, was the greatest amateur mathematician who ever lived. One day in the mid-seventeenth century he scribbled a note in the margin of an old book on arithmetic. He had discovered, he wrote, a "truly marvelous" proof that if n is a number greater than 2, there are no whole numbers X, Y, Z such that $x^n + y^n = z^n$. Unfortunately, he added, the margin was too narrow to contain it. Did Fermat really have a valid proof? Nobody knows. The theorem is so simple that a ten-year-old can grasp it, yet no mathematician has been able to establish either its truth or falsity.

The Last Problem (Simon and Schuster, 1961) is a book in which this theorem of Fermat's serves as a peg on which to hang nothing less than a popular history of number theory. The project could not have found a better author. Bell was not only an expert in the theory of numbers, he was also a skillful writer of popular books on mathematics, even a one-time writer (under the pseudonym of John Taine) of lurid science-fiction. He died in 1960 before completing *The Last Problem*, leaving a curious manuscript that is, like all his other books, a delight to read.

I say "curious" because Bell permitted himself to wander into all sorts of historical by-ways that fascinated him, though they are largely irrelevant to his story. What does mathematics have to do with the fertility rites of

This review originally appeared in the *New York Times Book Review*, February 4, 1962, ©1962 by The New York Times Company. Reprinted by permission.

Babylon, the amours of Cleopatra, or the lack of sanitation in the Paris streets of Louis XIV? Bell himself tells us that Fermat did much of his best work while the Thirty Years' War raged around him, yet he never mentioned the war in his correspondence.

Bell closes an admirable hatchet job on Alexander the Great by concluding that the Macedonian made his finest contribution to learning by drinking himself to death at an early age. We all know that social and political conditions can influence mathematics (and vice versa!), but by and large, Bell's excursions into such matters, though entertaining, cast only a dim light on his major themes.

Bell is more to the point when he discusses such topics as the mathematical contributions of Babylonia, magnificent beside the meager work of Egypt. The legend that Egyptian rope-stretchers laid out right angles by using an endless rope knotted at the vertices of a triangle with the sides 3, 4, 5 has, as Bell points out, been exploded.

He summarizes well the contributions of the Pythagoreans and the speculations about Plato's "nuptial number." He also summarizes the work on Archimedes' monstrous "cattle problem," a two-part problem in which the number of animals is to be calculated after certain mathematical conditions are given. The virtues and defects of Euclid are discussed and there are crisp biographies of a dozen lesser mathematicians who made important contributions allied to Fermat's last theorem. Toward the end, the book tends to dribble off; due, one suspects, to its unfinished state. Even the two chapters on Fermat are short and sketchy compared with the robust treatment of him in Bell's own *Men of Mathematics*.

Someone once sent to Augustin-Louis Cauchy, the great eighteenth-century French mathematician, a paper in which he tried to show that $x^3 + y^3 + z^3 = t^3$ had no solution in integers. Cauchy returned the manuscript, Bell tells us, with no comment save the note: $3^3 + 4^3 + 5^3 = 6^3$.[1] Alas, if there is a counterexample to Fermat's theorem, it is not so simple. The book's aftermath, an excellent summary by D. H. Lehmer, of the University of California, of recent work on the problem, discloses that an electronic computer has proved the theorem true for n up to 4,001. This means that z, if there is a z, must have more than 43,255 digits.[2]

Bell does not mention the grim possibility—perhaps more horrible for him to contemplate than the end of civilization—that Fermat's last theorem is true but unprovable. Worse still, it may be impossible to prove it unprovable. Mathematicians would thus be doomed to go on forever seeking a proof, never finding it, never knowing the search to be futile.

NOTES

1. Unfortunately, this lovely extension of $3^2 + 4^2 = 5^2$ does not continue to higher powers. The simplest known solution to $a^4 + b^4 + c^4 + d^4 = e^4$ is $30^4 + 120^4 + 315^4 + 272^4 = 353^4$.

2. This has been raised by modern computer searches to $n = $ more than 100,000, which means that the numbers involved would have more than a million digits. It is still possible that Fermat's last theorem fails for some extremely large prime exponent, or even for all prime exponents higher than the first counterexample, but very few number-theorists think the theorem is false.

13

Mathematical Magpie

Clifton Fadiman is a man of varied interests, impeccable taste, a sense of humor, a flair for showmanship, and a knowledge of mathematics greater than he likes to admit. The success of his previous anthology, *Fantasia Mathematica*, has prompted him to compile a second one. Like the first, *The Mathematical Magpie* (Simon and Schuster, 1962) is a bright, brassy carnival of stories, essays, poems, limericks, jokes, and what have you, all derived, as the dust jacket says, from the infinite domain of mathematics.

Step right up, ladies and gentlemen, and see the fabulous Ta-Ta, Sidney Sime's topological beast who turns himself inside out to enter a room in his skull; watch Lewis Carroll make a "cross cap" (a closed surface with no inside or outside) by sewing two handkerchiefs together; shudder at Bertrand Russell's masked Pi, whose enigmatic face no mortal can behold and live; observe Dr. Breuer remove an appendix by way of the fourth dimension; question Karl, the giant computer that can solve any problem except a military one; operate the Moebius strip conveyor belt.

In the lecture hall, hear Isaac Asimov explain his startling discovery about the mathematical powers of the unaided human brain; listen to Robert Coates's chilling account of what happened in New York when the Law of Averages began to fail; hear Frederick Soddy recite in rhyme his famous discovery about the diameters of five mutually kissing spheres; watch Johnny Hart, chalk-talk virtuoso, sketch the story of a primitive Euclidian's magnificent failure to prove, with a forked stick, that parallel lines never meet; learn from Elliot Paul how a distinguished mathematician was led to his profession by contemplating the combinations and permutations in a photographic album owned by a certain Parisian house of ill fame. A wonderful anthology; let's hope there are more to come.

This review originally appeared in the *New York Herald Tribune*, August 19, 1962.

14

Computers and Cybernetics

Who would have guessed, ten years ago, that the *New Yorker* magazine would someday hire a physicist as staff writer? Jeremy Bernstein, thirty-five-year-old associate professor at New York University, now holds this distinction; for several years his contributions to the *New Yorker* have been models of science writing at its best. *The Analytical Engine* (Random House, 1964) derives from his recent series of articles about computers. They were written to provide the intelligent layman with some elementary insights into those rapidly proliferating robots that threaten to alter our lives more drastically than do atomic energy and spaceships.

In a skillfully compressed section on the history of computers, Bernstein stresses the remarkable pioneer work of the English mathematician Charles Babbage. Small calculating devices had previously been designed by Pascal and Leibniz, but not until the early nineteenth century, when Joseph Jacquard invented a way to control weaving looms with punch cards, was it possible to conceive of a mechanical computer on a truly giant scale.

For forty years Babbage tried to obtain sufficient funds for constructing his "analytical engine." By today's standards it was a crude behemoth, operating with punch cards, gears and cranks, but it embodied almost all the basic design elements of modern computers.

Babbage succeeded in building only a few parts of his engine. Curiously, almost all we know about his machine comes from the writings of Lord Byron's daughter, Ada Augusta, the Countess of Lovelace. She combined a pretty face with a fine head for mathematics and extraordinary insight into the potentials of Babbage's dream. At one time she and Babbage even tried to work out a scheme for beating the horses to raise money for the project! (Babbage had many such schemes, including a mechanical tick-tack-toe machine for exhibition at fairs.)

This review originally appeared in the *New York Herald Tribune*'s *Book Week*, June 28, 1964.

Electricity later provided the means by which Babbage's successors could carry out his untimely program. Bernstein sketches the rapid evolution of the modern electrical computer from the crude, bulky models of the 1940s to the compact, transistorized systems of today. He explains well the recent revolution in programming made possible by such computer languages as FORTRAN (from "formula translation"), the difference between an analogue and digital computer (it is the difference between the slide rule and an abacus), the advantages of the binary over the decimal system.

After pointing out the striking ways in which a human brain does and does not resemble an electrical computer, Bernstein turns to the Perceptron, one of many "learning machines" now being developed. Like a human brain, the Perceptron learns from experience. Parts of its network can be destroyed without seriously impairing its abilities; other circuits simply take over, as they do in an injured animal brain. Does such a machine actually learn to think? It is a tricky linguistic question, obviously unapproachable without a sharp meaning analysis of the word *think*. A learning machine quickly reaches a level of sophistication beyond which no one knows exactly what circuit patterns are inside it or how it does what it does. It is precisely after making this point that Bernstein's book ends and Norbert Wiener's book *God and Golem, Inc.* (MIT Press, 1964) begins.

Professor Wiener was, of course, a major architect of the computer revolution (or the "cybernetic revolution," to use the broader term Wiener himself invented). His wise little book, based on lectures at Yale University and elsewhere, concentrates on those areas of the revolution that bear on traditional problems of religion and philosophy.

First, the learning machines. Is history itself, Wiener asks, some sort of transcendental game that God is playing with his own learning machines: human animals perfected by the long, ingenious process of evolution? Is it possible God can lose? Wiener reminds us that Arthur L. Samuel of IBM taught a computer how to play checkers so well that he consistently lost to the machine (though he later brushed up on the game and began winning again) and that, within ten to twenty-five years, chess learning machines are expected to reach master class. (This prophecy, by the way, arouses uncontrollable rage and disbelief among some chess experts.)[1]

One of the great distinguishing features of living things, as opposed to nonliving, is the ability to replicate, to make copies of themselves. But computers can be designed to do this also. Wiener outlines his own clever "existence proof" that such devices can be made. Since all traits of "life" seem to involve the body's structure on a molecular level, might it be possible to scan a human, molecule by molecule, and by the use of a pulsed code, and a suitable supply of chemicals, construct an exact duplicate? Could an individual be teleported, say, to Mars, at the speed of light, by breaking down his body, particle by particle, sending the information to a machine on Mars that would then reassemble the person from elements on Mars?

This suggestion—and Wiener agrees it is conceptually possible—has often been exploited in science fiction. "Dark Nuptial," a story by Robert Locke, is about a man of the future whose wife dies before their honeymoon. Fortunately, she had once been teleported from Mars to Earth, and her "matrix" is still on file. From this matrix, he has a new wife printed. Now he is sorely troubled. Is it *really* his wife? One smiles, but it is not a trivial problem. Although Wiener does not mention it, his former philosophy teacher at Harvard, Josiah Royce, once discussed essentially this question in considerable detail and depth.

Finally, there are the incalculable ethical, social, political, and military consequences of the computer revolution. While the population explosion expands the working force, automation whittles down the number of jobs. War is more and more being studied as a game, and it will probably not be long until learning machines are taught how to play it. How far can they be trusted? "I should very much hate to ride on the first trial of an automobile regulated by photoelectric feedback devices," Wiener writes metaphorically, "unless there were somewhere a handle by which I could take over control if I found myself driving smack into a tree."

Wiener spends a few pages on happier matters—the use of computers for artificial limbs, the growing success of language translation machines, the use of computers for medical diagnosis. He is mainly concerned, however, with what he fears is a lack of flexibility in the thinking of today's social scientists and political leaders as they struggle to cope with industrial changes far greater than they yet realize.

He sees this rigidity on both sides of the Iron Curtain. Karl Marx, he reminds us, lived in the middle of the *first* industrial revolution, and Adam Smith "belongs to a still earlier and more obsolete phase" of that same revolution. The danger to both East and West is a "homeostasis" of thought; an equilibrium unable to adapt to the dynamics of an automated society. Wiener sees the computer as analogous to the golem of Jewish folklore. It is an embryonic, half-witted intelligence, a monster of our own creation, difficult to control, capable of enormous evil.

So we move, whether we like it or not, with accelerating speed into a strange, unknown future. Old rules of ethics and politics are rapidly becoming obsolete. Wiener does not offer any new ones; he simply insists that, before such rules can be devised, the new problems must be recognized. It is part of his greatness that he was willing to take time off from his technical work to contribute what he could toward this first essential step.

POSTSCRIPT

Since 1964 the second industrial revolution has been gathering momentum as expected. Transistors have been replaced by silicon microchips, and soon even smaller, more powerful computers will be available, based on who knows what breakthroughs. At the moment, the two most promising techniques are magnetic bubble memories and the use of Josephson junctions. Looking further ahead, there are such possibilities as computing with light instead of electricity, or using "biochips" made by synthesizing organic molecules or by growing micro-organisms to produce them. In any case, unless the United States manages to restructure its economy, it looks as if Japan will be leading the world into the fantastic electronic future that lies ahead.

NOTE

1. This prophecy has been fulfilled. By 1982 Belle, a chess program developed at Bell Laboratories, was playing on a master level. Many chess programs will now defeat any human player, including grandmasters, if a very short time limit is allowed for each move.

15

Up from Adam

Except among Protestant fundamentalists and a fast-evaporating minority of ultraconservative Catholics, the theory of evolution is no longer a topic of dispute. There are, of course, all sorts of philosophical and logical attitudes one can take toward the fact of evolution. Biologists working on evolutionary theory are reluctant these days to talk about their metaphysical commitments, but Theodosius Dobzhansky, a distinguished Russian-born geneticist now at The Rockefeller University, is a refreshing exception. His previous books have often stressed the creative aspects of the evolutionary process; now he has pulled together his philosophical thoughts, as they have matured over a fifty-year period, to write *The Biology of Ultimate Concern* (New American Library, 1967). This little book is intended as a testament, an expression of a metaphysical vision in which biological evolution has the central role.

Dobzhansky is careful at all times to keep his vision separated from scientific knowledge. It is in no way implied, he fully realizes, by the scientific data. He has no quarrel with the prevailing mutation theory of evolution, sharpened by the recent discovery that "genes" are sections of the genetic code along helical DNA molecules. Mutations are random, with natural selection acting as a cybernetic device, feeding back information about the environment, information that the species uses to improve its survival chances. Prodded by chance and natural laws, species grope their way through space and time, exploring new habitats, changing, adapting, sometimes backsliding, often becoming extinct. Dobzhansky has little patience with neo-Lamarckian theories or the vitalistic views of such biologists as E. W. Sinnott and his predecessor Hans Driesch, who postulated mysterious, yet-undiscovered "entelechies" that guide biological groups toward predetermined ends. Muta-

This review originally appeared in the *New York Herald Tribune*'s *Book Week*, April 23, 1967.

tion theory, with its random trial-and-error technique, is quite sufficient, Dobzhansky believes, to explain what has occurred.

There are no discontinuities in the evolutionary process that require the intervention of transcendent fingers, no "gods of the gaps," as the author puts it. Differences in degree obviously generate differences in kind, and of course unpredictable features are always emerging along branches of the still-growing evolutionary tree. The two greatest transitions were the emergence of the first self-replicating molecules from lifeless matter and the recent emergence of man with his curious self-awareness and his revolutionary ability, denied the beasts, of directing his own evolutionary future.

Neither transition, miraculous though it may appear, demands supernatural string-pulling to explain it. Dobzhansky is unconcerned with the bizarre question that bugs so many of today's Catholics and conservative Protestants: Were the newly born Adam and Eve, or Adams and Eves, suckled and reared by soulless parents? The big transition from beast to man was not a sudden leap over a critical threshold, like the abrupt boiling or freezing of water. It was the result of small, imperceptible changes. There were hundreds of thousands of in-between individuals, creatures about whom it is as useless to ask if they were beasts or men as it is to ask if girls of fifteen are children or women.

The human species, with its complex nervous system and its self-awareness, is obviously the earth's most advanced life form. Darwin, Dobzhansky writes, should have called one of his books *The Ascent of Man*, not *The Descent of Man*. It may even be, the author surprisingly asserts, that man is the only rational, self-aware creature in the entire universe. How should one look upon the preposterous history of sexual gene-shuffling and random change by which man became what he is? Was it all no more than an accident, fulfilling no higher purpose, ultimately as absurd as the existentialists say it is? Dobzhansky thinks not. The absurdity vanishes, and with it our existential anxiety, if we surround evolution with a pious halo. The halo Dobzhansky recommends is one that he derived, he says, partly from the writings of Arnold Toynbee, the Protestant historian, and Paul Tillich, the Protestant theologian, but mostly from the books of the French Jesuit priest and paleontologist Pierre Teilhard de Chardin.

This is how the trick is done. Instead of looking for miraculous events at spots of time in the past—the creation of the first living molecules, the creation of the first humans, perhaps other events—one looks upon the entire history of the universe as a single monstrous miracle. The whole of nature becomes the mechanism by which God is carrying out His stupendous Plan. But exactly what is meant by "God"? What sort of "Plan" is being carried out? At this point, alas, Dobzhansky's words take on that mushy Hegelian quality so characteristic of Tillich's own writing. It is difficult to know where he stands.

Although Dobzhansky praises Teilhard as an "inspired seer" and calls his last chapter "The Teilhard Synthesis," one despairs of determining how much of Teilhard's vision he actually shares. Teilhard was a Christian mystic who never doubted that persons have immortal souls. His speculations are not so much denials of Catholic doctrine as they are reinterpretations and additions. Teilhard was convinced that a mere belief in immortality is not enough to give a Christian a strong incentive to cooperate in the great secular task of building a better earth. It is necessary that he participate somehow, even after death, in the coming *earthly* Paradise. In Teilhard's incredible eschatology, the forces of love will draw persons closer and closer together, irrespective of race, into a world community that in turn will evolve, over the eons, into a superorganism. Individuals will keep their unique personalities, but together they will form a "hyperpersonal" unity that has its own "Soul of souls." A great convergence eventually will occur at what Teilhard calls the "Omega Point," the end of human history. The souls of all who have lived, except possibly the souls of the damned, will combine with the earthly community and with God to form the mystical body of Christ about which St. Paul wrote. The transcendent, eternal Paradise, prophesied in the New Testament, will be beyond space and time. Death will be no more.

How much of this Christian vision does Dobzhansky want to keep? It is hard to say, but one guesses: not much. He does not accept Teilhard's conviction that the threshold between man and beast was crossed at a "single stride." He seems not to believe in life after death. He seems not to believe in Teilhard's personal deity, but rather, like Tillich, to equate God with being itself, and the highest religion with an "ultimate concern" that has Tillich's "God behind the gods" as its object. Is this pantheistic piety to be identified with some variety of Christianity? "My upbringing and education make me biased in favor of Christianity as the framework of the synthesis," he writes, but immediately he adds, "I can, however, understand people who would prefer a different framework."

It is all hints and haze. As far as I can tell, Dobzhansky's synthesis of science and religion differs in no essential way from the naturalism of such writers and scientists as H. G. Wells, Julian Huxley, John Dewey, George Gaylord Simpson, and other humanists who were and are much preoccupied with evolution. The books of all these men express the hope that human reason and love will eventually bring about a world order in which poverty and disease will become things of the past. "Gathered together at last under the leadership of man," Wells closed his *Outline of History*, "the student-teacher of the universe, unified, disciplined, armed with the secret powers of the atom, and with knowledge as yet beyond dreaming, Life, for ever dying to be born afresh, for ever young and eager, will presently stand upon earth as upon a footstool, and stretch out its realm amidst the stars."

Does Dobzhansky have an ultimate concern greater than that? If so, I am at a loss to know what it is. Indeed, his vision seems in some respects narrower than Wells's, for Wells considered the possibility of mankind colonizing other planets and cooperating with intelligent life that had evolved elsewhere, whereas Dobzhansky's vision, like Teilhard's, seems unaccountably confined to creatures of earth. As for Teilhard's emphasis on love, I cannot see that Dobzhansky has taken from it anything more than what earlier writers on evolution had in mind when they wrote about the role of altruism in the struggle for survival. The anarchist Prince Peter Kropotkin, as early as 1902, published a remarkable book called *Mutual Aid: A Factor of Evolution* in which he argued that love plays a greater role in the natural selection of higher animals than had previously been recognized. (His book is still worth reading as a counterbalance to books overstressing the role of aggression and competition, such as Robert Ardrey's recent *Territorial Imperative*, with its crude nineteenth-century approach to man's animal heritage.) It seems to me that Dobzhansky has done little more than take the old familiar humanist vision of a future world community and dress it up with some poetic phrases that he has taken from Tillich and Teilhard without the inconvenience of taking their theologies.

One wishes that Dobzhansky would give us his opinions about earlier philosophers of evolution, especially the leading proponents of what the histories of philosophy call "emergent evolution." He makes no mention, for example, of Samuel Alexander, the British philosopher whose famous work, *Space, Time and Deity* (reprinted in Dover paperback), so strongly emphasized the natural emergence of new levels of existence. One would expect Dobzhansky to find Alexander's eschatological ladder, with its infinite rungs of higher, yet-to-evolve life forms, more exciting than Teilhard's, with its two remaining rungs. At any rate, it would be interesting to know what Dobzhansky thinks of Alexander's more sophisticated, less eccentric non-Christian but theistically tinged picture of the future of our fantastic fidgety universe.

16

How About a Little Game?

It is hard to tell, looking through mass-circulation magazines, whether the two-culture gap in the United States is widening or narrowing. *Harper's Bazaar, Town & Country, Cosmopolitan*, and *Ladies' Home Journal* now carry regular horoscope columns. On the other hand, perhaps more surprisingly, the *New Yorker* now has on its staff a professional physicist, Jeremy Bernstein, age thirty-eight, who teaches at New York University and has written more than thirty-seven technical papers.

In the introduction to his new book *A Comprehensible World* (Random House, 1967), Bernstein tells how he got the job. He had just returned to his post at Brookhaven National Laboratory, Upton, Long Island, after a year in France on a National Science Foundation fellowship. Lacking anything better to do—he was a bachelor living in a quiet wooded area—an old ambition to be a journalist seized him. After typing out some sparkling recollections of his summer on the island of Corsica, where he had taught physics to French students, he sent the manuscript to the *New Yorker* and forgot about it. Several months later William Shawn, the magazine's editor, phoned to say he wanted to publish it. That was in 1961 and Bernstein has been writing for the *New Yorker* ever since. His first two books, *The Analytical Engine*, about computers, and *Ascent*, about his hobby of mountain climbing, were based on *New Yorker* contributions. His third book, *A Comprehensible World*, is a collection of varied *New Yorker* articles and book reviews.

They are a delight to read or reread. Bernstein has an ability, uncommon among his peers, to write about difficult topics in a way that intelligent laymen can understand, and to write about them with wit and literary distinction. When mirror-reflection symmetry, known to particle physicists as the law

This review originally appeared in *Commentary*, October 1967, ©1967 by Commentary, and is reprinted with permission.

of parity conservation, was overthrown in 1957 most physicists despaired of explaining to any nonphysicist what had happened. To oversimplify, the law of parity says that nature, in all her basic laws, shows no preference for left or right. If a motion picture is taken of any event, the film reversed, then projected on a screen, the mirror-reflected events look perfectly natural. This ambidexterity of the universe was shattered when it was discovered that there is, so to speak, a left-handed bias in all weak interactions of particles. If a film of such events could be shown in mirror-reversed form, it would depict events that cannot occur. Physicists are still struggling with the full, revolutionary implications of the discovery. Bernstein not only was capable of explaining it, he also was a friend of T. D. Lee and C. N. Yang, the two Chinese physicists who later shared a Nobel Prize for their theoretical work that had led to the overthrow of parity. Bernstein had even collaborated with them on a technical paper. His long *New Yorker* article about them, which provides the second chapter of his book, is a masterpiece of science writing. It documents a major turning-point in the history of modern physics, draws a vivid picture of two remarkable scientists, and is a superb popular account of why physicists were so astonished and agitated when the news that parity was not conserved first flashed from laboratory to laboratory.

Most of the other chapters are crisp, admirably written reviews of important books about science, illuminated by Bernstein's wide-ranging knowledge of literature and politics, and a philosophical attitude strongly influenced by his Harvard teacher, Philipp P. Frank, to whose memory the book is dedicated. Among the books reviewed are Erwin Schrödinger's *My View of the World*, Barbara Cline's *The Questioners: Physicists and the Quantum Theory*, George Gamow's *A Planet Called Earth*, Stephen and Jane Toulmin's *The Discovery of Time*, Marie Boas's *The Scientific Renaissance*, Jacques Barzun's *Science: The Glorious Entertainment*, and Walter Sullivan's *We Are Not Alone*. There is also a short but generous tribute to Arthur Clarke, whom Bernstein rightly considers one of the best, perhaps the best, of living science-fiction authors, followed by a longer tribute to Stanley Kubrick, the film-maker who directed *Lolita, Paths of Glory,* and *Dr. Strangelove.* Clarke collaborated with Kubrick on the screenplay for *2001: A Space Odyssey.* Through Clarke, Bernstein got to know Kubrick and to watch the filming of some of the movie's spectacular scenes.

"How About a Little Game?"—the title of the chapter on Kubrick—is so appropriately metaphorical that Random House could have used it for the title of the book. *"A Comprehensible World"* comes from a charmingly paradoxical statement by Einstein—"One may say the eternal mystery of the world is its comprehensibility"—which Bernstein puts at the front of his volume; but isolated from its context it strikes me as too ambiguous, too unpoetic. "How about a little game?" is the question Kubrick was always asking Bernstein. In his twenties Kubrick had been a chess hustler, earning a precarious living by playing for cash at those stone chess tables in the southwest corner of Greenwich Village's Washington Square Park. In a series of chess contests with Kubrick, Bernstein was inexplicably winning every fifth game until the twentieth, when he tentatively reached for one of Kubrick's knights. Kubrick pulled an old hustler's trick. He slapped his forehead as if in great pain. Bernstein immediately followed through with what he believed to be a clever coup, only to hear Kubrick cry out as he leaped to his feet and pounced on Bernstein's queen, "I knew you were a *potzer*!"

Potzer? It is a chess hustler's term. Bernstein defines the potzer as "a relatively weak player with an inflated ego." How about a little game? This is the ancient question that the Universe, or Something in back of the universe, began to ask those bewildered featherless bipeds who had started to proliferate on the sun's third planet, as soon as their apish brains could comprehend the science game. It is a curious game. There is no definitive rule-book, and part of the game is trying to find out what the basic rules are. They seem to be mathematically simple, beautiful, multifarious, arbitrary, and increasingly difficult to discover. The game has never been more exciting or dangerous than at present. No one is better than Bernstein at conveying this contemporary scientific mood of exhilaration — There's an exposed knight! Grab it! — but he is also wise enough to know that, even though the planet's players keep improving, they are all still potzers.

17

Numbers and Their Symbols

"It must have required many ages," Bertrand Russell once wrote, "to discover that a brace of pheasants and a couple of days were both instances of the number 2." *Number Words and Number Symbols* (MIT Press, 1969), by Karl W. Menninger, is a magnificent history of how mankind discovered numbers, invented a bewildering variety of ways to name, symbolize, and manipulate them, and how those ways altered over the millennia.

Menninger was a German mathematician of such panoramic interests and expository skill that he became one of his country's most widely read authors of nontechnical books on mathematics. This splendid translation of the revised 1958 edition of Menninger's most ambitious work is a beautiful volume. Its large pages are handsomely bound, carefully indexed, and enriched by 282 pictures, mostly photographs, that are as fascinating as the lively text itself.

Menninger's story is a colorful mix of mathematics, linguistics, and cultural anthropology. It begins with primitive counting methods, some so crude that there were no words for numbers greater than two, some as sophisticated as the 60-base system of ancient Babylonia, which not only used positional notation but also had a zero. Any number can be the base of a number system, and Menninger covers with awesome erudition the many base-systems that were used before the decimal system, so closely tied to finger counting, finally vanquished all the others.

No reviews can do justice to a survey that ranges over all the number words and symbols of every major culture of world history. The reader will learn about the practice of "back-counting" (e.g., the Latin word for 19, *unde-viginti* or "1 from 20"), of "hidden number words" such as "bicycle" in

---

This review originally appeared in the *Chicago Tribune Book World,* November 16, 1969, and is reprinted with permission.

which old number words lie concealed, of the medieval view that 1 is not a number but the source of all numbers, and a thousand other curious sidelights illuminated by quotations and anecdotes. The book is especially good on early counting and calculating devices: primitive tally sticks, the knotted cords of ancient Peru, the elaborate finger symbols once used for numbers, counting boards with movable counters, and of course the abacus.

The abacus, so simple yet so efficient, is still more widely used in China, Japan, and Russia than modern desk computers. The Chinese *suan pan* has two beads above the bar, five below. The Japanese *soroban* has one bead above, four below. A Russian *tschotu* has horizontal rods with ten beads on each, the two in the middle colored differently from the others. Our kindergarten abacus, Menninger reminds us, is an indirect descendant (by way of France) of the Russian abacus.

The ancient Romans and European medievals also had their abaci. One of the mysteries of number history, Menninger observes, is why those cultures did not realize that the vertical grooves of their abaci, to which sliding beads were attached, corresponded to a positional notation, an empty space equivalent to a zero. For some fifteen centuries "accountants" used positional notation on their calculating devices, but when doing arithmetic with written symbols they clung to the unspeakably clumsy Roman numerals. The ancient Greeks, too, used positional notation on their counting boards. Archimedes, in his book *The Sand-Reckoner*, explained his complicated method of symbolizing numbers as large as one pleased, yet even he did not hit upon the place system with its zero "place holder." It was a curious cultural mental block, an inability to see, as Menninger puts it, "that a symbol must be there in order to say that nothing is there."

The climax of the story is how our modern decimal system, with its place notation and zero, developed in India, was taught to the great Italian mathematician Leonardo of Pisa, better known as Fibonacci, who introduced it to merchants of the West in his famous *Liber Abaci* of 1202. A good notation has remarkable power to suggest new theorems. It is impossible to see how modern mathematics, so essential to science, could have developed without such a notation.

Chinese writing is unique, Menninger notes, in having numerals that are identical with its number words. Modern China has now adopted Western numerals, but in its traditional writing the numeral for, say, five is identical with the word for five. Chinese written words are (to me) more aesthetically pleasing than the black brush-strokes of an abstraction by Franz Kline. Their word for "calculate" is a picture of an abacus held by two hands over the symbol for bamboo. Chinese writing often uses three symbols to suggest a multitude. "Forest" is a triplet of trees, "fur" a triplet of hairs, "all" a triplet of men, "gossip" a triplet of women.

Although Menninger does not take up the philosophy of numbers, it is hard to put down his encyclopedic volume without asking what a number really is. The abstract "two" obviously is not the numeral "2." A numeral is only a symbol, just as a wooden chess queen is a symbol of the abstract queen defined by chess rules. There is a sense in which numbers are mental constructs, but it is also true that they snugly fit large portions of the outside world. Objects that remain (for a time) units — sheep, pebbles, people, fingers, stars — combine and separate in strict conformity with the iron laws of arithmetic. Long before man was on earth, if three trilobites crawled toward four trilobites they produced a set of seven. Pure mathematics is indeed a human invention, abstract, empty of empirical content, but applied mathematics does apply with uncanny accuracy to a world man did *not* invent. This plunges us straight into the old metaphysical controversy between realists and nominalists. Even without taking sides, one of the great wonders of it all is that there are almost as many mysteries about those ten little Indian digits as there are mysteries about physical things.

18

Gregory's Intelligent Eye

The more biologists learn about the process of seeing, the more complex and fantastic it turns out to be. We all know that the eye acts like a small camera, its flexible lens casting an upside-down image on the retina. Fibers of the optic nerve carry electrical impulses from the retina to the brain. The two optic nerves cross in a crazy way. All fibers from the left sides of each retina go to the brain's left half, all fibers from the right sides of each retina go to the brain's right half. There is, therefore, an invisible vertical line in our visual field. Points very close together at the center of the field, but on opposite sides of this line, are interpreted by opposite sides of the brain. It is the brain's evaluation of the pulsed input data that completes the total process of "seeing."

Richard L. Gregory, a psychologist formerly at the universities of Cambridge and Edinburgh (he is presently at Bristol University), is one of the world's experts on visual perception. *The Intelligent Eye* (McGraw-Hill, 1970) is based on a series of six brilliant, dramatic lectures that he gave in 1967-68 for England's Royal Institution, which were televised in color by the BBC. The book is a delight both to read and look at. Most of its abundant drawings and photographs concern optical illusions as amazing as good magic tricks. (Some of the demonstrations in Gregory's BBC lectures *were* conjuring tricks, but of course these could not be included in the book.) Particularly amusing are the newly discovered "impossible figures," the best known of which is the shape that has two or three prongs depending on where your attention is focused. Gregory explains how certain impossible figures actually can be constructed as "possible objects" even though viewing them continues to befuddle the mind. He reproduces two startling lithographs by the Dutch

This review originally appeared in the *Chicago Tribune's Book World*, August 2, 1970, and is reprinted with permission.

artist M. C. Escher, one showing a perpetual motion device based on an "impossible stairway," the other showing a belvedere replete with contradictions of perspective. An earlier engraving by William Hogarth, also in the book, is equally crammed with visual impossibilities. And there are several reproductions of eye-twisting Op paintings to illustrate the roles of eye movements and afterimages in perception.

To add to the fun, Gregory supplies the reader with a pair of red-green spectacles for viewing three-dimensional illusions. The glasses also are used in a clever proof that five flat illusions are deceptions in the mind rather than in the eyes. Two circular disks can be cut from their pages to be rotated on a turntable. If you stare for thirty seconds at one disk, watching its spiral line appear to expand, then shift your gaze to someone's face, the face seems to shrink, although it remains, paradoxically, the same size. It is an important experiment, because some psychologists have argued that illusions of this type (the most familiar is the feeling that scenery seen through a train window is drifting forward after the train has stopped) originate in tiny jerky movements of the eyeballs. The explanation is plausible in the case of the train but obviously cannot apply to the head-shrinking illusion.[1]

Gregory's other disk is a "Benham top," a black-and-white pattern that generates "subjective colors" when spun. As Gregory discloses, such devices have been rediscovered no less than eight times since a French monk, Benedict Prévost, first described one in 1826. The flickering pattern induces electrical impulses of different frequencies in the retina's three color receptors (red, green, blue), forcing them to transmit pulses that the brain wrongly interprets as color signals. Benham tops also produce colors when seen on black-and-white television screens. If the set is in color, the colors are even stronger because, as Gregory explains, the set's three color receptors are disturbed in precisely the same way as the retina's receptors.

The underlying theme of *The Intelligent Eye*, as well as Gregory's two earlier books, *Recovery from Early Blindness* (written with Jean Wallace) and *Eye and Brain*, is that perception is essentially a "look up" system. The brain receives sensory data, then searches its memories of past experience (how this is done remains totally unknown) to decide on the most probable interpretation, the "best bet," that makes sense of the input data. Optical illusions result when the brain's choice of a hypothesis fails to correspond with the physical structure of what the eyes are seeing. As Gregory puts it: "The brain makes a wrong bet. It loses."

A striking instance, discussed in detail, is how the brain reacts to the back of a molded face-mask. Seen close up, in a good light, there are enough depth clues for one's mind to decide the mask is hollow. In a poor light, or even a good but diffuse light that casts no shadows, the brain's search through its memory bank turns up so few experiences of faces that go the other way, with hollow noses projecting *backward*, that it is impossible to see the mask as anything but convex even when one knows it isn't.[2] Hundreds of other illusions have equally convincing explanations in the context of Gregory's primary posit.

I have one bone to pick. On page 146 Gregory attributes to Aristotle the belief that names of objects are parts of the essences of objects rather than labels attached to them by a culture. One thinks of the old joke about Adam telling Eve he named the tiger a "tiger" because it looked like a tiger. Aristotle certainly did not hold such a childish view, nor can I recall any philosopher who did. Perhaps Gregory meant that Aristotle believed all languages to possess a structure that, to some degree, corresponds to the structure of the physical world. If so, the view is neither childish nor out of date. Such a structure is none other than the "deep structure" in Noam Chomsky's linguistic approach, which Gregory discusses sympathetically in his last chapter.

But this is a small objection to a beautiful, stimulating book. I cannot imagine anyone reading it without being entertained and enlightened on every page by the author's descriptions of strange visual phenomena, his ingenious explanations, and his concise remarks about their bearing on ancient philosophical questions concerning how the tiny computer inside our skull maps and interprets the monstrous universe that surrounds it.

NOTES

1. This is sometimes called the waterfall illusion, because it is unusually strong when you stare at a waterfall for about a minute, then look away to watch the scenery drift upward. Jerry Andrus, an Oregon magician, discovered that the spiral effect is intensified by putting on a large rotating disk a spiral that goes one way near the center, the other way in the middle, then reverses again on the outside third of the circle. When you shift your gaze from this rotating pattern to, say, a sky of clouds, the clouds writhe and bubble like the surface of boiling soup. You can purchase a cardboard disk of this sort, suitable for a turntable, by writing to Andrus at 1638 E. First Avenue, Albany, OR 97321.

2. If such an inside-out mask is hung on a wall, the face appears to rotate the wrong way as you walk past it. You can demonstrate this illusion easily by attaching three cardboard squares along their edges to form the corner of a cube. Hold it on your palm with the concave side facing you, close one eye, and stare at the corner for a while. Soon the structure will snap into convexity and you will think you are seeing a normal cube. If you now move your hand, the cube will appear to rotate in a direction opposite to your hand's movements. It seems to be floating above the hand and moving independently. A correspondent, Fred Duncan, discovered that the illusion is intensified by putting black spots on the three square faces to simulate a die. In 1980 the El Paso (Texas) Science Center was distributing this as a card premium, designed by Fred and Ellen Duncan.

Jerry Andrus (see note 1) has devised dozens of remarkable illusions based on this principle, using inside-out model houses and other structures. You can obtain from him pieces of cardboard for folding into what he calls the "parabox," as well as other models of a similar nature.

19

Off to Gloss the Wizard

A young student of English literature at Bard College, Michael Patrick Hearn, is busy on a curious project. He is writing scholarly footnotes for a volume to be published in Clarkson Potter's well-known series of annotated classics. The book? *The Wonderful Wizard of Oz*!

This surely will strike many people, especially librarians, as an outlandish undertaking. Annotate *The Wizard of Oz*? What sort of erudition could possibly be appropriate for such a simple, straightforward fairy tale? And who said it was a classic anyhow?

Well, first of all, the children have said so. Since *The Wizard* was published in 1900, by a small Chicago house called George M. Hill, it has outsold every other juvenile. (If you should have in your attic a copy with the Hill imprint it could be worth a thousand dollars.) Alice Payne Hackett, in her recent book, *70 Years of Best Sellers*, lists the fifteen best-selling American children's books from 1875 to 1965. *The Wizard* heads the list with an estimated 5,000,000 copies. It is a low estimate. Never out of print, the book has been on sale in the United States since 1965 in some twenty editions. It has been translated into every major language, including Chinese, Japanese, Polish, Persian, Bengali, Yugoslavian, Turkish, Armenian, and Lettish. In the USSR (where Munchkins are called Chewing People) there is even a 1963 sequel by a Russian writer—an Oz book not yet in English.

Is it possible, as certain humorless critics have repeated for seventy years, that Lyman Frank Baum was no more than a clever hack whose fantasies do not deserve serious attention? Is it possible that adults who praise Baum are merely recalling sentimentally a parent reading to them a book as ephemeral as an Uncle Wiggily story?

It is not possible. Too many distinguished critics have spoken out in recent years against this incredible opinion. Too many valuable studies of Baum have appeared in influential literary journals. One of the best, "A Late Wanderer in Oz," by Jordan Brotman, who teaches English at Sacramento State College, opens with "I never read an Oz book when I was a child!" (Brotman's splendid appreciation is reprinted in *Only Connect*, readings on children's literature edited by Sheila Egoff and others, Oxford University Press, 1969.)

But there is no longer a need to defend Baum's genius. The tide turned several years ago. The question I wish to consider is how America's best-loved fairy tale lends itself to glossing. Since I had the honor of starting Potter's series with my *Annotated Alice* and have written several articles about Baum as well as introductions to Dover's facsimile editions of four Baum fantasies, I am sometimes asked why *I* have not attempted to annotate *The Wizard*. The answer is simple: I do not know enough about Oz.

Let's take a quick look at the sources. First there is the canon: fourteen novels by the Royal Historian, as Baum called himself. Next in importance are Baum's own non-Oz fantasies (some better, in my opinion, than *The Wizard*), which intersect his Oz books in numerous ways. Most of them are set in lands near Oz but on the other side of the Deadly Desert, which surrounds Oz. These enchanted kingdoms—Mo, Ix, Noland, Yew, Pingaree, and scores of others, many of them islands in the Nonestic Ocean—are sometimes visited by adventurers in Oz books. And characters from non-Oz fantasies (notably Trot, a California girl, and Cap'n Bill, her peg-legged sailor friend) sometimes find their way to Oz. There are Baum's lesser Oz documents: *Little Wizard Stories* (six short tales), *The Woggle-Bug Book*, and an Oz comic strip he wrote for Sunday "funny papers" in 1904-1905. Nor should we omit Baum's script and lyrics for his fabulously successful musical of *The Wizard*, which resembled his own book far less than did the Judy Garland movie. It opened in Chicago in 1902, propelling Fred Stone to instant fame as the Scarecrow, then moved to Broadway for eighteen months before going on the road. There are Baum's scripts and songs for two other Oz musicals, *The Woggle-Bug* and *The Tik-Tok Man of Oz*. The Royal Historian also wrote what he called Radio Plays about Oz (this was before radio), which he read from a stage to accompany hand-tinted films. As head of his own film company in Hollywood, he produced several silent motion pictures about Oz.

This far from exhausts the sources. After Baum died in Hollywood in 1919 a twenty-year-old Philadelphia girl, Ruth Plumly Thompson, continued the series with 19 more Oz books. Three Oz books were by John R. Neill, the Royal Illustrator for all the Baum and Thompson books except *The Wizard*; two are by Jack Snow; and single Oz books were written by Rachel Cosgrove, Eloise McGraw and Lauren Wagner, and Baum's eldest son, Frank Joslyn Baum. Finally, there are the Oz recordings, television shows, animated cartoons, and motion pictures, of which MGM's 1939 color extravaganza is the most memorable.

To annotate an Oz book properly one should be thoroughly familiar (as I am not) with this fantastic mass of data. *The Wizard* raises hundreds of questions that lead into twisted trails through later Oz references. What was the Tin Woodman's former name when he was a "meat person" in love with a Munchkin girl, and what bizarre marriage did the poor girl finally make? What breed of dog is Toto? (He appears to be a terrier in *The Wizard*, a bulldog in *The Road to Oz*.) Is Toto unable to talk in Oz or does he just prefer not to? What is the name of the pretty "green girl" who waits on Dorothy in the Wizard's palace and what is her subsequent history? What was the Wizard's full name, the initials of which form an embarrassing acrostic, when he lived in Omaha? Where and after what cataclysmic events, triggered by the San Francisco earthquake, did Dorothy and the Wizard meet again? What eventually happens to Uncle Henry and Aunt Em? Is there a second Yellow Brick Road? What is the name and color of the wild northern region of Oz? If no one ages in Oz, why does the Wizard speak of growing older there?

Such questions as these, unanswered in the first Oz book, are legion and sometimes not easily answered. Like the Baker Street Irregulars, who never tire of inventing explanations for Dr. Watson's memory lapses, there is now a growing society of Ozmapolitans, armed with an awesome knowledge of Oziana, who are masters at concocting delightful resolutions of the Royal Historian's many ambiguities and careless contradictions.

The International Wizard of Oz Club was founded in New York City in 1957 by Justin G. Schiller, then a thirteen-year-old collector of Baum, now a rare-book dealer. Annual dues include a subscription to the *Baum Bugle*—three issues a year—and the privilege of attending conventions.

At Oz conventions, there are vigorous discussions about those thorny problems that club member Hearn will be taking up in his notes. *The Wizard*, for instance, mentions pennies in Oz, yet we are told in later books by Baum that money is not used in Oz. "Money! Money in Oz!" the Tin Woodman exclaims in *The Road to Oz*. "What a queer idea? Did you suppose we are so vulgar as to use money here? If we used money to buy things with, instead of love and kindness and the desire to please one another, then we should be no better than the rest of the world."

Knowledge of the socioeconomic-political structure of Oz, as well as its pre-Wizard history, is beset with enigmas. Essentially the country is a happy, rural, unpolluted, anarchist Utopia. Although Ozma becomes the absolute ruler, backed by the powerful sorcery of Glinda the Good, it is seldom necessary for her to interfere in any way with the varied, often outrageous life-styles of her people. There are no fuzz in Oz, because each citizen loves his neighbor and freely gives him whatever he needs. The Royal Army usually consists solely of the Soldier with the Green Whiskers. His musket is so seldom fired that William Wallace Denslow (a Chicago newspaper artist), who illustrated *The Wizard*, drew flowers growing out of its barrel.

There are times, however, when it is necessary to defend Oz against wicked invaders; but the defense is always expertly managed with a minimum of bloodshed. The most famous invasion (in *The Emerald City of Oz*) was plotted by Baum's comic villain, the Nome King. He recruits a fearsome army of Growleywogs (led by their Grand Gallipoot), Phanfasms (headed by their First and Foremost) and Whimsies. The Whimsies have huge bodies but heads the size of doorknobs. They are so ashamed of their tiny heads that they conceal them under enormous false heads of pasteboard, with two small eyeholes in the chin. The Nomes and their evil allies tunnel under the Deadly Desert, from Ev to the Emerald City, where they intend to blitz the Palace. The Scarecrow's excellent brains devise a clever scheme. Ozma, using her Magic Belt, fills the tunnel with dust. When the thirsty invaders emerge they drink from the Fountain of Oblivion, placed near the Palace ages ago by Glinda. The magic water, no doubt the same water that flowed in the ancient river of Lethe, makes them forget who they are and why they came there. Babbling like children, they simply go back home.

It is this gentle, quaint, nonviolent Utopianism that has made Baum's Oz books so appealing to that part of our youth counterculture unhooked on heroin or hate. Oz is in the names of many hippie communes. Charles Reich's *The Greening of America* defends far-off ideals that, like the distant (oh so distant!) anarchist ideals of Marx and Lenin, have much in common with the Emerald City's permissive culture—the city, that is, after its humbug ruler left the throne and green spectacles no longer were necessary to make the capitol look greener than it was.

I hope these scattered remarks suggest some of the ways in which an annotated *Wizard* can deepen the uninitiated reader's comprehension of Baum's marvelous total achievement. As the Irregulars have great fun pretending that Holmes was an actual person, so Oz buffs like to pretend that Oz is a genuine place. Indeed, the club sells handsome colored maps of Oz and its environs. One can expect Hearn's notes to have the same mock-serious tone as those of the late William S. Baring-Gould in his monumental Potter-published *The Annotated Sherlock Holmes*

There is an Ozzy sense in which Holmes *is* easier to believe in than Conan Doyle, a man who convinced himself that winged fairies actually do exist and even wrote an unbelievably stupid book about it. In the same odd way Oz, too, may turn out to be more enduring than Kansas. It is entirely possible that five hundred years from now citizens of the earth, studying twentieth-century children's literature, will know of Kansas only because Dorothy Gale once lived there.

POSTSCRIPT

I wrote the foregoing piece before Hearn completed the manuscript for *The Annotated Wizard of Oz*. When the book finally appeared in 1973, it was even more superb than I had anticipated. Hearn has since annotated *A*

Christmas Carol and *Huckleberry Finn*, coauthored a book on Denslow, and edited *The Art of the Broadway Poster*. He is now working on an authorized biography of Baum.

20

Can a Computer
Become a Person?

Ancient metaphysical debates, unlike scientific quarrels and old soldiers, almost never fade away. Philosophers utter maledictions, announce that a problem has been permanently exorcised, then a few decades later they are furiously debating it again, dividing into the same old camps, and repeating in a new (sometimes worse) terminology the same old arguments. For centuries they worried over whether animals and people were machines. Today they ask: Are digital computers capable of simulating human thinking? If so, will they ever develop to the point at which it is legitimate to call them persons?

Hubert L. Dreyfus, who teaches philosophy at the University of California at Berkeley, answers both questions with resounding nos in his book *What Computers Can't Do* (Harper and Row, 1972). The most he will concede is that digital computers can imitate only the most trivial aspects of human thought and behavior. Over and over again he quotes with high glee the overoptimistic predictions of Marvin Minsky, Allen Newell, Herbert Simon, and other pioneers of what is now called artificial intelligence: A computer will in ten years be the chess champion of the world (Simon, 1957). Computers will soon be translating languages in a useful way, recognizing complicated patterns, discovering significant new mathematical theorems, and so on. Such hopes, Dreyfus is persuaded, are foredoomed.

Why? Because, he contends, human reasoning is so different from computer reasoning that it cannot be simulated to any important degree until we learn how to build an artificial person, with something like a human body,

This review originally appeared in the *Chicago Tribune*'s *Book World*, January 23, 1972.

capable of growing, perceiving the world by gestalts, interacting continuously with its environment; in short, until we build a humanoid. The brain, Minsky once declared, is only a computer made of meat. Dreyfus seems to imply that no computer, not made of meat, will ever calculate in a way that deserves to be called "thinking."

It is instructive to compare Dreyfus's attack on Minsky (his principal target) with Mortimer J. Adler's 1967 book, *The Difference of Man and the Difference It Makes.* Adler has the same skepticism about the future of artificial intelligence, but his skepticism rests on a theological base. For Adler, a Thomist or at least an ex-Thomist, there is a "radical qualitative difference" between a person and a chimpanzee, and between a person and any possible manmade machine. By this Adler means, though he is coy about saying it outright, that a person has a transcendent soul that cannot be trapped by the laws of this world.

Dreyfus's animadversions have different posits. Judging by his pronouncements and the philosophers he quotes most favorably, he is a phenomenologist influenced mainly by Maurice Merleau-Ponty, the French philosopher, who died in 1961. So far as I can tell, Dreyfus concedes that a person is no more than a fantastically intricate arrangement of molecules. But because the brain is imbedded in a body that can grow and amble about, it learns how to "zero in" (Dreyfus's favorite phrase) on the relevant aspects of a fuzzy perceptual totality and to think in a manner that no digital computer can, in principle, simulate.

This view sprouts prophecies as gloomy as Simon's were rosy. No digital computer, Dreyfus is convinced, will ever play grandmaster chess. Bobby Fischer just doesn't think digitally. It is true that MacHack, the famous chess program at Minsky's Artificial Intelligence Laboratory at MIT, does not play even master chess, although a few years ago, to the whoops of Dreyfus's critics, it trounced him in a game. Moreover, MacHack does not plan moves in the same way Fischer does. (No one knows how Fischer's brain or anybody else's brain works. We don't even know how it remembers anything.) But neither does a tick-tack-toe machine calculate the same way as a ten-year-old who plays an unbeatable game. Nowhere does Dreyfus make clear why MacHack could not learn to play master chess by its own electronic techniques.

Dreyfus praises (faintly) Minsky for developing a robot that perceives and picks up blocks, but he doubts if a robot can be digitally programmed to play ping-pong. I find these doubts unfathomable. A computer may never write a good poem, feel love and hate, be amused or sad, or wonder why it exists, but playing chess, translating Chinese, and playing ping-pong are exactly the kinds of tasks a computer *can* learn to do well.

There are curious gaps in Dreyfus's philosophical polemics. Consider free will. The important thing about B.F. Skinner's books is not that they say anything new about free will—they say nothing philosophically new about anything—but that by taking such an uncompromising stand for determinism Skinner has aroused a lot of sleepy readers to the full implications of determinism. It is astonishing that Dreyfus, in a book on how computers differ from "meat people" (as they are called in Oz), can refer to Pascal, Kant, Kierkegaard, Husserl, Heidegger, and Merleau-Ponty without once explicitly discussing the mystery of personal freedom.

I was equally surprised by Dreyfus's attitude toward Plato. Although Plato believed that human personality has a transcendent aspect that survives death, Dreyfus considers Plato the father of those modern naturalists, such as Minsky, who are convinced that all human thought and behavior can, in principle, be pinned down by rules and expressed in the formal language of logic and mathematics. The matter is complicated, but my opinion is that Plato, more justifiably, should be called the father of those contemporary thinkers who, like Dreyfus, are most upset by the suggestion that a digital computer can someday do a creditable imitation of a human being.

Dreyfus is right in chiding the experts on artificial intelligence for their early euphoria. He is right in saying that their quick, early progress leveled off as formidable difficulties were encountered. He may be right in predicting painfully slow future advances. But his pessimism about computer simulation of certain kinds of human problem-solving and acting is supported by arguments that impress this reader as peevish, murky, and unconvincing.[1]

NOTE

1. A systematic refutation of Dreyfus's main arguments is provided by Seymour Papert in MIT Artificial Intelligence Memo, No. 54, January 1968. It is titled *The Artificial Intelligence of Hubert L. Dreyfus: A Budget of Fallacies.*

21

Lewis Carroll's Semiotics

The Reverend Charles L. Dodgson, better known as Lewis Carroll, was a professional mathematician who taught at Christ Church, Oxford. He had a great love for mathematics and logic, especially in their recreational aspects, and a lively interest in linguistics, again especially in what can be called recreational linguistics or, less pompously, word play. His original puzzles and games (mathematical and verbal) appeared in numerous British newspapers and magazines, in dozens of pamphlets printed at his own expense, and in his many books. His nonsense fiction, notably the two *Alice* books, abounds in linguistic play and outrageous humor closely linked to mathematical and logical themes.

Carroll devoted several books to serious mathematics, the most important—it contains some genuine discoveries—being his *Elementary Treatise on Determinants*. He did not write formally about linguistics, but his interest in logic and epistemology led him to reflect more than most people about language and the theory of signs. The theme of Robert D. Sutherland's admirable book, *Language and Lewis Carroll* (The Hague: Mouton, 1970), is that Carroll's understanding of semiotics was deeper than hitherto recognized and that, by studying his word play and his informal pronouncements on language, one can reconstruct Carroll's essential linguistic views.

Sutherland, an associate professor of English at Illinois State University, is well aware, indeed explicitly states, that Carroll did not have a scientific, consistent philosophy of language. He believes, nevertheless, that it is worthwhile to make a systematic study of Carroll's incomparable word play and to guess as much as one can about the assumptions underlying it. The result is a greater appreciation of Carroll's grasp of semiotics and a heightened

This review originally appeared in *Semiotica*, vol. 5, no. 1, 1972.

understanding of that marvelous mix of logic and word play that has come to be called Carrollian nonsense. Such a study was initiated by the authors of a few magazine articles and by Daniel F. Kirk in his monograph, *Charles Dodgson, Semeiotician* (University of Florida Press, 1963). The task has now been completed by Sutherland in a treatise so comprehensive that it is unlikely it will be attempted again.

Instead of detailing the excellent classificatory scheme by which Sutherland orders his varied, chaotic material, I limit my remarks to two of Carroll's insights. His most important surely was his realization that words "are merely conventional signs." (Quotation marks enclose the phrase because it appears in a familiar stanza of *The Hunting of the Snark*.) Since there is no connection between words and what they signify except by way of human minds, a word means whatever the user intends by it or whatever the listener (or reader) thinks it means. As Humpty Dumpty put it in his famous discourse on semantics, "When *I* use a word . . . it means just what I choose it to mean—neither more nor less." In many passages, both serious and comic, Carroll defended the right of a philosopher, logician, or mathematician to define a word any way he pleases provided he makes clear exactly what his meaning is.

There is another side, however, to this license, a kind of semantic moral obligation not to depart too widely from commonly agreed-upon meanings, either among ordinary persons, living experts in a particular field, or earlier experts in a tradition. The obligation is especially binding when all three groups agree. The high price for violating the rule is to risk being misunderstood, which in turn stirs up unnecessary obfuscation.

Carroll was less explicit in advocating this moral obligation, but Sutherland makes a good case for Carroll's approval of it. In his *Symbolic Logic* Carroll asserts that, were he to find an author saying that by "black" he means "white," and vice versa, he would "meekly accept the ruling" even though he considered it "injudicious." That word *injudicious* conveys Carroll's awareness of the moral rule. Humpty Dumpty does nothing but bewilder poor Alice by his radical redefinition of "glory" as "a nice knock-down argument," and Alice is quite right, Sutherland contends, in rebuking Humpty for it. (An amusing nonverbal sign in this scene, by the way, missed by all *Alice* commentators, including me, occurs when Humpty offers Alice one finger in shaking hands. It was a practice of some upper-class members of Victorian society to use only two fingers when shaking hands with their inferiors. Humpty, in his vast pride, goes one better.)

An outstanding instance of this sort of semantic confusion in recent philosophical history was the attempt by William James, John Dewey, and other pragmatists to redefine or eliminate the word *truth* from philosophical and scientific discourse. Since the time of Aristotle most philosophers, almost all scientists, and all men-in-the-street have agreed on a correspondence meaning for "true" when applied to assertions about the external world; correspondence, that is, with an external structure and not merely a phe-nomenological correspondence with one's remembered experience. Ask any physicist or bartender what is *meant* by saying that the statement "There is a penny in this box" is true, and he will answer that it is true if there actually *is* a penny in the box. Need I add that we are not concerned here with ways of *testing* truth, of evaluating the degree to which such assertions should be believed?

Since Alfred Tarski made this utterly commonplace meaning of "truth" extremely precise, the pragmatists' attempt to discard it has become a hopelessly lost cause. Indeed, so much confusion was created by the pragmatists' campaign to eliminate a pragmatically indispensable meaning for a useful ancient word that James and Dewey wasted fantastic amounts of energy trying to clear up false impressions created by their radical redefini-tions. "There's glory for you!" James's book *Pragmatism* befuddled so many intelligent readers that he had to write an unintentionally funny sequel, *The Meaning of Truth*, to explain how he was misunderstood. Dewey was perpetually rebuking Bertrand Russell and other critics of pragmatism for identical misunderstandings. Not that there was anything "wrong" about what the pragmatists had to say. The point is that they chose to say it in an "in-judicious" language that proved not to be viable.

More relevant to contemporary polemics is another Carrollian insight, also stressed by Sutherland, into the misty ambiguity of so many emotion-ally charged words. The term *New Left* is now applied to naive anarchist views that predated Karl Marx. "If you want to have an increase in black employ-ment," Daniel Bell remarked (*New York Times* [November 12, 1970], 48), "you've got to crack the union monopoly. Does that mean you're Left or Right?" The almost total meaninglessness today of "Left" and "Right," especial-ly in the nice, knock-down, or rather blow-up, arguments of the Weathermen, is a still-untapped source for grim Carrollian satire. "Down with everything," someone once remarked, "and up with what's left." Mirror reversals of mean-ing are all over the place. Radicals talk like conservatives and conservatives talk like radicals (e.g., "conservative" economist Milton Friedman's proposed negative income tax or his views on free trade, and "radical" Paul Good-man's passionate pleas for decentralized government). "Liberal" and "con-servative," in the complexity of contemporary economics, political science, and religion, are rapidly becoming as empty of agreed-upon meaning as "realism" and "idealism" long ago became in philosophical discourse.

Nothing in Carroll's writings or in Sutherland's study casts light on cer-tain profound questions in linguistic philosophy; for example, on the extent to which all natural languages may have an infrastructure independent of a particular culture because it corresponds in certain ways with the structure of the physical world in which all cultures evolve, as well as with basic ex-periences common to all humans. But on less controversial levels of linguistics

Carroll's work is a rich collection of comic illustrations for significant insights. There is no better guide to this aspect of Carrollian nonsense than Sutherland's definitive, splendidly written book.

22

The Red Bugaboo

Periodically throughout history political leaders, sometimes entire nations, are smitten by paranoia. The bugaboo varies (Satan, a church, a country, a race, a social class, an idea), but the behavior of the extremists is invariant: hysterical actions that do more damage than the dreaded malevolence.

In the United States, from the thirties throughout the fifties, the bugaboo was Communism. The struggle to exorcise it may not have been a major plague, as world plagues go, yet the harm done was real enough, and nowhere more visible than in the entertainment world. There have been previous efforts to document parts of the crazy affair—Merle Miller's ACLU analysis of the television blacklist, John Cogley's *Report on Blacklisting*, Robert Vaughan's Ph.D. thesis, memoirs by various victims and observers. Not until the appearance of *A Journal of the Plague Years* (Atheneum, 1973), an astringent study by *Time* editor Stefan Kanfer, has the full story been told so well.

From the beginning, the plague was spread mainly by fuzzy-minded Christians. Their witless rhetoric had nothing in common with the anti-Communism of the democratic Left; indeed, the liberal anti-Communist usually found *himself* on the blacklist. Mrs. Elizabeth Dilling's *Red Network*, the first published blacklist, was divided into two parts: organizations and people. The people included Norman Thomas, John Dewey, Eleanor Roosevelt, Jane Addams, Robert Hutchins, Freud, Einstein, H. L. Mencken, Harry Emerson Fosdick, Sinclair Lewis, and Thornton Wilder. Among the subversive organizations were the NAACP, the New School for Social Research, even the YM and YWCA. "An ex-Communist tells me," wrote Mrs. Dilling (this and all later quotes are from Kanfer's book), "that Eleanor

This review originally appeared in the *New Leader*, July 23, 1973, and is reprinted with permission.

Copenhaver, National Industrial Secretary of the YWCA, has recently married Sherwood Anderson, prominent Communist worker. There should be a thorough investigation . . . Why should *Christians* support those who . . . etc." Colonel McCormick, publisher of the *Chicago Tribune*, hoped the *Red Network* would have a big sale "so that Americans will know who are the enemies of society within our gate."

Later blacklists were less preposterous, but not much. There was Myron C. Fagan's *Red Treason in Hollywood* and *Documentation of Red Stars in Hollywood*, the latter containing what Kanfer calls a white list of "touchables": John Wayne, Adolphe Menjou, Robert Taylor, Edgar Bergen, Charlie McCarthy. "Two Thousand Years ago a Man named Jesus died on a Cross," wrote Fagan (like Mrs. Dilling he was a Protestant fundamentalist). "It is possible that this year *I* shall die — on a different kind of cross — for the safety of America and, God grant, the Peace of the Universe." Kanfer adds a footnote: "Fagan was still thriving in 1973."

Red Channels, the deadliest of the blacklists, was issued in 1950 by Vincent Hartnett, an ex-Naval Intelligence officer who quickly became the leading foe of Communism in American show business. Eschewing the crimson cover of Mrs. Dilling's handbook, it showed a microphone leaning to the left, a scarlet hand about to seize it. In addition, California State Senator Jack Tenney published a report of his Committee of Un-American Activities. The names it included plus many more dotted the pages of such periodicals as Ed Gibbons's *Alert*, Alfred Kohlberg's *Plain Talk*, and *Counterattack*, mimeographed by three former FBI agents who had founded ABC (American Business Consultants) to investigate suspects for a fee. It was a marvelous and profitable racket. In 1953 Catholic lawyer Godfrey Schmidt established Aware, Inc., an even bigger investigative organization.

Hundreds of actors, writers, and directors were infected by the plague, and Kanfer examines it all. The bigger personalities survived by various strategems, some by weeping and naming the same old names, but on the lower levels of show business there were permanently blighted careers. A few may have been indirectly killed by the plague. Mady Christians, of *I Remember Mama*, was hounded until her ordeal ended in a massive attack of hypertension. A similar fate cut down the black actor, Canada Lee. John Garfield tried to salvage his career by agreeing to put his name on a *Look* confession, "I Was a Sucker for a Left Hook," but before it could be printed he died of a heart attack in the bedroom of an actress friend. Philip Loeb, papa of the *Molly Goldberg* television show, committed suicide after a long period of unemployment.

There were hundreds of lesser tragedies. Some of the victims had indeed been members of the Communist party, or fellow-travelers, but most of them had done little more than join a front group or sign a petition or march in a May Day parade. No act was too trivial to escape the eagle eyes of the Red-chasers. There were endless cases of mistaken identity and false hearsay. Some actors were denied work solely because their last names were the same as those of blacklistees. It made them "controversial."

Although Kanfer does not cover Joe McCarthy's antics, mainly because the senator from Wisconsin had little interest in show-business subversion, he does devote several incredible chapters to the hearings of HUAC (House Un-American Activities Committee), chaired by J. Parnell Thomas before he was packed off to prison for padding payrolls. The committee's most famous victims, the "Hollywood Ten," were jailed for refusing to talk about their Communist ties. Was their strategy admirable or craven? Socialists of an earlier, less covert American radicalism never hesitated to stand up and be counted. On the other hand, HUAC and everyone in Hollywood knew about the ten (eight were active party members), so their defiance was less an effort at concealment than a first attempt to resist the plague.

The most talented among the eight was Dalton Trumbo. His grim pacifist novel, *Johnny Got His Gun*, is the one literary product by members of the ten likely to escape the dustbin. Kanfer reminds us that it was first serialized in the *Daily Worker* during the period of the Hitler-Stalin treaty. When Hitler turned on Russia, the novel dropped out of sight for three decades, only to surface again after the United States became involved in Vietnam. Trumbo's skyrocket success since he emerged from limbo, about fifteen years ago, has made him Hollywood's richest radical. No film scripter lives in a larger, more ostentatious mansion. A few years ago he made a movie out of *Johnny Got His Gun* and won the International Film Critics Award.

There were moments of comedy during the HUAC hearings. Gary Cooper solemnly said he was opposed to Communism because "from what I hear . . . it isn't on the level." Director Leo McCarey boasted that the Russians had panned his films *Going My Way* and *The Bells of St. Mary's* because he had "a character in there they do not like." "Bing Crosby?" asked the committee's chief investigator. "No, God." Ginger Rogers's mother explained why she wouldn't let her daughter appear in Trumbo's *Tender Comrade*. The script called for Ginger to say "Share and share alike—that's democracy." Walt Disney's tongue slipped. He called the League of Women Voters a Commie front when he meant the League of Women Shoppers.

How much influence did the Hollywood party-liners have on the political views of moviegoers? It is hard to quarrel with Kanfer's opinion. None. True, they did their best to sneak propaganda into films, but whenever a producer or director spotted such a ploy, he chopped it out. A few scenes did slip by. Lionel Stander whistled the *Internationale*. A Jewish veteran said he couldn't get a job because his name wasn't Jones. Someone on the deck of a warship shouted, "It's ours!" before the film cut to a close-up of a Soviet plane.

After the fifties the plague began to fizzle even faster than the Communist party. Louis Nizer delivered the knockout punch. A radio talk-show moderator, John Henry Faulk, sued Aware for libel and Nizer was his attorney. Hartnett, the officer of Aware who had fingered Faulk, admitted he had been "sold a barrel of false information," and in 1962 the jury awarded Faulk $3.5 million. A few days before the trial ended, when it was clear that Hartnett had blown the case, his sidekick, Lawrence Johnson, a Syracuse grocer who had somehow become the nation's number two Red-hunter, checked into a motel and killed himself with sleeping pills.

How can we sum up? Even at the top of its influence, the American Communist party was nine-tenths bombast. It is easy now, writes Kanfer, to see the old Leftists of show business as ridiculous. "But, in the end, they deserve more. At their worst they were blind visionaries who believed that by walking forward they ascended into the air. They were furtive when they should have been open, romantic in an era that needed social realism, molten when they should have been crystalline. But at their meanest, they did subscribe to a faith in, and not against, the human potential. . . . If they were strident or philistine, they have paid their dues, paid them at usurious rates."

Residues of the plague still linger. The Reverend Billy Hargis is still fighting Communism in Tulsa, and books and pamphlets about the Red Menace still bemuse the innocent. "Farce is tragedy out for a good time; the rats make funny sounds as they gnaw at the walls." When Kanfer wrote that sentence, the last sentence of his book, he did not know that the funny sounds would soon be coming from the white walls surrounding a former HUAC member, Richard Nixon.

The bugaboo, of course, is not quite the same. It is now a vague monster compounded of Black Panthers, Maoists, Castroists, remnants of the Weathermen, Democratic party liberals, the *New York Times*, Daniel Ellsberg, Jack Anderson, and so on, but it's the same old paranoia. Those papers preserved by John Dean are probably funnier and more frightening than Mrs. Dilling's papers. Still, watching the Watergate hearings with their (so far) scrupulous regard for decency, catching sight of a bumper sticker that says "Honk if you think he's guilty," and reading this balanced and witty book, I'm inclined to think our freedoms are going to survive.

POSTSCRIPT

To update this a bit:

Dalton Trumbo died in 1976. According to his *New York Times* obit (September 11) he recalled in 1970: "I joined the Communist Party in 1943 and left it in 1948 on the ground that in the future I should be far too busy to attend its meetings, which were, in any event, dull beyond description." He rejoined briefly in 1954 to protest the conviction in California of fourteen Communist officials, but left the party again when the convictions were reversed. During the fifties and sixties he wrote screenplays under other names. In 1957 one Robert Rich (actually Trumbo) was awarded an Oscar for the script of *The Brave One*. In 1960 when Otto Preminger announced that the screenplay for *Exodus* was by Trumbo, nobody seemed to mind.

"I never considered the working class anything other than something to get out of," Trumbo once remarked.

Billy Hargis's career came to an abrupt end in 1974 when he admitted to charges of having had sexual relations with five students in his college, four of them male.

Stefan Kanfer has written two novels, and is now book editor of *Time*.

We all know what happened to Nixon.

23

The Magic of Lewis Carroll

It is possible, I suppose, for someone who is bored by magic tricks, dislikes puzzles, and has never played a chess game to enjoy Lewis Carroll's *Alice* books and *The Hunting of the Snark*. But can such a person ever get to the center of Carroll's mind or fully appreciate all his writings? It is like asking a landlubber who hates the ocean to tell us about the novels of Melville and Conrad, or expecting a city-dweller who never spent a night in the woods to give us insights into *Walden*.

The Magic of Lewis Carroll (Simon and Schuster, 1973) is a marvelous anthology of the kinds of things Carroll loved best, aside from little girls. Carroll performed magic as a boy and throughout his life enjoyed mystifying children with legerdemain and taking them to magic shows. The book contains just about everything Carroll ever wrote on tricks, games, and puzzles, ably edited (with an introduction and extensive commentary) by an eminently qualified Carrollian. John Fisher is currently doing television production work for the BBC in London. He studied literature at Oxford (where Carroll taught mathematics), he is addicted to word play and recreational mathematics and, best of all, he is a member of the International Brotherhood of Magicians.

It was Fisher's happy inspiration to do more than just reprint excerpts from Carroll's books, articles, and privately printed pamphlets. Not only has he accompanied his selections with appropriate illustrations—the book is almost as much fun to look at as to read—but he has taken off from the texts to proffer fascinating new material.

For example, Fisher begins with a quote from Alice: "The Mouse gave a sudden leap out of the water, and seemed to quiver all over with fright." This reminds Fisher of a passage in Isa Bowman's charming little book, *Lewis*

This review originally appeared in the *Chicago Tribune's Book World,* October 14, 1973.

Carroll As I Knew Him (available, by the way, as a Dover reprint): "Everyone when a child has, I suppose, seen the trick in which a handkerchief is rolled up to look like a mouse, then made to jump about by a movement of the hand. He did this better than any one I ever saw . . ." The quotation is followed by picture instructions on exactly how to make the mouse, though you'll have to ask a magician to teach you how to animate it.

Isa spoke of other "wonderful things" Carroll made with his handkerchief. We don't know what those other things were, but one of them could have been the magician's (and Carroll's) White Rabbit that nibbles bits of food. So, for a bonus, Fisher reveals how to make the rabbit, too.

Carroll was so excited when a boy showed him how to fold a sheet of paper and make it pop by swishing it through the air that he recorded the memorable occasion in his diary. Later he writes of the "remarkable day" on which he taught the fold to the children of the Duchess of Albany. That's all the excuse Fisher needs to explain how to fold the "paper pistol."

Tenniel's drawing of the Walrus and the Carpenter shows the Carpenter wearing a boxlike paper hat, still folded today by newspaper pressmen to keep ink out of their hair. How is it made? Fisher gives the steps. One of Carroll's child-friends wrote in a letter about the time she was playing on the Fort at Margate when "a gentleman on a seat near asked us if we could make a paper boat, with a seat at each end, and a basket in the middle for fish!" How did Carroll fold the boat? It's in Fisher's book.

And the book is jammed with a hundred other wondrous things: an intricate under-over maze Carroll drew as a youth; rules for his original games with a backgammon board, cards, numbers, and croquet; how to play billiards on a circular table; how to appear to bite a piece out of a teacup (like the witness at the Knave of Hearts's trial); how to make an egg stand on end (as did the Sheep in the Looking-glass shop when she placed an egg — soon to enlarge to Humpty Dumpty — "upright on a shelf"). There are selections of Carroll's best double acrostics, anagrams, verse enigmas, and word-ladders (ARMY, arms, aims, dims, dams, dame, name, nave, NAVY). You can learn how to play his board game, Lanrick; solve syllogisms by putting red and grey counters on a diagram; write secret messages in an ingenious, hard-to-break cipher; determine quickly the day of the week for any date; memorize numbers by a simple mnemonic system.

Fisher has included selections from Carroll's two books of mathematical puzzles, *Pillow-Problems* and *A Tangled Tale*, as well as dozens of other brain teasers, logic and time paradoxes, and mind-twisting curiosities found in Carroll's writings. What happens to the weight on one side of a pulley when a monkey climbs the other side? Why do the digits of 142,857 keep reappearing in cyclic order when you multiply the "magic number" by 2, 3, 4, 5, or 6? What is the topological secret of Fortunatus's Purse (from *Sylvie and Bruno*), which holds all the world's wealth because everything outside is also inside?

"Invented what I think is a *new* kind of riddle," Fisher quotes from Carroll's diary. "A Russian had three sons. The first, named Rab, became a lawyer; the second, Yrma, became a soldier. The third became a sailor: what was his name?"

Much of the material in Fisher's book is not elsewhere available. I had never before read Carroll's instructions for his Nyctograph, a cardboard stencil device designed to simplify scribbling notes in pitch darkness.

"Anyone who has tried," Carroll wrote in a ladies' magazine, "as I have often done, the process of getting out of bed at 2 A.M. in a winter night, lighting a candle, and recording some happy thought which would probably be otherwise forgotten, will agree with me it entails much discomfort. All I have now to do, if I wake and think of something I wish to record, is to draw from under the pillow a small memorandum book, containing my Nyctograph, write a few lines, or even a few pages, without even putting the hands outside the bed-clothes, replace the book, and go to sleep again."

Today, with our bedside lamps and overheated sleeping rooms, the need for such a device is less, but there is more to Carroll's invention than meets the eye. To use it properly, the Oxford don was forced to invent what he called a "square alphabet": a way of drawing each letter, inside a square hole, with a minimum number of lines and dots. Alphabets of just this type are in use today on the display screens of computers, and in printing designed to be read easily by scanning machines.

For many years Carroll planned to gather in one volume all the games and puzzles he had originated. At one time he considered calling it *Alice's Puzzle-Book*, and there was even an advertisement for it in *Sylvie and Bruno*. He never got around to writing it. Now Fisher has given it to us, and in a form more bountiful than Carroll could have imagined. Had the Reverend Charles Lutwidge Dodgson been able, in a dream of precognitive clairvoyance, to see its pages, I think he would have been delighted.

24

So-called Books for Children

My first reaction to these two handsome volumes—*Cobwebs to Catch Flies: Illustrated Books for the Nursery and Schoolroom 1700-1900*, by Joyce Irene Whalley (University of California Press, 1974); and *Early Children's Books and Their Illustration*, text by Gerald Gottlieb, essay by J. H. Plumb (New York: Pierpont Morgan Library, 1975)—was delight in the old illustrations, many in sumptuous color, and with the richly informative commentary. But the more pages I turned the more something troubled me. Suddenly I understood. The writing, selling, and buying of children's books has always been, by and large, in the hands of grownups who know little about the minds and hearts of children.

In the early eighteenth century, when juvenile books started to proliferate, the purveyors had one central aim: Give the young ones what they ought to read whether they like it or not. Joyce Whalley, a researcher at the Victoria and Albert Museum in London (which owns one of the world's finest collections of juveniles), is concerned almost solely with this grim didactic literature. As she bluntly puts it, the earliest of these books were aimed "at saving the soul from hell, a necessity which continued until well into the nineteenth century."

It's no good to argue that children were different in those days and really liked these dreadful volumes. They weren't different and they didn't like them. We know because when they grew up many of them wrote about their childhood. It is nice to see photographs of rare first editions of such pious "children's books" as Isaac Watts's *Divine Songs* or Mrs. Barbauld's *Hymns in Prose*, but there is no reason to think that children were inspired by them. "Damn them!" wrote Charles Lamb to Coleridge, "I mean the cursed Bar-

This review originally appeared in the *New York Times Book Review*, January 18, 1976. ©1976 by The New York Times Company. Reprinted by permission.

bauld Crew, those Blights and Blasts of all that is Human in man and child."
When Gerald Gottlieb tells us that *Pilgrim's Progress* "was enthusiastically
seized upon" by youngsters who found it "an exciting adventure story," you
don't have to believe him.

Religious fervor finally cooled, but not the notion that children were eager
to obtain books that taught them morals and manners, how to read and count,
and dry facts about geography, history, and science. Give the child what you
think it likes became, as Miss Whalley writes, the modified rule. This was
the period in England when certain popular adult novels were believed to
be of great interest to children.

Gulliver's Travels is the most preposterous example. Gottlieb says it
became a "children's favorite." He means it became a favorite for grownups
to give to children. Swift's savage satire was as unintelligible to children then
as now. When it became obvious that it had to be cut and rewritten, the
abridgers naturally left out such scenes as Gulliver putting out a Lilliputian
Palace fire by urinating, or Gulliver sitting astride the nipple of a frolicsome
Brobdingnagian lass, and other pleasantries that boys and girls really *would*
have enjoyed.

Robinson Crusoe is another vaunted "children's classic" that had to be
rehashed. It is hard to believe, but *Clarissa* and *Tom Jones* were also rewritten for the long-suffering kiddies. Pictures of first editions are in Gottlieb's
book to prove it. He may even be right when he tells us they were widely read.

Nineteenth-century adults in England and America continued to give their
captive audiences what they thought they liked: *Water Babies, The Rose and
the Ring* (illustrated by Thackeray himself), *Ivanhoe, A Christmas Carol*,
nonsense by Lear, and of course the two immortal *Alice* books. Most people assume that *Alice* was enormously popular with Victorian children, but
when you investigate the matter you find it was popular mainly with teenagers and grownups. One could fill pages with confessions by the most ardent British admirers of *Alice* about how they disliked the books as children.
(Carroll's *Sylvie and Bruno*, reprinted in facsimile last year as a "children's
classic," was avoided by children *and* adults.)

Alice was, of course, a great improvement over *Pilgrim's Progress*—
children were happy with anything that didn't preach or teach—and besides,
a wondrous heresy was taking root. Publishers were actually publishing fiction that children liked whether their parents did or not. On the hack level
were the penny dreadfuls in England, the dime novels and the series books
in the United States, but there were also authentic masterpieces: *Pinocchio,
Treasure Island, Peter Rabbit, Just So Stories, The Wonderful Wizard of Oz*.

If you wonder why Gottlieb, who stops short of the current century, left
out so many earlier classics—the fantasies of Irving, Hawthorne, MacDonald,
and Lang, for instance, or such favorites as *Heidi, Little Women*, and
Huckleberry Finn—the reason is that his big book is essentially an exhibition catalogue. It is limited to the prominent holdings of the Pierpont Morgan

Library, where Gottlieb is a curator: the early hornbooks, battledores, street cries, broadside ballads, riddles, games, and especially those books whose first editions are so scarce that only the wealthiest collector could own one.

Juvenile book illustrations naturally reflect fashionable trends in adult art. Happily we have now passed through that curious phase when abstract art dominated the galleries, producing illustrations that mimic the mistakes children try to avoid when they draw. It is hard enough today to get young ones to look at pictures that don't move, but impossible to get them to look at unmoving pictures they can't understand. If you doubt this, try showing a little girl one of Brian Wildsmith's distorted scenes for *Mother Goose* alongside Kate Greenaway's marvelous illustration for Browning's *Pied Piper*—it's the frontispiece of Gottlieb's book—and ask her which she likes best and why. The most objectionable books pictured in the two volumes under review were tolerated by children, I suspect, because they liked the realistic pictures.

Both books are of interest mainly to librarians, rare book dealers, collectors, and students of juvenile literature. For the rest of us they teach a moral. The next time you read the 300 words of an expensive book to a child in ten minutes, and are never asked to read them again, don't be too angry with the publisher. It used to be worse.

25

The Popperism of Sir Karl

The first volume in the Library of Living Philosophers, *The Philosophy of John Dewey*, appeared thirty-five years ago. Today, this incomparable series, edited by Paul Arthur Schilpp, numbers fourteen works, of which *The Philosophy of Karl Popper* (Open Court, 1974) is the latest, largest, and most expensive. It is the only publication in the collection thus far to require two volumes, and to sell for the horrendous price of $30.00. Nevertheless, for anyone seriously concerned with the philosophy of science, the book is a bargain.

In keeping with the series' established format, *The Philosophy of Karl Popper* opens with a lengthy intellectual autobiography by Sir Karl himself (a splendid introduction to the man and his ideas), followed by thirty-three descriptive and critical essays by eminent thinkers. These, in turn, receive detailed, often caustic, replies from Popper. The book concludes with a massive bibliography of the philosopher's writings, and a comprehensive index.

Like Bertrand Russell, whom Popper considers his greatest predecessor since Kant, Sir Karl is a passionate "realist." That is, he accepts the commonsense belief in an external world, existing independent of our minds, and possessing a structure not made by us yet partially comprehensible to us. Science is a never-ending search for truth about that structure. ("Truth" is taken in the classic correspondence sense that goes back to Aristotle and received precise definition from the twentieth-century mathematician and logician Alfred Tarski; it is objective and absolute.) Of course we can never be certain we have caught it, but we do have reasons for believing science is getting closer to it.

This review originally appeared in the *New Leader*, October 14, 1974, and is reprinted with permission.

Whereas Popper's realism is unobjectionable to most modern philosophers of science, other aspects of his thought have brought him into bitter conflict with his peers. (There has long been a rumor that he and Ludwig Wittgenstein once battled each other with pokers: Sir Karl's account of this incident is even funnier than the mythology.)

His most publicized contention is that the more easily a theory can be proved false, the better and bolder it is, and that one which cannot be refuted is useless because it has no "informative content." Marxist and psychoanalytic theory, he insists, have become empty in this way, for each has been so vaguely generalized, twisted, and patched, one can no longer imagine a historical event or experimental outcome that would persuade a Marxist or a Freudian to discard his core beliefs. In his autobiography, Popper gives a colorful account of how he came to realize the sharp difference between such vapid theories and theories that take genuine risks. "If the redshift of spectral lines due to the gravitational potential should not exist," Popper quotes Einstein, "then the general theory of relativity will be untenable." One would be hard put, Popper argues, to get a statement of comparable humility from a Marxist or Freudian. By ingeniously "immunizing" their views against all possible falsifications, they have rendered those views uninteresting.

Sir Karl is at odds with his critics on many other important topics as well. He has, for example, defended indeterminism throughout his life against the determinism of Einstein and others. Most physicists are probably indeterminists on the microlevel and determinists on the macrolevel. Popper is an indeterminist on all levels.

"If God had wanted to put everything into the world from the beginning," Sir Karl writes, quoting himself from an early lecture, "He would have created a universe without change, without organisms and evolution, and without man and man's experience of change. But He seems to have thought that a live universe with events unexpected even by Himself would be more interesting than a dead one." This emotional bias toward what William James called the "open universe," as against the "block universe," underlies Popper's great defense of democracy in his best-known work, *The Open Society and Its Enemies*.

Popper's most notable clashes were with Rudolf Carnap over induction. Carnap was convinced that inductive logics could be constructed for formalized scientific languages, and that these would become useful tools for measuring a theory's "degree of confirmation" in the light of total available evidence. Sir Karl considers this nonsense.

Not only is Popper scornful of any attempt to formulate a logic of induction; in his language, induction does not exist. He is persuaded he has completely solved Hume's famous problem (How can induction be justified?) by replying: It can't because there is no such thing.

To be sure, says Popper, scientists can and do prefer one hypothesis over another. This preference, though, is not based on Carnapian "confirming instances" but on how successfully a theory passes attempts to refute it. Yet hasn't Popper merely introduced induction through the back door? To oversimplify one case in point, he does not believe the discovery of Neptune confirmed Newton's theory of gravitation. Instead, he argues, the new planet "corroborated" the theory by not falsifying it. This sounds like denying that a man is happy because the horse he bet on won the race, and asserting, on the contrary, that he is jumping up and down because his horse failed to lose. (For Carnap's side of this acrimonious debate, see *The Philosophy of Rudolf Carnap*, Open Court's earlier work in the same series, pp. 995-98.)[1]

On the problem of induction it is too early to know whether future thinking will follow a Popperian or Carnapian road, or find other directions. But in this, as in all his concerns, Popper has opened myriads of new speculative paths. Even his strongest critics must admit that the publication of this new work is a major event in the history of modern philosophy.

NOTE

1. It was Carnap's opinion that Popper consistently tried to exaggerate the differences between them by finding ways to say the same things Carnap said, but say them in a less ordinary language. Suppose, for instance, a scientist, convinced that Neptune probably has a ring around it, supervises a space probe that succeeds in photographing the ring. Carnap would say that the purpose of the probe was to confirm the theory, and that it succeeded. Popper would say that the probe's purpose was to falsify the theory, and having failed, the theory was corroborated.

In the mid-sixties Carnap and Popper both attended a conference in London where some of their differences were discussed by Popperians. At the close, Carnap declared that the main thing he had learned from the conference was that the distance function is not symmetric. The distance from me to Popper, he said, is small. But the distance from Popper to me appears to be enormous.

26

The Adventures of Stanislaw Ulam

Not many mathematicians write autobiographies, and it is easy to understand why. Even a great mathematician is almost always unknown to the public. His "adventures" are usually so confined to the interior of his skull that only another mathematician cares to read about them. And when a great mathematician has nonmathematical adventures he may consider them too trivial to record. ("They don't do anything very much," John von Neumann once said to Ulam. He was speaking of women.) There have been some recent exceptions: Bertrand Russell, for instance, and Norbert Wiener, who became famous enough to get his life story published. Einstein wrote a marvelous short "autobiography," but it was entirely about ideas.

Now Stanislaw Marcin Ulam has put down the story of his "adventures" and Scribner's has had the courage to publish it (*Adventures of a Mathematician*, 1976). Ulam? He is certainly not well known outside mathematical and scientific circles, but let me assure the reader that Ulam is a creative thinker of the highest rank and that his remarkable book is worth reading even by those who flunked high school algebra.

It is worth reading if for no other reason than to dispel the myth that political leaders are the main causes of historical change. Had Napoleon died in his crib, thousands of men might not have expired for the glory of France, but would the world today have been much different? Imagine Aristotle revivified and visiting Manhattan. Nothing much in our social, political, economic, artistic, sexual, or religious life would mystify him, but he would be staggered by the products of technology. A pocket calculator would seem

This review originally appeared in the *New York Times Book Review*, May 9, 1976. ©1976 by The New York Times Company. Reprinted by permission.

a miracle; as the man who invented formal logic, he would be more eager to understand the calculator than the workings of Congress. It is not politics but science that alters history. And behind science is mathematics.

To most people the mathematician is a harmless fellow who likes to write strange symbols that no one else understands. The funny thing is that those symbols, arranged in a certain order, have the power to destroy the world. "Steinmetz jotted a formula on his cuff," writes Dos Passos in *The 42nd Parallel*, "and next morning a thousand new powerplants had sprung up . . . and they let him be a Socialist and believe that human society could be improved the way you improve a dynamo . . . because mathematicians are so impractical who make up formulas by which you can build powerplants, factories, subway systems. . . ."

Consider $e = mc^2$. Hitler, Stalin, Churchill, and FDR had only the dimmest notion of what it means. Yet this simple equation is the product of a theory as beautiful as a Mozart concerto, more useful to humanity in the long run than the stock market, more revolutionary than the Communist party. And this theory, the theory of relativity, was something a funky mathematician, kicked out of Germany because the practical men who were running the Fatherland couldn't stand Jews, made up in his head. If Hitler had understood the formula he might not have lost the war.

At the moment, the most terrifying embodiment of that formula is the H-bomb. Who invented it? Let's try a multiple-choice test (check one): (*a*) Fermi, (*b*) Oppenheimer, (*c*) Teller, (*d*) General Groves, (*e*) someone else.

The answer is (*e*). It was Ulam.

To this day we don't know what it was that came into Ulam's head, because it is still top secret. The most he says about it is that it was an "iterative scheme" that modified a previous scheme by Teller. Ulam's calculations had proved that Teller's approach wouldn't work, but by "injecting a repetition of certain arrangements" Ulam found a way to make it work. Teller was at first skeptical, then enthusiastic. Later he made some changes and additions, wrote a report, and the new scheme led to the first successful thermonuclear reactions. Ulam and Teller actually hold a patent on the first H-bomb.

Ulam has little to say about the merits of either side in the great controversy that raged over whether the Super should be built or not. Teller led the yes faction, Oppenheimer the no. (A recent book by Herbert F. York, *The Advisors*, defends Oppenheimer's side.) As for his own role, Ulam has no moral qualms. "Even the simplest calculation in the purest mathematics can have terrible consequences. Without the invention of the infinitesimal calculus most of our technology would have been impossible. Should we say therefore that calculus is bad?"

Ulam was born in 1909 in Lwow, Poland, the son of Jewish parents. His father was a lawyer. Does one tend to recall early childhood events because they symbolize later concerns? Ulam has a vivid memory of playing on an Oriental rug at the age of four, while his father watched and smiled. He remembers thinking: "He smiles because he thinks I am childish, but I know these are curious patterns. I know something my father does not know."

Mathematicians are popularly supposed to have at least one eccentricity. Ulam's eccentricity is his eyesight. One eye is extremely nearsighted, the other farsighted. He has never worn glasses. When he looks in the distance he uses one eye. When he reads he brings the page close to his nose and uses the other. Has this peculiar eyesight, he wonders, affected his thinking habits?

As a child Ulam became, as he puts it, drunk with mathematics. His student years at the Polytechnic Institute in Lwow, where he got his doctorate, threw him into contact with the eminent Polish mathematicians: Kuratowski, Tarski, Banach, Sierpinski, Mazur, Kac, Steinhaus, and others. There were endless conversations in cafés, especially at a coffee house called the Scottish Café, where mathematicians recorded unusual problems in what became known as *The Scottish Book*. (Ulam later translated it for publication.) A few months at Cambridge University put him in touch with the great British mathematicians. He recalls that someone once asked Whitehead (who lived above him in Cambridge, Massachusetts), "Which is more important, ideas or things?" "Ideas about things," was Whitehead's instant reply. It is another symbolic memory. Ulam has always shuttled easily back and forth between pure and applied mathematics.

It was von Neumann who invited Ulam to the Institute of Advanced Studies at Princeton. This was followed by several years of teaching, first at Harvard, then at the University of Wisconsin. At Madison Ulam became a U.S. citizen and married Francoise, a beautiful French girl he had met at Cambridge. In his acknowledgments he thanks his wife for "having managed to decrease substantially the entropy" of his memoirs. ("Entropy" is a technical term for a kind of disorder.) Today he is retired from the University of Colorado, but still a research professor at the University of Florida.

It was also Johnny (as von Neumann was known to his friends) who invited Ulam to Los Alamos when work was just beginning on the atom bomb. Ulam had no notion of what was going on. "I don't know much about engineering or experimental physics," he told Johnny. "In fact I don't even know how the toilet flusher works, except that it is a sort of autocatalytic effect." Johnny paled. Later Ulam discovered that "autocatalytic" was a word used in connection with plans for the bomb. A few months later he was admitting to a friend that he had "sunk so low" from his earlier work in topology that his latest paper actually contained numbers with decimal points.

One of Ulam's great seminal ideas at Los Alamos was his invention of the Monte Carlo method. This is a way of simulating physical processes, such as chain reactions and particle diffusion, by using computer-generated random numbers.

There is now a vast technical literature on the method. Ulam remembers proposing the idea to Johnny in 1946 on a drive from Los Alamos to nearby Lamy. To this day, he says, he can recall what he said at specific turns in the road, a curious kind of multiple memory storage that he likens to recalling the spot on a page where one long ago read a memorable passage.

It has been characteristic of Ulam's distinguished career that his mind was always making creative leaps that produced simple but unconventional ideas that quickly became new branches of mathematics. The suggestion of cellular automata theory is another instance. Von Neumann published a famous proof that robots can be programmed to pick up spare parts and build replicas of themselves. The proof is based on a matrix of cells that change states according to specified transition rules—a beautiful notion that Ulam happened to think of.

Ulam's many contributions to set theory and logic, group theory, probability theory, and the theory of infinite games are too technical for anything but the barest mention in his book. Mathematically sophisticated readers will find his major papers on pure mathematics in a 710-page anthology, *Stanislaw Ulam: Sets, Numbers and Universes*, published by MIT Press in 1974. A volume of equal bulk is contemplated for his contributions to biology, fluid mechanics, nuclear physics, astronomy, and pattern recognitions. Ulam and a collaborator, C. J. Everett, hold a patent on a device for propelling spaceships with small nuclear explosions (the Orion project). He helped write the first computer program for chess.

Ulam is well aware that his genius consists of a knack for thinking of significant problems. "I am of the type that likes to start new things rather than improve or elaborate. The simpler and 'lower' I can start the better I like it. . . . I cannot claim that I know much of the technical material of mathematics. What I may have is a feeling for the gist, or maybe only the gist of the gist. . . ." Over and over again Ulam has obtained profound results in fields about which he knew little. Perhaps because of that he was able to see the problems in fresh ways.

Here we touch on the mystery of creativity. How was it that Einstein, who would have been lost in a laboratory, was able to seize upon such crazy notions as the constancy of the speed of light relative to any observer (the heart of special relativity), or the even crazier notion that gravity and inertia are one and the same (the heart of general relativity)? In wondering about this Ulam tosses in an observation about poetry that surely is old hat, but I had not come upon it before. "When I was a boy," he writes, "I felt that the role of rhyme in poetry was to compel one to find the unobvious because of the necessity of finding a word which rhymes. This forces novel associations and almost guarantees deviations from routine chains or trains of thought. It becomes paradoxically a sort of automatic mechanism of originality. I am pretty sure this 'habit' of originality exists in mathematical research. . . ."

Most mathematicians, Ulam reminds us, are almost as vain as opera tenors. Ulam is no exception, but his vanity is so unself-conscious, who could be offended? He considers himself "good looking." He believes he teaches "rather well." Johnny always leaned backward to appear modest, but Ulam always took pleasure in boasting—especially about minor accomplishments, such as his athletic prowess (soccer, tennis, track), his ability at chess, and his wit.

Because Ulam speaks Polish, French, German, and English, his word play tends to be (like that of Nabokov, whom he admires) bilingual. One Christmas when the Ulams and the von Neumanns were staying at a hotel in Las Cruces, New Mexico, that had once been a brothel, the old swing in the lobby reminded them of a Foucault pendulum. This led to "a learned and improper bilingual joke" that Ulam refrains from repeating. A programmer at Los Alamos, pretty and well endowed, had a habit of unfolding computer printouts in front of Fermi and Ulam, and below her low-cut Spanish blouse. "How do they look?" she would ask. "Marvelous!" Ulam would exclaim. (Not bilingual but binary.) Once when his wife accused him of bragging Ulam responded, "True. My faults are infinite, but modesty prevents me from mentioning them all."

Johnny is the book's second hero. He and Ulam were firm friends, and there are no better portraits of the man than those found here and in a biography of Johnny that Ulam wrote for a 1958 issue of the *Bulletin of the Mathematical Society*. Ulam had considered expanding this into a book before he changed his mind and wrote about himself. Although von Neumann's achievements were monumental (his work on computer design, the invention of game theory, his famous treatise on the foundations of quantum mechanics, to mention only three), he was disappointed that he had not been the first to discover Kurt Gödel's deep undecidability theorems. He had an encyclopedic knowledge of history, reading Greek and Roman historians in the original and knowing all the major incidents of America's Civil War. Ulam's book abounds in anecdotes about Johnny, about his wives, about his jokes. The account of von Neumann's lingering death from cancer, and his last-hour conversion to Roman Catholicism, is heart-breaking.

Ulam devotes several pages to Norbert Wiener: his egotism, his childishness, his absent-mindedness. Yes, Virginia, mathematicians are absentminded. It is because, Ulam explains, unlike scientists they can work in their heads while they are walking, eating, and talking.

Among the dozens of other mathematicians with whom Ulam has collaborated, surely the most colorful is Paul Erdös. Since he was a child prodigy in Hungary, Erdös has thought about almost nothing but mathematics. His more than 700 technical papers have given rise to what mathematicians call the "Erdös number." If you have written a paper with Erdös your Erdos number is 1. If you have come no closer to him than writing a paper with someone who has written a paper with Erdös, your Erdös number is 2. And so on. Mathematicians even draw a graph of these relations—it is called the Erdös graph—and argue about its topological properties.

When Erdös enters a room his first remark is about mathematics. His letters begin: "Suppose that x is . . ." At the end, he may add a few remarks about getting old, a worry that started, Ulam says, when Erdös was thirty. He has no job, supporting himself by lectures here and there, and staying with friends. He speaks a peculiar Erdösian language. A child is an "epsilon," husband is "boss," wife is "slave," marriage is "capture," lecturing is "preaching," and God is the SF (supreme fascist). Erdös is always meditating about a mathematical problem. If an amusing thought strikes him, he leaps up, flaps his hands, sits down again. "You are not a real mathematician," declares Ulam, "if you don't know Paul Erdös."

Among the great physicists who walk through Ulam's life, Fermi gets the highest praise. He, too, died of cancer. After Ulam's last visit, in a Chicago hospital, he could only weep and think of Plato's account of the death of Socrates. Shortly after Fermi died Ulam was in Chicago calling on Fermi's widow. He gave the address to a cab driver, adding that it was the house of the famous Italian scientist who had just died. The driver, who happened to be Italian, refused to let Ulam pay the fare.

Of the other physicists in Ulam's book I will mention only four. Niels Bohr is characterized as possessing great wisdom but not the genius of Newton or Einstein. Oppenheimer is a brilliant but "very sad man" who lacked the "ultimate creative spark of originality." Teller impresses Ulam as "a comedian whose ambition is to be a great tragedian or vice-versa." George Gamow comes through as egocentric, likable, addicted to alcohol and practical jokes, perceptive in his espousal of the Big Bang, and the first to realize that the four substances of DNA, in varying combinations, could encode the structure of all living things.

Ulam is continually amazed by the fact that mathematics, a creation of the mind, so accurately fits the structure of the outside world. He cites the title of a paper by Eugene Wigner: "The Unreasonable Effectiveness of Mathematics." It is a deep question about which philosophers argue. To Ulam the correspondence remains a mystery. Somehow it is closely bound to the fantastic amount of uniformity in the universe. "The miracle is," Ulam writes, "that science would not be possible, physics would not be conceivable if there was not this similarity or identity of vast numbers of points or subsets or groups of points in this universe. All individual protons seem to resemble each other, all electrons seem to resemble each other. . . ."

Objects not only are duplicated, they go on doing the same thing over and over again. Think of the countless billions of electrons spinning around in hydrogen atoms. Perhaps, G. K. Chesterton once said, it is because God, like a small child, never gets tired of doing it again. "The repetition in Nature may not be a mere reoccurrence; it may be a theatrical encore. Heaven may encore the bird who laid an egg. . . . Perhaps God is strong enough to exult in monotony. It is possible that God says every morning, 'Do it again' to the sun; and every evening, 'Do it again' to the moon."

The formulas of physics are no more than compressed descriptions of nature's weird repetitions. The accuracy of these formulas, coupled with nature's tirelessness, give the formulas their incredible power. Ulam has never ceased to be surprised by "how a few scribbles on a blackboard or on a sheet of paper could change the course of human affairs." That this kind of symbol manipulation can indeed shape history, for good and for evil, is the apocalyptic center of Ulam's autobiography.

God geometrizes. Behind the scenes, invisible to all but a few, are the discoverers of these curious patterns in the Father's cosmic carpet. They scribble their hieroglyphics and men go to the moon, harness the atom, crack the genetic code, transform the planet's face. It is no tribute to our culture that men and women who fancy themselves educated can look upon these towering intellects as irrelevant, absent-minded professors who pour syrup down their backs while they scratch their pancakes.

POSTSCRIPT

A publication asked me for a long review of Ulam's book, but they did not care for what I wrote, mainly because I did not go into details about the conflict between Ulam and Teller over the building of an H-bomb, and the social implications of its construction. When the *New York Times* asked for a short review, I compressed the original to about 800 words. It appeared in the *New York Times Book Review*, May 9, 1976.

The review printed here is the original. In reading it over I realize that I should not have called Ulam *the* inventor of the bomb. It was a collaboration, and until the full story is told (it is still top secret), it is impossible to know who contributed what. Ulam put it this way in a letter (we are friends) after my review appeared: "I think your calling me the inventor of the H-bomb is a tremendous overstatement. My own estimate would be that I might have contributed indeed, and perhaps my suggestions did accelerate the actual solution of the problem, but that is far from being an inventor of that terrible thing."

27

Updike Going Down

According to *Time*'s cover story on John Updike (April 26, 1968), he was raised a Unitarian, joined the Congregationalist church in his late twenties, and shortly thereafter was felled by a religious crisis. For several months, says *Time*, Updike brooded on the horror of his mortality, an experience that reverberates throughout his writing, but most explicitly in his short story "Pigeon Feathers." Karl Barth once wrote that God can speak through Russian communism, a flute concert, a blossoming branch, or a dead dog. In "Pigeon Feathers" it is a dead pigeon. Only by clinging to the theology of Karl Barth, Updike has declared, was he able to survive.

Since then Updike has cooled toward many of Barth's dogmas, but he has never abandoned Barth's conviction that liberal Protestant theology, pushed to its ultimate in the "theology" of Paul Tillich, is almost the opposite of everything that Jesus preached. Tillich's God is another name for Being, and it takes a lot of verbal acrobatics to show wherein this "theism" differs from what everybody else calls atheism. Middle-class suburban Protestantism, as Updike still sees it through his quasi-Barthian eyes, is what Barth called a modern Tower of Babel, a confusion of pagan tongues babbling about everything except what Kierkegaard called the scandal of Christianity.

When God goes, the half-gods come. Among the young who have not rushed joyfully back to fundamentalism (Billy Graham, Oral Roberts, Reverend Sun Moon), the void is now being filled by astrology, occultism, and fragments of Eastern faiths. Among the middle-aged, the god is sex. Glorious, unrestricted sex! It is this new Church of Eros that Updike celebrated in *Couples*. The Congregational Church of Tarbox, Massachusetts

---

This review is reprinted from vol. 28, no. 1, February 1976 edition of the *Virginia Seminary Journal* of the Protestant Episcopal Theological Seminary in Alexandria, Virginia, by permission of the editor.

(where the three main streets of the business district are Hope, Charity, and Divinity), finally goes up in flames, while the unwinking eye of God, on the old weathercock, looks down from transcendent heights. The book was Updike's first whopping money maker. We all know why. Readers cared not a rap about its Barthian moral.

Most readers of Updike's latest religious novel, *A Month of Sundays* (Knopf, 1975), won't care a rap about its Barthian moral either. Here and there a Christian or ex-Christian reader, who takes time to ask himself what he believes, may discover the message under the pubic hair; but most Americans who shell out seven bucks for the book will be buying it for just another peep through Updike's witty and poetic keyhole.

First, enough of the plot to see what Updike is up (or down) to. The narrator is the Reverend Thomas Marshfield: Thomas for doubting Thomas—"I doubt (verily, my name *is* Thomas)"—and Marshfield for, I take it, the marshy field in which he and his merry parishioners are sinking. Marshfield is forty-one, self-centered, egotistical, blue-eyed, muscular, balding, long-nosed, and (he assures us) the possessor of an average-size penis. He does not reveal his denomination, though one assumes from references to back collar studs and other clues that it is Episcopalian. Nor do we learn the town where his fashionable church flourishes.

Marshfield's father, senile and in a nursing home, had been a liberal minister, having rebelled against *his* father's fundamentalism. Tom (as I will call him henceforth) in turn reacted against his father's faith by becoming a Barthian. "Let us have it in its original stony jars or not at all!" At divinity school he met and married the daughter of his professor of ethics, Jane nee Chillingworth. This mate of Tarzan Tom is a cool cookie. She is the same age as Tom (they even look alike) and a firm atheist. Her ultimate concern, Tom tells us, is the "Right Thing."

Tom and Jane were technical virgins when they first met, and Tom remained faithful until middle-age crept up on him, his faith soured, and his marriage went stale. Into this void strides his organist, Mrs. Alicia Crick. She is a squat, nearsighted "blonde bimbo," divorced, with rabbit-pink eyes behind octagonal spectacles, a thick waist and homely feet. Her ultimate concerns are "music and men." She is in Tom's church only for access to its organ, which she plays with such abandon that it eclipses the spoken Word. It is only a coincidence, Tom says in a footnote, that her name is Alicia; he did not invent it to symbolize the Wonderland of suburban religiosity. Most of the novel's action occurs, however, in the "surreal early summer of the Watergate disclosures," thus underscoring the symbolism Tom's footnote pretends to deny.

Soon Alicia is playing with abandon on a different organ, and pulling out all the Puritan stops. We learn that Tom prefers her on top, that he enjoys "going down," but has a "probably political prejudice" against anal violation. Tom has momentary thoughts of leaving Jane. To provide excuse for a divorce, he even tries to entice her into an affair with his neighbor and assistant minister, young Thaddeus Bork.

Ned Bork is a bearded flower-child, bachelor, and bisexual, whose "limp-wristed theology" is a "custardly confection of Jungian-Reichian soma-mysticism swimming in a soupy caramel of Tillichic, Jasperian, Bultmannish blather." Ned punctuates his conversation with "you knows," helps drug-hooked kids, joins peace marches (in contrast to politically indifferent Tom), and wears a sweatshirt with "Jesus Christ Superstar" emblazoned on the front. Everybody in the parish loves him.

Ned and Jane never make it. Meanwhile, Alicia is more and more bugged by Tom's inability (as she puts it so delicately when she "spills the beans" to Tom's wife) to "shit or get off the pot." But Tom is no more able to leave Jane than to leave his job. What would he do? Learn to fix cars? Partly to spite Tom, Alicia begins sleeping with Ned. One of the novel's funniest episodes is Tom's account of how he once slipped out into the night to spy on Alicia, then hid in the back seat of her parked car until she left Ned's house and drove away with him.

After Tom and Alicia part company, word of Tom's prowess gets around the parish. "There was a smell about me now. Women sensed it." Some of the girls who seek him out are chafing at the bit. None take their religion seriously. Tom is shocked by how "unfussily" these damsels seek the "scrotal concealed in the sacerdotal." They teach him the "continuum" between faith and sex.

Tom is unimpressed by any of these stray lays, but there is one gorgeous creature in his church, Mrs. Francis Harlow, with whom he is most anxious to connect. She is the parish's only believer. The width of her lovely gray eyes (wide with faith?) is "disorienting." Frankie disorients, all right. So much so that for the first time in his life Tom is impotent. Frankie loves him for it, and sees their relationship as holy.

Angry because Tom has fired her as the church organist (Jane protested, Ned didn't), Alicia gets her revenge. She tells Deacon Harlow about Tom's adulteries (except for Mrs. Harlow, of whom she isn't sure), and Harlow in turn tells the bishop. Rather than put Tom through the "frolicksome rite of defrocking," the bishop dispatches Tom to a sanatorium in some unidentified southwestern desert state. His therapy is to write daily about whatever he likes, and to play games with other clerical misfits, principally golf (the hole symbolism is not missed) and poker (poke her?).

Tom is there for exactly one month, the month of December, "at some point in the time of Richard Nixon's unraveling." (Updike likes to give his novels a symbolic historical backdrop.) Chapters 1 to 31 are what Tom types from December 1 to 31. On each of the month's four Sundays he pecks out a sermon.

The style is Updikean with more Nabokov than usual, although it gets less "defiantly tricksome" near the end. Tom is addicted to word play. He enjoys making sophisticated puns (such as Andman Willsin for Edmund Wilson) and portmanteau words. When his fingers slip on the keys, he lets it stand, appending a footnote of mocking Freudian analysis. He even plays "word golf," Nabokov's term for Lewis Carroll's game of "doublets" in which a word is turned into its opposite by successive changes of single letters, each change producing another dictionary word. (Evolution proceeds by just such tiny changes along the DNA molecule. So does a denomination evolve, by imperceptible little jumps, into the opposite of what it once was.)

The plot, which I have so loutishly summarized, constitutes the burden of Tom's typescript, but after the main story is unraveled, there is more to come. Tom, cut off from his harem, is masturbating regularly. The only available female on the scene is the sanitorium's efficient manager, a stern, hefty, dark-haired lady, "undeformed but unattractive." Tom calls her only Ms. Prynne. (Like Chillingworth, her name is another obvious echo of *The Scarlet Letter*.) Slowly, as the winter nights slip by, Tom realizes that Ms. Prynne is his only chance for one last bang before he "topples off" the novel's edge.

This final episode is handled with consummate skill and humor. Tom, although not sure whether Ms. Prynne is reading his typing, frequently addresses himself directly to her. When he finishes a daily chore, he attaches a paperclip just so, to see if its position is later altered. He is seeking a sign. There are none.

Tom's first sermon is on Christ's forgiveness of the woman taken in adultery. His second, on the miracles of Jesus, takes the Barthian view that the miracles were not intended primarily to heal (after all, only a small number of sufferers were made whole), but to demonstrate God's power. His third sermon edges still closer to Barth. Its text: "He found him in a desert place."

The desert is the world apart from God. Like T. S. Eliot's dry Wasteland, it is creeping over the earth, especially into our cities. It has engulfed the White House. Where has our vaunted technology taken us? To the "absolute desert" of the moon—a metaphor Updike had used effectively in *Rabbit Redux,* where the Apollo moon-shot provided the timely backdrop. But it is precisely in Death Valley that we are found. It is not we who find God. God finds us.

The next morning Tom thinks he sees the faint mark of an erased capital N on his last page. Had Ms. Prynne started to write "Nice"?

His third sermon is pure Barth. The faith of "Dear Tillich, that great amorous jellyfish," is no more than a "recession of beyonds." "Better Barth, who gives us opacity triumphant, and bids us adore; we do adore, what we also love in the world is its residue of resistance—these motel walls that hold us to this solitude, the woman who resists being rolled over, who is *herself*. Ms. Prynne, forgive me. . . ."

Tom is now penitent. He confesses he has been cruel to his wife. But after all, what is right and wrong in God's sight? Is not our ethics a "hobgoblin of little minds"? We should be concerned "not with the goodly but the godly. Not living well but living forever."

"Ms. Prynne," Tom types, "am I trying to seduce you?" Yes, of course, and one of the many subtleties of this short but complicated novel is that we never know whether Tom's seeming return to Barth is genuine or merely a device to arouse Ms. Prynne. Tom himself probably does not know.

The final sermon, written December 27, is on the resurrection of the body. Tom approves the emphasis — in Paul, in Barth, in Unamuno — on the Christian hope for another life with real bodies, not a "gaseous survival of a personal essence, or one's perpetuation through children or good deeds or masterworks of art, or identification with the race of Man. . . ." The resurrection hope is impossible to believe, but has it not, writes Tom, *always* been impossible? We can only "profess to believe." After quoting from Pascal on the mystery of our existence, Tom closes with an affirmation that there is a Who. "We have been placed."

Next morning, Tom finds a penciled note at the end of his sermon: "Yes — at last, a sermon that could be preached."

Tom is overjoyed. "You spoke. You exist." He is finding Ms. Prynne not so unattractive after all. There is her graceful neck, the "generous curve" of her mouth, her "sable eyes," her large behind, which he now finds "manageable" as well as "grabbable, huggable, caressable, kissable." He lets her know that the kindness she had displayed toward a drunken Indian, when she took her clerics for an outing, had not gone unobserved. He speculates on the darkness of her pudenda, like a "heap of coal," and on the "few teasing dark hairs about her nipples." "You who were kind to a drunken Indian, be kind to me, poor Wasp stung by the new work-ethic of sufficient sex. . . ."

There is no word from Ms. Prynne on the next two days, but Tom does not abandon hope. Has he not been a good patient? He wants his merit badge. "You, Ms., pynn it on me." He lists three reasons why he loves her, and two why she should love him: "(a) I am here (b) I need you." He ends his penultimate day's typing with the penultimate verse of the Bible, castrated of its last two words: "Even so, come." What happens on December 31 is best left (I must leave *some* surprises) for the curious reader.

What should we make of all this? Opposite the copyright page Updike quotes a typical line from Tillich: "The principle of soul, universally and individually, is the principle of ambiguity." The novel is, above all, a novel about spiritual fog. Tom does not know what he believes. "Something's gone wrong. I have no faith. Or rather, I have faith, but it doesn't seem to apply," he says to his senile father. "Daddy, I'm frightened. Tell me what to do. What shall I become? I wanted to become better than *you*." But his father's head is empty. Daddy can only pat Tom's hand and say, "There's none of that until we get to be a little bit older."

Tom is, quite obviously, Updike's symbol of Protestant unraveling. The church does not know what to become or what to do. It does not know how to be better than it was. Like Tom, it is caught in the middle, between Frankie and Jane, faith and faithless ethics. Tom's treachery (he realizes) is not his adultery, but staying with his wife, with a parsonage that he should have cursed as Christ cursed the barren fig tree.

A Month of Sundays reaches its symbolic climax in Chapter 19 with the thunderous absence of a climax. Tom, in a motel room with Frankie, is making his last desperate attempt to sustain an erection. His only hope is blasphemy. "Say you don't believe in God. Say you think God is an old Israeli fart. Say it." He slaps her. ". . . How can you be so dumb as to believe in God the Father, God the Son, and God, the Holy Ghost? Tell me you really don't. . . . Tell me you know deep down there's nothing. The dead stink, Frankie; for a while they stink and then they're just bones and then there's not even that. Forever and ever. Isn't that so? Say it."

But Frankie can't.

It is important to understand that Tom is not shouting his own beliefs. He is shouting only the dark side of his beliefs. Stung by the irrationality of faith, by his and his church's impotence, he is trying to convince himself as much as Mrs. Harlow that there is no God. But—he lets us know later— he had been secretly praying for an erection. For a moment, he thinks he has it. But it collapses and all is lost again.

Need the symbolism be spelled out? Yes, because most reviewers of the novel missed it—which is to say, they missed the main point of the book. It is a religious tract disguised as a porno novel. The main theme is that Protestantism—not evangelical faith but the nonfaith of suburban churches—is impotent. Confronted by its virile historic past it has nothing to do but go limp. Frankie is sure that in time "it would have happened, and been beautiful," and when Tom is sent west, she is willing to go with him. The poor, simple-minded soul does not yet know that in her presence Tom and the church are beyond reviving. The denomination sinks slowly into the marshfield, going down, or (to change the sexual metaphor), going off into the leafless purple desert where it masturbates with ancient memories.

Is Updike telling us more than this? Is he saying that the church *should* go back to Barth—that is, back to Saint Paul? Is he telling us it *cannot* go back? Should it continue to crawl Tillichwise in a direction opposite to the plain teachings of Jesus? (Was any religious leader ever *less* ambiguous about faith in a wholly other, yet personal, God who provides for another life, a genuine life beyond the grave?) Is there some third way, not yet revealed to us? Updike does not answer *these* questions. Ambiguity is the essence. At the front of the novel he could have quoted not Tillich but Mrs. Crick's "Shit or get off the pot." But that would have been a ringing Kierkegaardian, Barthian "either/or." The novel is an "and/but" book. My guess is (I could be wrong) that Updike himself does not know what he believes.[1]

The novel is beautifully, intricately constructed with unobtrusive threads that weave back and forth, and, like all of Updike's prose, dazzling in tones and rhythms, in figures of speech, in resonating words. It is a comic novel. It is rich in nontrivial ideas. It touches on questions no Christian worth his salt can evade.

Descriptions of the sexual acrobatics are as elegantly contrived as those in *Couples*. Will hassle-free readers a hundred years from now marvel at how marvelously Updike blended sex and theology, or will they wonder why all the Hawthorne was so deeply buried under piles of fashionable porn? On this let my review be ambiguous. Nor shall I presume to speculate on whether Updike is up-tight to the point at which his writing suffers, or whether his increasing preoccupation with sex is no more than a pro's knowledge of what smells.[2]

Perhaps a more interesting criticism is that somehow, I'm not sure exactly why, the novel failed to arouse my suspension of disbelief. Not once did I think I was reading a document typed by a Protestant minister. Not that I haven't met clerics who resemble the Reverend Marshfield in behavior and belief! It's just that I was always conscious of Updike pretending to write like a Protestant minister.

Maybe it's because Tom writes too much like John. Maybe it's because Tom seems unaware of recent Protestant trends. Would a minister who bothered to read Allen Ginsberg (as Tom does) not also bother to read, say, Harvey Cox? (My fingers almost slipped on that one.) And the big religious news of the past ten years, for both Catholics and Protestants, surely is not the movement of the young toward occultism, which Tom mentions, but toward Pentecostalism and conservative Evangelicalism, which he doesn't.

I put down the book in a mood strangely like that with which I once put down *Tender Is the Night*. Fitzgerald's novel was filled with superb writing, but I was never able to persuade myself that Dick Diver was a psychiatrist. He was just F. Scott, bewildered, going down, playing a puppet in another novel about himself.

POSTSCRIPT

My theological novel, *The Flight of Peter Fromm*, was published in 1973. To my vast surprise, by far the best review it received was in the *Virginia Seminary Journal*, published by the Protestant Episcopal Theological Seminary, Alexandria, Virginia. I sent the journal and the reviewer a letter of appreciation, and this led the editor to ask me to review Updike's religious novel. The two books have some features in common. I had spoken in my novel of Updike's Barthian phase and even quoted in full his marvelous poem about the Resurrection.

My second surprise was the seminary journal's willingness to print my review. I can't blame them for excising a few passages in which I quoted lines from Updike's novel that would have been in bad taste for such a journal. Here I have restored several of the offensive passages, but omitted one that dealt with Updike's minister placing a communion wafer "between the parted lips of a mouth that, earlier in the very week . . . had received one's throbbingly ejaculated seed."

Much as I admire Updike's skill, I find myself in agreement with the conclusion of Thomas R. Edwards's review in the *New York Review of Books* (April 3, 1975):

> It may be that God has put us here to serve Him by breaking what we believe are His laws; it may be too that Marshfield's discovery of this, even at the expense of so much unhappiness, in others and himself, is admirable. But *A Month of Sundays* doesn't hang together well enough to prove that Updike's interest in sex and his interest in religion have come together to say something that is impressive or interesting about love. Perhaps to my shame, I can't see the novel as being a great deal more than disappointing self-indulgence by a very gifted writer.

NOTES

1. In an introduction to *Soundings in Satanism*, ed. by F. J. Sheed (Sheed and Ward, 1972), Updike described his Christian beliefs as follows:

> I call myself Christian by defining "a Christian" as "a person willing to profess the Apostles' Creed." I am willing, unlike most of my friends — many more moral than myself — to profess it (which does not mean understand it, or fill its every syllable with the breath of sainthood), because I know of no other combination of words that gives such life, that so seeks the *crux*.

Unless Updike interprets the creed in some curious and perverse way, I take this to mean that in 1972 Updike was a conservative, orthodox Protestant. Strange!

2. A typo. I meant, of course, "sells."

28

The First Three Minutes

There is a famous passage in *A Study in Scarlet* where Sherlock Holmes explains to Watson why, whenever he is told a fact about astronomy, he does his best to forget it.

"But the solar system!" Watson exclaims.

"What the deuce is it to me?" Holmes interrupts. "You say that we go round the sun. If we went round the moon it would not make a pennyworth of difference to me or to my work."

I would guess that most Europeans felt the same way during the great debates over the Copernican and Ptolemaic theories and that even today most laymen have a similar indifference toward the debates over contemporary models of the universe. No branch of physical science is more remote from the practical. What does it matter to you and me whether spacetime is infinite, or finite and closed like the surface of a sphere? What difference does it make if the universe expands forever until it dies from the cold, or if, after many billions of years it starts to contract? Who cares whether the contraction will end in a black hole or whether the universe will bounce back into existence, as foretold by Hindu myths, to start another cycle in an endless round of cosmic rebirths?

Well, astronomers, physicists, and philosophers care, and it has always been impossible for them not to consider such questions. Why does a chicken cross the road? Because it's there. Why do astrophysicists build models of the universe? Because the universe is there, and because they have in their heads the materials and the mathematical tools for constructing such models.

Indeed, the materials and tools are available in an abundance far exceeding that of earlier centuries. By "materials" I mean, of course, the entire body of scientific knowledge—never certain, always changing, but steadily improving in its power to explain and predict the peculiar behavior of the outside world. There are, therefore, excellent reasons to believe that today's models of the universe "fit" reality better than the old ones.

Modern cosmology began with Einstein's model of a finite yet unbounded universe. Although it cannot be visualized, it is easy to understand. A straight line is infinite and unbounded, but bend it through a space of two dimensions and it can form a circle. This "closed universe" is still one-dimensional, with no boundaries, but now it has a finite size. A plane is infinite and unbounded. Bend it through "three-space" (i.e., three-dimensional space) and it can be the closed surface of a sphere. Perhaps, said Einstein, our three-space bends through four-space to form the "surface" of a hypersphere. Like the circle and the sphere's surface, such a space is unbounded in the sense that you can travel through it as far as you like, in any direction, and never reach an end. Nevertheless it is finite in size. To prevent gravity from collapsing the universe, Einstein posited an unknown repulsive force that preserves the cosmos in static equilibrium. Such serious flaws were found in this model that Einstein reluctantly abandoned it even before the evidence for an expanding universe became overwhelming.

Since then hundreds of books and thousands of papers have explored a bewildering variety of other models. Twenty years ago the two most fashionable were the Big Bang, skillfully defended by George Gamow in his widely read book, *The Creation of the Universe*, and the steady state, ably defended by Fred Hoyle in his equally popular book, *The Nature of the Universe*. The titles differ significantly in a single word. For Hoyle the universe had no moment of creation. It has always been the way it is, perpetually expanding, preserving its overall structure by a continual creation of hydrogen in empty space.

To the great astonishment of Hoyle and his friends, the steady-state theory was suddenly shot down in the mid-sixties by one of the major astronomical discoveries of the century. The universe was found to be permeated with a microwave radiation that is extremely difficult to explain unless one assumes it to be an electromagnetic glow produced by a primeval explosion. The Big Bang theory at once became the preferred "standard" model.

It is as hard today to find two astrophysicists who agree on all aspects of this model as it is to find two economists who agree on how to model the nation's economy, but almost all astronomers now believe that the universe began, ten to twenty billion years ago, with a monstrous fireball that flung out matter and energy in all directions. The resulting universe has been expanding ever since.

Will the expansion ever stop? This depends on whether the amount of matter in the universe does or does not exceed a certain "critical density." In relativity theory space is "bent" by the presence of matter, and the denser the matter the greater the curvature. Beyond the critical density the curvature is strong enough to close space back on itself as in Einstein's static model. In such a closed cosmos gravity would be strong enough to slow the expansion and eventually reverse it. At the moment the density seems far short of the critical amount. There may, however, be enough matter hidden somewhere to alter the picture, so work is still being done by cosmologists who favor oscillating models.

What will be the ultimate fate of the universe if it goes into a contracting phase? Here again there is little agreement among experts. It could become a super black hole that would just sit there, wherever "there" is, doing nothing much except maybe rotate and radiate. It might go through what John Wheeler calls a worm hole to emerge as a white hole in some other spacetime. It might explode, producing another fireball that would start the whole show over again, perhaps (as Wheeler likes to think) with new kinds of particles and laws that would make a universe utterly unlike the one we know.

In spite of these wild controversies there is now surprising agreement on the nature of the last (if not only) fireball, and that is what Steven Weinberg's excellent book *The First Three Minutes* (Basic Books, 1977) is all about. He has not tried to write another book about the present structure of the universe. He has tried instead to put down in detail, but in a way that laymen can understand, what the best minds among today's astrophysicists believe to be the most probable history of the universe during its *first three minutes* after the zero moment of explosion.

The standard model rests on a wondrous mix of astronomical data, relativity theory, and particle physics. Dr. Weinberg, a physics professor at Harvard and senior scientist at the Smithsonian Astrophysical Observatory, has a distinguished record of prize-winning work in all three fields. His book is science writing at its best. There is no sacrifice of accuracy for sensational effects; at the same time the difficult mathematics is kept to a minimum. The back of the book has a useful glossary, formulas for those who can understand, a selected list of references, and a good index.

Four preliminary chapters give the reader what he needs to know to follow the second part of the book, in which Weinberg reconstructs what may have happened in the first few minutes of the universe's existence. The reconstruction is in the format of a motion picture. At intervals the picture is stopped, and the frame is carefully examined.

The film begins (how could it be otherwise?) in mystery. What was the nature of the fireball at zero time? Weinberg postpones this question to a later chapter where he takes a few tentative peeks "behind the veil." His first frame assumes a beginning, then stops the film at one-hundredth of a second after zero time. The temperature of the universe is 100,000 million degrees Kelvin. We see an undifferentiated soup of primitive particles and radiation, expanding with unimaginable rapidity, and in a state of almost perfect thermal equilibrium. "The universe is simpler and easier to describe than it ever will be again."

The particles are electrons, positrons (antiparticles of electrons), and the massless particles: photons, neutrinos, and antineutrinos. (There are no "antiphotons" because the photon is its own antiparticle.) These particles are so closely packed that the soup's density is almost 4,000 million times that of ordinary water.

This picture of the universe and the film of what happens next rest on such technical reasoning that most readers will find this the hardest part of the book to follow. The deductions draw on the laws of thermodynamics, relativity theory, and quantum mechanics, but in essence the reasoning is very much like that of Holmes when he reconstructed a crime.

The procedure is first to get all the relevant observational evidence one can. Holmes had his hand magnifier. The cosmologist has optical and radio telescopes, bubble chambers, and cyclotrons. To this evidence he applies logic, mathematics, and physical laws. For example, a well-established law says that the net electric charge of the universe cannot vary. Charged particles can be created and destroyed, but only in pairs of equal and opposite charge. Similar "conservation laws" apply to other "quantum numbers." They put severe restraints on the composition and behavior of the universe in its first three minutes.

Slowly, bit by bit, like the investigators of a bombing, the cosmologist fits the broken pieces together and tries to reconstruct what must have happened. There is no way to identify the Mad Bomber, but shrewd guesses can be made about the bomb's construction and what it did. It is, of course, a bizarre kind of bomb. The big explosion is not something that takes place *in* a universe. The explosion *is* the universe. From the observed rate of the universe's expansion, the present state of its matter, the temperature of the microwave radiation, and a thousand other things, the cosmologist does his best to run the movie backward. His deductions are so complicated, so dependent on laws that could be scrapped tomorrow, that the wonder is that a standard model can be constructed at all. But back to our film.

Eleven-hundredths of a second after the first frame the temperature has dropped to 30,000 million degrees and the density to thirty million times that of water. A second later the temperature is down to 10,000 million degrees and the density to 380,000 times that of water. After thirteen more seconds the temperature is 3,000 million degrees. Electrons and positrons are now furiously annihilating each other, and nuclei of deuterium (heavy hydrogen) are starting to form.

The fifth frame stops the action about three minutes after the first frame. The temperature is now a mere 1,000 million degrees, or seventy times as hot as the sun's center. Tritium and helium nuclei are shaping up. A half-hour later the soup is still too hot for electrons and nuclei to unite in stable atoms. This doesn't happen until 700,000 years later. At that time the soup—mostly hydrogen and a smaller amount of helium—is starting to form galaxies and stars. "After another 10,000 million years or so, living beings will begin to reconstruct this story."

One must not suppose that Weinberg's breathtaking documentary, given in more vivid detail than my skimpy synopsis suggests, is put forth as "true." Many earlier cosmologists, when they wrote for laymen, had an embarrassing habit of describing their favorite model as if they were describing astronomical facts, only to have the model fall apart a decade or so later. Weinberg is too good a scientist to harbor such illusions. He makes it quite clear that he is doing no more than giving an account of the first few minutes of the best model now available. He does maintain that for the first time in history there is enough data and sufficiently adequate theory to take this reconstruction seriously.

The reconstruction could not have been made had not the microwave radiation been detected in 1965 and found to have a temperature of three degrees Kelvin. This raises a puzzling question: Why was this historic discovery not made earlier? In 1948, Gamow and his associates Ralph Alpher and Robert Herman had predicted a radiation of about five degrees, and the details had been refined by them and others in 1953. Yet nobody thought it worthwhile to look for this dim remnant of the ancient fireball.

In what he calls a diversionary chapter Weinberg speculates on why the search was delayed. He finds three reasons: difficulties in the early Big Bang theories, a woeful lack of communication between theorists and experimentalists (radio astronomers simply did not know how easily the microwave radiation could be detected), and finally, physicists were in no mood to take seriously *any* theory about the universe's origin.

The situation was indeed curious. Here was a respectable theory, along with a relatively simple way to confirm it, but radio astronomers did not bother to make the test. What happened was a reversal of the usual sequence. The observations were made casually by two teams of scientists working near each other geographically (one at Bell Telephone Laboratories, one at Princeton University), neither aware of what the other was doing or of the previous calculations by Gamow, Alpher, and Herman. Not until the results were announced did radio astronomers suddenly become interested in a theory they should have tested fifteen years before. We are so accustomed, writes Weinberg, to think of science history as "the great magical leaps of a Newton or an Einstein" that we forget "how easy it is to be led astray, how difficult it is to know at any time what is the next thing to be done."

As to what happened at zero time, one scientist's guess is as good as another, because the temperature and density of the fireball would have been beyond the point at which quantum laws apply. There may have been a zero moment before which time itself has no meaning, a singularity about which nothing can be said. Perhaps, as one irreverent aphorism has it, the "big blast was produced by our farter who art in heaven." Or the blast may have been the universe rebounding from a previous contraction, the fireball never reaching a temperature and density at which quantum theory is irrelevant.

On such mysteries let me quote a once popular writer before disclosing his name: "How their [modern cosmologists'] theories conflict is soon apparent. Next-door neighbors? No, they are miles apart. . . . Some say the world had no beginning, and cannot end; others boldly talk of a creation . . . though it is by no means obvious how there could be place or time before the universe came into being. . . . Some circumscribe the All, others will have it unlimited."

This is from an essay by Lucian, written in Greek in the second century! Today's models of the universe are more complicated than those of the old Greeks and Romans, and presumably better confirmed, but they remain swathed in ultimate questions as familiar to the ancients as to us. We are no closer to answering them.

This brings me to my only caveat. Weinberg closes his valuable little book with a touch of metaphysics. Whatever cosmic model survives the rapidly expanding data, he writes, there is little comfort for us. "It is almost irresistible for humans to believe that we have some special relation to the universe, that human life is not just a more-or-less farcical outcome of a chain of accidents reaching back to the first three minutes, but that we were somehow built in from the beginning."

After a brief description of how beautiful the earth looks below the airplane in which he is riding while he writes his epilogue, Weinberg continues: "It is very hard to realize that this all is just a tiny part of an overwhelmingly hostile universe. It is even harder to realize that this present universe has evolved from an unspeakably unfamiliar early condition, and faces a future extinction of endless cold or intolerable heat. The more the universe seems comprehensible, the more it also seems pointless."

What does that last sentence mean? I take it to mean that in earlier ages, when little was known about natural laws, it was easier to suppose that the gods or God had designed the universe, including us, with some beneficent end in view. As a corollary, the more we learn about the universe, without finding any evidence of such purpose, the more meaningless the whole thing seems.

This certainly is how Weinberg feels. His final paragraph about science lifting human life above the level of farce and giving it the "grace of tragedy" is in the spirit of Bertrand Russell's famous essay, "A Free Man's Worship." But if Weinberg is suggesting that the new cosmologies make the universe seem more pointless to scientists and thinkers in general, I believe he is mistaken. Of those great physicists and philosophers who thought the universe had a point, I am unable to think of a single one who would have been dismayed by any current model. A Russian astronaut may bring back the news that he failed to see God in outer space, but surely this observation, or rather the lack of one, has nothing to do with serious philosophy or theology. Scientists like to imagine that advances in their specialty somehow have grave metaphysical consequences. The dull truth is that the great eternal questions are unaffected by oscillating cosmological fashions.

If God or the gods, or the Old One (as Einstein liked to call Everything), had a transcendent reason for bringing us into existence, what does it matter whether the first man and woman were formed in one day from the dust of the ground, as Genesis has it, or evolved over billions of years from the dust of a primeval fireball? The fact that we are here proves that we derive, in some crazy sense, from the fireball, and I for one find this more miraculous than the Genesis story. We know we are fated to die and to return to the dust. *That* is a stark fact that does indeed seem pointless, and the writers of Ecclesiastes and Job understood it as well as any modern physicist.

As a layman I like to keep up with the latest developments in cosmology, and I am fascinated by the arguments of rival authorities. Weinberg's book, to quote Isaac Asimov on the back cover, "is a tremendous service to us all." But when it comes to deciding on the basis of the latest model whether the universe has a point or not, I find myself in sympathy with the youthful Sherlock Holmes.

29

The Tao Is Silent

Fifty years ago a funny thing happened to Western philosophers on their way to work. They got lost in the mathematics building. As a result, their books became so splattered with arcane symbols that nobody could understand them except mathematicians, and *they* weren't interested.

Raymond M. Smullyan is a mathematician who *is* interested, but the funny thing about him is that he is more interested in the great themes of traditional philosophy than the philosophers are. Not that he doesn't understand their newfangled jargon. He studied philosophy under Rudolf Carnap, received his doctorate in mathematics at Princeton, and is now a professor of mathematics at Lehman College. His *Theory of Formal Systems* is an elegant treatise that has had enormous influence on mathematicians working with recursive functions, proof theory, and artificial intelligence.

Into this expertise in logic and set theory, stir the following: a love of music (Smullyan is an accomplished classical pianist), a love of magic (in his youth he was a part-time performing conjuror), a love of chess (his brilliant problems have been featured in *Scientific American*),[1] a subtle sense of humor, a relaxed literary style, and eight years of absorption in Chinese and Japanese philosophy, art, and literature. The result can be seen in *The Tao Is Silent* (Harper & Row, 1977), Smullyan's first nontechnical work.

Harper & Row, a leading purveyor of worthless books on occultism, probably published this volume in the hope of reaching the enthusiasts of pseudo-Eastern cults who are seeking shortcuts to satori. Such purchasers will find Smullyan disappointing. He prescribes no new Yoga exercises, no new diets, no new meditation techniques, no devices that will intensify one's orgasms and psychic powers. What he does offer are forty-seven crisp essays, in a

This review originally appeared in the *New Leader*, May 23, 1977, and is reprinted with permission.

quaint, friendly voice, on themes central to one of the great traditions of Eastern wisdom.

Part 1 is on the fundamental concept of Taoism, the Tao. Does it "exist"? Why is it formless, nameless, and like a "mysterious female"? To say the Tao is vague, writes Smullyan, "is one of the vaguest statements I know. . . . It is beautifully and wonderfully vague—almost as vague as the Tao itself." Why does the Tao "refuse to argue"? "Could you, in your wildest imagination, conceive anything as preposterous as arguing with the Tao?"

Part 2 defends the view that the Tao is "good" but not "moral." Several of these essays have the form of Platonic dialogues. In one of them a Taoist disputes a Moralist; in another, God and a Mortal discuss free will. Part 3, "The Tao Is Leisurely," deals with, among other things, gardening, altruism versus egotism, the Taoist principle of *wu-wei* (or "effortless action"), and a very funny tale about what happened to a boy who believed passionately that a person should not amount to something. To an essay on dogs opening, "I am very partial to dogs—one reason being that I am a dog lover," Smullyan appends a characteristic footnote: "If the more sophisticated reader objects to this statement on the grounds of its being a mere tautology, then please at least give the statement credit for not being inconsistent."

Part 9, "The Tao Is a Delightful Paradox," is Smullyan at his whimsical best. He begins by explaining why he prefers crazy philosophies to sensible ones. "Crazy philosophies are characterized by their madness, spontaneity, sense of humor, total freedom from the most basic conventions of thought, amorality, beauty, divinity, naturalness, poesy, absolute honesty, freedom from inhibitions, contrariness, paradoxicalness, lack of discipline, and general yum-yummyness. Their most important advantage over the sensible philosophies is that they come far closer to the truth!" Smullyan hastens to add that he is in no way *against* sensible philosophy: "It only serves to show how wonderful crazy philosophy is by contrast."

This is followed by a remarkable discussion of personal identity. Smullyan asks you to imagine that your body is no more than a dream in the circuitry of a sleeping computer that will eventually awaken. After a few billion years, when the entire universe is about to run down, you will *really* wake up and will discover you are a totally different kind of intelligence (that you cannot now even comprehend) and had merely been dreaming you were a computer.

Essay 38 is the finest defense of astrology I have ever read. I am always amused when someone—Velikovsky for instance—comes along and tries to explain biblical miracles by inventing scientific causes for them. Surely the best justification for miracles is that God is beyond the natural world. Why should God, or the Tao, need scientific laws to do anything?

"Who knows," Smullyan writes, "perhaps the Universe is a great magician who does not want us to suspect his magical powers and so arranges most of the visible phenomena in a scientific and orderly fashion in order to fool us and prevent us from knowing him as he really is!" This is pure

Platonism, and only a sensible Aristotelian or an admirer of the thoughts
of Chairman Mao could be disturbed by it. Not that Smullyan believes in
astrology, you understand. He merely thinks that the best way to view the
phenomenon is as pure sorcery—in other words, as what Jung called
synchronicity.

The book ends with a witty dialogue between a Moralist, a Practical Man,
a Mystic, a Logical Positivist, a Psychologist, a Dissenter, and a Metaphysi-
cian. Their topic is the future of philosophy. "Metaphysics is essentially one
giant koan," argues the Mystic (Smullyan), "not for an individual, but for
the human race as a whole—a koan whose purpose is to force the realization
of the impossibility of metaphysical methods being pushed any further. Stated
otherwise, metaphysics is the necessary ripening process of the human race
to prepare it for mysticism."

Smullyan is telling his readers that he cares not a rap whether they agree
with him or not. Indeed, from his point of view his book is not an argument,
but the Tao talking to itself. Waving his (her, its?) hands over Smullyan's
typewriter, the Tao has created little Zen illusions on the pages, and decorated
them with startling anecdotes, amusing koans and lovely haikus:

Upon the temple bell, asleep, a butterfly.

NOTE.

1. Since I wrote this review, two collections of Smullyan's fantastic chess problems have been published: *The Chess Mysteries of Sherlock Holmes* (Knopf, 1979),
and *The Chess Mysteries of the Arabian Knights* (Knopf, 1981). And there are now
four books of Smullyan's original logic puzzles: *What Is the Name of This Book?*
(Prentice-Hall, 1978), *This Book Needs No Title* (Prentice-Hall, 1980), *The Lady or
the Tiger?* (Knopf, 1982), and *Alice in Puzzleland* (Morrow, 1982), for which I had
the pleasure of writing a foreword. There are many more Smullyan books on the way.

"If Professor Smullyan did not exist," a colleague once said in introducing him
to an audience, "it would be necessary to invent him, as he will now demonstrate."

30

People Shapers

To this day I have never troubled about the ethics of the matter.
—Dr. Moreau

One of the most extraordinary of all the human abilities denied to beasts is the power to shape, accelerate, even to terminate the very process of evolution itself. It's as if God said to us: "I've done the best I could to bring your world and you into existence. Now you're on your own. Let's see how you manage it."

The realization that humanity can control its own destiny is as ancient as it is awesome, but not until recent decades have techniques been discovered that make it possible for people shapers to do the job in extreme ways that their predecessors would not have dreamed possible. As usual, science continues to rocket ahead of education and political wisdom, and some of the new techniques are more frightening, in their potential for good and evil, than nuclear energy. Vance Packard's latest book, *The People Shapers* (Little, Brown, 1977), which covers a wider ground than most of the similar books currently proliferating, is a valuable, skin-crawling compendium of these revolutionary developments.

The book's first half, about behavior control, discusses sophisticated conditioned-reflex methods pioneered by B. F. Skinner, alterations of personality by psychosurgery, by drugs, by hypnotism, by devices inserted in the brain. Other chapters report on new advertising and public-relations tools and the growing power of big government to keep its eye on everybody. A famous experiment by the Spanish scientist José Delgado, recorded on film, says it all. Over and over again a furious bull, his head wired for remote

This review originally appeared in the *New York Times Book Review*, October 23, 1977. ©1977 by The New York Times Company. Reprinted by permission.

control, charges toward Delgado. Each time Delgado pushes a button. The bull skids to a halt, meekly walks away.

The second half of Packard's book, on genetic reshaping, is even more staggering, although some of the techniques are as old as Plato. In the fifth chapter of *The Republic* (the first great document, by the way, on women's lib) Socrates defends both negative and positive eugenics: enforced birth control, forbidding the coupling of inferiors, encouraging the mating of superiors—in brief, a state-controlled human breeding program. Packard gives excellent capsule reports on what is being done and contemplated along such lines.

Male sperm is now widely collected in "ejaculatoriums" for use in artificial insemination. The test-tube babies of *Brave New World* are starting to crawl from the pages of science fiction into reality. A human egg already can be fertilized *in vitro* (in glass), then later implanted in a womb to grow naturally. It soon may be possible for a couple to rent a young lady's womb as an incubator for their child. Cow wombs are cheaper. That too is a coming possibility.

J. B. Gurdon, using one cell from a frog's leg, clones an exact duplicate of the frog. Beatrice Mintz combines two fertilized mice eggs to grow a single mouse that has four parents. Progress in organ transplanting is so rapid that the hybrid monsters of H. G. Wells's great allegory, *The Island of Doctor Moreau*, are beginning to haunt experimenters' dreams. A Russian scientist keeps alive a two-headed dog. At Case Western Reserve Medical School, Robert J. White transplants monkey heads to monkey bodies.

He really does. A grafted monkey head is unable to manipulate its new body, but it functions well until tissue rejection sets in. When it becomes possible to repair severed spinal cords, White tells Packard, it will be possible to transplant human heads and produce normal people. "Oz" buffs think instantly of Princess Langwidere (languid air) and her collection of thirty beautiful heads, one of which "she" selects every morning the way a woman chooses a dress.

Packard touches occasionally on age-old philosophical debates and takes them up in a brief final chapter. Too often his comments are trivial. For example, he lists six goals that all individuals should strive to achieve: "responsible self-direction, individual fulfillment, the rearing of fine children, clear-cut uniqueness as a person, a spontaneous way of life, a capacity for independent thinking." Impressive until you realize that a Nazi, Stalinist, Christian, Buddhist, Skinnerian, and every school of psychiatry would agree.

We live at a time when many scientists are as indifferent to ethics as Doctor Moreau, and our philosophers are lost in far-off labyrinths of logic and mathematics. Alas, science can only tell us how to get somewhere. It cannot tell us where we ought to go. There is no substitute for "wisdom" in choosing goals, but now we are back to Plato's fifth chapter with its talk of philosopher kings. Whatever you may think of philosophy, there is no escape from it if you are concerned about how to distinguish right from wrong, and how to control controllers. For better or worse, it provides the only language in which the monstrous dilemmas raised in Packard's book can be talked about at all.

POSTSCRIPT

Genetics is advancing at such a rapid rate that much of Packard's book is now dated, but there are so many new books on the promise and the dangers of genetic engineering that there is no point in listing them. On new trends in human reproduction I particularly recommend *Utopian Motherhood*, by the embryologist Robert T. Francoeur (A. S. Barnes, 1973), even though it was written more than a decade ago.

31

The Glory of Everything

When a new book by an American about children's fiction comes along, I have a simple test for deciding whether it is worth reading. If it fails to mention L. Frank Baum, the author is an ignoramus. Roger Sale, professor of English at the University of Washington, Seattle, and author of several respected books of criticism, is no ignoramus. His appreciation of Baum and Oz, which appeared six years ago in the *Hudson Review,* is in *Fairy Tales and After* (Harvard University Press, 1978) as the penultimate essay.

As soon as young children learn to read, they divide into little people with widely varying tastes. Sale tells us at once that he is not writing a survey in which he draws dogmatic lines between juvenile books he deems great and those he believes to be mediocre. He is merely reflecting on those books he himself loved as a child and found that he enjoyed rereading when older.

He doesn't write about Pinocchio, Mary Poppins, Raggedy Ann, Dr. Dolittle, Tom Sawyer, Narnia, or Rootabaga, and he confesses that he now finds Milne's Pooh books boring. We needn't worry about these omissions because of his enthusiasms for and fresh insights into books just as good or better.

Sale's first chapter, an enchanting discussion of traditional European fairy tales, contains an unusually beautiful explication of "Beauty and the Beast," almost the last great fairy tale with explicit sexual elements.

This is followed by a discussion of Hans Christian Andersen as the first major teller of fairy tales not based on oral tradition. A chapter on animals introduces Randall Jarrell's *The Animal Family* and Selma Lagerlof's *The Wonderful Adventures of Nils.* Beatrix Potter's *Peter 'Rabbit* and other miniature books rate a special chapter later on.

This review originally appeared in the *Chicago Tribune*'s *Book World,* October 23, 1978.

In a perceptive essay on Lewis Carroll, Sale displays little patience for Freudian critics, not because Carroll's eccentricities are irrelevant to his fiction but because "Dodgson seems really to have been the person he presented himself as being . . . a fact many psychologists find difficult to live with."

Sale's finger rests squarely on why the Alice books, even in Victorian England, were read mainly by adults. It is because both stories lack strong narrative lines. A great movie or stage musical can be made of *The Wizard of Oz,* but you can't do much with poor Alice. Witness the recent failure on the New York stage, though written by the best of writers and composers, to imitate *The Wiz* with an all-black cast for *Alice.*

It is because both of Alice's dreams are (like dreams) patchworks of disheveled bits and pieces that disturb rather than please most children unless they enjoy chess and can appreciate subtle logical paradoxes and mathematical and verbal jokes. Perhaps the Alice books also appeal, suggests Sale, to adults who see life as a disconnected "succession of follies and errors," not as a battle between good and evil or a meaningful quest. Dorothy at least tries to destroy the Wicked Witch and get back to Kansas, but Alice doesn't try hard to do anything or go anywhere except get to the last row of a chessboard to become a queen.

Kenneth Grahame's *The Wind in the Willows* gets a splendid chapter, as does Kipling for his *Jungle Book, Just-so Stories,* and *Kim.* After his tribute to Baum, Sale closes with an essay entitled "Two Pigs." The first is Freddy, the hero of Walter Brooks's popular series. The second is Wilbur—who else?—of E. B. White's *Charlotte's Web,* a book that Sale is surely right in calling *the* classic children's novel of the last thirty years. The essay almost ends with Wilbur's marvelous "hymn" to the barn:

> It was the best place to be, thought Wilbur, this warm delicious cellar, with the garrulous geese, the changing seasons, the heat of the sun, the passage of swallows, the nearness of rats, the sameness of sheep, the love of spiders, the smell of manure, the glory of everything.

The glory of everthing. This is the luminous secret behind all great books for children, including the fantasies. As Sale reminds us, *The Road to Oz* begins with Dorothy offering to show a lovable bum, the Shaggy Man, how to get to Butterfield. Fortunately they are soon lost and wind up in Oz. Sale's essays are about some of the classics that help children (and adults) escape for a while from Butterfield. They return from the enchanted lands with a heightened awareness of the mystery and magic of what Baum called the "big outside world"—the real universe with its own incredible glories that the human race, still in its babyhood, is only starting to explore.

32

Hello and Goodbye

"A sad spectacle!" exclaimed Thomas Carlyle, contemplating the possibility that millions of planets circle other suns. "If they be inhabited, what a scope for pain and folly; and if they be not inhabited, what a waste of space!"

Much more is now known about the universe than in Carlyle's time, but the question of whether ETI (a fashionable new acronym for Extraterrestrial Intelligence) exists is as open as it ever was. However, one incredible new fact has entered the picture. For the first time in history we have the technology for maybe answering the question. This mere possibility is so overwhelming in its implications that a new science called "exobiology" has already been named even though its entire subject matter may not exist.

We do know that our Milky Way galaxy contains more than 200 billion suns, and that there are billions of other galaxies. Are there other planets? Fifty years ago the two most popular theories about the origin of the solar system each made such planetary systems so unlikely that top astronomers believed that ours was the only one in the galaxy. After flaws were found in both theories, astronomers returned to a model proposed by Immanuel Kant (later by Laplace) in which solar systems are so likely that most of the Milky Way's stars must have them. The wobblings of a few nearby suns suggest big planets close to them, but no one really knows.

If solar systems are plentiful, our galaxy could contain billions of planets earthlike enough to support carbon-based life. Biologists have a strong case for confining life to carbon compounds (silicon and boron are the next best bets), but no one has any notion of how earthlike a planet must be to permit carbon life to arise. Our two nearest neighbors, Venus and Mars, were probably formed the same time the earth was, yet their atmospheres are strik-

Reprinted with permission from the *New York Review of Books,* November 23, 1978. © 1978 by Nyrev, Inc.

ingly different from each other and from ours. Even if a planet goes through an early history exactly like our earth's, no one knows the probability that life on its surface can get started. If it does start, no one knows the probability that it will evolve anything as intelligent as a fish.

Our probes of Mars have been great disappointments in SETI (Search for ETI). I can still recall the tingling of my spine when as a boy I read on the first page of H. G. Wells's *War of the Worlds:*

> Yet across the gulf of space, minds that are to our minds as ours are to those of the beasts that perish, intellects vast and cool and unsympathetic, regarded this earth with envious eyes, and slowly and surely drew their plans against us.

Not even Wells guessed how quickly the Martians would vanish from science fiction.

If we can trust recent polls, half of America believes that ETIs are regularly visiting the earth in UFOs, but this is no more than part of the big upsurge of enthusiasm for parascience and the occult. It is not taken seriously by the vast majority of scientists, least of all by Carl Sagan, who has repeatedly said that there is not one scintilla of evidence that ETIs have ever visited us. His arguments have had the same notable absence of effect on UFO buffs as his demolition of Velikovsky's crank theories has had on Velikovsky and his admirers.

Nevertheless Sagan is the most tireless of all exobiologists in his efforts to persuade fellow scientists and the government that ETI is an idea whose time has come. A few years ago his book *The Cosmic Connection* was a lyrical outburst of a firm belief that our galaxy teems with ETI. *Murmurs of Earth* (Random House, 1978), to which Sagan contributes a lively preface, essay, and epilogue, is a collection of essays by the six persons most responsible for a remarkable LP recording placed on each of the Voyager spacecraft launched last fall. After photographing Jupiter next year, they will proceed to Saturn. One may be diverted toward Uranus, but both are destined to leave the solar system to wander through the galaxy, making a round trip every quarter billion years.

SETI (the Search for . . .) must be distinguished from CETI (Communication with . . .). The search began with a historic paper by physicists Philip Morrison and Giuseppe Coconni, "Searching for Interstellar Communications," *Nature,* 1959. There are good reasons to suspect, the authors argued, that ETIs exist. If so, the probability seems high that many are far ahead of us in both brain power and technology. We now have the means to send radio messages to other stars, therefore so do they. Perhaps they are doing just this. Since we have the ability to detect such messages, a systematic search seems desirable. "The probability of success is difficult to estimate," the authors concluded, "but if we never search, the chance of success is zero."

The first search for ETI was made by the astronomer Frank Drake in

1960, using radio telescopes he had assembled at Green Bank, West Virginia. The effort was minor and no signals were detected. Drake's initial thoughts about CETI concerned pulsed codes that would begin with simple arithmetical facts such as the sequence of prime numbers. It is assumed by all exobiologists that on any planet where there are "things" that keep their identities (pebbles, fingers, stars . . .), two things plus two things make four things. (No one doubts this except a small group of extreme cultural relativists with a meager grasp of logic and mathematics.) By starting with simple theorems about counting numbers, it is possible slowly to construct a scientific language by which we could communicate with aliens across interstellar distances. A Yale mathematician, Hans Freudenthal, wrote an entire book to show how this can be done.

There is an easier way. It occurred to Drake early in the game (he writes about this in Sagan's book) that excellent pictures can be transmitted in pulsed codes simply by drawing a rectangular matrix of cells and coloring each cell black or white. After a few preliminary explanations, one would proceed to send pictures in a binary code that used say, 1 for black, 0 for white. Any ETI capable of detecting the message would surely be able to figure out how to scan the matrix, and in this way enormous amounts of information could be quickly transmitted.

But do ETIs have eyes? It seems likely. An organ sensitive to electromagnetic waves is by far the most efficient way for an intelligent creature to map its environment. On earth, for instance, the eye has independently evolved three times: on vertebrates, insects, and mollusks. An octopus has excellent eyes, yet evolution produced them entirely apart from those of insects and vertebrates. Even if ETIs are eyeless and explore their world by other senses, a picture composed of two kinds of cells would still be meaningful in terms of whatever senses they use. A cube has the same structure to the touch of a blind person as it has to the eyes of one who can see.

Although radio is by far the best way to contact ETIs, it occurred to several scientists that it might be worthwhile to add a visual message to Pioneer 10 and 11 when they were launched in 1971 and 1972. These spacecraft have already taken spectacular pictures of Jupiter. After photographing Saturn next year they will leave the solar system to travel for eons, like the Voyager craft, around the galaxy. Each Pioneer carries a metal plate designed by Sagan. It bears a picture of a nude man and woman, drawn by Sagan's wife, Linda, as well as some basic information about our solar system. It was the first visual message fired from earth into space.

When Sagan was asked by NASA to prepare a more elaborate message for the Voyagers, he vowed to squeeze into it as much information as he could. His first step was to seek the advice of distinguished consultants, including Morrison, who started it all, and three science-fiction writers: Isaac Asimov, Arthur Clarke, and Robert Heinlein.

The Voyager message finally took the form of a gold-plated copper record in an aluminum cover containing instruments for playing. It is an aural not a visual message. Sagan is under no illusion about the probability that ETIs will intercept the craft and play the record. The chances are infinitesimal. However, the Voyager message will become available to earthlings (first in the book under review, later as a record), so its main function is public relations—to arouse among people the expectation of ETI contact and to cushion the violent cultural shock that is sure to follow if such contact is made.

Murmurs of Earth is an eloquent account of this recording, how it got made, why it was made, and what it contains. Linda Sagan somehow managed to write a delightful essay about the record's weakest aspect, a section in which short inane greetings to aliens are spoken in almost sixty languages. Burma asks, "Are you well?" Indonesia's message is, "Good night, ladies and gentlemen. Goodbye and see you next time." Turkey sends: "Dear Turkish-speaking friends, may the honors of the morning be upon your heads." China: "Friends of space, how are you? Have you eaten yet? Come and visit us if you have time." (To eat us?)

Delegates to the Outer Space Committee of the United Nations also recorded greetings. The French delegate read a poem by Baudelaire. The Australian delegate decided to speak in Esperanto. The Nigerian delegate said, ". . . as you probably know, my country is situated on the west coast of the continent of Africa. . . ."

Kurt Waldheim, the UN's Secretary-General, read a statement about how we step "into the universe seeking only peace and friendship." If we are capable of saying this, in the light of our history, should we not beware of similar statements from ETI? Jimmy Carter's message speaks of earth as "rapidly becoming a single global civilization," and hoping someday "to join a community of galactic civilizations." A strange message from an evangelical Baptist, who, if he accepts New Testament prophecy, must believe with Billy Graham that our world is going to get worse and worse until finally—for Billy, soon!—world history will end in the thunder and lightning of the Second Coming and the final overthrow of Satan.

It was wise of Sagan and his friends to put nothing on the disk about major religions—there was just no way to include one without the others—but was it cricket to omit all hints of earthly war, famine, disease, crime, and poverty? No inquisitions, no pogroms, no holocausts, no Hiroshima or Nagasaki! The only merit I can see in this decision is that it will alert us to similar lapses in case we start getting messages. ETIs may consider us a nuisance, the way our colonists regarded native Indians, or lowgrade organisms to slaughter for some desired protein the way we kill turtles to get oil for beauty creams.

Sir Martin Ryle, the Royal Astronomer of England, has vigorously opposed sending any kind of message into space. However, as Sagan and Morrison often have said, the distances between us and the most likely nearest ETI are so great that there is almost no chance of personal contact. A "cosmic quarantine" ensures only dialogue at safe distances. Also, as Drake points out, our presence has already been announced to ETIs by the expanding sphere of our radio and radar transmissions, and by the infrared heat generated by our technology. This provides, of course, other ways we can detect *them*. We, too, can eavesdrop.

Sagan's disk carries in aural form 116 pictures that advanced ETIs should have no difficulty in reconstructing. All are in the book with an accompanying essay by Jon Lomberg. The first picture is simply a circle, a clever suggestion of Morrison's to show ETIs they have hit on the proper way to make the pictures. The rest are photographs, mostly black and white silhouettes, though some are in color. The color photos are recorded in red, blue, and green separations that can be superimposed to give a full color range. The photographs were carefully selected to represent such diverse aspects of earth as our companion planets, DNA, cell division, human anatomy, conception, birth, rivers, sand dunes, flowers, animals, houses, cities, factories, bridges, cars, trains, planes, and other familiar things.

Most of the record is devoted to sounds and music. Ann Druyan writes about the sounds: earthquakes, volcanoes, thunder, wind, rain, surf, crickets, frogs, birds, hyenas, elephants, dogs, chimps, whales, footsteps, heartbeats, laughter, infant cries, even a kiss that NASA gave strict orders to keep heterosexual. The music section, discussed by Timothy Ferris, includes twenty-seven pieces and runs a full ninety minutes. Bach, Mozart, Beethoven, and Stravinsky supply the Western classics. Louis Armstrong blows "Melancholy Blues." There are pygmy songs, African drums, Japanese bamboo flutes, bagpipes, and other forms of ethnic music.

No one expects the Voyagers to reach any ETIs until after a few tens of millions of years; even then the craft may fly unnoticed by inhabited planets. However, in his epilogue Sagan injects a more optimistic note. There is a Red Dwarf star, called AC + 79 3888, that the craft could reach in only 60,000 years. When one Voyager is about to leave the solar system we could make a firing adjustment that would direct it toward this dwarf. It just might have planets that just might have intelligent life, and they just might. . . .

Nigel Calder's latest book, *Spaceships of the Mind,* (Viking, 1978), is written from a viewpoint almost the opposite of Sagan's. Not that Sagan isn't gung ho for exploring the solar system, landing astronauts on Mars, and starting colonies in space. It's just that Sagan has confined his attention to SETI, CETI, and ETI, on the assumption that ETIs really are out there. It may surprise the reader to learn that there is a growing body of respectable scientific opinion that ETIs may not be there at all.

To begin with, some astronomers, unhappy with accepted models of solar system history, are considering new models in which planets again are exceptional. Secondly, most biologists are persuaded that life is impossible without proteins, and this entails an exceedingly narrow range of conditions on a planet before life can even get started. Finally, if life does begin they see its evolution on earth as a sequence of such unlikely events that there is a large probability against the rise of intelligence.

The physicist John Wheeler has carried this view to its ultimate. In his cosmic vision an infinite number of Big Bangs are constantly taking place in "superspace," and with each explosion random factors produce different physical constants. As a result, every universe has its peculiar set of mathematically consistent particles and laws. In most of these universes the formation of suns, let alone planets, is not possible. The universe has to be "finely tuned" to permit planets, still more finely tuned to permit life. As Wheeler sees it, billions upon billions of lifeless universes are being produced. Since they contain no creatures to "observe" them, there is a Berkeleyan sense—which Wheeler, Eugene Wigner, and a few other physicists believe to be supported by quantum mechanics—in which they do not even exist. (So far as I know, Wheeler and Wigner have never followed Bishop Berkeley in restoring existence to unobserved objects by allowing God to observe them.[1]) When chance elements form a universe that permits it, life barely squeaks through on one planet. "Chances are overwhelming," Wheeler wrote in 1973, "that earth is the sole outpost of life in the universe."

Cosmologists have coined a new phrase called the "anthropic principle." As the physicist P. C. W. Davies explains in "The Tailor-Made Universe" (*The Sciences,* May 1978), the principle's essence is that "we observe the world that we do because we are here. This is not meant to imply that our existence *causes* the observed features to arise, only that it crucially depends on their having arisen." The most surprising aspect of the principle is that is permits answering certain questions about cosmology and microphysics by considering the nature of life. Instead of asking what sort of life can evolve in a universe, we turn it around and ask what laws of a universe allow us to exist. Why are our laws what they are? Because if they were otherwise we wouldn't be here to discover them!

Nigel Calder, England's leading popularizer of science, discloses in *Spaceships of the Mind* that he favors this new view and is inclined, therefore, to think we are the galaxy's only ETIs. It is, as Calder admits, a minority opinion, but one likely to grow if it turns out that Mars is totally barren of life and if no radio messages from the stars are detected in the next few decades. It is amusing that the pendulum seems to be swinging back to a point of view that dominated Western thought for centuries before Bruno was incinerated for (among other things) suggesting that the cosmos swarms with inhabited worlds!

Spaceships of the Mind, based on a television series that Calder presented on the BBC, is concerned mainly with humanity's great leap into uninhabited space. The book surveys what Calder calls the "Big Ideas" about this leap, the wild extrapolations. Will we soon be building "Santa Claus machines"—automatic factories in space that take material from the moon, planets, or asteroids and process it to make substances needed for a space colony?

Will we at some future date be constructing "Dyson spheres" (proposed by the physicist Freeman Dyson)—space cities that cluster in a massive shell around a star to make maximum use of the star's energy? Will we colonize large asteroids, explore the moons of Saturn, rendezvous with comets? Will spaceships obtain economical thrust from ion engines that eject electrified atoms? Will they unfurl huge metal-foil sails to catch the feeble pressure of sunlight and tack around the solar system?

A chapter in Calder's book is devoted to the Big Ideas of Gerard O'Neill, a former Princeton physicist now at the center of a thriving counterculture space cult dedicated to the planning of gigantic space settlements. It produces books, issues a periodical, and runs workshops. The Crystal Palace is one of O'Neill's smaller ideas. Imagine an enormous structure that resembles a dozen bicycle tires stacked together inside a thick cylinder to provide shielding from deadly cosmic rays. Inside the tubes: atmosphere, soil for farms, and housing for 6,000 colonists. The whole thing rotates to generate pseudogravity.

Calder's book is on the borderline between science and fantasy, but no matter. What came to mind as I marveled at its lurid illustrations was the favorite magazine of my boyhood, Hugo Gernsback's *Science and Invention*. Its cover pictures, on gold paper to symbolize the golden age of science, were a crazy mixture of hits and misses. One big miss was a marvelous cover showing what a Martian should look like. Other covers were amazingly prophetic. My guess is that fifty years from now Calder's book will seem the same quaint mixture of hits and misses. But Calder knows his science, and between discussions of outrageous plans there are solid facts about the universe, and informed speculation about the awesome possibilities that lie ahead as population pressures and energy needs propel us into what O'Neill calls the High Frontier.

At the close of *The Great Gatsby,* F. Scott Fitzgerald imagines that "enchanted moment" when the old Dutch sailors held their breath in the presence of the new continent, "face to face for the last time in history with something commensurate to . . . [humanity's] capacity for wonder." The paragraph is beautifully written, but how provincial it now seems! Let us not fault Fitzgerald for scientific ignorance. As late as 1931 a widely used astronomy text by Forest Ray Moulton ridiculed tales about travel to the moon and Mars. "Only those who are unfamiliar with the physical forces involved," wrote Moulton, "believe that such adventures will ever pass beyond the realm of fancy."[2]

In the Center of Immensities (Harper & Row, 1978), by Sir Bernard Lovell, the eminent British radio astronomer, is the most scholarly book of the three. It is essentially a history of cosmology, written with wisdom and grace, with a sound knowledge of the history of science and philosophy, and from the perspective of today's preparation for the Big Jump.

Lovell, too, favors the anthropic principle. Our presence on earth, he believes, is the outcome of events that have near zero probability. "It seems that the chances of the existence of man on Earth today, or of intelligent life anywhere in the Universe, *are* vanishingly small." Even the expansion rate of the cosmos has to be just so to permit life.

> If the rate had been less by an almost insignificant amount in the first second [after the primeval bang], then the Universe would have collapsed long before any biological evolution could have taken place. Conversely, if the rate had been marginally greater, then the expansion would have reached such magnitudes that no gravitationally bound systems (that is, galaxies and stars) could have formed.

We Are Not Alone is the title of a book on ETI by the science writer Walter Sullivan. We *are* alone say Wheeler and Lovell and Calder. Sagan's Voyager message will be heard only by ourselves. Who is right? Is the new revival of this ancient notion sad and lonely, or should we greet it with elation? I don't know.

NOTES

1. That many cosmologists, including Einstein, were reluctant to accept an exploding universe because it seems to suggest an outside Creator, whereas cosmologists who believed in God welcomed the Big Bang with enthusiasm, is the thesis of a pleasant, informal little book by Robert Jastrow, *God and the Astronomers* (Norton, 1978). Jastrow's thesis is weakened by the fact that devout theists such as Sir Arthur Stanley Eddington at first found the exploding universe distasteful, and that many of the architects of the Big Bang cosmology were and are atheists. My own view is that the question of the existence of a creator God is not in any way affected by the truth or falsity of any cosmology.

2. Great philosophers have no clearer crystal balls than great scientists. In a 1934 lecture on cosmology, Alfred North Whitehead said, "In ten thousand years men may go to the moon." (This is reported by Joseph Gerhard Brennan in an essay on Whitehead in *American Scholar,* Fall 1978.) Brennan adds, "His estimate erred a bit on the conservative side."

33

Keeping Up With Einstein

This being the hundred-year anniversary of Albert Einstein's birth in Ulm, publishers are eager to take advantage of the occasion. Every month, it seems, a new book bearing his name appears. The formats vary. At one extreme is Nigel Calder's *Einstein's Universe*, crammed with splashy art, up-to-the-minute information, and nimble popular expositions of difficult concepts. At the other extreme is *Einstein* (Peebles Press, 1979), a translation of a 1966 collection of pedestrian essays by French scientists and writers, of whom the most eminent is Count Louis De Broglie, holder of a Nobel Prize for his great contributions to early quantum mechanics.

The book will be of value to anyone unfamiliar with Einstein's life and work; but so much has been learned about him since 1966, and so much has happened in physics and cosmology, that today it seems quaintly dated. Surely any person interested in modern science knows how, simply by thinking deeply, the unpretentious young Einstein somehow managed a stupendous leap of creative imagination that resulted in the greatest revolution in physics since the days of Isaac Newton.

"Newton, forgive me," Einstein once wrote. Although he contradicted Newton in many ways, his theory of relativity absorbed Newton's laws in the sense that they became special cases of a vaster, more complex theory. You will find all this covered sketchily and sometimes technically in the essays of this volume, along with many of the now-familiar personal details about its subject: his poor record as a student, his years as a humble clerk in the Swiss patent office, his modesty, his humor, his Zionism, his pacifism (temporarily abandoned when he urged the American government to start work on an atom bomb), his absent-mindedness, the monkish simplicity of his life,

---

This essay originally appeared in the *New Leader*, May 21, 1979, and is reprinted with permission.

and so on. Also included are fifty excellent photographs, from youth to old age, some not previously published.

In Hilaire Cuny's essay, "Such as We Knew Him," quotations about Einstein's appearance rise to embarrassing heights of adulation. Five pages are devoted to the glory of his face: ". . . the kindness of his expression which envelops his whole being with a kind of radiant softness. His nose isn't Jewish, but large and fleshy. The severe bone structure which softens near the mouth, just at the chin, frankly, becomes feminine in appearance. He has the Jews' beautiful eyes. I've never met anyone with a head like that." Such sentimental rhapsodizing reaches the ultimate in David Ben Gurion's tribute: "His face resembles that of God." How Einstein would have roared with laughter over that remark!

One day, Cuny tells us, Einstein and his friend Charles Chaplin "proposed to make a huge fire with bank notes and material possessions from all over the world, and have all peoples form a circle around it to celebrate their deliverance." One can easily imagine Einstein making such a suggestion in jest—no scientist of his eminence had less respect for money and conspicuous waste—but Chaplin? One wonders where Cuny picked up this preposterous anecdote.

To me the book's most interesting chapter is "The Philosopher-Scientist" by François Russo. He is the only contributor who deals in more than a cursory way with the biggest intellectual dispute in the history of modern physics—the debate between Einstein and Niels Bohr.

In quantum theory the causality and determinism of classical physics is replaced by a mathematical formalism in which nature makes decisions—on the basis of pure chance—whenever a particle is measured. As a consequence, quantum mechanics swarms with paradoxes that wrench the mind to a far greater degree than any paradox of relativity. Einstein could not believe, as he often said, that God (he meant Spinoza's pantheistic deity) plays dice with the universe. It was his conviction that quantum mechanics is "incomplete." He fully accepted its remarkable achievements and its internal consistency, but he was convinced that it was not the final word.

To dramatize this distrust of quantum theory, in 1935 Einstein and two associates, Boris Podolsky and Nathan Rosen, published a notorious paper titled, "Can the Description of Physical Reality by Quantum Mechanics Be Considered as Complete?" The paper described a thought experiment that came to be known as the EPR paradox, after the initials of the authors. Its subtle argument is too technical to explain here—even Russo does not attempt it—but it seems to show that under certain conditions the information obtained by measuring a particle in one part of the universe is instantly transmitted to a "correlated" particle that may be light-years away and not in any spacetime causal relation with the measured particle. Bohr replied to Einstein that same year, and in 1949 they again argued the issue in a volume of essays honoring Einstein.

Several chapters of the collection under review take a position toward this historic debate that was commonplace in 1966. Einstein is depicted as a genius who revolutionized physics in his youth, yet later behaved exactly like the early opponents of relativity. "In this he probably showed a weakness common to all men," writes Roger Nataf, "that of refusing to change their concepts after arriving at a certain age."

Russo puts it this way: "Einstein perhaps didn't have the intellectual courage which had allowed him, in his youth, to surmount the concepts and habits of mind then considered as indisputable . . . . It was Bohr and his disciples who had the courage this time." The older Einstein is portrayed as a rather sad and lonely figure, isolated from his colleagues because of his foolish opposition to the new physics.

Einstein was indeed isolated from the mainstream of theoretical physics in his later years, but one reason this book is dated is that since 1966 the EPR paradox has suddenly become one of the hottest topics in physics. New laboratory results based on Bell's theorem (a theoretical result obtained by J. S. Bell) have sharpened the EPR paradox and made it more mysterious than ever. The Copenhagen interpretation of quantum mechanics (the approach of Bohr and his friends) has meanwhile come under heavy fire from many younger physicists who share Einstein's suspicion that something — no one knows just what — is radically wrong with it.

If at the same time it does not seem possible to go beyond quantum theory the way Einstein hoped, we cannot fault him for not knowing of results obtained after his death. The essential point is that a new respect is developing for his intuition about the magical, seemingly mad events that take place on the level of particle interactions.

There are a few amusing lapses of translation in *Einstein*, such as the one where François Le Lionnais is supposed to have written, "Contrary to what the public thinks, Einstein wasn't a great mathematician, but essentially a physician . . . ." (maybe it's a printer's error). On the whole, though, the English text seems adequate.

My main complaint is that the writers had no opportunity to revise their essays in the light of three recent trends: a fantastic increase in the number of experiments that strongly confirm the general theory of relativity; exciting new developments in cosmology that are closely tied to relativity; and the latest speculation—e.g., Roger Penrose's twistor theory—about the possibility of going behind quantum mechanics to a deeper level of understanding.

Once, Russo tells us, when someone taxed Einstein over having lost the open-mindedness of his youth, he responded: "A good joke shouldn't be repeated too often." The "joke" is repeated too often in this book. It was stale even in Einstein's day, and is especially so now when physicists are smiling much less broadly than they used to over Einstein's animadversions about God the dice-tosser.

34

How Not to Talk
About Mathematics

In precisely what sense do universals (such as blueness, goodness, cowness, squareness, and threeness) exist? For Plato they are transcendent things, independent of the universe. Aristotle agreed that they are outside human minds, but he pulled them down from Plato's heaven to make them inseparable from the world. During the Middle Ages the nominalists and conceptualists shifted universals sideways from the outside world to the inside of human heads.

In the philosophy of mathematics, with which *The Mathematical Experience* (Birkhäuser, 1980) is primarily concerned, this ancient controversy over universals takes the form of speculating on what it means to say that such abstractions as the number three, a triangle, or an infinite set "exist," and the companion problem of what it means to say that a theorem about these ideal objects has been "proved." Let us not get bogged down in the technical and ambiguous differences between such schools as the logicism of Bertrand Russell, the formalism of David Hilbert, and the constructivism (or intuitionism) of L. E. J. Brouwer. All of these are briskly discussed, along with many other central mathematical issues, by the book's two distinguished authors, mathematicians Philip Davis and Reuben Hersh. Let us consider instead the more fundamental question that cuts across all the schools. Do mathematical structures have a reality independent of human minds?

It is easy to caricature what mathematicians mean when they call themselves realists. They certainly do not suppose (I doubt if Plato did) that were we transported to some far-off realm we would see luminous objects

Reprinted with permission from the *New York Review of Books*, August 13, 1981. Copyright © 1981 by Nyrev, Inc.

floating about that we would recognize as pi, the square root of minus one, transfinite sets, pure circles, and so on; not symbols or models, but the undefiled universals themselves. Realists mean something less exotic. They mean that, if all intelligent minds in the universe disappeared, the universe would still have a mathematical structure and in some sense even the theorems of pure mathematics would continue to be "true." On its ultimate microlevel (if it has one) the universe may be nothing but mathematical structure. "Matter" has a way of vanishing on the microlevel, leaving only patterns. To say that these patterns have no reality outside minds is to take a giant step toward solipsism; for, if you refuse to put the patterns outside human experience, why must you put them outside your experience?

For a mathematical realist a tree not only exists when nobody looks at it, but its branches have a "tree" pattern even when no graph theorist looks at them. Not only that, but when two dinosaurs met two dinosaurs there were four dinosaurs. In this prehistoric tableau "2 + 2 = 4" was accurately modeled by the beasts, even though they were too stupid to know it and even though no humans were there to observe it. The symbols for this equality are, obviously, human creations, and our mental concepts of two, four, plus, and equals are by definition mind-dependent. If mathematical structure is taken to mean only what is inside the brains of those who do mathematics, it is as trivial to say all mathematics is mind-dependent as it is to define sound as a mental phenomenon, then proclaim that the falling tree makes no sound when nobody hears it.

Fortunately scientists, mathematicians, and ordinary people seldom talk this way. The existence of an external world, mathematically ordered, is taken for granted. I have yet to meet a mathematician willing to say that if the human race ceased to exist the moon would no longer be spherical. I suspect Davis and Hersh would not care to say this, yet the troubling thing about their book is that it does not make clear why.

Although there are hints of the authors' philosophical perspective throughout the book, it is not explicitly stated until the last page but one:

> Mathematics is not the study of an ideal, preexisting nontemporal reality. Neither is it a chess-like game with made-up symbols and formulas. Rather, it is the part of human studies which is capable of achieving a science-like consensus. . . .
>
> Mathematics does have a subject matter, and its statements are meaningful. The meaning, however, is to be found in the shared understanding of human beings, not in an external nonhuman reality. In this respect, mathematics is similar to an ideology, a religion, or an art form; it deals with human meanings, and is intelligible only within the context of culture. In other words, mathematics is a humanistic study. It is one of the humanities.

Davis and Hersh do not deny that mathematical concepts are objective in the sense that they are "outside the consciousness of any one person," but they are not outside the collective consciousness of humanity. Mathematicians do not discover preexisting, timeless things like pi and dodecahedrons; they construct them. Once constructed, however, they can be studied in much the same way that astronomers study Saturn. They acquire from the culture's consensus a permanence of structure that cannot be altered by the whims of individual mathematicians.

What is one to make of this extreme conceptualist view? All that mathematicians do is certainly part of culture for the simple reason that everything human beings do is part of culture. But to talk as if mathematical objects are no more than cultural artifacts is to adopt a language that quickly becomes awkward because it is so out of step with ordinary language. It is like insisting that all birds are pink, then distinguishing between the pinkness of cardinals and the pinkness of crows. Conceptualism in mathematics has its strongest appeal among anthropologists and sociologists who have a vested interest in making culture central.[1] It is a language that also appeals to those historians, psychologists, and philosophers who cannot bring themselves to talk about anything that transcends human experience.

Mathematical realists avoid this language for a variety of reasons, one of which is its obvious clumsiness in explaining some things everybody knows are true. For example, why do mathematical theorems fit the universe so accurately that they have enormous explanatory and predictive power? The authors call attention to Eugene Wigner's well-known paper, "The Unreasonable Effectiveness of Mathematics in the Natural Sciences." For a nonrealist this effectiveness is indeed an awesome mystery. And if mathematical concepts have no locus outside human culture, how has nature managed to produce such a boundless profusion of beautiful models of mathematical objects: orbits that are conic-section curves, snowflakes, coastlines that model fractal curves, carbon molecules that are tetrahedral, and on and on?

If mathematical entities are no more than cultural products, one would expect independent cultures to fabricate widely disparate laws of arithmetic and geometry. But they don't. Number systems may differ in their notational base, but of course this is only a difference in how numbers are symbolized. If theorems of elementary geometry are created, not discovered, why has no culture found it expedient to suppose that the cube of the hypotenuse of a right triangle equals the sum of the cubes of the other two sides? Who can believe that on some distant planet intelligent beings have constructed a planar map of five regions, each pair sharing a common portion of a border? The mere existence of extraterrestrial mathematicians would at once place some mathematical objects outside human culture, but even here on earth are apes aware, albeit dimly, of the difference between a ball and a cube, and between one and two bananas? Of course, if one believes in a God who knows all that can be known, then all mathematical objects are not only "out there," beyond the folkways, they are way out there.

For the realist, mathematical progress, like scientific progress, mixes creativity with discovery. Never would Newton have entertained the fantastic notion that he had invented the law of gravity, or Einstein the wild belief that he had invented the law $E = MC^2$. There is an obvious sense in which scientists create theories, but there is an equally obvious sense in which theories penetrate the secret chambers of what Einstein liked to call the Old One. Einstein did not impose his equations on the universe. The Old One imposed its equations on Einstein.

What does a conceptualist gain by talking as though the spirality of Andromeda is projected onto the galaxy by human experience? Of course if spirality is defined as entirely a mental concept, then the spirality cannot be "out there." But what astronomer, seeing a photograph of a newly discovered galaxy, is likely to exclaim: "How astonishing! When I look at this photograph I perceive that lovely spirality stamped on my brain by the shared experience of my race"? Not that there is anything inconsistent about such a language. Rudolf Carnap was able to show, in his *Logical Structure of the World*, that a phenomenological language, never going beyond human experience, is capable of expressing the same empirical content as any realistic language, but he quickly opted for realism as the only workable language for science.

It is also the most efficient language for most mathematical discourse. Although I am an unabashed realist (for emotional reasons) I agree with Carnap's application of his "principle of tolerance" to the various schools of mathematical philosophy. The choice of a language for talking about mathematics is not so much which language is "right" (in logic, said Carnap, there are no morals) as it is which language is most convenient in a given context. With reference to the book under review, the context is not a technical discussion about the flimsy foundations of set theory. As the authors make clear in their preface, the book is an attempt to convey to nonprofessionals what mathematics is all about.

No mathematician hesitates to speak of "existence proofs" about objects even when they are nowhere modeled, or known to be modeled, by the external world. And most mathematicians, including the very greatest, think of such objects as independent of the human mind, though not of course existing in the same way Mars exists. Last year Robert Griess, Jr., constructed a finite simple group called the "Monster." It has 808,017,424,794,512,-875,886,459,904,961,710,757,005,754,368,000,000,000 elements, each a matrix of 196,883 by 196,883 numbers. Griess prefers to call it "The Friendly Giant from the 196,883rd Dimension" because it is a symmetry group of the packing of identical hyperspheres in a space of 196,883 dimensions. There is nothing "wrong" in thinking of the Friendly Giant as composed by Griess the way Mozart composed a symphony, but there also is nothing wrong in thinking of the Giant as having existed as timelessly as a large prime, waiting to be discovered.

Artists can paint anything they like; but, if a Russian mathematician had constructed the Monster before Griess had, the group would have had exactly the same properties as Griess's group. A conceptualist can explain this, but not without using a language both curious and cumbersome. Davis and Hersh, overwhelmed by the mysteries of infinite sets and modern proof theory, have chosen a language of considerable value in analyzing the obscure foundations of mathematics, but it serves only to confuse us ordinary folk when applied to all of mathematics.

Closely related to the anti-realism of Davis and Hersh is their attack on the infallibility of mathematical reasoning. Most philosophers have found it useful to distinguish mathematics from science by saying that mathematicians can prove some things in ways scientists cannot. Awareness that all science is fallible (I think it was the mathematical realist Charles Peirce who first applied the term "fallibilism" to science) goes back to the ancient Greek skeptics and is taken for granted by all modern scientists and philosophers. (It is not a doctrine first stressed by Karl Popper, as the authors imply on page 345.)

This fallibilism follows at once from the absence of any logical reason why a natural law cannot alter tomorrow. Science has no way of establishing facts, laws, or theories except by assigning them what Carnap called degrees of confirmation and Popper likes to call degrees of corroboration. The borderline between this corrigible synthetic truth (based on observation of the world) and infallible analytic truth (based on consistency in the use of words) may not be as sharp as Hume thought, but the distinction is too useful to throw away. "There are three feet in a yard" clearly is not the same sort of statement as "Mars has two moons."

Now a large portion of mathematics is analytic; and, where it is, there is no harm in speaking of certainty. The truth of $2 + 2 = 4$ does not depend (as John Stuart Mill contended) on the pleasant fact that two fingers plus two fingers make four fingers. It follows from the way terms are defined in a formal system that constructs integers. Davis and Hersh devote several pages to instances where arithmetic addition fails to apply—for example, a cup of milk added to a cup of popcorn does not produce two cups of the mixture. No realist would deny the authors' assertion that "there is and there can be no comprehensive systemization of all the situations in which it is appropriate to add." In relativity theory, to give another example, addition of relative velocities does not obey the usual arithmetical laws.[2]

But it does not follow from the misapplication of mathematics to the world that there are no infallible proofs in pure mathematics. On this point the arguments of Davis and Hersh become careless. A good instance is on page 326, where they speak of Euclid's theorem that the angles of a triangle add to a straight angle. This, they declare, has been "proved false" by non-Euclidean geometry. A better way to put it—it is what they really mean—is that in a formal non-Euclidean geometry the theorem is false. But in the Euclidean system it remains true for all possible (noncontradictory) worlds because it expresses a tautology that follows from the system's axioms and rules. It says nothing at all about the structure of physical space.

To blur the distinction between analytic and synthetic truth (as Willard Van Orman Quine and others have done) is to blur the difference between science and mathematics. A colorful recent effort along these lines is a monograph called *Proofs and Refutations*,[3] by the Hungarian philosopher Imre Lakatos, who died suddenly in 1974, age fifty-one, of a brain tumor. Lakatos's fiery broadsides against mathematical certainty have acquired something of a cult following, especially among social scientists. Davis and Hersh devote a chapter to this eccentric book, which they deem brilliant, overwhelming, and a masterpiece of complex reasoning and historical erudition.

Fascinating though this book by Lakatos is, in my opinion Davis and Hersh greatly overrate its merits. Lakatos had been a student of Popper. Impressed by Popper's vision of science as an ever-growing body of constantly altering conjectures, *Proofs and Refutations* tries to show that mathematical progress follows a similar zigzag course. The book has been called more Popperian than Popper. Later Lakatos and Popper clashed over the problem of induction. (Lakatos's acid tongue got him into brawls with almost everybody.) You will find Popper's low opinion of Lakatos vigorously detailed in *The Philosophy of Karl Popper*,[4] where he replies to Lakatos's contribution to that anthology.

Now it is quite true, as Davis and Hersh emphasize, that mathematicians seldom use deductive reasoning to create theorems. First they have a hunch. Then, like scientists, they make experiments (in their heads or on paper) and search for proofs that the hunch is sound. (The fact that they can tinker with drawings and discover elegant theorems is not easily justified in a nonrealist language.) This fumbling process is unlikely to be reflected in their papers. As Davis and Hersh remind us, only after a published proof has met the approval of peers is it eventually accepted. Sometimes, as in the case of the celebrated four-color-map theorem, a proof is taken to be valid for years before someone punches a deductive hole in it.

Recently the four-color theorem was proved with the aid of a computer, but the proof is buried in such an ugly mass of printouts that it requires other computers to check it. Davis and Hersh are right, in my opinion, in denying that this reliance on computers adds a new empirical element to mathematics. Many proofs, especially in group theory, are so horrendously complex that the possibility of human error becomes large. To say such proofs may be invalid is not different in principle from saying that mortals can fumble when they do long division by hand or on an abacus. Because waitresses make mistakes when they add your check, however, it does not follow that the laws of arithmetic are corrigible, or that geometers should keep trying to trisect the angle.

Lakatos's book takes the form of an entertaining dialogue between a teacher and his students. First the teacher gives Cauchy's clever proof, using graph theory, of Euler's famous conjecture that the number of vertices of any polyhedron, minus the number of edges and plus the number of faces, equal two. Thus for a cube: $8 - 12 + 6 = 2$. This formula, with its apparently ironclad proof, is then shot down by the students, who describe a zoo of "monster" counterexamples. Consider a cube with a smaller cube glued to the center of one face. The number of vertices is 16, the edges 24, the faces 11. Plugging these values into Euler's formula gives $16 - 24 + 11 = 3$. Does this undermine Cauchy's proof?

It does not. For Euler and Cauchy a polyhedron was assumed to be simply-connected (topologically like a ball), with nonintersecting faces that are simply-connected polygons (topologically like a circle). Lakatos writes as though Cauchy, had someone showed him the cube-on-cube monster, would have slapped his forehead and exclaimed: "What a fool I am! Euler's formula is false!" But the formula is not false. The face around the base of the smaller cube is a polygon with a square hole, and therefore the solid is not what Cauchy meant by a "polyhedron." And the same for the other monsters: polyhedrons with intersecting faces, polyhedrons joined at edges or at corners, polyhedrons with tunnels or interior hollow spaces, and so on. In a footnote Lakatos actually speaks of Cauchy's "inability to imagine" a polyhedron not topologically equivalent to a ball, as though this eminent French mathematician could not conceive of a cube with a square hole through it!

What happened historically has little resemblance to the distorted history sketched in Lakatos's seemingly learned notes. Mathematicians simply generalized Euler's formula to other kinds of solids; and, as this commonplace process continued, terms like polygon and polyhedron broadened in meaning. Steady generalization, with inevitable language modification, is more characteristic of mathematical growth than revisions forced by oversights and faulty proofs. The discovery of irrational numbers did not demolish proofs that all integers are either odd or even, nor did the discovery of quaternions invalidate the commutative law of arithmetic. Both discoveries simply pushed along the social process of enlarging the way mathematicians decided to use the word *number*.

Lakatos was aware of these obviosities. In fact, they are expressed by students in his dialogue. But he seemed to think that the final moral of his book—Euler's formula holds only for "Eulerian polyhedrons"—is somehow an indictment of formalism. But this is just what formalism is all about. For a formalist, a theorem never holds except in a formal system in which it holds.

Although Lakatos's historiography is, as Gerald Holton put it, "parody that makes one's hair stand on end," his book does suggest the shaggy, meandering way in which mathematics, like science, advances. As for providing any evidence that all proofs are suspect, as Davis and Hersh suggest, the book is irrelevant. Proofs naturally are fallible in the pragmatic sense, and they become ambiguous and controversial when applied to such queer objects as transfinite sets. Mathematicians do make errors, and proofs are often naïve, incomplete, and plain wrong. No complicated proofs are ever wholly formalized, because of printing costs and limits of time, space, and energy.

Moreover, thanks to the work of Kurt Gödel (whose Platonic realism was extreme), we know that in any formal system complicated enough to include arithmetic there are theorems that cannot be proved within the system. The structure of a brick may indeed have mathematical properties that can never be completely captured within a deductive system. None of this touches the realist view that the brick and its properties are independent of human minds and that where proofs are simple enough to be formalized they can be considered "certain" in a way that does not apply to any scientific claim.

Many aspects of *The Mathematical Experience* deserve high praise. It contains discussions, often quite technical, of topics not usually found in books for general readers. The authors are skillful in describing the monumental task of classifying finite simple groups—a task completed after the book went to press. They do an excellent job on the notorious and still unproved Riemann conjecture. There are admirable chapters on non-Cantorian set theory and nonstandard analysis.

The book jumps around a lot from topic to topic, but this hopscotch effect was inevitable since many of the chapters are excerpts from previously published articles, some by Davis alone, some by Hersh alone, some by both, and some by one of them in collaboration with somebody else. An excellent chapter on Fourier analysis is by Reuben and Phyllis Hersh. Not least of the book's merits are the many photographs of mathematicians whose faces are unfamiliar even to most professionals.

In my opinion, *The Mathematical Experience* is a stimulating book that is marred by its preference for an ancient way of talking about mathematics that has recently become fashionable in some mathematical circles,[5] but that seems to me so inappropriate in a book for general readers that it spreads more confusion than light. It is possible to scratch your left ear with your right hand, but why bother?

POSTSCRIPT

My review prompted much correspondence pro and con. The following letter from Robert Farrell, of La Trovi University, Bundoona, Victoria, Australia, appeared in the January 21, 1982, issue of the *New York Review of Books:*

> Martin Gardner's criticisms of the mathematical conceptualism he found in Davis and Hersh's *The Mathematical Experience* ring true. That kind of conceptualism is of a piece with the various "philosophies" mathematicians—and

scientists—espouse not as a result of argument and reflection but as, one suspects, a means of deflecting them. One can appreciate that working mathematicians and scientists will typically find philosophical enquiry into their disciplines distracting while wishing that they didn't dress up their irritation or mere lack of interest as a rival "philosophy."

Conceptualism, though espoused in order to deflect problems, faces, as Gardner rightly pointed out, problems of its own. Most notable is conceptualism's inability to give any convincing account of the role mathematics plays in successful science and technology. If mathematics is just a human conceptual or cultural creation, how is it that it stands so strikingly apart from other such human creations in being applicable to reality? Conceptualism has no answer; it presents us with a mystery. Gardner is surely right, too, to see part of conceptualism's appeal as being to those with an abhorrence of "talk of anything that transcends human experience."

Gardner attacks conceptualism in the name of mathematical realism, the view that "if all intelligent minds in the universe disappeared, the universe would still have a mathematical structure and in some sense even the theorems of pure mathematics would continue to be 'true.' " The correctness or otherwise of such a view I won't discuss here; one thing that is sure, though, is that mathematical realism is not so easily dismissed as conceptualists will have it. Gardner's comments on Davis and Hersh indicate why.

Unfortunately, having done such a good job in realism's behalf, Gardner then proceeds to undo it. Just when one takes him to have offered strong arguments for mathematical realism, one finds Gardner writing that his "unabashed" realism is held for mainly "emotional reasons"; his only other announced ground for being a realist is the "efficiency" of the language of realism. Gardner sees the dispute between realists and conceptualists as one to be settled not by evidence and argument, but by choice. He takes Rudolf Carnap as his philosophical guide, modeling his view of mathematics on the view he takes Carnap to have held about rival theories of physical reality: "Rudolf Carnap was able to show, in his *Logical Structure of the World*, that a phenomenological language, never going beyond human experience, is capable of expressing the same empirical content as any realistic language. . . ." Carnap showed no such thing; at most that was what he *tried* to show. Most later philosophers—Carnap's later self included—have taken him to have failed in his attempt. (Gardner's metaphysically tolerant attitude, by the way, fits rather more Carnap's views of 1950, as expressed in the essay "Empiricism, Semantics and Ontology.")

Gardner's mathematical realism now looks rather abashed, having no more philosophic worth than someone else's unabashed conceptualism, perhaps also held for "emotional reasons."

Gardner's realism takes another beating when he, later in his review, informs us that mathematics, in particular Euclidean geometry, is analytic; that is, that the theorems of Euclidean geometry are true solely in virtue of their logical structures and of the meanings of the terms in them. According to Gardner, Euclidean geometry can't be wrong—though many have thought it so—because its theorems are "logical tautologies," without content. But if geometrical—and, in general, mathematical—theorems are without content, what becomes of Gardner's mathematical "realism"? A genuine realist about geometry will see it as being about points, lines, planes and such. If the realist wants geometry to be necessarily true, the necessity will have to come from elsewhere than analyticity. Gardner's Carnapian tolerance of various geometries is but another symptom of a deeper antirealism, one which affects his view of all mathematics.

The question of whether mathematical realism is correct or not will only get settled if one is, first of all, clear as to what it is, and, second, clear as to what the criteria for settling such questions are. Anyone interested in the question would do well to ignore any "emotional reasons" one way or the other, and look to the work of those who have approached it with those two desiderata in mind; to them I recommend Hartry Field's recent *Science Without Numbers*, an impressive—and rather technical—attempt to answer the question in the negative, though not in favor of conceptualism, but of a version of Hilbert's formalism.

My reply (in the same issue) was as follows:

Robert Farrell is right in chiding me for saying Carnap "was able to show." I should have said "believed he could show." But Farrell is wrong in suggesting that Carnap later gave up his "metaphysical tolerance" toward the rival languages of phenomenalism and realism, or toward the rival languages for talking about the foundations of mathematics.

Der logische Aufbau der Welt (The Logical Structure of the World, which I will henceforth call the *Aufbau* program) was Carnap's first major work. Carnap himself considered it no more than a tentative sketch of a program. He early recognized its many faults, and became his own severest critic. The *Aufbau*'s major error, he declares in his 1961 preface to the second edition, was basing the program on a single primitive relation (similarity) instead of a multiplicity of relations. He remains convinced, however, that his thesis of the "reducibility of thing concepts to autopsychological concepts remains valid."

Carnap's *Aufbau* program was taken up by Nelson Goodman in his book *The Structure of Appearance*, and later vigorously championed in his contribution to *The Philosophy of Rudolf Carnap* (edited by P. A. Schilpp, 1963). Goodman argues that the incompleteness of a phenomenal language no more counts against it than the inability to trisect any angle counts against Euclidean geometry. Equally irrelevant is the charge that a phenomenal language is epistemologically false, because the language is not designed to say anything about an external world. Goodman concludes that Carnap's errors were "serious, unoriginal, and worthwhile."

Commenting favorably on Goodman's paper, in the same volume, Carnap left no doubt that he considered the choice between a phenomenal language and the realistic language of physics to be based only on the "practical decision" as to which language is the most efficient. Phenomenalism is rejected because "it is an absolutely private language which can only be used for soliloquy, but not for common communication between two persons."

If realism is taken as an ontological thesis, Carnap writes, he is not a realist. But "if 'realism' is understood as preference for the reistic language [Carnap's term for a language about material, observable things] over the phenomenal language, then I am also a realist." This metaphysical neutrality was never abandoned by Carnap, and I cannot comprehend why Farrell seems to think it applies only to the Carnap of 1950.

The problem of "realism" with respect to the entities of pure mathematics is an altogether different question, but here again Carnap never discarded his "principle of tolerance." When Farrell says: "A genuine realist about geometry will see it as being about points, lines, planes and such," I don't know what he means. Euclidean geometry was formalized by Hilbert, and others, as an uninterpreted system. One interpretation is to take its symbols as representing abstract points, lines, planes and so on. Even so, one is still inside a formal system which says nothing about the world "out there." To get to *that* world one must apply what Carnap called correspondence rules which link such ideal concepts as points and lines to observed physical structures.

Insofar as geometry applies to the outside world, it loses its certainty. By the same token, it is necessarily true only when its empirical meanings are abandoned. I am sure Farrell intends to say something important in his paragraph about this, but exactly what he wants to say eludes me. I am unfamiliar with the book Farrell recommends, so I cannot comment on it.

The notion that there is no mathematical reality outside human minds seems to appeal strongly to some contemporary writers who look favorably on Eastern religions. Here, for instance, is a passage from Robert Pirsig's *Zen and the Art of Motorcycle Maintenance* (Morrow, 1974):

> Laws of nature are human *inventions,* like ghosts. Laws of logic, of mathematics are also human inventions, like ghosts. The whole blessed thing is a human invention, including the idea that it *isn't* a human invention. The world has no existence whatsoever outside the human imagination. It's all a ghost, and in antiquity was so recognized as a ghost, the whole blessed world we live in. It's run by ghosts.

Contrast this with the Platonic realism defended by G. H. Hardy in his *Mathematician's Apology:*

> A chair or a star is not in the least like what it seems to be; the more we think of it, the fuzzier its outlines become in the haze of sensation which surrounds it; but "2" or "317" has nothing to do with sensation, and its properties stand out the more clearly the more closely we scrutinze it. It may be that modern physics fits best into some framework of idealistic philosophy—I do not believe it, but there are eminent physicists who say so. Pure mathematics, on the other hand, seems to me a rock on which all idealism founders: 317 is a prime, not because we think so, or because our minds are shaped in one way rather than another, but *because it is so*, because mathematical reality is built that way.

Hardy's realism is certainly shared by most professional mathematicians, including those working on the foundations of mathematics. Just to be sure

I was not biased in this opinion, I phoned my friend Raymond Smullyan, an expert on formal systems who also happens to be a Taoist. My first question was "Do you consider yourself a realist?" He replied, "Of course." My next question was "Among today's leading authorities on set theory who are doing creative work in the field, how many would you say are anti-realists?" Smullyan said: "Almost none."

William James, in his book *The Meaning of Truth*, argues for a mind-dependent view of mathematics very close to that of Davis, Hersh, and Kline. It is marred by the fact that James had only a meager understanding of mathematics; he never heeded his friend Charles Peirce's continual urging that he take time to study the subject.[6] For example, to bolster the view that even logics are man-made, James speaks of Boole and Jevons as having created different logics, without realizing that Boole and Jevons merely proposed different systems of notation for the same logic. Nevertheless, in spite of such mistakes, James makes a good case for a cultural approach to mathematics that was shared by F. C. S. Schiller and (I think) by John Dewey.

Truths of science and mathematics, not yet verified, are what James calls "sleeping truths." The thousandth decimal of pi, for example, "sleeps" in "the world of geometrical relations," even though "no one may ever try to compute it." Of course it sleeps just as much in the world of arithmetic, where pi is the limit of a series of fractions; or rather I should say it "slept," because pi's thousandth decimal is now known. To make the point today one would have to speak of, say, pi's billionth decimal digit.

There are, James writes, coats and shoes that "fit" backs and feet even though they are not yet made. "In the same way countless opinions 'fit' realities, and countless truths are valid, though no thinker ever thinks them." James doesn't mention it, but this includes countless scientific facts and laws not yet discovered.

To the anti-pragmatist, James continues, these sleeping relations are the fundamental ones. To the pragmatist, they are "static, impotent, and relatively spectral" until they are verified in human experience. For a Jamesian, the thousandth decimal of pi was a ghost that did not spring into full-bloodied reality until someone calculated it. "To attribute a superior degree of glory to [an unverified truth] seems little more than a piece of perverse abstraction worship."

What James seems to be claiming here is that although facts about the world, and even theorems of pure mathematics, exist in some vague way before they are discovered, as soon as they enter human experience they acquire a stronger reality. I can think of few philosophical tasks less rewarding than defending the view that the planet Neptune became more real after humanity knew it existed, or that a giant prime becomes more real when it is proved to be prime.

Of course Neptune did not exist as a known object before it was found, and nobody knew that $2^{44497} - 1$ is a prime until 1979; but these statements are vapid tautologies. Obviously nothing is known by a mind until a mind knows it. The trouble with a pragmatic language that limits full reality to human experience is that there are excellent pragmatic reasons for not adopting such a strange way of speaking.

NOTES

1. See Part 1, Chapter 5 for my evaluation of anthropologist Leslie White's paper, "The Locus of Mathematical Reality," which defends the same cultural approach to mathematics taken by Davis and Hersh, and by Morris Kline in the book mentioned in note 5 below.

2. In an interview in *Omni* (June 1981) Kline makes the same mistake of confusing the certainty of a formal system with the uncertainty of applying it to nature. Asked if he could think of an algebra that violated the rules of arithmetic, Kline replied:

> I can think of several. Take a quart of water at forty degrees and mix it with another quart of water at fifty degrees. Do you get two quarts at ninety degrees? You do not. It's more like forty-five degrees. So you can't just say I'm going to add forty and fifty and automatically get ninety. It depends on the physical situation.

Kline, Davis, and Hersh of course fully understand the distinction between a formal system and its applicability, but that is not the point. The point is that fallibilism in the application of a formal system to nature in no way introduces uncertainty into the system.

3. Imre Lakatos, *Proofs and Refutations*, ed. by John Worrall and Elie Zahar (Cambridge University Press, 1976).

4. *The Philosophy of Karl Popper*, ed. by Paul A. Schilpp (Open Court, 1974).

5. See, for example, Morris Kline's book, *Mathematics: The Loss of Certainty* (Oxford University Press, 1980), which takes the same extreme anthropocentric point of view as the book by Davis and Hersh. All mathematics, Kline tells us, is a "purely human creation," all laws of logic are the products of human experience, and "today the belief in the mathematical design of nature seems far-fetched." No mathematical design in nature? My mind reels at the infelicity of this phrasing. I am in complete agreement with Ernest Nagel's criticisms, expressed in his restrained review (*New York Review of Books*, November 6, 1980) of this quirkish volume.

6. F. C. S. Schiller, England's leading pragmatist, knew almost as little mathematics as James. In Chapter 19 of *Logic for Use* (1930), enormous confusion results from his failure to distinguish the certainty of abstract arithmetic from the uncertainty of applied arithmetic. What is worse, he seems to think that laws of arithmetic vary with the notation used:

> A dialectical victory over the rash assertion that $2 + 2 = 4$ *absolutely and unconditionally*, is easy to gain. For what the sum works out at depends on the *scale of notation* we choose to adopt. Ordinarily we use 10. But in the scale of 4, $2 + 2$ would $= 10$, which would also be the sum of $7 + 5$, in the scale of 12. Moreover, each of these results is as true and necessary in its context as that $7 + 5 = 12$ in decimal notation.

Of course translating $2 + 2 = 4$ into another base notation no more alters its truth than translating "two plus two equals four" into French.

35

Eureka!

How do creative geniuses produce great works of art or invent great scientific theories? Most philosophers answer: We don't know. The creative act is a mystery, a leap across a chasm not bridgeable by reason.

David N. Perkins, a Harvard psychologist, thinks otherwise. Like his mentor, Herbert Simon, one of the pioneers in the field of artificial intelligence, he believes that the creative act does not differ essentially from ordinary problem solving, and that the "heuristics" involved in creativity are slowly being understood. When the process is finally comprehended, it should be possible (though Mr. Perkins does not go into this aspect of Mr. Simon's views) to program computers to invent scientific theories, perhaps even to create great works of art. The purpose of *The Mind's Best Work* (Harvard University Press, 1981) is to demystify both kinds of creativity.

It is a delightful book, easy to read, amusing and jammed with intriguing "personal experiments," puzzles for the reader that offer insights into creative thinking. It is a valuable book because it summarizes well the results of recent investigations and effectively debunks a variety of cherished myths.

The most widespread myth is that creativity is spontaneous and nonrational. Archimedes broods over a problem, something in his unconscious flashes up, and he leaps from the bathtub to shout "Eureka!" Such flashes of insight do occur, but they are rare and easily exaggerated. Poincaré solves a difficult problem at the instant of stepping on a bus. Darwin and Wallace each suddenly think of natural selection while reading Malthus. The lines of "Kubla Khan" come to Coleridge in an opium dream. But can we trust the memories of these men? Mr. Perkins argues that we can't. More often the "Aha!" is only a burst of satisfaction felt when a solution is obtained

This review originally appeared in the *New York Times Book Review,* January 3, 1982. © 1982 by The New York Times Company. Reprinted by permission.

after a long mental struggle, like the elation of a climber finally reaching a summit. Whenever the thought process is reviewed immediately after reaching a solution, Mr. Perkins writes, "I have never heard of a completely out-of-the-blue insight."

Mr. Perkins sees a great creative act as the outcome of a tedious process of searching through possibilities that involve both reasoning and emotion. In the case of the arts, there is a trade-off between "premature closure" (psychologese for giving up too soon) and continuing a search so long that it wastes time. Great artists know that they never reach perfection. Instead of "maximizing," they do what Mr. Simon calls "satisficing." They stop when a work of art is reasonably good. Only lesser artists, studies have shown, deem a work to be unique in its perfection. Greater artists readily admit that their products (poem, novel, painting, symphony, . . .) can be altered without damage. And Mr. Perkins is particularly effective in downgrading much of the current nonsense about the merits of brainstorming and the alleged influences of left and right sides of the brain on creativity.

Then, halfway through his book, something strange happens, though Mr. Perkins seems not to notice it. The creative act starts to grow mysterious again. We are told that creative people are not stupid, but that beyond a certain level of intelligence, higher IQs have no bearing on creativity. We are told that searching for a solution is more than just a routine testing of all combinations of ideas, but precisely how the creative mind narrows the search remains obscure. We are told that programs to teach creativity have been singularly unsuccessful. "I think I have seen people gain . . . from heuristics in my own teaching," Mr. Perkins writes, but he isn't sure. "Heuristics do work, sort of. . . ." Clever tests designed to measure creative skills fail to do so. Attempts to find a common personality profile of creative individuals have done little more than isolate a few traits obviously linked to creativity: independence of opinion, willingness to try unusual approaches and so on. (Cut an apple in half the wrong way—Mr. Perkins closes his book with this metaphor—and you will be surprised to see a five-pointed star.)

In his last chapter, under the heading "The Sum of It All," Mr. Perkins lists fourteen points to express "what creating seems to be all about." They are, alas, obviosities. Point 1: "Creating is the process by which a maker achieves a creative product." Point 4: "It is useful to view creating as a process of selecting from among the many possible outcomes—arrays of words, formulas, pigments on a surface, and so on." Want to write a great poem? Just find the right words. Want to carve a great statue? Just chip away all the excess marble. Want to invent a great scientific theory? Discard the wrong formulas.

Read the book for fun. Read it to find out what psychologists are up to. Don't expect to learn much about how the mind does its best work. My own view is that creativity, like intelligence, is an enormously complex process that operates quite differently in different situations. I think Mr. Perkins's biggest mistake was to try to encompass within one book an investigation of creativity in science and mathematics and creativity in the arts. It's like writing a single monograph on how great chefs cook and how grandmasters play chess.

The final "sum of it all" is this: Psychologists are doing interesting work, but they have miles to go before they understand creativity well enough to be able to teach either a person or a computer how to write a noteworthy melody.

36

The Bible and God's Numerology

Jerry Lucas, a former All-American basketball star of the New York Knicks, used to be seen often during the mid-seventies on television shows. He was then teamed up with magician Harry Lorayne to promote Lorayne's books and instruction courses on how to improve your memory. Lucas and Lorayne coauthored *The Memory Book* before they had a falling out and went their separate ways.

One day, at the urging of his wife, Lucas began to read the Bible. He was "born again" and soon was conducting "Memory Ministries," where he taught Christians how to remember Scripture. At one of these, he met a young Protestant fundamentalist, Del Washburn, who had made a truly astounding discovery about the Bible.

This discovery is revealed in the opening sentence of the book, *Theomatics: God's Best Kept Secret Revealed* (Stein and Day, 1977), which he "coauthored" with Lucas: "Guess what the Lord has done? God has written His entire word mathematically!" The book's dust jacket is even more dramatic: "God's best kept secret revealed . . . scientifically proves that a Mind— far beyond human capabilities and understanding—planned, constructed, and formed every word in the Bible."

One opens the volume with shaking hands, only to discover that God's "best kept secret" is nothing more than "gematria," the ancient system of assigning numbers to each letter of the Hebrew alphabet, then adding up biblical words and phrases to obtain curious mathematical correlations. Medieval Christians took over the technique by numbering the Greek letters

---

This review originally appeared in *The Vector*, April 1982, and is reprinted with permission.

of the New Testament. If Washburn and Lucas are aware of this old tradition, it is their own "best kept secret." Maybe they had memory lapses and forgot to mention it.

Washburn tells us that he spent eight months going carefully through the Bible, using the best Hebrew and Greek texts he could find, to determine the sum of every word. He calls these sums "theomatic" values. The next step was to decide on key numbers for basic biblical names and concepts. For example, "Jesus" has a theomatic value of 888. This is 8 times 111, so Washburn picked 111 as the key number for "Jesus." The third step: search the Bible diligently for phrases and passages that relate to a basic word such as "Jesus," and which have a theomatic sum that is a multiple of the key number. The finding of such passages is the art of "theomatics."

Consider, for instance, the passage "it came and stood over where the child lay." This refers to the star of Bethlehem, which in turn relates to "Jesus." Lo and behold, the passage has a theomatic sum of 28 times 111.

The key number for "Satan" is 276. Here is a typical "Satanic" passage: "For it has been appointed unto man once to die and then the judgment." The passage sums to 17 times 276. And so on.

In looking over the hundreds of theomatic passages that Lucas and Washburn have found in the Bible, one is overwhelmed by the arbitrariness of their great art. Many of the passages are only remotely connected with the key concept assigned to them, and the authors do not hesitate in deciding where a passage is to begin and end. Moreover, they have a marvelous gimmick that gives them even greater leeway with Greek texts. They feel free to include or exclude *the* wherever they like on the grounds that *the*'s are not essential to a passage's meaning. Nevertheless, with the aid of some statistician friends, they snow the reader with "demonstrations" that the probabilities against their correlations arising from chance, or from selective choices, are astronomical.

The book also has chapters on such famous biblical numbers as 666 (the number of the Beast), 153 (the number of fishes caught in Peter's net), and 144,000 (the number of the redeemed in the Apocalypse). The authors explore all three numbers, again with no references to the vast literature already devoted to such nonsense.

Is it possible, they wonder in the book's last chapter, that someday they will be shown to have been sincere but mistaken? "We can assure the reader that that day will never come. God may allow man to condemn, criticize, and even abuse this truth, but He will never allow anyone to duplicate these designs with any random assignment of numbers to the letters of the Greek alphabet other than those that He Himself placed in the papyrus. In fact, no one will even come close."

Why would anyone even try?

Given today's resurgences of fundamentalism, numerology, and pseudoscience, it is perhaps not surprising that two immature born-againers, with no sense of humor or history, would rediscover one of the cherished secrets of the ancient Kabbala. What is truly surprising is that Stein and Day would believe that such a book deserved publication.

To publish *Theomatics* was a great disservice to the authors, who may someday grow up and find themselves deeply ashamed of their sad, simple-minded, outlandish, and (in my opinion) subtly blasphemous book. God may well be a great mathematician—witness the intricate, beautiful mathematics of relativity and quantum mechanics—but gematria lowers the mind of God to a level far below the mind of my crazy numerologist friend Dr. Matrix. At least Dr. Matrix knows something about number theory. The God of *Theomatics* calculates on a level no higher than grade-school arithmetic.

37

Life and Rubik's Cube

One of the big surprises of the creation-science trial in Arkansas in December 1981 was the appearance, as a key witness against Darwinian evolution, of Chandra Wickramasinghe, a distinguished astrophysicist from University College, Cardiff, in Wales. Even more surprising was his revelation that he and his older, more eminent collaborator, the British astronomer Sir Fred Hoyle, both former disbelievers in a life-creating god, are now persuaded that such a god exists. Not only that, but they believe that the existence of a creator can be established by mathematics, with a probability greater than $10^{40,000}$ (1 followed by 40,000 zeros) to 1.

Hoyle and Wickramasinghe have written a colorful book about all this, *Evolution from Space*, (Simon and Schuster, 1982). In a lecture at the Royal Institution in London, Hoyle gave a startling account of their revolutionary new theory.[1] Already it bids fair to arouse more antagonism than Hoyle's now abandoned steady-state cosmology, a model of the universe that he vigorously promoted until the evidence for a Big Bang became overwhelming.

Hoyle and his friend do not deny that most of life on earth, including human beings, evolved from simple forms that first appeared on the planet several billion years ago. What they do claim is that natural laws cannot account for life's origin and that Darwinian natural selection cannot explain its development.

Their argument is a mathematically sophisticated form of the ancient proof of God by design. Put all the parts of a watch in a barrel, goes a familiar version, and you can shake the barrel until doomsday without producing a watch. Hoyle's favorite analogy concerns Rubik's Cube. Give a scrambled cube to a blindfolded person, let him make a random move each second, and it will take a hundred times as long as the age of the earth to solve the

This review is reprinted with permission from *Discover* magazine, March 1982.

358

cube. Life depends on long amino-acid chains, each link selected from twenty possible amino acids. Calculations show, Hoyle reported, that the chances of forming a typical chain by randomly combining amino acids are about the same as the chances of solving Rubik's Cube by haphazard twists.

Conventional evolutionary theory says: Given the size of earth's primeval seas, and millions of years for molecules to swirl around in this "organic soup," amino-acid chains could take shape by blind chance alone. No way, says Hoyle. Even if you assume that all of space is an organic soup, the universe is still too young to make it likely that the necessary amino-acid chains could have resulted from blind shuffling. Moreover, there is no way random mutations can account for the rapidity with which new species arose after life began on earth.

Then how can life be explained? One must assume, Hoyle declared, that an intelligence within the universe is directing the constant creation of microörganisms in interstellar gas. These organisms ride the galaxy on light waves. A few billion years ago some of them were carried to the earth by comets, according to a theory proposed by Hoyle and Wickramasinghe in their earlier book, *Lifecloud,* and more recently, in a somewhat different form, defended by Francis Crick in *Life Itself.*[2]

But that is only half the story. To direct the course of evolution, the intelligence has for billions of years been showering microörganisms (perhaps even insects!) on the earth, where they interact with life forms to promote the large mutations necessary to explain what seem to be sudden jumps in the fossil record. Small DNA copy-error mutations do no more than fine-tune a species. The last big leap, from beast to human, is so enormous that Hoyle cannot conceive of it as being the result of DNA replication errors. He says there is no way a Darwinian struggle for survival can explain "the emergence of a Mozart, a Shakespeare, or a Karl Friedrich Gauss."

Sometimes viruses from outer space cause flu epidemics and other dread diseases, a wild hypothesis advanced by Hoyle and Wickramasinghe in *Space Travelers* and in an earlier book, *Diseases from Space.* Why would a deity allow such suffering? Either God wants us to endure pain and hence is not all good, or God is unable to prevent pain and hence is not all powerful. Hoyle counters this oldest of arguments for atheism with a view that goes back to David Hume. God is indeed good but not omnipotent. "The creator of carbonaceous life," said Hoyle, "was motivated by a harsh necessity out of which the present situation may well be as optimal as could be managed."

But if an intelligence inside our universe directed all this, by what process did this intelligence come into being? Did it arise from the actions of some now extinct intelligence in a cycle of the universe that preceded the Big Bang, or from the action of a higher intelligence outside the universe? Is there an infinite hierarchy of intelligences? Hoyle has no answers to these transcendent questions.

What can a skeptic say about this latest bombshell from the greatest maverick among living astronomers? On the apparent gaps in the fossil record, Stephen Jay Gould and other "punctuationists" (none of whom is mentioned by Sir Fred) are providing plausible hypotheses. As for the old argument that blind chance cannot explain the origin of life, who ever imagined, as Isaac Asimov asked many years ago, that molecules combine by blind chance? Spill a thousand jelly beans on a rug and the probability that they will form beautiful hexagonal patterns is indeed near zero. But myriads of such patterns form when snow is falling.

When agitated by outside energy, said Asimov, organic molecules in earth's primeval soup could form the required building blocks of life by the workings of "unblind chance." It would be chance guided by natural laws — laws about which so little is yet known that no one can even begin to figure the odds. Not even Hoyle.

POSTSCRIPT

My review was of the British edition of *Evolution from Space.* When Simon & Schuster brought out the U.S. edition, they covered the entire back of the dust jacket with excerpts from the review, taken out of context, and conveying the impression that I enthusiastically endorsed the book. I find this practice morally reprehensible.

NOTES

1. This lecture, sponsored by *Omni* magazine and delivered at the Royal Institution, London, on January 12, 1982, is reprinted in *Evolution from Space (The Omni Lecture), and Other Papers on the Origin of Life,* by Fred Hoyle (Enslow, 1982).

2. See also the interview with Crick in *Omni*, March 1982. The person who interviewed him was David Rorvik, author of the book *In His Image: The Cloning of a Man* (Lippincott, 1978) All geneticists immediately recognized this book as a fraud, but it was not until Lippincott was sued by a British biologist, whose name Rorvik had exploited in the book, that Lippincott publicly conceded that the book's account of the cloning of a man was untrue. (For details on the lawsuit and its out-of-court settlement, see *Discover*, June 1982, page 12.) *Omni*, of course, knew all about Rorvik when they assigned the interview to him, but did Crick?

38

Colin Wilson Prowls Again

The seventies' obsession with the occult, not just in the United States but also in most countries around the world, is still producing addlepated books, but none more addlepated than those of England's Colin Wilson. This is something of a tragedy, because Colin is an intelligent, nimble writer who at one time had before him the promise of a brilliant career.

In the mid-fifties, when he was 24, Colin burst on the literary scene with a best-selling book called *The Outsider*. Prominent critics hailed him as a major writer, and Colin himself declared: "I am as conceited and as certain of my future importance as Shaw . . . and may as well be regarded as a young prodigy now as a centurian prodigy in 75 years." His book's theme was as bold as it was simple. An "outsider" is a person of religious insight who refuses to affiliate with an established church, yet is unable to accept the secular humanism of modern science. Alienated from his culture, a social misfit, he searches desperately for a new religious faith. The book was subtitled: *An Inquiry into the Nature and Sickness of Mankind in the Mid-Twentieth Century*.

More than ten years ago, while exploring the steamy jungles of the paranormal, Colin found the faith he was seeking. His 600-page work, *The Occult*, covered every aspect of the topic from ancient times to Wilhelm Reich's orgone energy and the ability of Ted Serios, a Chicago bellhop, to project thought-pictures onto Polaroid film. Colin bought it all. With unparalleled egotism and scientific ignorance he believed almost everything he read about the paranormal, no matter how outrageous. Nothing by believers escaped his notice, nothing by skeptics held his attention. *The Occult,* he once told me, outsold all his many previous books put together. A 1978 se-

This review originally appeared in *Inquiry*, June 1982, and is reprinted with permission.

quel, *Mysteries* (667 pages!), was more of the same. He edited the twenty volumes of a lurid, worthless set called *A New Library of the Supernatural*. His own contribution to this series, *The Geller Phenomenon,* is surely the most gullible book ever written about the Israeli charlatan, now thoroughly discredited in the eyes of almost everybody except Colin's.

Now comes his latest potboiler, *Poltergeist* (Putnam, 1982), in which he discloses once again that colossal narcissism that renders him incapable of learning from others wiser than he, or of doubting his own ability to evaluate paranormal claims. Before the end of page 2 we have been introduced to a young lady who could see through her nose and left ear, another who smelled with her chin, others who heard with their elbows and read books with their stomach. One woman, we are solemnly told, looked into her intestines and counted 33 worms. Later "she excreted precisely this number." Colin wasn't there to count them, but he trusts the person who did. Mediums float about rooms. They levitate massive tables. Geller is back, still bending his spoons. The book's pages swarm with dreary ghosts and demons, all as real to Colin as elephants. Because ghosts usually look like solid people, he informs us, "it is probable that most people have at some time seen a ghost without realizing it."

In a chapter on fairies, Wilson not only thinks they exist but he tells once again, with nary a hint of humor, the story of the two little girls at Cottingley whose photographs of the wee folk persuaded Conan Doyle to write his hilarious monograph about them. I have been chastised by some readers of my recent book *Science: Good, Bad and Bogus* for including a chapter on the Cottingley photographs, on the grounds that everybody now knows they were faked. Not Colin. What about the discovery four years ago that some fairies in the photos had been copied line for line from an illustration in a 1915 book? I read Colin's chapter with mounting suspense, wondering how he would handle this "smoking gun." His technique was masterful. He never mentioned it.

One might have thought that psychic surgery would be too far out even for Colin, but this is to overestimate his acuity. He tells how Edivaldo, a Brazilian psychic surgeon, ripped open a man's stomach, exposing his entrails "sloshing around in blood." A few seconds later, all is "neat and tidy," and the man gets up and goes home. Colin buys this because did not his good friend Guy Playfair, another hack writer on the occult, see it with his own eyes? Naturally Colin made no effort to check with his New Jersey acquaintance, the magician Randi, who could have explained exactly how this dramatic trick is done with the aid of a transparent membrane like Saran wrap; but it's just as well, because Colin never believes anything magicians try to tell him. When Playfair himself was operated on by Edivaldo, he told Colin he could feel the "surgeon's" hands descend into his belly "with a distinct plop," but no pain. This failed to cure Playfair's stomach complaint, though it was "considerably eased."

Although Colin rambles all over the psychic landscape, most of his book focuses on dwellings haunted by destructive poltergeists. After combing the literature on such phenomena, finding thousands of "authenticated" cases, he retells some of the classic horror tales as if he were describing events that no one but an ignoramus could dispute. There is almost always a neurotic teen-ager, usually a girl, living in the haunted house; but the theory that she could be producing the manifestations by clever tricks is beneath Colin's contempt. Yes, the girl may at times throw things, but that is because the poltergeist is compelling her to.

Colin freely admits that tables and chairs cannot fly across a room unless propelled by far stronger forces than those conjured up by psychics who bend cutlery and slide little plastic pill bottles. From where do poltergeists get this awesome energy? Not until page 170 is the dark secret revealed. It comes from the ground. Colin modestly allows that he doesn't know exactly what this "peculiar force" is; but he suspects it is electrical, because dowsers often experience a tingling in their hands. Both Colin and his wife have become excellent dowsers, and they themselves have felt the mysterious force tug on their dowsing rods. The force obviously is *very* peculiar, because it can make bottles alter their course in midair and even go through solid walls.

What about the popular conjecture by parapsychologists that poltergeist phenomena are the result of RSPK (recurrent spontaneous psychokinesis) generated by the omnipresent teen-ager? Colin reluctantly rejects this theory. The evidence that an actual "earth-bound spirit" is present in the house is just too overwhelming. In fact, Colin says, it is as "positively established" as the existence of the duck-billed platypus. You'd never guess what bothers him most. Why is it that these low-order spirits never kill anyone? They can hurl heavy wardrobes that miss people by a fraction of an inch, and they can start fires, but for some strange reason nobody is ever seriously injured. "Is there some sort of psychic law that prevents poltergeists from being more destructive?"

Colin's answer, in his final chapter, is that the poltergeist has "only the most rudimentary powers of reason. It may be mischievous, but it is not evil. . . . Where evil is concerned, human beings have a monopoly." On this profound philosophical note the crazy book ends.

I have throughout referred to Wilson by his first name because we are supposed to be friends. Colin had been much taken by my 1952 book on pseudoscience, *Fads and Fallacies*. I naively supposed then that this was because he agreed with my attitude toward cranks, but it soon became clear that he liked the book for another reason. It introduced him to dozens of cranks he had not known about before. Many of them are mentioned in his early novel, *The World of Violence*.

In 1966, when my wife and I lived in a Manhattan suburb, Colin came to visit us. During his stay of several days he talked nonstop, often pacing the floor while great thoughts agitated his brain. Nothing I had to say about anything was of the slightest interest to him. I recall interrupting his monologues only once. "Colin," I said, "it seems to me that what is bugging you the most is that you are not God." To my amazement, he found this perceptive. Shortly after he left we received a courteous thank-you note in which he said that his visit had provided the most stimulating exchange of ideas he had had in America.

Colin is still talking to himself, and hawking his wild soliloquys to all scientific illiterates who care to read them. For years the central notion behind his "phenomenological existentialism," as he pompously calls it, is that each of us has multiple personalities. Our lowest self is the unconscious mind. Above the conscious self rises a "ladder" of superconscious selves, a concept Colin discusses at length in *Mysteries*. It is on these higher rungs that we are capable of such paranormal powers as telepathy, clairvoyance, psychokinesis, precognition, out-of-body travel, and so on. History is the slow perfection of these talents as we evolve through successive reincarnations into gods.

Now in his fifties, Colin hasn't yet made much progress toward godhood, but he *has* learned how to dowse—and there are all those future lives to look forward to. Is there any likelihood that before he shuffles off his present body he will fulfill his youthful dream of being respected, like George Bernard Shaw, as a prodigy of old age? This was a bright prospect until Colin blew it. The former boy wonder, tall and handsome in his turtleneck sweater, has now decayed into one of those amiable occult eccentrics for which the land of Conan Doyle is noted. They prowl comically about the lunatic fringes of science, looking for ever more sensational wonders and scribbling ever more boring books about them for shameless publishers to feed to hungry readers as long as the boom in occultism lasts.

39

The Gribbin Effect

The Jupiter Effect Reconsidered (Vintage Books, 1982) is the latest manifestation of a strange phenomenon known as the Gribbin effect. This is the process by which irresponsible science writers, flourishing Ph.D. diplomas, are able to persuade naïve editors that they have something valuable to say.

Remember the great flap in March 1982 about a rare "alignment" of planets that would set off terrible earthquakes? The cause of this false alarm was a 1974 book, *The Jupiter Effect,* published by Walker, of which the new paperback is a revision. Its two authors, British astrophysicist John Gribbin and American astronomer Stephen Plagemann, bear impressive credentials—each earned a doctorate at Cambridge University.

Here is the way they ended their original book: "In 1982 'When the Moon is in the Seventh House, and Jupiter aligns with Mars' and with the other seven planets of the Solar System, Los Angeles will be destroyed. The astrological link with the dawning of the age of Aquarius may or may not be coincidence; that is outside the scope of this book, which contains only solid scientific evidence and reasoning."

The book's "reasoning" was as follows. In 1982 all nine planets would huddle together on the same side of the sun. Because Jupiter's pull on the sun would be augmented by the other planets, higher solar tides would result. These tides would increase the number of sunspots. Flares associated with the spots would intensify solar winds. The solar winds would stir up storms on earth. This movement of large air masses would cause slight alterations of the earth's spin, triggering the release of stresses in the earth's crust, especially along California's San Andreas fault. The conclusion: in 1982 Los

This review originally appeared in *Discover* magazine, July 1982, and is reprinted with permission.

Angeles would experience "the most massive earthquake known in the populated regions of the earth in this century."

This shaky chain of arguments and the book's "solid evidence" were blasted by scientists, who called attention to a startling omission. The book contained no pictures to show how the planets would cluster. Unsophisticated readers naturally assumed that alignment meant more or less in a straight line. Actually, in 1982 the nine planets spread over a sector never smaller than 95 degrees.

Gribbin and Plagemann also failed to disclose that Jupiter is so small relative to the sun, and so far away, that its gravity raises the sun's surface only about one millimeter. If all the planets were in a straight line (which they never are) their combined pull would cause a solar tide of less than a tenth of an inch. Because the sun's diameter is about 865,000 miles, and its surface is constantly fluctuating up and down by five or six miles, it is hard to see how a tide of one-tenth of an inch could have much effect on its turbulence. (In their afterword, Gribbin and Plagemann give the combined tidal effect of all nine planets as 20 meters, but how they arrived at this preposterous figure is known only to them and Jupiter.)

There was an even stranger lacuna in the first book. The authors reported no checks on previous planetary clusterings to see whether they correlated with earthquakes—the obvious way to test their screwball theory. Jean Meeus, a noted Belgian astronomer, took the trouble to check. He found no past correlations between bunching and quakes, none between bunchings and sunspots, and none between sunspots and quakes.[1] No one denies that solar activity affects the ionosphere, or that big storms have a minuscule effect on the earth's rotation, but the kinds of correlations needed to establish the Jupiter effect are as missing as those needed to support crank theories that relate sunspots to economic booms and busts.

When it became apparent that the sun's activity was peaking in 1980, instead of 1982 as *The Jupiter Effect* predicted, Gribbin wrote an article on "Jupiter's Noneffect."[2] Said he, flatly, "The book has been proved wrong." But when he and his friend began work on their paperback revision, they found their prophecy to be "not so bad, after all." They had made, they said, only one tiny error. The period of maximum sunspots arrived two years before they had expected. This, they confess, throws doubt on the relation of planetary patterns to sunspots, but they still refuse to rule out the effect. Did not 1980 see a "ripple of seismic activity around the world, including the eruptions of Mount St. Helens in a region of the globe related, in geological terms, to the San Andreas fault"? An exploding Mount St. Helens is on the cover of their new book. "The Jupiter effect did happen," they write, "almost as forecast—but it came two years early." Unfortunately, evidence that sunspots correlate with volcanic activity is as nonexistent as evidence of correlation with earthquakes.

One of the most glaring blunders by Gribbin and Plagemann was their neglect of the fact that solar tides appear simultaneously on opposite sides of the sun, just as the moon raises tides on opposite sides of the earth. Any planetary influence on solar activity would therefore be just as great when the planets bunched on opposite sides of the sun. As Meeus points out, on January 16, 1901, the four giant planets (Saturn, Jupiter, Uranus, and Neptune) were on opposite sides of the sun within a combined arc width of only 25 degrees, as compared to their 60-degree spread this year. And 1901 was a year of minimum sunspots.

But wait! In their new afterword Gribbin and Plagemann report another great discovery. Periods of *minimum* solar activity also trigger earthquakes! Did not the last big Chinese quake take place in 1976? In juggling their statistics, the authors consider quakes within two years of a maximum. Add two years on either side of a minimum and you cover eight of the eleven years of the average sunspot cycle. How can you lose? Periods of maximum quakes, maximum volcanic activity, and maximum and minimum sunspots are like economic depressions. The boundaries are so fuzzy that with hindsight a clever researcher can fudge almost anything.

As former prophets of doom, the authors have now acquired commendable modesty. Can we expect seismic quiet from now until the next sunspot minimum in the mid-eighties? "The answer is not entirely clear-cut. But a look at past history, and a nagging suspicion that the coming unusual sequence of planetary alignments must have some effect on the changing sun, suggests that the best answer is 'probably not.' The *worst* may be over; but peace and quiet may not yet be on the agenda."

In view of such vagueness, why do the authors let stand in their new edition the statement that Los Angeles will be destroyed this year? Can it be that, if by sheer coincidence a major quake hits the city in 1982, they know that no one will care about their retractions and that they will become world famous?

Meanwhile, Gribbin keeps churning out potboilers. His worst book since *The Jupiter Effect* is *Timewarps* (1979). In this he explains how we may someday travel to parallel universes by popping in and out of black holes, defends reincarnation, regards ESP and precognition as "proven," and declares that tachyons (conjectured particles that go faster than light) now have the "balance of evidence" supporting their reality. Who knows what strange theory Gribbin will take up next? Whatever it is, you can be sure that if he writes a book about it, the Gribbin effect will take over and the book will find a ready publisher.[3]

NOTES

1. See Meeus, "Comments on *The Jupiter Effect*," in *Icarus*, vol. 26, 1975, pp. 257-68, and "Planets, Sunspots and Earthquakes," in *Mercury*, July-August 1979, pp. 72-74. Neither paper is listed by Gribbin and Plagemann in their bibliography of

33 "key publications" since the first edition of their book. Indeed, they list not a single paper critical of their theory.

2. Gribbin's temporary retraction appeared in *Omni,* June 1980.

3. This prophecy was fulfilled late in 1982 by Pantheon's publication of *The Monkey Puzzle,* written by Gribbin and British science writer Jeremy Cherfas. Most experts on evolution believe that human beings and apes diverged from a common ancestor about 15 to 20 million years ago. Arguing from genetic evidence, Gribbin and Cherfas maintain that the common ancester flourished about 4.5 million years ago.

The Jupiter Effect Reconsidered has a publisher's note in back saying that Gribbin is an editor of *Nature,* but he has not been with *Nature* since 1975. He and Cherfas are consultants for England's *New Scientist* magazine.

40

The Power and the Gory

Steven Spielberg, still enjoying the reputation of a Peter Pan who never grows up, has done it again. He has hired excellent actors and cameramen, a talented director, superlative special-effects experts, and put them to work on another blockbuster with an imbecilic plot. I refer not to *E.T.,*[1] a heart-warming fantasy for young and old, but to his simultaneously released *Poltergeist.* Like *The Exorcist* and its counterparts, it is craftily designed to rake in millions by pandering to our country's continuing obsessions with demonology and the paranormal.

For *Close Encounters of the Third Kind,* Spielberg courted scientific respectability by hiring the astronomer J. Allen Hynek as a consultant and even putting him in the movie. To give similar authenticity to *Poltergeist,* Spielberg has the film's haunted suburban home investigated by Martha Lesh, a University of California scientist played by Beatrice Straight and apparently modeled on Thelma Moss, a UCLA parapsychologist.

Lesh conducts her research with the help of two male assistants and a truckload of electronic equipment. Later she brings to the house, to exorcise its malevolent spirits, a medium who is called a dwarf in the novel (a tie-in paperback by James Kahn), but who on the screen turns out to be a large midget with a funny voice. After lots of mumbo jumbo and garbled commands about moving to or from "the light," she finally rescues Carol Anne, the lovable five-year-old daughter of crack real-estate salesman Steve Freeling. The spooks had kidnapped the girl by teleporting her through her bedroom closet to another astral plane.

"This house is clean," declares the small medium, and you think, thank goodness, the picture is over. Then suddenly all the rotting corpses buried

This review originally appeared in *Discover,* August 1982, and is reprinted with permission in a graveyard under the housing tract push up through the ground in a Grand Guignol climax that has the audience screaming. What the troubled dead expect to gain by this ploy, which ends by sucking the entire Freeling house into the closet's vortex, remains as unintelligible as why, when the ghosts first entered the house, they had to come through a television screen.

Young children in the theater of course never stop giggling and screeching, especially when a steak comes alive and bubbles into a mass of maggots, or while a parapsychologist claws his decaying face into a bloody, putrefying mess. When events like this occur, events that would render anyone insane for months, characters in the story uncork such vapid remarks as "This is for real," "This is awesome," and "I think we need a Jungian analyst to interpret the meaning of these visions." After one mind-boggling incident on the screen, the best a parapsychologist can muster is "Fantastic!"

Is not all this delightful, unwholesome nonsense for the kiddies, even if it gives them nightmares? Why take such a crazy picture seriously as propaganda for the occult? One reason is that Spielberg himself so takes it. The film's previews feature noted parapsychologists William Roll and Charles Tart and the occult journalist D. Scott Rogo solemnly pontificating about poltergeists. A press kit supplied by MGM contains an eleven-page document with quotations from leading parapsychologists on the reality of poltergeists, and a listing of notable poltergeist hauntings from A.D. 30 to 1968. In it, Thelma Moss takes pains to clear up some misconceptions about such hauntings: "In contrast to popular superstition, most Los Angeles haunted houses are not old, abandoned mansions. They are typically middle-class, recently built, comfortable homes which are lived in by several members of a family, most of whom have had some experience with the apparitions."

Another MGM press release describes the firsthand experiences with poltergeists of Tobe Hooper (the film's director), Beatrice Straight, Jobeth Williams (Mrs. Freeling), and Dominique Dunne (the older Freeling daughter). Says Spielberg, "It is a very personal thing, which I won't discuss. I've come much closer to a poltergeist than I have to a UFO. I've always wanted to see a UFO but never have. Ghosts? That's another story."

Most parapsychologists have no doubts about the reality of poltergeist manifestations. They disagree only on the cause. Do poltergeists spring from the psychokinetic powers of the disturbed adolescent who invariably occupies the haunted house, or from prank-playing spirits who are either demons from hell or souls of the dead, or (as in Spielberg's film) both? (Ordinary psychologists believe that the adolescent deliberately fakes all the phenomena, but parapsychologists treat this theory with contempt.) In his 1979 Penguin paperback, *The Poltergeist Experience,* Rogo is sure that discarnates are involved. As for coming through television screens, why not? In the Prentice-Hall book *Phone Calls from the Dead,* which Rogo coauthored, he tells how spirits talk to us through telephones.

Spielberg's unholy ghosts are aided by devils, including perhaps the Antichrist himself, who howls through the book and movie as "the Beast." One of the film's curious visual effects gives the audience the sensation of looking down through a glowing tube that leads from the bewitched bedroom closet, now the Beast's mouth, straight into the crimson maw of hell.

Here is how Kahn's book describes it: ". . . a giant mouth, all gums and lips and blinding light transilluminating the pink-yellow tissues, all the way back to the bottom of the mucoid pit, where a pale, oily esophagus could be seen generating its peristaltic spasms down to the abysmal depths."

Last June, Spielberg paid $60,500 for the balsa wood sled with "Rosebud" painted on it, featured in the poignant last scene of *Citizen Kane*. He said he wants to hang it over his desk to remind him of how important quality is in films. Maybe some day Rosebud will remind him that bigger, louder, schlockier gimmicks, mixed with blood, violence, and ersatz science, are not enough to make a motion picture memorable.

NOTE

1. I enjoyed *E.T.*, although I thought George Will scored some good points against it in his *Newsweek* column (July 19, 1982) "Well, *I* Don't Love You, E.T."

41

The Case Against Creationism

After Clarence Darrow made a monkey out of William Jennings Bryan at the Scopes trial in Tennessee, most scientists thought the battle for evolution had been won. Today, as a spin-off from the resurgence of fundamentalism, the dreary battle is being waged all over again,[1] but with one startling difference. Fundamentalists no longer argue that creationism should be taught in the public schools solely because the Bible supports it. They now want it taught because, they maintain, it is scientifically superior to evolution.

This is nonsense, of course. Creationist arguments are so moth-eaten that scientists are inclined to ignore the new attacks on evolution as the work of cranks. Philip Stuart Kitcher, a London-born philosopher of science at the University of Vermont, has written a book (*Abusing Science: The Case Against Creationism,* MIT Press, 1982) that not only tells the sad story but also provides a marvelously lucid summary of the evidence for evolution and the overwhelming case against its enemies.

Although fundamentalist orators are increasingly strident in branding evolution theory the work of Satan, the intellectual leaders of the onslaught are a small group of men whose ignorance of modern science is almost as great as that of the electronic preachers. Some actually have doctorates, though mainly in fields other than biology or geology. Dr. Henry M. Morris, who heads the Institute for Creation Research, in San Diego, is a hydraulics engineer. His 1974 book, *Scientific Creationism,* has been enormously influential. Dr. Duane Gish is a biochemist whose 1979 book, *Evolution? The Fossils Say No!,* punches even harder at the scientific establishment.

Morris and Gish are not even willing to take the days of Genesis symbolically and allow God billions of years to structure the cosmos. The entire universe, it is argued, is probably only thousands of years old, not millions.

This review originally appeared in *Discover,* September 1982, and is reprinted with permission

372

much less billions; God created it all in six ordinary solar days. Methods of dating rocks by radioactivity and other techniques are tossed aside as worthless. What about galaxies so distant that it took light millions of years to reach the earth? No problem. God created the universe with this light already on its way!

Moreover, say the creationists, fossils are the records of plants and animals destroyed by Noah's great flood. Why do those records seem ordered in time from simple to more complex? Because, according to creationists, the ordering is a swindle. Paleontologists reason in a vicious circle. Assuming evolution, they date strata by their fossils. Then they point to the time ordering of fossils as proof of evolution. They are fond of citing outcrops where fossils are in reverse order, and suggesting that these anomalies are embarrassments to paleontologists. On the contrary. As Kitcher makes clear, geologists find in such regions conclusive evidence of massive thrust faults or folds that shuffle the strata, sometimes literally turning fossils upside down.

Abusing Science does more than just explode moldy arguments. As a philosopher concerned with the way science operates, Kitcher is good at showing how creationists distort Karl Popper's views on scientific method, and how they misuse such books as Thomas Kuhn's *Structure of Scientific Revolutions*. He is equally skillful at showing how creationists persist in quoting out of context Stephen Jay Gould and other "punctuationists" (who believe evolution is not as gradual as Darwin thought) to give the false impression that even the experts now doubt the fact of evolution.

Every devotee of a fringe science should read Kitcher's pages on Alfred Wegener, whose theory of continental drift was long rejected by geologists. Cranks are forever citing this as proof that orthodox scientists oppose novel theories for irrational reasons. The truth is that the establishment had excellent reasons for not embracing Wegener's theory until the discovery of plate tectonics provided a mechanism for it. "An ideally rational and open-minded scientific community," writes Kitcher, "faced with Wegener's theory and Wegener's evidence, would have done what the actual scientific community actually did."

Must believers in evolution abandon faith in a Creator? Kitcher takes great pains to rebut the Moral Majority's foolish charge that evolution leads straight to atheism. For a theist, evolution is God's way of creating. It conflicts with no religion, only with a primitive Christianity that takes every sentence of Genesis as literally true.

I have one small criticism. Kitcher does not cover the monumental contributions to modern creationism by George McCready Price. Ninety percent of the arguments in books by Morris and Gish are lifted from Price's 1923 textbook, *The New Geology*. Even Velikovsky relies on Price to support some of his eccentric geological opinions. But Price was a Seventh Day Adventist with no academic credentials, which probably explains why creationists of other fundamentalist denominations are reluctant to acknowledge their massive debt to him.

NOTE

1. A Gallup Poll, reported in newspapers of August 29, 1982, found that 44 percent of the American public, about a quarter of whom are college graduates, believe that God created man by fiat within the last ten thousand years. Thirty-eight percent accept evolution, including the evolution of man, but think God guided the process. Nine percent are evolutionists who believe God had no part in the process, and 9 percent have no opinion. Protestants are more likely to take Genesis literally (creation in six solar days) than Catholics, and this fundamentalist view is only slightly more prevalent in the north and middle west than elsewhere.

42

Eysenck's Folly

Imagine that you are reading a book, by an eminent British astronomer, called *Flat Earth: Science or Superstition?* You find that the first three-fourths of the volume marshals impressive evidence against flatness, then the rest of the book proves that the earth is shaped like the Great Pyramid. Would you not be incredulous?

That was precisely how I felt when I finished Hans Eysenck's latest and most controversial book, *Astrology: Science or Superstition* (St. Martin's, 1982), written with D. K. B. Nias, an associate at the London University Institute of Psychiatry, where Eysenck is a professor. The first nine chapters give all the reasons why traditional astrology is humbug. The remaining two chapters vigorously champion a strange new astrology concocted about thirty years ago by a French psychologist, Michel Gauquelin.

The chapters attacking astrology are admirable. There are crisp accounts of flawed efforts by believers to confirm astrology, reports of carefully controlled tests by skeptics that failed to support it, and strong general reasons for disbelief. For example, China and India have ancient astrological traditions just as impressive as the West's, yet based on entirely different star patterns. If one tradition is right, the other two are wrong. If birth charts can give subtle insights into personality and destiny, why are they unable to tell a person's sex, intelligence, or race, or recognize the criminally insane? Why is there no clustering of birth dates of thousands who are killed in a single earthquake?

What about people born in northern countries where some astrological signs never rise? Why do astrologers not adjust for changes in the zodiac caused by the precession of the earth's axis? As Eysenck and Nias write, "In

This review originally appeared in *Discover,* October 1982, and is reprinted with permission.

the time of Ptolemy, the sun was in constellation Aries on the day of the spring equinox . . . today it is in Pisces."

After demolishing traditional astrology, the authors turn to the work of Gauquelin, done in conjunction with his wife, Françoise. As a young man, Gauquelin was a passionate believer in astrology. His faith wavered when he tried to prove its worth. In the course of his efforts, which convinced him that astrology had no merit, he uncovered what he became convinced were mysterious correlations between personality traits and the positions of certain planets at the moment of birth.

Among his findings: Famous doctors are more likely to be born when Mars or Saturn is in one of two "critical zones"—having just risen or having just passed its highest point. Military leaders tend to be born with Mars or Jupiter in a critical zone. Top athletes with "iron wills" correlate with Mars, those with "weak wills" correlate negatively. Extroverts incline to births "under" Mars or Jupiter, introverts under Saturn. Soldiers and musicians have different planetary patterns, but musicians specializing in military music fall midway between the two groups!

The authors reproduce Gauquelin's table of eighty personality traits that are linked to Mars, Jupiter, Saturn, or the moon. Recent research, they solemnly tell us, has found traits associated with Venus, but none that relate to the sun, Mercury, or the distant planets. Correlations are hereditary. Children tend to be born under the same planets as one parent. If both parents were born under the same sign, the effect on a child doubles in intensity.

Gauquelinology has other bizarre aspects. Correlations with planets do not hold for ordinary professionals, only for the most eminent. They fail completely for drug-induced births. This suggests to Eysenck and Nias that the planets "are somehow acting as celestial midwives. Some kind of signal emanating from the planets may somehow interact with the fetus in the womb, stimulating it to struggle into birth at a certain time."

The authors answer many objections, but ignore the most crucial. How trustworthy are Gauquelin's raw data? To determine their accuracy, a skeptical statistician would have to check the tens of thousands of birth records, from all over Europe, that Gauquelin used in his numerous studies. Such records, especially old ones, are often vague. Only a slight amount of selectivity, an unconscious "experimenter effect" in deciding what records to use and what to discard as unreliable, can produce a strong overall bias.

Most scientists think Gauquelin's challenge is too crazy and flimsy to justify the time, cost, and labor of having a skeptical outsider verify his data or attempt a major replication. More likely, there will continue to be minor efforts to repeat his tests, with believers getting positive results, doubters negative results, and each side accusing the other of sloppy controls. Meanwhile, astrology buffs will loudly proclaim that Gauquelin's popular books somehow support astrology, when actually all they support is Gauquelinology.

As for Eysenck's own competence as a statistician, it is worth-while to recall his maverick record. For instance, he has long infuriated colleagues by insisting there is no good evidence that I.Q. differences between races are not genetic. In another field of inquiry, Eysenck snagged a quarter of a million dollars in research grants from the tobacco industry (see *Discover,* March 1981) and later published his findings: no good evidence of any causal link between lung cancer and smoking.

For these and many other reasons, you don't have to believe Eysenck when he claims that Gauquelin's work "compares favorably with the best that has been done in psychology, psychiatry, sociology, or any of the social sciences," much less when he asserts that "the time has come to state quite unequivocally that a new science is in the process of being born."

POSTSCRIPT

A portion of a letter from Gauquelin was published in *Discover* (January 1983):

> In his article "Eysenck's Folly," Martin Gardner asks, "How trustworthy are Gauquelin's raw data?" It is very easy to check the accuracy of my data for everyone who really wants to do so. Actually, *all* my birth data were published in eighteen volumes by my Laboratoire d'Étude des Relations entre Rythmes Cosmiques et Psychophysiologiques. Every volume provides complete information explaining how my samples were drawn. I never discarded any birth record, and I am keeping all of them in the files of my laboratory. Several people have inspected them. Nobody found them faulty.

To which I replied:

> Few doubt that Gauquelin's documents support his data. But did unconscious selection bias the gathering and preservation of that data? Only a costly investigation by a top statistician could answer this question.

43

The Sting

When people are told by reputable doctors that they have an incurable disease, the impulse to seek help from a quack can be overwhelming. I know of no sadder or funnier account of a victim trapped in this terrible dilemma than Andrew Potok's *Ordinary Daylight* (Holt, Rinehart and Winston, 1981), a book now available in a Bantam reprint edition.

Potok is a former painter who lives in Vermont, intelligent, handsome, and slowly going blind with a degenerative disease of the retina called retinitis pigmentosa. A few years ago when he was forty, Potok read in the *London Observer* about a cure for his disease, unorthodox but so marvelous that improvement is sometimes noticeable in two or three days.

Who discovered this miracle therapy? A former mid-European named Helga Barnes (a pseudonym, used by Potok's publisher for legal reasons; her real name is Julia Owen), now seventy and twice widowed. For fifty years Helga has been treating the near-blind by stinging the back of their necks with bees. Not just ordinary bees, you understand. They are bees fed with a secret formula that she refuses to divulge to all those "filthy parasite doctors," as she calls them, who consider her therapy worthless.

"I had come to that point in my life," Potok begins his remarkable narrative, "when I felt that no matter what I did I had nothing to lose." Off he goes to London, with his compliant but skeptical wife, Charlotte. Soon he is allowing his neck to be stung by Helga's "angel bees," while Helga chatters like a madwoman about how her treatment never fails, and how she will "wipe the floor" with all those "money-grubbing" ophthalmologists who are trying to steal her precious secrets.

Signs of quackery are everywhere, but Potok is too desperate to face up

This review originally appeared in the *Skeptical Inquirer,* Fall 1982, and is reprinted with permission.

to them. When he asks Helga about his incipient cataracts, a familiar compli-
cation of his disease, she tells him flatly that he has none. On a later occasion,
while Helga looks into his eyes and shouts, "The pigment is dehydrating faster
than I expected!" Potok notices that she has forgotten to turn on her ophthal-
moscope. One of the stirring testimonials in Helga's literature turns out to have
been written by her chauffeur. (License plates on her car read BEE 008.)

The daily beestings, five or more at a time, are making Potok violently
ill, but Helga is ecstatic. The venom, she assures him on the phone just before
he passes out, are "pushing out all the filth," dissolving the "terrible fungus."
When he tells her his sight is not improving, she is furious and accuses him
of lying.

Charlotte, who from the beginning has seen clearly through the scam,
tries to read Helga's two medically illiterate books, both published by the
Helga Barnes Press. She finds them "horrible and disgusting." Convinced
that her husband is crazy for staying, she packs up and leaves.

Potok not only stays; he brings his young daughter, Sarah, who has inherited his disease, to London for the bee therapy. Fearful that Helga will
drop them as patients, Potok lies to her about his progress. There are even
times when both he and Sarah imagine with joy that they are seeing better.
At Helga's insistence, each writes a testimonial letter in which details are
fabricated to placate the terrible-tempered Mrs. Barnes.

Newspaper stories had said that Helga never asked for money, but after
several months of free therapy Helga flies into a rage. She calls Potok a scoundrel, a cheater, and a thief. She is washing her hands of him unless he comes
through with a thousand pounds. "No fees, no bees!" she screams. Poor
Potok, still hoping against hope, borrows the money from a friend.

Sarah is pronounced completely cured and sent home. Potok hangs on.
Helga is now mixing new bees with old ones, but doing it gradually "lest we
bust your liver." After six months in England, and many hundreds of
beestings, Potok leaves. Back home his eye doctor finds no change whatever
in his or his daughter's retinas.

Helga, Potok tells us, is still going strong. British newspapers continue
to run glowing accounts of her cures—not just for eye ailments but also for
arthritis, asthma, diabetes—you name it, the angel bees cure it. On a recent
BBC television program she claimed 100 percent successes. Her fees now start
at 3,000 pounds and go up to 12,000.

Potok, reunited with Charlotte, finally accepts his blindness. No longer
able to paint, he turns to writing, and a publisher buys his candid account
of how he has been stung. It is a brave, splendidly written, deeply moving
story about one man's struggle against self-pity and the inexorable vanishing
of ordinary daylight. It is also a sharply etched portrait of a type of personality that haunts the fringes of modern medicine—the ignorant, neurotic,
partly self-deluded charlatan who, aided by the uncaring print and electronic
media, preys on human gullibility and despair.

44

How Well Can
Animals Converse?

Because some animals look and behave in many ways like human beings, there has always been a strong tendency to humanize what goes on inside their little, sometimes not so little, heads. The impulse extends even toward birds. John Locke (1690), in his *Essay Concerning Human Understanding,* writes about a Brazilian parrot that engaged in human conversation. John Audubon often painted his birds with human facial expressions and body poses that made his pictures less accurate but more salable. We all know the almost irresistible impulse to believe that a loved pet understands far more than it does when we talk to it.

Words that symbolize activities of the human mind—thinking, talking, laughing, and so on—are notoriously fuzzy because they mark portions of complex continua. Is an animal aware of its self-identity? A few years ago George Gallup (1977) reported some experiments he thought proved that apes have a self-consciousness not possessed by other animals, not even by monkeys. Gallup put spots of odorless, nonirritating red dye on the heads of anesthetized apes. As soon as the awakened apes saw a red spot in a mirror, they tried to rub it off. Does this prove self-awareness?

The experiment seemed persuasive until Robert Epstein, Robert Lanza, and B. F. Skinner (1981) reported a similar experiment with pigeons. The birds pecked at blue dots on their breasts, concealed by bibs, only when they saw the dots in a mirror. What does this prove? It proves, said Epstein, "that a pigeon can use a mirror to locate an object on its body that it cannot see." The experiment certainly does not prove that chimps have no rudimentary

---

This review originally appeared in *Semiotica,* vol. 38, nos. 3-4, 1982.

self-awareness, but it does cast doubt on the significance of Gallup's test.

A popular stage act of the nineteenth century featured a dog, cat, horse, goat, pig, or bird that appeared capable of doing arithmetic, and answering difficult questions. The animal used body movements for counting, and for indicating yes and no, or it picked out the correct answering sequence of cards that bore numbers, letters, or pictures. Similar acts have appeared recently on television. The secret, now well known, is to train the animal to respond to cues too subtle to be perceived by a human audience. The cues can be almost anything, but because visual cues are easier to detect, the signals are usually auditory—a slight sniff, or the click of fingernails on a hand kept in a pocket or behind the back. The person cuing is seldom on stage, rather someone watching from the wings or sitting in a front row disguised as a spectator.

The most famous of European "thinking" horses was Clever Hans, trained by Wilhelm von Osten, a retired Berlin teacher of mathematics. What made Hans unique was that it had been trained to respond to unconscious visual cues from onlookers. This was firmly established by Oskar Pfungst (1965), a German psychologist, who reported his findings in a classic 1907 German book. Pfungst was careful to absolve von Osten of conscious deception, but this could have been a ploy to avoid libel action or just to be kind. Hans had been conditioned to react to an imperceptible raising of the head of one or more onlookers at just the moment when a sequence of hoof taps had reached the correct number. Von Osten always wore a large-brimmed hat that would, of course, greatly magnify this signal. After Pfungst made everything crystal clear, von Osten angrily refused to allow further testing. Until he died he maintained that Hans was capable of "inner speech" and of doing mathematical calculations.

After von Osten's death, Hans was acquired by Karl Krall, of Elberfeld, who trained several other horses (one of them blind) to perform like Hans. Maurice Maeterlinck (1914) was so impressed that he devoted a chapter of praise to these horses in his book *The Unknown Guest*. Gustav Wolff, a Basel psychiatrist, wrote an entire book (1914) about the horses in which he expressed his belief that the animals could think and talk like humans. The claims in Krall's *Denkende Tiere* (1912) were demolished by Stefan von Máday (1914) in his book, *Gibt es denkende Tiere?*

The "Clever Hans effect"—the responses of an animal to unconsciously given cues—has cast its shadow over the sudden burst in recent years of research on the ability of apes to "talk" by using sign language or by manipulating visual symbols. The trainers of these clever apes contend that their experiments have scrupulously ruled out Hans. Skeptics insist that the effect is harder to eliminate than trainers realize, and that in fact their controls have not been adequate.

The controversy grew in bitterness when Herbert Terrace (1979), a psychologist at Columbia University, published *Nim*. In this book he revealed disenchantment with his own research involving Nim Chimpsky, a baby male chimp named after Noam Chomsky, who has been sharply critical of talking-ape claims. After four years of teaching sign language to Nim, Terrace reluctantly concluded that the chimp was incapable of comprehending the simplest grammar. It had merely learned to respond to signs in ways that differed in no fundamental respect from the way dogs learn to "sing" or turn back-flips on command. The controversy heated up more when Thomas A. Sebeok and Donna Jean Umiker-Sebeok (1980) published their anthology, *Speaking of Apes,* which opens with their strong arguments that the recent work on talking apes is seriously marred by failures to exorcise the ghost of Clever Hans.

It is not hard to understand the acrimony that prevailed in May, 1980, when the New York Academy of Sciences sponsored a two-day conference, organized by Sebeok, on "The Clever Hans Phenomenon: Communication with Horses, Whales, Apes, and People."[1] The book under review, published by the New York Academy of Sciences (1981), bears the same title. Edited by the two chairmen of the conference, Sebeok and Robert Rosenthal, a Harvard psychologist, it contains papers read at this historic meeting.

Part 1, on man-animal communication, begins with a paper by Heini Hediger, a Swiss zoologist, who stresses the acuteness with which animals can observe subtle human expressions. Trained dogs frequently execute an order before it is given, simply by watching the trainer's face. Hediger calls attention to William McDougall's notoriously flawed experiment with rats, designed to prove the inheritance of acquired learning. It is hard to believe now, but McDougall's experimenter always knew what a rat was supposed to do when he put it in water. (The rats had been trained to avoid electric shocks by swimming through a certain channel.) Each generation of rats improved in ability except the last, which was handled by a new assistant after the former assistant died. The possibility of a Clever Hans effect is alone sufficient to render McDougall's results worthless.

Paul Bouissac (I am taking the papers in order) brings out the fact that circus animals never "perform" the way humans do; they merely display carefully conditioned behavior designed to arouse pathetic fallacies in the minds of viewers. Thus a bear in a 1980 Ringling Brothers circus act gives its semi-nude lady trainer a seemingly dangerous "kiss of death," but the audience does not see the tiny piece of carrot in her teeth. Bouissac reminds us of the serious accidents that sometimes occur when a circus beast, supposedly fond of a trainer, misinterprets a careless gesture. There have been several such incidents involving Washoe, the most famous of the talking chimps, but only the latest found its way into print: the time Washoe bit off a middle finger of the eminent psychologist Karl Pribram, as told by Dick Teresi (1981) in *Omni.*

Duane Rumbaugh, who trains apes to speak "Yerkish" (a language using a computer console with keys bearing geometrical symbols for words), and his wife, Sue Savage-Rumbaugh, were the only two ape trainers, aside from Terrace, who spoke at the conference. (Other trainers had been invited, but declined to come.) Duane Rumbaugh vigorously denies that Hans infected his own research. He lashes out at critics for unfamiliarity with the tests they belabor, for closed minds, and for not seeking clarification by letters and phone calls. "Broad, blatant injection of Clever Hans into every study of the ape-language area," he writes, "smacks of a witch hunt. Every scientist, behavioral or otherwise, has heard Clever Hans neighing in the stable. Every scientist of repute will do all that is possible to keep Clever Hans where he belongs—in the stable."

No experiment, Rumbaugh reminds us, can ever be totally controlled. Always there are ways to punch holes in it. He accuses the Sebeoks in particular of misrepresenting his work with the ape Lana, and closes his paper with heavy sarcasm by saying that he made no attempts to control barometric pressure, alternations in the amperage of electrical lines to his laboratory, or people going about their chores in adjacent rooms.

Sue Savage-Rumbaugh does not consider the question of whether apes comprehend syntax. She limits her attention to reasons for believing that apes understand the meanings of Yerkish symbols in a way that goes "far beyond the training context." By this she means that her apes do more than just associate a symbol with an object or an act; they are capable of categorizing symbols in such groups as "food" and "tools." In a revealing passage, which suggests the intense rivalry among ape trainers, she expresses "doubts that other apes [a footnote refers to reports by the Gardners, Fouts, Premack, and Terrace] have achieved the level of symbolic functioning" reached by her two chimps, Sherman and Austin.

Suzanne Chevalier-Skolnikoff, an anthropologist who believes devoutly in the ability of apes to understand the syntax of human language, applies a Piagetian analysis to ape signing. Her instances are taken mainly from the work of her friend, psychologist Francine ("Penny") Patterson, who claims to have found in Koko, a lady gorilla, an intelligence and a grasp of human language that far exceeds that of any other talking ape. Dr. Patterson's latest report on this is *The Education of Koko,* a book by Patterson (1981) as told to Eugene Linden. The book is a tribute to Patterson's good looks (lots of photographs, some in color), but, alas, no tribute to her scientific competence. Patterson's willingness to attribute human thoughts and behavior to Koko, on the basis of shaky anecdotal evidence, seems boundless.

In Patterson's eyes, Koko invents brilliant metaphors (such as "elephant baby" for a Pinocchio doll), tells deliberate lies, draws representational pictures ("her favorite subjects are birds and alligators"), makes up English rhymes, understands Pig Latin, develops "crushes" on men, can give opposites (e.g., asked for the opposite of *first,* she responded with *last*), and delights in playing subtle practical jokes, after which she usually "laughs heartily." Other ape trainers tell me they have never heard a gorilla laugh, but to Penny,

"Koko's laugh is a chuckling sound that is like a suppressed human laugh."
A typical Koko joke: asked to find a "scary picture," Koko picks up a mirror and thrusts it in front of a trainer's face.

Patterson gives many instances of Koko's ability to rhyme. Here is a sample (the *signs* are in italics):

BARBARA: Which animal rhymes with hat?
KOKO: *Cat.*
BARBARA: Which rhymes with big?
KOKO: *Pig there.* (She points to the pig.)
BARBARA: Which rhymes with hair?
KOKO: *That.* (She points to the bear.)
BARBARA: What is that?
KOKO: *Pig cat.*
BARBARA: Oh, come on.
KOKO: *Bear hair.*
BARBARA: Good girl. Which rhymes with goose?
KOKO: *Think that.* (Points to the moose.)

Koko also invents "gestural rhymes." These are gestures in sign language that look similar. For example, Penny asks Koko to make a gestural rhyme. Koko responds with *time* and *bellybutton. Time* is signaled by tapping the wrist with a crooked index finger, *bellybutton* by tapping the navel the same way. Ten minutes later, Penny adds, Koko spontaneously signed *bread red head.*

Koko not only has a good comprehension of time, fully understanding the meaning of *before* and *after,* but she also knows the meaning of *birth* and *death.* Asked where gorilla babies come from, Koko first replied *Koko.* She was then asked where in Koko do babies come from? The gorilla pointed to her abdomen. Did the trainer unconsciously look at her own stomach, as Patterson herself speculates? Or did Koko make a series of random gestures, unremembered by the trainer, before she scratched her belly? Who knows? Later, when Patterson asked the same question, Koko signaled *up* and touched the ceiling. As for death, here is the book's most unbelievable snatch of dialogue:

MAUREEN: *Where* do *gorillas* go *when* they *die?*
KOKO: *Comfortable hole bye.*
MAUREEN: *When* do *gorillas die?*
KOKO: *Trouble old.*

"We do not know," Patterson comments, "where Koko got the idea that the dead go to a hole unless it was from leafing through magazines (she is an avid 'reader' of *National Geographic*)."

Are any of these extraordinary conversations recorded on videotape? If so, it would be possible to determine how much of the dialogue is genuine, and how much of it is something eager trainers read into vague gestures or recall in distorted ways when they later write it down. Patterson never mentions videotapes of these sensational conversations, though it is easy to run a videotape machine continually and later erase whatever is not worth preserving.

In reading Chevalier-Skolnikoff's contribution to the volume under review, I thought I had finally come upon a "joke" episode with Koko that had been preserved on film. Chevalier-Skolnikoff recalls an occasion when Patterson pointed to her eyes, nose, mouth, ear, forehead, and chin. Koko imitated each gesture perfectly while Chevalier-Skolnikoff recorded it on Super 8 film. Two weeks later she returned with a photographer to capture this on 16 mm film. Here is how she tells it:

> Again, Patterson modeled the behaviors. She pointed to her eye and Koko put her face close up to Patterson's, as if trying to examine as well as possible what Patterson was doing, and then she clearly pointed to her ear. Patterson modeled pointing to her nose, and again Koko closely examined the modeled behavior, and then pointed to her chin. Koko continued to point to inappropriate parts of her face for about 5 minutes. Finally Patterson became exasperated and scolded her and signed to her that she was a "bad gorilla" whereupon Koko signed that she was a "funny gorilla," and laughed.

Now this is a much more remarkable tableau than the earlier one in which Koko exhibited only routine imitative behavior. Koko seems to be joking, and even "laughs" at her own pranks. Struck by the fact that there is no specific mention of filming this episode even though a photographer was taken there to film it, and recalling Rumbaugh's advice to skeptics about seeking information before sounding off, I wrote to Chevalier-Skolnikoff to ask if this was indeed photographed. She replied that she had about four minutes of the five-minute sequence on two rolls of 16mm film, but had not yet viewed it in "real time." She kindly offered to have it copied for me if I paid the cost, which she estimated at about $50. I sent $60 to include incidental expenses.

When the film arrived it was accompanied by a letter from Chevalier-Skolnikoff saying she had now viewed the print and found that, unfortunately, the "funny gorilla" remark is not on the filmed portion. Also, the deceptive pointing to wrong parts of the face is missing. Since the aim of the filming session was to record imitation, she explained, deception was the last thing they were concerned with. Evidently the photographer stopped shooting when he saw that Koko was being uncooperative.

The film does show a preceding episode in which Koko is totally uncooperative, moving about and paying no attention to Patterson. And there is another segment, shot just after the joke, in which Koko is cooperative, pointing to the right places and kissing Patterson on corresponding parts of the face.

Thus the joking episode, like so many of the incredible conversations reported by Patterson, remains an unrecorded anecdote. Terrace, who viewed the film for me, reported that Koko is seen doing nothing except occasionally imitating Patterson's gestures in a manner characteristic of signing apes. The gesture for *funny* is brushing the index and middle fingers across the tip of the nose. *Bad* is indicated by touching the mouth with the fingertips, then moving the hand away with the palm outward. *Eat* is made by touching fingertips to mouth. All three signs are similar. *Gorilla* is made by touching fists to the chest, something Koko often does without any intent to sign. Did Koko imitate *bad gorilla* in a vague way, as apes usually do? Did Koko make the sign for *eat,* or some other similar sign that, in other contexts, Patterson might have taken to be a gestural pun? And did Patterson, eager to prove that Koko has a human sense of humor, misinterpret Koko's gestures as meaning *funny gorilla?* We will never know.

Not only does Koko philosophize, she also corrects trainers. Chevalier-Skolnikoff gives several instances taken from Patterson's Ph.D. dissertation. On one occasion a teacher said to a visitor: "No, she's not an adolescent yet, she is still a juvenile." Koko, who has been trained to understand spoken English, overheard. "No, gorilla," said Koko. On the basis of such anecdotal marvels, Chevalier-Skolnikoff concludes that talking-ape skills cannot be attributed to unconscious cuing.

Terrace's apostate paper follows, in which he summarizes his reasons for thinking that just such cuing explains all the work so far reported. "In view of the discoveries about the nature of Nim's signing that were made through videotape analysis," he writes, "it is essential for any new project to maintain a permanent and unedited visual record of the ape's discourse with its teachers. Indeed, the absence of such documentation would make it impossible to substantiate any claims concerning the spontaneity and novelty of the ape's signing. Requiring proof that an ape is not just mirroring the signs of its teachers is not unreasonable . . ."

After examining the objections that ape researchers have raised against Terrace, Mark Seidenberg and Laura Petitto together decide that Terrace's work cannot be dismissed and that "there is no basis on which to conclude that signing apes acquired linguistic skills." They deplore the widespread hype given to talking apes by the media and hope that future research will be more carefully designed.

John Prescott reports on how easily one is moved by the pathetic fallacy while watching porpoises perform, and Karen Pryor calls attention to similar errors that have been made by those who work with these lovable little whales. One of John Lilly's most absurd mistakes was interpreting a male dolphin's actions toward a human female teacher as indicative of sexual attraction, ignoring the fact that male porpoises in captivity behave sexually toward almost anything, which "we do not find intelligent or endearing in male dogs." It is just as easy to mistake a dolphin's gaping jaw as a "smile" as it is to mistake a performing ape's bared teeth as a "grin," as though the ape is amused by what is going on rather than responding to a cue.

Part 2, on human communication, opens with a paper by Starkey Duncan, Jr., on the strategies people adopt in everyday conversation. Psychiatrist Martin Orne cites examples of how Hans trots into therapy sessions, and how unwitting cues from a hypnotist can seriously distort a hypnotized subject's memories of a past event."[2] "It is possible to talk to a computer, to an ape, to a plant, or to a pet rock," writes Karl Scheibe in the next paper, but he agrees with Terrace and Sebeok that apes do not participate in anything that can justly be called a conversation. Ray Hyman, a magician as well as a psychologist, explains how psychics give "readings" to people about whom they have no prior information—a technique known in the trade as "cold reading." Robert Rosenthal, who edited the last printing in English of Pfungst's book on Clever Hans, cites examples of how an experimenter's facial expressions and voice tones can subtly convey to a human subject what the experimenter wants the outcome of a test to be. This can play havoc in grade schools, where teachers often have positive expectations for favorite pupils and low expectations for children of minority groups. Sebeok cites numerous cases of self-deception triggered by intense belief, from wart curing to stigmatization, and death from voodoo curses.

Barbara Foorman, the first speaker of Section 3, a section on deceptive communication, recounts an amusing instance of how feedback deceived some experimenters who were testing four-year-olds. Theodore Sarbin presents some striking examples of self-deception by neurotics, hypnotic subjects, military leaders, and ordinary people, and speculates on the parameters underlying such deception. Statistician Persi Diaconis shows how easily experimenter belief can distort the statistical analysis of raw data. Bella DePaulo reports on studies of why some people are better than others in detecting lies. Daniel Moerman considers the placebo effect and its mysteries. Paul Ekman writes about studies of the facial expressions and body movements of persons who are lying. Vernon Allen and Michael Atkinson report the results of an interesting test on how well adults can decide, when viewing a videotape of a child, whether the tape was secretly filmed or whether the child was acting. Professional magician James Randi closed the session with what was essentially a magic performance that regrettably can be described only by bracketed asides.

The book's final section consists of a single lecture by Marcello Truzzi, a sociologist who calls himself a "zetetic," an ancient Greek word for skeptic. True to his peculiar brand of zeteticism, Truzzi takes no sides in the controversy. He warns against skeptical "hit men" (by whom he means such persons as Randi and myself) who unfairly, in his opinion, discredit unorthodox science, to the cheers of the establishment; but he is equally opposed to similar dogmatism and tactics on the part of true believers. "Though I began my investigations [I assume he means his reading] completely convinced by Pfungst's arguments, I am now wary of extending them to new areas and find myself . . . forced to suspend judgment even about Hans. I offer you doubts rather than conclusions."

A great admirer of Charles Fort, and editor of a whimsical Fortean publication called *Zetetic Scholar,* Truzzi has recently come under the influence of philosopher-physicist Paul Feyerabend, for whom "anything goes" in science, including the serious investigation of astrology. It was unthinkable that Truzzi would betray whether his private views lean toward Terrace and the Sebeoks, or toward Patterson. On this vague, delicately balanced note, the book ends.

I am less comfortable on a fence. Some Greek skeptics did indeed refuse to judge any hypothesis. Pyrrho liked to say there is no difference between being alive or dead. When someone asked why he didn't die, he replied, "Because there is no difference." Other Greek skeptics were closer to the modern skepticism of, say, Bertrand Russell — that is, dubious about metaphysical dogmas, and aware of the fallibilism of science, but willing to take vigorous stands on scientific, moral, and political controversies. Carneades, a later skeptic, enjoyed defending an argument with great eloquence, then defending the opposite side with equal passion. But Carneades also supported value judgements based on probability: the weight of empirical evidence together with the degree to which a hypothesis is consistent with well-established opinions. He liked to illustrate progressive levels of belief with the following fable:

A man entered a cave and thought he saw a snake. After running out of the cave, he started to reflect on the possibility it was not a snake. Going back inside, he perceived that the object was not moving. This tended to confirm, though only to a weak degree, the conjecture that it was not a snake. Finally, he poked the snake with a stick and discovered it was a piece of rope.

From where I sit at the moment, with limited information, it seems to me that Terrace has poked at a snake and found it to be a piece of rope. I could of course be wrong, but the views of Terrace and the Sebeoks impress me as more credible than those of their opponents, especially Patterson's. Whatever your subjective feelings may be, *The Clever Hans Phenomenon* is a fascinating, invaluable reference on the intensifying debate.

Although the proponents of ape language may be losing some ground in academic circles, there is little evidence that the media hype is subsiding. Adrian Desmond's (1979) *The Ape's Reflexion,* and Keith Laidler's (1980) *The Talking Ape* are the latest nonfiction books to praise the ape trainers, and Michael Crichton's (1980) *Congo* is the most recent fictional abomination along similar lines. The debate is likely to be generating scholarly fireworks, and outrageous popular books, articles, and motion pictures, for a long, long time.

NOTES

1. The word *babies* should now be added to this list. In *Teach Your Baby Math,* Glenn Doman (1979) explains how you can use flash cards to train a one-year-old infant, who cannot yet talk, to solve in its head such problems as: "Seventy-five minus fifty multiplied by two plus ten and divided by three equals what?" The child proves it has calculated correctly by crawling toward numbered cards on the floor and picking out (most of the time) the card with 20 on it, while its proud mother, who has trained the child, watches with adoration and awe. Doman is the founder and director of what he calls the Institutes for the Achievement of Human Potential, in Philadelphia. His earlier book *How to Teach Your Baby to Read,* sold over a million copies.

2. A likely instance of Clever Hans feedback in hypnotic revelations is provided by *The Control of Candy Jones,* a potboiler by Donald Bain (1977). Candy Jones, the well-known former model, now a radio talk-show host in Manhattan, had at one time worked for the CIA. Under hypnosis, she spun fantastic tales of harrowing torture by CIA operatives. The amateur hypnotist was her husband, the late Long John Nebel, whose radio show Candy acquired. One thinks also of the many recent books about persons who under hypnosis recall being taken aboard UFOs by extraterrestrials, and similar books about persons who under hypnosis remember details about their lives in past incarnations.

REFERENCES

Bain, Donald (1977). *The Control of Candy Jones.* New York: Playboy.

Crichton, Michael (1980). *Congo.* New York: Knopf. Reviewed by Thomas A. Sebeok: Amy and the apes. *Times Literary Supplement,* July 17, 1981, p. 802.

Desmond, Adrian J. (1979). *The Ape's Reflexion.* New York: Dial/Wade. Reviewed by Thomas A. Sebeok: On hard facts and misleading data. *Reviews in Anthropology* 8 (1), 1981, 9-15.

Doman, Glenn (1979). *Teach Your Baby Math.* New York: Simon and Schuster.

Epstein, Robert, Lanza, Robert P., and Skinner, B. F. (1981). *Science,* May 8, 1981; *Discover,* July 1981, pp. 11-12.

Gallup, George (1977). Self-recognition in primates. *American Psychologist* 32, 329-338.

Krall, Karl (1912). *Denkende Tiere,* 2nd ed. Leipzig: Friedrich Engelmann.

Laidler, Keith (1980). *The Talking Ape.* New York: Stein and Day.

Locke, John (1690). *Essay Concerning Human Understanding,* Book II, Chapter 27.

Maeterlinck, Maurice (1914). *The Unknown Guest,* Chapter IV. New York: Dodd, Mead.

Patterson, Francine, and Linden, Eugene (1981). *The Education of Koko.* New York: Holt, Rinehart and Winston.

Pfungst, Oskar (1965). *Clever Hans,* edited by Robert Rosenthal. New York: Holt, Rinehart and Winston.

Sebeok, Thomas A. and Umiker-Sebeok, Donna Jean (eds.) (1980). *Speaking of Apes: A Critical Anthology of Two-Way Communication with Man.* New York: Plenum.

———(1981). Clever Hans and smart simians: The self-fulfilling prophecy and kindred methodological pitfalls, *Anthropos* 76, 89-165.

Teresi, Dick (1981). Sorry, sorry, sorry. *Omni* (February), 114.

Terrace, Herbert (1979). *Nim: A Chimpanzee Who Learned Sign Language*. New York: Knopf.

Von Maday, Stefan (1914). *Gibt es denkende Tiere?* Leipzig: Wilhelm Englemann.

Wolff, Gustav (1914). *Die denkenden Tiere von Elberfeld und Mannheim. Süddeutsche Monatshefte* 11 (4), 456-467.

Index

Abell, George O., 203, 216
acupuncture, 207, 208
Addams, Jane, 284
Adler, Mortimer J., 13–28, 40–41, 42, 45 n5, 278
aesthetics, 30, 40, 44, 45 n3, 89
Andersen, Hans Christian, 142, 326
anthropic principle, 333, 334
Aquinas, Saint Thomas, 14, 15, 17, 20, 21, 22, 25 n8, 40
Archimedes, 112, 252, 267
Aristotle, 14, 31, 32–33, 38, 39, 40, 41, 45 n4, 46 n8, 247, 271, 281, 295, 298, 339
art as propaganda, 29–46
Asimov, Isaac, 211, 214, 216, 254, 319, 330, 360
astrology, 205, 207, 208, 375
Augustine, Saint, 22, 25 n8, 41

Barclay, Kate, 178, 185 n3
Barr, Stringfellow, 22, 23
Barth, Karl, 232–33, 305
Baruch, Bernard, 82–83
Bates, David, 176–87
Bates, Stockton, 176, 177, 181, 184–85, 187
Baughman, Roland, 134, 139
Baum, Frank J., 134, 137 n18, 273
Baum, L. Frank, 115–37, 139–46, 155, 164, 166–68, 171, 172 n5, 193, 272–77, 326, 327
Baum, Maud Gage, 118, 120, 122, 123, 124, 126, 130, 132, 136 n9
Beardsley, Aubrey, 47, 48–49
Beerbolm, Max 56, 157
Bell, E. T., 251–53
Ben-Gurion, David, 337
Benedict, Ruth, 88–89, 92, 95, 96, 239
Berkeley, Bishop George, 70, 195–96, 198, 203 n2, 333
Bernstein, Jeremy, 255–56, 263–65

Big Bang theory, 313–19
blacklisting, 284–88
Blackmore, Susan, 214
Boas, George, 76, 96, 239, 242 n4
Bohr, Niels, 199, 245, 303, 337
Boucher, Anthony, 134, 140
Bowman, Isa, 289–90
Bradbury, Ray, 132, 134, 140, 145
Browne, Lewis Allen, 150, 151
Bryan, William Jennings, 123, 372
Buchanan, Scott, 15, 22, 24 n7, 42

Cabell, James Branch, 62, 67 n11
Calder, Nigel, 332–36 passim
Campbell, John, Jr., 212–13
Carnap, Rudolf, 41, 42, 57, 59, 60, 65, 66, 70, 72, 80 n1, 160, 161, 243, 248, 296–97, 320, 342, 343, 347, 348, 349
Carneiro, Robert, 78, 241 n2, 242 n4, 241
Carpenter, J. E., 178, 181
Carroll, Lewis, 115, 120, 155, 164–68, 172 n4, 173–75, 179, 180, 181, 184, 191, 254, 280–83, 289–91, 327
Cauchy, Augustin-Louis, 252, 345
Center for the Study of Democratic Institutions, 19, 28 n11
Chesterton, G. K., 14, 21, 41, 44, 59, 61–62, 67 n5, n8, n9, n10, 145, 167, 219, 220
Chevalier-Skolnikoff, Suzanne, 385–86
Chicago, University of, 13–27, 40, 42, 43, 44 n1, 45 n5, 46 n10, 65, 71
Chomsky, Noam, 96, 382
Churchill, Winston, 102, 250, 299
Clarke, Arthur C., 264, 330
Clever Hans, 381–89 passim
Cogley, John, 284
Coleridge, Samuel T., 292–93, 352
color perception, 69–70, 77
Comfort, Alexander, 19–20